Bewitching Women, Pious Men

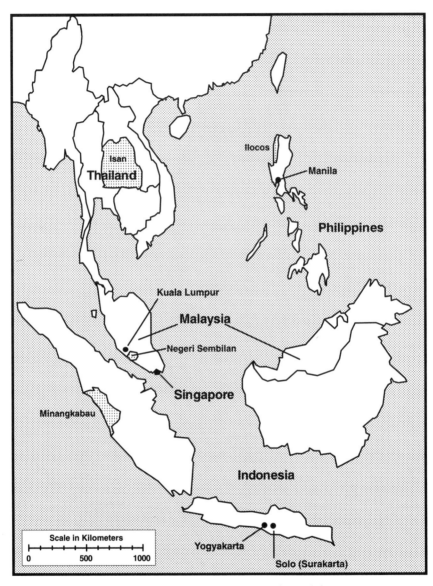

Location of research sites in Southeast Asia

Bewitching Women, Pious Men

Gender and Body Politics in Southeast Asia

EDITED BY

Aihwa Ong and Michael G. Peletz

UNIVERSITY OF CALIFORNIA PRESS
Berkeley   Los Angeles   London

HQ 1075.5
.A 785
B49
1995

0 30892841

University of California Press
Berkeley and Los Angeles, California

University of California Press, Ltd.
London, England

New material © 1995 by the Regents of the University of California.

Parts of this book were published in earlier versions.
Chapter 3: "Neither Reasonable Nor Responsible: Contrasting
Representations of Masculinity in a Malay Society," *Cultural Anthropology* 9,
no. 2 (1994): 135–78. © 1994 by the American Anthropological Association. Reprinted
by permission. Not for sale or further reproduction.
Chapter 5: "State versus Islam: Malay Families, Women's Bodies, and the
Body Politic in Malaysia," *American Ethnologist* 17, no. 2 (May 1990): 258–76.
© by the American Anthropological Association. Reprinted by
permission. Nor for sale or further reproduction.
Chapter 6: "State Fatherhood: The Politics of Nationalism, Sexuality, and Race
in Singapore," in *Nationalisms and Sexualities,* ed. Andrew Parker et al.
(Routledge, 1991), pp. 344–64. Reprinted by permission.
Chapter 9: "Narratives of Masculinity and Transnational Migration: Filipino
Workers in the Middle East," *masculinities* 2, no. 3 (fall 1994): 18–36.
Reprinted by permission.

Library of Congress Cataloging-in-Publication Data

Bewitching women, pious men : gender and body politics in
   Southeast Asia / edited by Aihwa Ong and Michael G. Peletz.
      p.   cm.
   Includes bibliographical references and index.
   ISBN 0-520-08860-3. — ISBN 0-520-08861-1 (pbk.)
   1. Sex role—Asia, Southeastern.   2. Power (Social sciences)—
Asia, Southeastern.   3. Asia, Southeastern—Social life and
customs.   I. Ong, Aihwa.   II. Peletz, Michael G.
HQ1075.5.A785B49   1995
305.3'0959—dc20   94-22740
                                                                        CIP

Printed in the United States of America
9 8 7 6 5 4 3 2 1

CONTENTS

CONTRIBUTORS

Evelyn Blackwood is Assistant Professor of Women's Studies and Anthropology at Purdue University. She has published articles on Native American berdache/two-spirit people and lesbian relations cross-culturally, and is the editor of *The Many Faces of Homosexuality: Anthropology and Homosexual Behavior* (1986).

Suzanne A. Brenner is Assistant Professor of Anthropology at the University of California, San Diego. Her research has focused on gender, hierarchy, and social change in Java. She is currently working on a book that analyzes gendered discourses of tradition, modernity, and social order in contemporary Indonesia.

Janadas Devan is a lecturer in English at the Nanyang Institute of Technology, Singapore. His scholarship concerns neo-Confucianism and nationalism in Southeast Asia.

Geraldine Heng is Assistant Professor of English at the University of Texas, Austin. She is writing a book on medieval romance called *Empire of Magic: Romance and the Politics of Cultural Fantasy.*

Jennifer Krier wrote her Ph.D. dissertation on gender, power, and state-region relationships among the Minangkabau of West Sumatra, Indonesia. She is currently working on issues of property, gender, and citizenship as a Liberal Arts Fellow at Harvard Law School.

Jane A. Margold is a Visiting Scholar at the Center for Humanities, Wesleyan University. Her research deals with the transnational emergence of new political subjectivities; with masculinities; and with the persistence of servitude in the postcolonial world.

Mary Beth Mills is Assistant Professor of Anthropology at Colby College. Her most recent research examines changing gender and household relations as a result of rural-urban labor migration in Thailand. She is presently working on a book entitled *"We Are Not Like Our Mothers": Modernity and Identity among Thai Migrant Workers.*

Aihwa Ong is Associate Professor of Anthropology at the University of California, Berkeley. She is the author of *Spirits of Resistance and Capitalist Discipline: Factory Women in Malaysia* (1987). Her research concerns new Asian immigrants in California and overseas Chinese in the Asia-Pacific region.

Michael G. Peletz is Associate Professor of Anthropology and Director of Asian Studies at Colgate University. His publications include *A Share of the Harvest: Kinship, Property, and Social History Among the Malays of Rembau* (1988), and *Reason and Passion: Representations of Gender in a Malay Society* (1995).

Jacqueline Siapno is a Ph.D. candidate in the Department of South and Southeast Asian Studies at the University of California, Berkeley. Her research and writing focus on literature—traditional Malay, modern Indonesian, and Philippine.

PREFACE

This book had its beginnings in a conference on gender in Southeast Asian cultures that was held at the University of California, Berkeley, in the winter of 1992. The meetings were sponsored by the University's Center for Southeast Asian Studies as part of its annual conference series, and were organized by Aihwa Ong of the Department of Anthropology. Sylvia Tiwon of the Department of South and Southeast Asian Studies helped put together the program for the meetings. We appreciate the support and encouragement of Robert Reed, Director of the Center; we are also grateful to Eric Crystal and Cynthia Joysama, who made many of the administrative arrangements for the conference and were instrumental in its success.

Although we were not able to include in the present volume all the papers presented at the meetings, we would like to take this opportunity to express our gratitude to all the participants for the intellectual energy and excitement they brought to the formal sessions and the dialogues that followed. We are especially grateful to Anna L. Tsing and Vincente Rafael who (along with Michael Peletz) served as discussants, and not only raised provocative questions, but also sharpened our theoretical contributions. Subsequently, Michael Peletz agreed to be coeditor of the present volume, and jointly imagined how the entire collection would come together. One of our early decisions was to "round out" the collection by including two previously published papers (Ong, and Heng and Devan) that were not presented at the conference.

We would like to thank Naomi Schneider and William Murphy of the University of California Press, for their encouragement and support in publishing the book. We are also grateful to anonymous readers for the Press, who provided helpful comments, and to Herbert P. Philips, who drew our attention to the modernist Thai painting that graces the cover of the book.

In addition, we would like to express our gratitude to the contributors to the volume. Of the ten scholars represented here, the majority are young professors in their first jobs. They have been trained in different anthropology, English, and Southeast Asian departments in the country, but all share a critical, interdisciplinary approach to questions of gender, power, and postcoloniality. Important as well, the contributors have been diligent in their numerous revisions of what began as working papers, and enthusiastic in supporting our efforts to bring this book to press within a relatively short period of time. We trust that their essays, and the myriad questions raised in the volume as a whole, will engage anthropologists and Southeast Asianists as well as scholars involved in research and writing on cultural studies, political economy, women, and gender.

A. O.
M. G. P.

Introduction

Aihwa Ong and Michael G. Peletz

How can anthropologists and other scholars bring fresh perspectives to the study of femininity and masculinity in Southeast Asia? Dominant scholarly conceptions of gender in Southeast Asia focus on egalitarianism, complementarity, and the relative autonomy of women in relation to men—and are framed largely in local terms. For the contributors to this book, gender is a fluid, contingent process characterized by contestation, ambivalence, and change; their approaches, moreover, situate gender squarely within the interlocking ideological and material contexts of a dynamic, modernizing region.

In the postcolonial world, the intersections of the past and the present, the local and the global, define the axes for exploring the negotiation and reworking of gender. This volume brings together two streams of gender analysis in postcolonial societies. First, our studies of the everyday experience, understanding, representation—and reworking—of gender examine the entanglements of gendering processes with different types of social hierarchies in the region. Second, our essays show that different forms of knowledge and power focus on bodies and sexualities as the crucial sites of political, economic, and cultural transformations. In the course of exploring the gender politics that have emerged in late modern Southeast Asia, we reconsider the links between the gender meanings and material forces that shape communities, nations, and transnational arenas, and the negotiation of everyday life. As such, this collection, which is based on anthropological research and cuts across disciplinary boundaries, suggests new ways of studying how gender articulates with diverse forms of power, nationalism, and capitalism in Southeast Asia and beyond. More broadly, by interweaving anthropological insights on the construction of gender with theories bearing on postcoloniality, cultural struggle, marginality, and the body politic, we hope to enrich our understanding of all such phenomena.

POSTCOLONIALISM AND CULTURAL STRUGGLE

In recent years, ethnographies of everyday gender experience in relation to diverse forms of domination and subordination have suggested that the dynamics of gender are most appropriately contextualized in the ever shifting and ever widening fields of knowledge and power associated with specific modernities. The more general point emphasized by scholars such as Allan Pred and Michael Watts is that in the contemporary world, capital has reinvented itself as a "multiplicity of capitalisms" that have spawned "a multiplicity of experienced modernities" shaped by the heavily homegrown sense of the local and the global (Pred and Watts 1992:xiv). Insights of the latter sort have informed the thrust of this book, which differs from other works on gender in the region (Ward 1963; Van Esterik 1982; Eberhardt 1988; Atkinson and Errington 1990; Locher-Scholten and Niehof 1992) in that it places gender both in a framework of symbolic meaning and in relation to the specific historical and political economic forces shaping various postcolonial milieux. We argue that indigenous notions bearing on masculinity and femininity, on gender equality and complementarity, and on various criteria of prestige and stigma are being reworked in the dynamic postcolonial contexts of peasant outmigration, nation building, cultural nationalism, and international business. We also maintain that the experiences and images of gender are refracted in different ways not only through symbolic systems and class patterns, but also in relation to various types of "cultural struggles" (Ong 1991; B. Williams 1991) or Gramscian wars of position in which struggles over the ascendancy and authenticity of meanings and values are linked to the material conditions shaping the distribution of wealth, power, and prestige.

Since the 1960s, rapid economic growth has occurred in countries like Singapore, Malaysia, Thailand, and Indonesia, but has so far eluded countries such as the Philippines, thus accentuating the contrasts among Southeast Asia's different postcolonial formations, particularly the ways in which ideologies of religion, ethnicity, development, and nationhood shape the lived experiences and understandings of gender on the ground. By "postcolonialism"[1] we refer to the actual situations of postcolonial sites, caught up between colonial legacies, efforts to achieve consciousness of nationhood, and the politics of cultural struggles, in which different groups at once attempt to fashion their own identities in relation to each other and are heavily influenced by global hegemonies (B. Williams 1991). The postcolonial society, according to Achille Mbembe, is composed of "a plurality of 'spheres' and arenas, each having its own separate logic and yet nonetheless liable to be entangled with other logics when operating in specific contexts; hence the postcolonial 'subject' has had to learn to continuously bargain . . . and improvise" (1992:5).

This need to continuously negotiate and invent identity pervades life in postcolonial Southeast Asian countries, which are self-defined as "developing," "multiracial," "multicultural" societies. Most Southeast Asian countries are variously consumed with the fever of development and/or dealing with low intensity conflicts and continuing metropolitan dominance. Singapore, and increasingly Malaysia, Thailand, and Indonesia, for example, are frequently referred to as "Little Dragons," a term which denotes their newly affluent societies and simultaneously alludes to the authoritarian states overseeing the processes responsible for such affluence (see Appelbaum and Henderson 1992). In these and most other contexts, colonial legacies have receded from view as local populations are caught up with transregional Asian forces like resurgent Islam and neo-Confucianism. The Philippines, in contrast, is not only plagued by a weak state, irredentist movements, and continuing imperial domination by the United States and its global surrogate the World Bank (Bello et al. 1982); it is also the home of powerful Marxist-feminist movements with the clear potential to effect substantive change. In these conditions of upheaval and uncertainty, cultural struggles are framed by ideologies linked to religious orthodoxies, export capitalism, and postcolonial nationalisms expressed in "narratives of community" (Chatterjee 1993). Such interlocking postcolonial ideologies shape the conditions, contours, and possibilities of everyday negotiations and reworkings of gender. One of the central objectives of this book is to elucidate the ways in which these interlocking ideologies have helped transform "traditional" modes of gender within the particular postcolonial contexts of Southeast Asia.

CONTESTED GENDERS

Recent studies of gender as a performative and negotiated activity (Ginsburg and Tsing 1990b; Butler 1990) suggest that the contestation (or challenging) of meanings is most intensive at the borders of communities, classes, cultures, and nationalities (see also de Lauretis 1987). Faye Ginsburg and Anna L. Tsing demonstrate that in North American situations, pervasive uncertainty over gender constructs requires that gender meanings are subject to constant negotiation—in the dual sense of negotiating a deal and negotiating a stream (1990a:2). Taking the argument one step further, we suggest that in managing complex, hierarchical relations in postcolonial societies, gender is not only negotiable but also constantly evolving—and typically doing so with both ironic and unintended consequences. Men and women must deal with—and deal in—the tensions between poetics and politics, prestige and shame, homogeneity and heterogeneity, the dominant and the dominated, the local and the global. Thus, at particular historical and spatial junctures, the negotiation of gender meanings, obligations, and rights may escalate into outright contestations, if not at the national, then at the local, ritual, and personal levels of daily life. As James Clifford has noted, "Culture is contested, temporal, and emergent. Representation and explanation—both by insiders and outsiders—is implicated in this emergence" (1987:19).

In this volume, we situate and examine contested genders within specific contexts, tracing the different interpretations—male versus female, hegemonic versus counterhegemonic, official versus local, religious versus secular, this world versus the next, and capital versus labor—that follow the shifting faultlines of social change. We show that gender domination is never a thing in and of itself, and that it intersects with and is in a very basic sense constituted by other hierarchized domains like the body, the family, civil society, the nation, and the transnational arena, each of which is variously gendered (Ong 1991; Mohanty et al. 1991). We believe that an understanding of the working and reworking of gender at particular historical junctures and domains of social life will yield new insights on the nature of cultural production and contestations in centers and peripheries alike.

The central issues addressed in the pages that follow include questions such as, In what ways can women and men play havoc with gender ideologies and other forms of authority (ritual, cultural, political, and national) in their social universes? And, at what sites, and over what issues, are women and men most compelled to question, even to contest, hegemonic forms of gendered power? Raymond Williams has defined "hegemony" as a "lived system of meanings and values—constituting and constitutive," but he also reminds us that it is "always a process" and that it is "continually resisted, limited, altered, and challenged by pressures not all its own" (1977:110). Hegemony is never complete and is always vulnerable to subversion by counterhegemonic tactics (R. Williams 1977).[2] The chapters in this book analyze changing gender meanings within larger hegemonic contexts, revealing the entanglements of gender with other differences keyed to culture, class, and nationality. Such an approach suggests that gender relations in Southeast Asia and elsewhere cannot be considered fixed systems, if only because they are typically comprised of contradictory ideologies which are constantly undergoing change, and which are equally constantly creating new possibilities of subversion and resistance.

To the authors in this collection, this engendering of cultural conflict is a process fraught with ambivalence, which Andrew Weigert (1991) defines as "the experience of commingled contradictory emotions." Postcolonial forces of dislocation, ethnic heterogeneity, nation-building, and international business have blurred, confused, and made problematic cultural understandings of what it means to be male or female in local societies, the more general point being that consent in gender meanings increasingly gives way to contestation. Such processes and dilemmas are readily apparent among Filipino and Thai labor migrants, Javanese market women, matrilineal kin, citizens caught up in the Islamic–secularism competition, and members of the emerging middle classes in Southeast Asia—all discussed in the pages that follow—though they are certainly not unique to such groups. As we shall see, the sites of gender skirmishes and conflict include village squares and coffee-shops (chapters 2, by Suzanne Brenner, and 3, by Jennifer Krier), government offices and rural gatherings (chapters 3, by Michael Peletz, and 4, by Evelyn Blackwood), universities and the mass media (chapters 5, by Aihwa Ong, and 6, by Geraldine Heng and Janadas Devan), bourgeois homes and leftist circles (chapter 7, by Jacqueline Siapno), and labor exporting villages and labor circuits (chapters 8, by Mary Beth Mills, and 9, by Jane Margold). We will also see that these gender conflicts are affected by or spill over into the broader field of intersecting national and international interests.

In Southeast Asia, as in many other areas, the symbolic structuring of gender relations is commonly based on binary oppositions of prestige and stigma, the spiritually potent and the spiritually weak, the disciplined and the disruptive, and so on (Atkinson and Errington 1990). Such pairs of opposed values create the sort of social interdependencies that breed ambivalences between and within gender identities. Peter Stallybrass and Allon White point out that in a wide variety of symbolic constructions, the dependence of the "top" on the "bottom," and the "high" on the "low" produces a "mobile, conflictual fusion of power, fear, and desire in the construction of subjectivity." Thus, that which is considered low status (e.g., femininity) is both reviled and desired (1986:4–5; Douglas 1966). As formulated along such lines, gender(ed) ambivalence is produced and reworked through the process of negation, denial, and defiance of dominant moral logics (Stallybrass and White 1986:89). In our essays, we indicate how gender subjectivities are shaped by such contradictory constructions in changing fields of power relations as women enter the public spheres and popular consciousness of the wider society. Such ambivalences, both collective and individual, can be tapped by the regulatory schemes of consumer culture, nationalism, religion, or capital, on the one hand, but also channeled into resistance against dominant ideologies on the other.

BODY POLITICS

The postcolonial state, in its varied tasks of building a national identity, meeting challenges from communally-based interest groups, and representing itself as a modern nation, is continuously engaged in defining the composition and form of political society. This making and patrolling of the body politic is an ongoing struggle that often entails the inscription of state power on women's (and, to a lesser extent, men's) bodies. We therefore use the term "body politics" to refer to the inherently political nature of symbols and practices surrounding the body politic and the human body. These cross-referencing inscriptions of power—that is, the diverse ways society is mapped onto the body and the body is symbolized in society—are mutually dependent upon and entangled in each other. Indeed, the social regulation of bodies is inseparable from their incitement to subvert or resist social forces (Foucault 1979).

Such control of female bodies by the state or communal groups is in fact a recurring and striking theme in postcolonial nation-states. Observations along these lines might appear to (and to a certain degree do indeed) confirm Michel Foucault's (1979) argument that the body is a historically and culturally specific nexus of shifting power relations that inscribe different meanings as schemes of social control and resistance. But Foucault ignored the differential regulations of gendered, racial, and class bodies in colonial and postcolonial formations. Aihwa Ong (1987, 1988, 1989, 1990, 1991) has discussed both the series of knowledge-power schemes deployed in the colonial era to define Malays as racialized, lazy bodies, and the ways in which their postcolonial counterparts (in the form of corporate, media, and religious narratives) have likewise served to problematize young women's bodies and sexualities (see also Stoler 1985, 1989, 1990; Rafael 1988; Blanc–Szanton 1990). Reports from elsewhere in the world are quite relevant as well: some newly independent African states, for example, have required women's bodies and gestures to bear the markings of local traditions, in order to represent indigenous African modernities built upon pre-European cultures (Wipper 1972).

Studies such as these reveal that the discursive constructions of bodies are frequently plotted against divisions that maintain social order, and that women's bodies in particular are commonly used to symbolize and threaten transgressions of social boundaries (Douglas 1966). It is no accident that "body images 'speak' social relations and values with particular force," and that in highly ordered social spaces, women's bodies straying across borders are often symbolically constructed as deviant or grotesque (Stallybrass and White 1986:10). Nor is it surprising that, in our chapters, we encounter politically incorrect housewives, women with bewitching genitals, femmes fatales in the marketplace, disobedient Chinese mothers, and widow ghosts—all ideological images of transgression and deviance in the shifting constructions of values, boundaries, and behavior in Southeast Asia.

The representation of gendered bodies as problematic is of course especially blatant in nationalist (and, to a lesser extent, transnational) narratives. The female body in particular, with its softness and openings, has often been used to symbolize the endangered or dangerous social body in postcolonial nationalist discourses (see chapters 5, by Ong, and 6, by Heng and Devan). Such symbolic imagery is dialectically linked to hegemonic constructions of the state as masculine (Enloe 1994). Bodies are also the sites of conflicting relations of knowledge and power linked to transnational flows of labor, capital, and culture. Capitalism's grip on laboring bodies invariably includes the subverting of indigenous notions of gender and the regendering of migrant workers, rendering them as oversexed or desexed bodies servicing the geopolitics of production (chapters 8, by Mills, and 9, by Margold). The essays in this volume also make clear that the transcultural forces of Islam, neo-Confucianism, and Marxist-feminism often play a critical role in shaping women's bodies and the body politic at the local level. Gender meanings, we suggest, are also shaped by the effects of local, national, and global forces acting on the body.

THE ETHNOGRAPHY OF GENDER IN SOUTHEAST ASIA

All the essays in this collection are based on new research and are geared toward demonstrating that recent developments in gender analysis and social theory are changing our understandings of the ways in which gender identities are lived and experienced by contemporary social actors in Southeast Asia and beyond. Scholars of the region have long pointed to the "relatively high status" (autonomy and social control) of women in this area as an important feature which both underlies the region's tremendous diversity and simultaneously distinguishes it from India, China, Japan, other parts of South and East Asia, and most other "culture areas" (Ward 1963; Van Esterik 1982). For many years now scholars of Southeast Asia have also moved beyond the study of "women's status" and "gender roles" in order to substantiate their claims concerning women's relative equality vis-à-vis men. Yet careful analyses of men's and women's everyday experiences in relation to diverse forms of domination and subordination suggest that the dynamics of gender and social life must be contextualized in the ever shifting and ever widening fields of knowledge and power associated with Southeast Asian modernities (Ong 1987; Peletz 1987, 1988a, 1988b, 1993a, 1993b; Karim 1992; Wolf 1992; Tsing 1993). The important volume *Power and Difference: Gender in Island Southeast Asia,* edited by Jane Atkinson and Shelly Errington (1990), does in fact emphasize that many insular Southeast Asian cultures stress gender equality and complementarity, but it also illustrates, albeit perhaps less emphatically, that the prerogatives, spiritual power or "potency," and overall prestige enjoyed by men—

whether among scattered hill tribes in Kalimantan or urbanites in the densely populated cosmopolitan centers of Java—typically exceed those of women (see also Eberhardt 1988). The relative hegemony of themes of gender equality and complementarity in Indonesia (the focus of Atkinson and Errington's volume) and Southeast Asia as a whole thus needs to be explored rather than presumed. We also need to examine how indigenous notions bearing on masculinity and femininity, on gender equality and complementarity, and on various criteria and axes of prestige and stigma (the negative reciprocal of prestige) are being rewired or reworked in hierarchical and other ways in the context of capitalist development, nation-state formation, and globalization. More generally, the historicization of gender in varied political and economic contexts clearly distinguishes this volume from earlier works that tend to map gender formations onto divisions of Southeast Asia into "mainland" versus "insular" regions, "upland" versus "lowland" groups, "matrilineal" versus "bilateral" systems of kinship, or "inner" versus "outer" islands. Taking these distinctions as our starting point, our chapters seek to examine gender construction as also the effects of significant developments characteristic of postcolonial Southeast Asia: uneven capitalist development combined with enormous local diversity; de-peasantization, labor migration, and the growth of consumer culture; the rise of newly affluent middle classes; the relative strength and legitimacy of the state in the region; and the prevalence of overt state policies of ideological control.

In the late-twentieth-century world, gender identities are made not exclusively according to local knowledges, but in ever widening geographies of production, trade, and communications. Indeed, as Appadurai (1991:198–199) points out, "ethnographers can no longer simply be content with the 'thickness' they bring to the local and the particular; nor can they assume that as they approach the local, they approach something more elementary, more contingent, and thus more 'real' than life seen in larger-scale perspectives." Processes of state and nation formation, global economic restructuring, and overseas labor migration have created fluid geographies of gender, race, and class that cut across national boundaries. As a consequence, just as postcolonial subjects are increasingly hard put to balance the decentering and recentering forces of cultural and national upheavals, so too are cultural understandings of what it means to be male or female becoming increasingly blurred, varied, and problematic. These processes and conundrums are especially evident among, though clearly not confined to, the mobile peasants, labor migrants, and middle classes discussed in the pages that follow. As we shall see, the sites of disruption include the body, the household, the local community, and the transnational spaces where desires, fears, and power become entangled with the moral economies of religious "brotherhood," nationalism, and global capitalism.

Our understanding of gender and social life in this part of the world can benefit from an engagement with broader social theory that helps to reveal the hybridity and fluidity of gender forms—both feminine and masculine—that are negotiated, transmitted, or disrupted in the margins of cultural hegemonies and national narratives. More generally, we need to devote far more attention to "the political economy of contested symbols and meanings" (Peletz 1993b:68) at the local, national, and transnational levels. We have in fact just begun to understand the cultural work of gender in this vast and teeming peninsula-archipelago world. As the region becomes more closely integrated into the postcolonial world order, the shifting sources and sites of what constitutes vulnerability, danger, and difference merit sustained analytic scrutiny. As Southeast Asian societies are hurtled into the Pacific Century, these issues take on even greater salience and urgency.

THE SIGNIFICANCE AND OUTLINE OF THE VOLUME

This volume combines the methods and perspectives of anthropology, feminism, and cultural studies. By linking anthropological insights on the construction of gender with theories bearing on social location, marginality, body politics, and postcolonial formations, we hope to contribute to new ways of thinking about and interpreting gender and other planes of hierarchy and differentiation both in Southeast Asia and beyond. Our overriding theme is that gender (both masculinity and femininity) is highly contingent and fluid, taking shape as it does in the contexts created in different and overlapping webs of power. We pay special attention to the fact that the symbols and meanings of gender are reproduced historically and negotiated and contested in a myriad of both centrally located and out-of-the-way places and are, in any case, suffused with profound ambivalence. We also show that experiences, understandings, and representations of gender are refracted in different ways not only along class lines but also in relation to one's position(s) in various types of cultural struggles, many of which range far beyond issues of class. All of this is to underscore our earlier point that cultural struggles or positional wars not only need to be analyzed in the study of gender, but also that such forms of contestation clearly transcend class struggles as conventionally defined (see Hefner 1990, esp. chap. 7; Peletz n.d.).

In a departure from most earlier approaches to the study of gender in Southeast Asia and elsewhere, the essays in this volume look closely at the contestation and negotiation of femininity *and* masculinity, which are viewed in a dialectical relationship informed by everyday social process and the broader realities of political economy and historical change.[3] Indeed, masculinity as the unmarked category in many Western and other contexts becomes marked in various Southeast Asian situations as the emblem of nationhood, the deficient provider, or the subaltern of flexible accumulation. In some societies, moreover, we find culturally elaborated discourses on gender that depict men, especially lower-class men, as deficient in those qualities (e.g., "reason," "rationality") that endow humans with prestige and virtue and otherwise set them apart from the beastly world of nature. The juxtaposition and entanglement of such discourses with competing discourses which call them into question highlight the indeterminacy and ambivalent nature of gendering processes. They also make clear that serious efforts to describe and analyze the contingent, internally dissonant, and ambivalence-laden construction of masculinity will enhance our understanding of the multitude of ways in which hegemonies of all varieties are both challenged and subverted in the changing circumstances of postcolonial formations. By examining gender identities in relation to how bodies (including, most notably, their "passions") are imagined in political terms, we suggest in addition that there are multiple and shifting gendered bodies in Southeast Asia that escaped earlier anthropological formulations such as those that constructed the existence of monolithic, culturally specific bodies (e.g., of the Balinese) (Bateson and Mead 1942).

Some of the essays (chapters 1, by Brenner, and 3, by Peletz) also reveal that Islamic manhood is by no means always shaped by rigid, patriarchal discourses. In fact, Islam has long allowed a kind of flexibility and precariousness in the construction of masculinity (and femininity), although these features—along with the contradictory imperatives and indeterminacies—of Islamic masculinities have not received sufficient attention in Southeast Asia or elsewhere. (Siegel 1969 is an important exception; see also Abu-Lughod 1986; Peletz 1988b, 1995; Lavie 1990; and Karim 1992.) Studying Islamic and other masculinities as processes contingent on political and economic systems, bureaucratic interventions, nationalist ideologies, and militarist mobilizations is important for challenging essentializing positions on masculinity (Gilmore 1990) and on Islamic cultures.[4] More broadly, the study of manhood is of value not simply because it yields interesting ethnographic data on constructions of masculinity, which enhance our understanding of the dialectically related domain of feminity. It also helps bring into especially sharp focus the merits—indeed, the necessity—of describing and analyzing gender in relation to other forms of difference and inequality (class, race, etc.) which are in a very basic sense constituting and constitutive of masculinity and femininity alike.

The essays in this volume draw upon a range of sources including anthropological field observations, oral histories, literary texts, newspaper accounts, and radio reports. In the course of their essays, the authors bring disparate subjects into relation with one another: the writings of Filipina feminists, Thai stories of widow ghosts, and eyewitness accounts of beheadings, as well as narratives of state fatherhood and model mothers, middle-class Islamic revivalists, recalcitrant husbands, promiscuous market women, and "hard" and "soft" societies. Both individually and collectively, the essays illustrate that analyses of topics such as these yield important insights on the problematization and contestation of gender as processes through which social agents negotiate cultural borders and meanings and postcolonial states effect nation building and capitalist development. Our essays also demonstrate that everyday subjects and marginal sites of cultural contestation are especially worthy of our attention because as Barbara Babcock (1978:32) emphasizes, "What is socially peripheral is often symbolically central."

In terms of their regional orientation, three of the essays deal with materials from Indonesia, two focus on Malaysia, and two concern the Philippines; the other two essays deal with Singapore and Thailand. We should perhaps emphasize as well that most of the essays concern the major ethnic groups in Southeast Asia (Javanese, Malays, Thais, Tagalogs), rather than the national minorities which received considerable attention in the early years of anthropological scholarship on Southeast Asia (e.g., Leach 1954), and which have been the focus of recent work on gender as well (M. Rosaldo 1980; R. Rosaldo 1980; Eberhardt 1988; Atkinson and Errington 1990; Tsing 1993). Our collection shows in any case that the national majorities in Southeast Asia are by no means homogeneous groups, but are themselves internally divided along gender, economic, social, and spatial lines, and that these lines themselves shift and reform in both contradictory and unexpected ways.

The order of the book reflects our concerns with gender negotiation at the junctures of local, national, and transnational borders. The first three essays (Brenner, Krier, Peletz) deal with daily, largely subterranean struggles between men and women in Java, Minangkabau, and Negeri Sembilan—(Muslim) societies routinely referred to as "matrifocal" and, at least in the case of the latter two, "matrilineal." In all three cases we not only encounter trenchant local critiques of formal ideologies of gender, self-control, and/or "spiritual potency" that have long been assumed to effectively "sum up" indigenous experiences, understandings, and representations of gender. We also see that gender(ed) differences are ambivalently realized and negotiated across lines of silence and speech, male and female spaces, and gendered codes of bodily conduct. These negotiations and skirmishes are largely local, but they all involve discourses drawing on more or less pan-Islamic notions of "reason" and "passion," and are, more generally, heavily informed by changes in broader moral and political economies. The second group of essays (Blackwood, Ong, and Heng and Devan) discusses the reworking of gender in situations which are defined to one or another degree by official and national narratives, and which are also given form and meaning both by state-sponsored development programs and nationalist politics, and their intended and unintended results. These essays are especially concerned with describing and analyzing the concrete points of articulation between ideological apparatuses of the state and the dissemination of hegemonies throughout the wider society. In these cases, the reconfiguring of key symbols bearing on gender(ed) difference is motivated in part by attempts to render less permeable the shifting—hence doubly dangerous—boundaries between races, classes, and religious communities which serve "simultaneously to help constitute the ritual purity and political hegemony" of ruling elites (Peletz 1993b:92). Contestations over gender(ed) difference in private and public spheres, family and civil society, uterine and phallic nationalism, and women and men as family providers, have in some instances had unexpected consequences, ranging from the problematization of Malay masculinity and femininity alike to the "retraditionalization" (Ong 1995) of Minangkabau, Malay, and Singapore Chinese gender norms. We will also see that the ideological control of women's bodies and behavior is a recurring theme in attempts to retrieve a paternal essence in nationalist narratives. A more general leitmotif in these essays is that official discourses depicting men as fathers and breadwinners and women as mothers and housewives are variously invoked and contested by women and men who must traverse the new social boundaries defining the body politic while nonetheless negotiating the intertwined affiliations of locality, class, race, and nationality.

The essays in the third section (Siapno, Mills, Margold) deal with some of the ways in which repressive urban cultures and the transcultural effects of late capitalism constrain and otherwise inform gender identity and class situation. The counterposing of gender images across cultural, national, and ideological divides creates critical tensions in the choices and lived experiences of men and women. In two cases (Siapno, Mills) pairs of constrasting female images—privileged city matrons versus young female guerillas, and seductive young women versus voracious widow ghosts—become vehicles for expressing the desires, fears, and overdetermined ambivalences associated with the transformation of changing gender and kinship roles effected by class differentiation and development in postcolonial Southeast Asia. This theme of contested tropes and changing political economy is picked up in the last essay (Margold), which focuses on the narratives of Filipino men who are deployed in the labor circuits of Middle East economies, and who thus have to contend with the uncertainties and knowledge–power regimes of transnational industries that strive to resocialize and represent them as sexually neutered beasts of burden. The sacrificial sense of themselves that emerges from these men's narratives is clearly produced at the intersections of global business and labor struggles, as transnational discourses threaten to strip them of their indigenous sense of masculinity.

Our historically situated analyses are not meant primarily as case studies of "gender in Southeast Asia." They are offered instead as ethnographic studies that seek both to denaturalize and to historicize our understanding of gender, its location in webs of knowledge and power, and the ways in which the contestation of gender meanings can rework the linkages between behaviors, bodies, and discursive practices. In the course of our essays we have tacked back and forth between the local and the global, have critically engaged the modalities of social regulation effected by nationalism and capitalism, and have analyzed how social practices, narratives-as-texts, and flows of commodities have helped give rise to new ideologies of gender. By examining the reworking of gender in specific contexts defined by the intersection of local, national, and global fields of knowledge and power, we illustrate that the ways in which gender identities are produced, contested, and transformed have far-reaching implications for our understanding of domination and resistance, and cultural life at large. We believe that our explorations of the complex reworking of indigenous notions of gender in political economies of social change will help build bridges between anthropology, feminism, and cultural studies.

NOTES

We would like to thank Suzanne Brenner, Jane Margold, and Mary Beth Mills for their helpful comments on an earlier draft of this essay.

1. Our use of the term "postcolonialism" is to be distinguished from the term "postcolonial(ity)" as it is popularly employed in subaltern studies, cultural studies, and feminism to refer to a multiplicity of criticisms that seek to repudiate Eurocentric master discourses on colonialism, modernization, gender, race, and cultures in the third and first worlds (Spivak 1990; Mohanty et al. 1991; Frankenburg and Mani 1993; Gerwal and Kaplan 1994). (For an assessment of the various intellectual positions associated with the postcolonial, see Dirlik 1994.) While we share this oppositional subjectivity (see Ong n.d.), we also insist on the analytic importance of both the postcolonial in a literal sense and the critical job of explaining actual historical and social situations of postcoloniality in relation to global capitalism and domination by metropolitan powers. Worldwide, there is a broad range of postcolonial formations that includes, but is not limited to, the endemic crisis of the postcolony as vividly described by Achille Mbembe (1992) for West Africa. In the introduction we note some of the differences between two types of postcolonial

formation in Southeast Asia, including differences with respect to integration into international capitalism. One can also identify other types of postcolonies, such as those developing out of the dismantling of the socialist-dominated, war-ravaged countries of Vietnam, Cambodia, Laos, and Burma.

2. Raymond Williams, following Antonio Gramsci, has refined the concept of "hegemony" in the following ways:

> "Hegemony" goes beyond "culture" as previously defined, in its insistence on relating the "whole social process" to specific distributions of power and influence. . . . It is in [the] recognition of the wholeness of the process that the concept of "hegemony" goes beyond "ideology". What is decisive is not only the conscious system of ideas and beliefs, but the whole lived social process as practically organized by specific and dominant meanings and values (Williams 1977:108–109).

Williams goes on to emphasize that "a lived hegemony . . . does not just passively exist as a form of dominance." Rather, any given hegemony has "continually to be renewed, recreated, defended, and modified." For these and other reasons, Williams develops the concept of an "alternative hegemony," which refers both to norms, values, beliefs, etc., that are simply different from the hegemony and to those that are explicitly subversive of it and thus appropriately characterized as "counterhegemonic." The more general point is that while hegemonies are by definition always dominant, they are never "either total or exclusive"; at any given time, they find themselves up against alternative or directly oppositional political and cultural forms, the scope, force, and overall significance of which are of course highly variable. For an adaptation of the hegemony concept to gender domination, see Ortner (1989–90).

3. While the topic of masculinity has clearly received short shrift in the literature on gender in Southeast Asia (and elsewhere), we are not suggesting that it has never been broached in the context of Southeast Asian (or other) societies. In addition to Siegel's (1969) pioneering work on constructions of masculinity in Aceh (noted in the introduction), there is a rich corpus of material on the Ilongot (see, for example, M. Rosaldo 1980; R. Rosaldo 1980), and some recent work on the Wana (see Atkinson 1989). Peacock's early (1968) work on ritual transvestism and mercantile masculinity in Java also merits note in this connection, as do other important essays (e.g., Keyes 1986).

4. Essentializing perspectives on gender in the Islamic world are, unfortunately, extremely widespread. For a critical review of some of the literature on the topic, see Hale (1989); see also Leila Ahmed (1992).

REFERENCES

Abu-Lughod, Lila. 1986. *Veiled Sentiments: Honor and Poetry in a Bedouin Society.* Berkeley: University of California Press.

Ahmed, Leila. 1992. *Women and Gender in Islam: Historical Roots of a Modern Debate.* New Haven: Yale University Press.

Appadurai, Arjun. 1991. "Global Ethnoscapes: Notes and Queries for a Transnational Anthropology." In Richard G. Fox, ed., *Recapturing Anthropology: Working in the Present,* pp. 191–210. Santa Fe: School of American Research Press.

Appelbaum, Richard P., and Jeffrey Henderson, eds. 1992. *States and Development in the Asian Pacific Rim.* Newbury Park, Calif.: Sage Publications.

Atkinson, Jane M. 1989. *The Art and Politics of Wana Shamanship.* Berkeley: University of California Press.

Atkinson, Jane M., and Shelly Errington, eds. 1990. *Power and Difference: Gender in Island Southeast Asia.* Stanford: Stanford University Press.

Babcock, Barbara. 1978. *The Reversible World: Symbolic Inversion in Art and Society.* Ithaca: Cornell University Press.

Bateson, Gregory, and Margaret Mead. 1942. *Balinese Character: A Photographic Analysis.* New York: New York Academy of Sciences.

Bello, Walden, David Kinley, and Elaine Elinson. 1982. *Development Debacle: The World Bank in the Philippines.* San Francisco: Institute for Food and Development Policy.

Blanc-Szanton, Cristina. 1990. "Collision of Cultures: Historical Reformulations of Gender in the Lowland Visayas, Philippines." In Jane M. Atkinson and Shelly Errington, eds., *Power and Difference: Gender in Island Southeast Asia,* pp. 345–384. Stanford: Stanford University Press.

Butler, Judith. 1990. *Gender Trouble: Feminism and the Subversion of Identity.* New York: Routledge.

Chatterjee, Partha. 1993. *The Nation and Its Fragments: Colonial and Postcolonial Histories.* Princeton: Princeton University Press.

Clifford, James. 1987. "Introduction: Partial Truths." In James Clifford and George Marcus, eds., *Writing Culture,* pp. 1–26. Berkeley: University of California Press.

de Lauretis, Teresa. 1987. *Technologies of Gender: Essays on Theory, Film, and Fiction.* Bloomington: University of Indiana Press.

Dirlik, Arif. 1994. "The Postcolonial Aura: Third World Criticism in the Age of Global Capitalism." *Critical Inquiry* 20 (winter 1994): 328–356.

Douglas, Mary. 1966. *Purity and Danger: An Analysis of Concepts of Pollution and Taboo.* London: Routledge.

Eberhardt, Nancy, ed. 1988. *Gender, Power, and the Construction of the Moral Order.* Center for Southeast Asian Studies Monograph No. 4. Madison: University of Wisconsin.

Enloe, Cynthia. 1994. "Feminism, Militarism, Nationalism: Weariness Without Paralysis?" In Constance Sutton, ed., *Feminism, Militarism, Nationalism.* AAA-IWAF, Arlington: American Anthropological Association.

Foucault, Michel. 1979. *The History of Sexuality.* Vol. 1. New York: Vintage Books.

Frankenburg, Ruth, and Lata Mani. 1993. "Crosscurrents, Crosstalk: Race, 'Postcoloniality,' and the Politics of Location." *Cultural Studies* 7(2):292–310.

Gerwal, Inderpal, and Caren Kaplan, eds. 1994. *Scattered Hegemonies: Postmodernity and Transnational Practices.* Minneapolis: University of Minnesota Press.

Gilmore, David. 1990. *Manhood in the Making: Cultural Concepts of Masculinity.* New Haven: Yale University Press.

Ginsburg, Faye, and Anna Tsing. 1990a. "Introduction." In Faye Ginsburg and Anna Tsing, eds., *Uncertain Terms: Negotiating Gender in American Culture,* pp. 1–16. Boston: Beacon Press.

———, eds. 1990b. *Uncertain Terms: Negotiating Gender in American Culture.* Boston: Beacon Press.

Hale, Sondra. 1989. "The Politics of Gender in the Middle East." In Sandra Morgen, ed., *Gender and Anthropology: Critical Reviews for Research and Teaching,* pp. 246–267. Washington, D.C.: American Anthropological Association.

Hefner, Robert W. 1990. *The Political Economy of Mountain Java: An Interpretive History.* Berkeley: University of California Press.

Karim, Wazir Jahan. 1992. *Women and Culture: Between Malay Adat and Islam.* Boulder: Westview Press.

Keyes, Charles F. 1986. "Ambiguous Gender: Male Initiation in a Northern Thai Buddhist Society." In Caroline Walker Bynum, Stevan Harrell, and Paula Richman, eds., *Gender and Religion: On the Complexity of Symbols,* pp. 66–96. Boston: Beacon Press.

Lavie, Smadar. 1990. *The Poetics of Military Occupation: Mzeini Allegories of Bedouin Identity under Israeli and Egyptian Rule.* Berkeley: University of California Press.

Leach, Edmund. 1954. *Political Systems of Highland Burma: A Study of Kachin Social Structure.* London: Athlone Press.

Locher-Scholten, Elsbeth, and Anke Niehof, eds. 1992. *Indonesian Women in Focus: Past and Present Notions.* Leiden: Koninklijk Instituut Voor Taal-, Land-, en Volkenkunde.

Mbembe, Achille. 1992. "The Banality of Power and the Aesthetics of Vulgarity in the Postcolony." *Public Culture* 4(2):1–30.

Mohanty, Chandra T. 1991. "Introduction: Cartographies of Struggle." In Chandra T. Mohanty, Ann Russo, and Lourdes Torres, eds., *Third World Women and the Politics of Feminism,* pp. 1–50. Bloomington: Indiana University Press.

Mohanty, Chandra T., Ann Russo, and Lourdes Torres, eds. 1991. *Third World Women and the Politics of Feminism.* Bloomington: Indiana University Press.

Ong, Aihwa. 1987. *Spirits of Resistance and Capitalist Discipline: Factory Women in Malaysia.* Albany: SUNY Press.

———. 1988. "Colonialism and Modernity: Feminist Re-presentations of Women in Non-Western Societies." *Inscriptions* 3/4:79–93.

———. 1989. "Center, Periphery, and Hierarchy: Gender in Southeast Asia." In Sandra Morgen, ed., *Gender in Anthropology: Critical Reviews for Research and Teaching,* pp. 294–312. Washington, D.C.: American Anthropological Association.

———. 1990. "Japanese Factories, Malay Workers: Class and Sexual Metaphors in West Malaysia." In Jane M. Atkinson and Shelly Errington, eds., *Power and Difference: Gender in Island Southeast Asia,* pp. 385–422. Stanford: Stanford University Press.

———. 1991. "The Gender and Labor Politics of Postmodernity." *Annual Review of Anthropology* 20:279–309.

———. 1995. "Postcolonial Nationalisms: Women and Retraditionalization in the Islamic Imaginary." In Constance Sutton, ed., *Feminism, Militarism, Nationalism.* AFA-IWAC, Arlington: American Anthropological Association.

———. N.d. "Women out of China: Travelling Tales and Travelling Theories in Postcolonial Feminisms." In Ruth Behar and Deborah Gordon, eds., *Women Writing Culture/Culture Writing Women.* Berkeley: University of California Press. Forthcoming.

Ortner, Sherry. 1989–90. "Gender Hegemonies." *Cultural Critique* 14:35–80.

Peacock, James. 1968. *Rites of Modernization: Symbols and Social Aspects of Indonesian Proletarian Drama.* Chicago: University of Chicago Press.

Peletz, Michael G. 1987. "Female Heirship and the Autonomy of Women in Negeri Sembilan, Malaysia." In Barry Isaac, ed., *Research in Economic Anthropology,* vol. 8, pp. 61–101. Greenwich, Conn.: JAI Press.

———. 1988a. "Poisoning, Sorcery, and Healing Rituals in Negeri Sembilan." *Bijdragen tot de Taal-, Land-, en Volkenkunde* 144(1):132–164.

———. 1988b. *A Share of the Harvest: Kinship, Property, and Social History among the Malays of Rembau.* Berkeley: University of California Press.

———. 1993a. "Knowledge, Power, and Personal Misfortune in a Malay Context." In C. W. Watson and Roy F. Ellen, eds., *Understanding Witchcraft and Sorcery in Southeast Asia,* pp. 149–177. Honolulu: University of Hawaii Press.

———. 1993b. "Sacred Texts and Dangerous Words: The Politics of Law and Cultural Rationalization in Malaysia." *Comparative Studies in Society and History* 34(1):66–109.

———. 1995. *Reason and Passion: Representations of Gender in a Malay Society.* Berkeley: University of California Press.

———. N.d. " 'Ordinary Muslims' and Muslim Resurgents in Contemporary Malaysia: Notes on an Ambivalent Relationship." In Patricia Horvatich and Robert W. Hefner, eds., *Islam in an Era of Nation Building: Religions and Political Renewal in Muslim Southeast Asia.* Forthcoming.

Pred, Allan, and Michael J. Watts. 1992. *Reworking Modernity: Capitalisms and Symbolic Discontent.* New Brunswick: Rutgers University Press.

Rafael, Vincente. 1988. *Contracting Colonialism.* Ithaca: Cornell University Press.

Rosaldo, Michelle. 1980. *Knowledge and Passion: Ilongot Notions of Self and Social Life.* Stanford: Stanford University Press.

Rosaldo, Renato. 1980. *Ilongot Headhunting, 1883–1974: A Study in Society and History.* Stanford: Stanford University Press.

Siegel, James T. 1969. *The Rope of God.* Berkeley: University of California Press.

Spivak, Gayatri Chakravorty. 1990. *The Post-Colonial Critic: Interviews, Strategies, Dialogues.* New York: Routledge.

Stallybrass, Peter, and Allon White. 1986. *The Politics and Poetics of Transgression.* Ithaca: Cornell University Press.

Stoler, Ann L. 1985. *Capitalism and Confrontation in Sumatra's Plantation Belt, 1870–1979.* New Haven: Yale University Press.

———. 1989. "Rethinking Colonial Categories: European Communities and the Boundaries of Rule." *Comparative Studies in Society and History* 13(1):134–161.

———. 1991. "Carnal Knowledge and Imperial Power: Gender, Race, and Morality in Colonial Asia." In Micaela di Leonardo, ed., *Gender at the Crossroads of Knowledge: Feminist Anthropology in the Postmodern Era,* pp. 51–101. Berkeley: University of California Press.

Tsing, Anna L. 1993. *In the Realm of the Diamond Queen: Marginality in an Out-of-the-Way Place.* Princeton: Princeton University Press.

Van Esterik, Penny, ed. 1982. *Women of Southeast Asia.* Monograph Series on Southeast Asia, Occasional Paper no. 9. Dekalb, Ill.: Northern Illinois University, Center for Southeast Asian Studies.

Ward, Barbara, ed. 1963. *Women in the New Asia: The Changing Social Roles of Men and Women in South and Southeast Asia.* Paris: UNESCO.

Weigert, Andrew. 1991. *Mixed Emotions: Certain Steps toward Understanding Ambivalence.* Albany: SUNY Press.

Williams, Brackette F. 1991. *Stains on My Name, War in My Veins: Guyana and the Politics of Cultural Struggle.* Durham: Duke University Press.

Williams, Raymond. 1977. *Marxism and Literature.* Oxford: Oxford University Press.

Wipper, Audrey. 1972. "African Women, Fashion, and Scapegoating." *Canadian Journal of African Studies* 6(2):329–349.

Wolf, Diane L. 1992. *Factory Daughters: Gender, Household Dynamics, and Rural Industrialization in Java.* Berkeley: University of California Press.

ONE

Why Women Rule the Roost:
Rethinking Javanese Ideologies of
Gender and Self-Control

Suzanne A. Brenner

Suzanne Brenner's opening essay both draws upon and provides a vital, gendered critique of Benedict Anderson's pioneering (1972) work on Javanese notions of spiritual power or potency. Her main concern is to point up the limits and silences of the "official line" emphasized in the literature on Java—for example, that Javanese men tend to avoid trading in the marketplace and managing the domestic economy because of concerns that their involvement in such domains might undermine their spiritual potency or otherwise sully their status. Arguing that such explanations only go so far, Brenner delineates the alternative, largely counterhegemonic, view, heretofore given scant attention in the ethnographic literature, that men do not actively participate in such domains because they are, as Thomas Stamford Raffles put it early in the nineteenth century, "fools in money concerns" owing to their inability to control their passions or desires (nafsu) and thus act in accordance with their reason or rationality (akal). This alternative view holds that women, inherently more capable of controlling their base desires, are better suited than men to accumulating material and spiritual resources that can be invested in the production of the family's status in the wider society. It thus challenges the commonplace assumption that Javanese women are less concerned with matters of status. But what are the limits of women's self-control? As a domain long managed by women, the marketplace continues to be seen as a place where women cannot be controlled by men. Rumors of rampant sexuality among female traders point to the ambivalence with which women's self-control is viewed, further complicating the linkages that have been posited between self-control, status, and spiritual potency in Java.

Brenner's focus on contrasting representations of gender and shifting embodiments of power and status not only provides a vital corrective to the literature on Javanese ideologies of gender and self-control; it also contributes to our understanding of the contextually specific and highly variable and contingent ways in which masculinities and femininities are constructed, contested, and otherwise reworked in contemporary Islamic societies through discourses drawing on (more or less) pan-Islamic notions of "reason" and "passion." More fundamentally, it calls into question the value of totalizing models of power and prestige that take male dominance for granted without considering the multiple discourses and conflicting logics at play in any gendered field.

The ethnographic literature on Java has referred repeatedly over the years to a concept that can be glossed as "spiritual potency" (see Keeler 1987, 1990; C. Geertz 1960; Anderson 1972; Hatley 1990; S. Errington 1990). According to a number of ethnographic accounts, there is a common belief among Javanese people that individuals have the potential to develop a concentration of inner spiritual strength through the sustained practice of emotional and behavioral self-control. Individuals who have amassed this mystical power are said to be recognizable through their constantly calm demeanor, their refined speech styles and comportment, and their ability to elicit deferential behavior from others without apparent coercion or effort. Such individuals are lauded for achieving the goal of self-mastery, ultimately leading to the ability to master others (Anderson 1972; Keeler 1987).

Ideas about spiritual potency do seem to be widespread in Java. It is clear, however, that these ideas have been most highly elaborated and systematically perpetuated among the ranks of the traditional Javanese aristocratic-cum-bureaucratic elite, the *priyayi* (see C. Geertz 1960; J. Errington 1984, 1988; Sutherland 1979). The concept of spiritual potency and the practices associated with it reinforce the ethical codes, behavioral norms, and linguistic styles that uphold *priyayi* claims to high status and cultural superiority. This concept is thus part of a larger ideological system that legitimates the deeply entrenched social hierarchies of Javanese society, especially those that have developed in the environs of the courtly centers of Solo and Yogyakarta. The ideology of spiritual potency supports the notion that people of high social status are inherently deserving of that status, and deserving of the deferential behavior and language that high status commands, because of their superior spiritual strength and moral worth.

Although the elite *priyayi* class includes females as well as males, I suggest that these ideologies of spiritual potency reinforce the superiority of *priyayi* males in particular, while placing all females, regardless of social class, in a categorically inferior spiritual, moral, and social position. The assertion that males are spiritually stronger than females is used to justify *priyayi* declarations that women should defer to and faithfully serve men,

whether their husbands, fathers, or rulers. Within this ideological framework, it is often said that men have greater self-control than women over
their emotions and behavior, suggesting that men are "naturally" stronger
than women in a spiritual sense, and that women should "naturally" defer
to them as a result. The fact that these ideologies are not confined to the
ranks of the *priyayi* alone, but are also commonly voiced among other elements of the Javanese population, indicates that their influence on gender
relations and identities in Javanese society deserves some attention.

Several types of linguistic and behavioral "evidence" are used to support
the idea that men have greater self-control, and therefore greater spiritual
potency, than women. It is said, for example, that men have greater mastery over the hierarchical intricacies and etiquette of the Javanese language,[1] thereby indicating their superior personal refinement; that men
are more able and more inclined than women to perform various sorts of
ascetic practices, which both reflect upon and augment their power and
self-control; and that men's sexual prowess and potency is linked to a more
spiritual kind of potency that women lack.

While Javanese women sometimes express their agreement with these
assertions of male power and self-control, they frequently give accounts of
male and female behavior that directly contradict the same notions. This
paper will explore conflicting Javanese representations of gender, drawing
into question the stereotyped, male-centered visions of male potency—inevitably suggesting female impotency—that pervade Javanese cultural representations, and which have in turn shaped ethnographic accounts of how
gender "works" in Java. It will focus on ideas about human passions and
the ability to control those passions, and how these ideas underlie the negotiation of male and female identities and statuses within the broader
social order. The marketplace and the home—two places that are closely
associated with women in Javanese thought—will be seen not only as sites
of economic production and of social and biological reproduction, but
also as sites where conflicting understandings of male and female nature
are symbolically and ideologically negotiated.

Although many scholars have recognized the need to draw a distinction
between ideologies of gender and the actual social practices that may belie
those ideologies (e.g., Tsing 1990; Keeler 1990), there remains a persistent
tendency for ethnographic accounts to privilege dominant or hegemonic
representations of gender.[2] By "dominant" or "hegemonic" representations or ideologies, I refer to those models that support the claims of a
particular category of people to superior status and power, models which
are most likely to be invoked in formal discourse and which are most often
accorded a position of supremacy among other, potentially competing
models. Ideologies, particularly the clearly articulated gender ideologies
that many people seem to have ready at the tips of their tongues, tend to

have a simplicity and even elegance to them that is difficult to resist. These dominant representations have a way of taking over studies of gender even when the writer is fully aware that they do not exhaust the full range of cultural discourses or social practices.

As a result, the ethnographic record presents a somewhat uneven picture of gender in Java—a topic that has been treated quite shallowly to date. It emphasizes certain prevalent, generally male-focused gender ideologies, while paying scant attention to less systematically articulated conceptions of gender, especially those that are voiced more often by women. In this paper I will point to an alternative, sometimes submerged view of male and female nature that presents a counterpoint to more conventional depictions of gender in Java. In the final analysis, however, no single configuration of gender relations can be considered absolutely "correct" or total, because constructions of gender invariably encode conflicting and ambivalent meanings that can never be fully reconciled (Ong 1987, 1990; Flax 1990).

CONTESTED AUTHORITY IN THE JAVANESE HOUSEHOLD

At a certain point in many Javanese wedding ceremonies, the bride and groom approach each other. When a few paces still remain between them, each one takes up a small quantity of betel (*sirih*) and throws it at the other, the idea being that the one whose betel hits the other person first will be the dominant partner in the marriage. It is often said that the bride should make sure that she loses the contest, but apparently the outcome is not always predictable. In a tone of mild amusement, Augusta de Wit describes this nuptial ritual as she observed it early in this century:

> With measured steps, the two advanced towards each other; and whilst yet at some distance paused. Two small bags of sirih-leaves containing chalk and betel-nuts were handed them; and with a quick movement each threw his at the other's head. The bride's little bag struck the groom full in the face. "It is she that will rule the roost," said one of the women, chuckling. And I fancied I saw a gleam of satisfaction pass over the bride's demure little face, half hidden though it was by the strings of beads and jessamine flowers dependent from her head dress. The next moment however, she had humbly knelt down on the floor. One of the bridesmaids handed her a basin full of water and a towel; and she proceeded to wash her husband's feet, in token of loyalty and loving submission (De Wit [1912] 1984:306–307).

This small ritual seems to epitomize the ambivalence with which the gendered division of domestic power is viewed in Java. On the one hand, the dominant ideology dictates that the wife should defer to her husband's greater prestige and authority as the nominal head of the household; thus, the bride is supposed to make sure that the groom wins the betel battle, and washes his foot "in token of loyalty and loving submission." On the other hand, the reality of the situation is that in many Javanese households, women enjoy a de facto power which far outweighs that of their husbands. Consequently, no one is too surprised if the bride's betel strikes the groom first.[3]

The observations of a host of anthropologists confirm that in the majority of homes, the woman does indeed "rule the roost"; Robert Jay puts it quite bluntly when he writes that married men in rural Java are "probably among the most henpecked lot of husbands anywhere in the world" (Jay 1969:92). Scholars have remarked in particular on the prominent economic roles of women and their central position in the household (H. Geertz 1961; Jay 1969; Stoler 1977; Koentjaraningrat 1985; Siegel 1986; Papanek and Schwede 1988; Keeler 1987, 1990; Hatley 1990). The dominance of women in the household is almost invariably linked to their economic power, often both inside and outside the home. In *The Javanese Family*, for example, Hildred Geertz notes that within the domestic domain, "The wife makes most of the decisions; she controls all family finances, and although she gives her husband formal deference and consults with him on major matters, it is usually she who is dominant" (1961:46). Much earlier accounts of Javanese society reveal that women's economic clout is not a modern development; in 1817, Sir Thomas Stamford Raffles wrote, "It is usual for the husband to entrust his pecuniary affairs entirely to his wife. The women alone attend the markets, and conduct all the business of buying and selling. It is proverbial to say that the Javanese men are fools in money concerns" ([1817] 1965:353).

In most Javanese families today, regardless of social class or occupation, the wife continues to manage household finances.[4] Javanese women often voice the opinion that men are incompetent in managing money, and many men seem to agree (cf. H. Geertz 1961; Jay 1969). Husbands are expected to turn over most or all of their income to their wives, who in turn allocate it as they see fit for household expenditures, sometimes giving their husbands only pocket money with which to buy cigarettes or snacks. Although one hears complaints on both sides—the wife grumbling that her husband keeps more for himself than he should, while the husband feels that his wife demands too much from him—this financial arrangement is generally accepted as the proper one between husband and wife. At a wedding that I attended in a village in Central Java, the village headman delivered a typical lecture of fatherly advice to the bride and groom, amplified through the public address system for all the guests present to hear, during the course of which he drew attention to "the notion that we Javanese have of 'female money,' " (*dhuwit wédok*). "This means," he instructed the young couple, "that the husband should set aside a portion of his wage every month to turn over to his wife." However, many people—women in particular—would argue that a man should give his entire salary to his wife, not just a portion of it.

With regard to patterns of inheritance and property ownership, women also fare quite well relative to men. Both descent and inheritance are reckoned bilaterally in Java (as is true in many parts of Indonesia and in Southeast Asia more generally). Javanese custom prescribes that daughters and sons should inherit equal shares of property from their parents; this can include land, houses, jewelry, money, and other valuables.[5] Women often own property separately from their husbands, particularly property that they have inherited from their own parents, and they may dispose of it as they please (H. Geertz 1961). Husbands have no claim over their wives' property and, in the event of divorce, a woman may take with her whatever she inherited or otherwise brought with her into the marriage. Property that has been owned jointly by a husband and wife is usually divided evenly between them if they are divorced.

Women not only manage their husbands' incomes and control their own inherited property; they are also very important economic contributors to their households in their own right. In many households women earn as much as or more than their husbands. In fact, they are often the main or even sole breadwinners for their families. This is certainly the case in households where men are absent (many households are headed by women alone, in part because of the high divorce rate in Java), but it is also true in some households where both husband and wife are present. Women's earnings through agricultural or other wage labor, craft manufacture, trade, or employment in the informal sector (for instance, as domestic servants or sidewalk food vendors) not infrequently exceed their husbands' economic contributions to the household. Many Javanese women also pursue careers as civil servants, teachers, doctors, and owners or employees of shops and other private businesses.

In the merchant community of Solo, the city in Central Java where I conducted research, women were quite commonly the major providers for their families as textile merchants or market traders, while their husbands took a back seat to them in running the family businesses and in managing household finances.[6] What Raffles observed in the early nineteenth century continues to be true in Solo today: among the Javanese, women dominate the markets, from petty retail trade up to the lucrative large-scale wholesale trade in agricultural products, textiles, and other commodities.[7] In the region of Central Java that includes the court cities of Solo and Yogyakarta, it is a commonplace that a market stall entrusted to a Javanese man is doomed to failure (cf. Atmowiloto 1986). The prevailing stereotype in Solo is that while the wife goes off each day to the market to earn a living for her family, her husband stays at home, amusing himself by whistling to his songbirds.[8] In this sense, the relationship of men and women to money at the marketplace closely parallels the situation found in the home: just as men are deemed ill suited to handling household finances, they are also considered incapable of competently managing many kinds of businesses.

THE RELATIVE STATUSES OF WOMEN AND MEN

The dominance of women in their households, combined with their economic strength and autonomy, would seem to suggest a degree of social and economic status for women in Java which is comparable to that of men. To the extent that status can be measured by financial independence, influence in the family, and the freedom to make one's own decisions, women do indeed enjoy, at least in some respects, nearly equal standing to men.

Yet the notion of "status" itself is a very complex one in Java, not reducible to economic position or to any other simple factor.[9] Considerations of status shape every interpersonal encounter and linguistic utterance (C. Geertz 1960; Siegel 1986; Keeler 1987; J. Errington 1988). Status, always relative, is determined by a remarkably intricate set of considerations. These considerations include, but are not limited to, age and seniority, whether one is of noble descent, education, occupation, wealth, ethnicity, place of origin (e.g., village versus city), and gender. Status is also measured on the basis of somewhat less tangible qualities—for example, degree of cultural refinement, mastery of elaborate linguistic etiquette and social skills, and the reputed possession of spiritual strength. The concept of prestige is important in the evaluation of status, but is sometimes divorced from other determinants of status, such as wealth. For example, certain occupations, such as palace retainer, Muslim religious leader, or petty civil servant, are poorly paid but are still considered prestigious, at least in some circles. On the other hand, ethnic Chinese, many of whom are quite well-to-do, are categorically disrespected by many Javanese in spite of their wealth, due to the pervasive stereotypes that hold them to be unrefined, greedy, and incapable of mastering proper Javanese linguistic etiquette.[10]

Scholars of Javanese society are generally quick to point out that while women have economic power and considerable control over household affairs, in the realm of prestige they fall far short of men (Jay 1969; Hatley 1990; Keeler 1987, 1990). This detracts markedly from society's overall evaluation of their status. According to key ideological formulations, women have certain inborn character traits that doom them to an inferior station in life no matter how much money they earn or how much power they wield in the household (Hatley 1990; Keeler 1987, 1990). As these representations have it, most women are lacking in the qualities that lead individuals to be designated as "high status" even when they control substantial economic resources and domestic authority.

What is it about women that relegates them to this (ideologically, at least) inferior position? Ironically, one of the very characteristics that appears to give women so much autonomy and power in the household— their economic prowess—is also one of the main factors detracting from their prestige. In the central ideologies of Javanese society, there is an undeniable devaluation of the economic activities for which women and traders are known. Excessive attention to financial matters and the pursuit of wealth is said to indicate low status, lack of refinement, and a corresponding lack of spiritual potency (Anderson 1972; Keeler 1987, 1990; Djajadiningrat-Nieuwenhuis 1987; Hatley 1990; S. Errington 1990). Matters of money, especially where bargaining or the open pursuit of profit are involved, are seen as *kasar*—unrefined, uncivilized, coarse, and of low status.[11] Individuals who are mindful of their prestige must be careful never to show too much concern with money, lest they be seen as *kasar* too.

The idea that a preoccupation with money points to low status—an idea that is strongest among *priyayi* elites but which is also held, to some extent, by nonelites—shows how deeply ingrained *priyayi* ideologies are in Javanese society. *Priyayi* ideologies can be traced to the marriage of Javanese aristocratic values with nineteenth-century codes of proper conduct for indigenous servants of the colonial bureaucracy, espoused by Dutch and Javanese elites and legitimated by reference to Javanese tradition. It was in the interest of the well-entrenched colonial state and its Javanese functionaries, the members of the *priyayi* class, to support ideologies that made service to the state, rather than independent wealth, the primary source of prestige in Javanese society. The view that trade was inherently coarse protected *priyayi* and colonial interests against those of a monied elite that might otherwise have rivaled them for status and power (see Brenner 1991a). Particularly in the court centers of Solo and Yogyakarta, trade among the Javanese was considered the proper domain only of women and low-status men, as well as members of "foreign" ethnic groups such as Chinese, Arabs, or Europeans. While some *priyayi* women did engage in trade in order to supplement their husbands' incomes, their *priyayi* status was not questioned as long as their husbands were not openly involved in business. Dutch observers claimed that the Javanese were generally ill suited to trade (e.g., van Deventer 1904), noting that "only" the women seemed to have any business sense. It has been argued convincingly that the colonial dismissal of trade as an insignificant sideline activity for women served ideologically to legitimate state policies that limited Javanese participation in the most profitable areas of commerce (Alexander and Alexander 1991:373).

The broad influence of *priyayi* values in Javanese society has often been noted. This influence did not stop with the end of colonial rule, but has continued on into the present period, in a process that has been referred to as "priyayization," whereby *priyayi* norms and values are adopted by other elements of the population (see Djajadiningrat-Nieuwenhuis 1987). While Javanese men are increasingly involved in business, especially in the more modern sectors of the economy, and although wealth is, in practice, a very important source of status in Indonesian society, there remains a certain taint to business matters and to the handling of money, and a continued association of the less savory aspects of monetary and mercantile pursuits with women and ethnic minorities, all of which indicate that *priyayi* ideologies have not lost their hold upon the Javanese population.

Women, then, appear to be destined to inhabit the low-status, "coarse" realm of the social hierarchy. Their firm obligation as wives and mothers is to attend to financial matters: they are supposed to see to it that every last *rupiah* of the family's money is wisely spent. Those who are traders must bargain and calculate shrewdly in order to compete successfully in the overcrowded marketplace, where acting refined is out of the question. Other aspects of women's conduct also seem to support the conclusion that women are more *kasar,* and therefore of lower status, than men. Women are quicker than men to use low, or *kasar,* forms of Javanese language (*Jawa kasar, ngoko*), and to otherwise display behavior without embarrassment that many men would feel to be beneath their dignity. In the marketplace, even the wealthiest women traders can be seen slapping each other on the arm in a gesture of friendliness, shouting and laughing boisterously, and hurling pieces of cloth or wads of money across the aisles at each other. Few men of similar socioeconomic position would be willing to comport themselves this way in a public setting; they would consider such behavior demeaning and damaging to their prestige.

Men's interactions with each other, in contrast to women's, tend to be stiff and formal, marked by an attention to social and linguistic decorum that is almost painful to watch when one has become accustomed to the earthier, more relaxed styles of women (see H. Geertz 1961). The higher a man's social standing, the more circumscribed his range of behavioral and speech styles must be in order to protect and regenerate his status, style being a critical element of an individual's status image (cf. Keeler 1987, 1990; J. Errington 1988). Although this is also true for women, the latter are not expected to control their language and conduct to the same degree as men.[12] Ward Keeler (1990) remarks that "Women can disaggregate status and style more than men can in part because . . . women's status is defined in considerable measure by that of their husbands" (Keeler 1990:144; cf. Hatley 1990:184). As he also observes, to the extent that women's behavior and speech styles are accorded less weight than men's, women have the freedom to engage with relative impunity in behavior that would be compromising to men's status. Women are not thought *incapable* of speaking or behaving in an *alus* or refined manner—indeed, it is primarily women, not men, who are given the task of educating their female *and* male children in linguistic and behavioral politesse—but the wider range of social styles deemed acceptable for women gives them the reputation for behaving erratically, and not always in accordance with common standards of refined behavior.

IDEOLOGIES OF GENDER AND SELF-CONTROL

In a highly influential article entitled "The Idea of Power in Javanese Culture," Benedict Anderson (1972) explores Javanese ideologies of spiritual potency, which he terms "Power." To grossly simplify his more elaborate explanation: this form of Power goes beyond ordinary worldly power as it is generally understood in the West. It is a kind of divine energy and mystical inner strength that enables an individual to control himself, other people, and his environment without the use of crude physical, political, or material force. This Power is said to be accumulated and concentrated through ascetic exercise and through other forms of self-discipline that involve sustained control over one's personal passions and desires. The more self-discipline an individual has, the more spiritual power he amasses, which in turn leads to further self-control as well as the ability to master supernatural forces and the wills of human beings.

A calm, refined (*alus*) demeanor is taken to indicate that an individual possesses a large store of personal Power. Achieving high status is contingent upon having this Power, and consequently upon projecting an image of having total but effortless mastery over the inner passions. Powerful persons can thus be recognized from their poise, restraint, and equanimity in all situations. Conversely, those who are unable to control their emotions, speech, or behavior demonstrate their lack of spiritual potency (Anderson 1972; see also Keeler 1987; Hatley 1990). Excessive attention to the pursuit of personal gain, including economic profit, is seen as a sign of greed and self-interest, betokening lack of Power and low status.

Anderson does not directly address the issue of gender in his article, which, as he writes in a later retrospective paper, was intended primarily to offer an alternative, culturally unique perspective to Weber's concept of charisma (Anderson 1990). Whether this model of Power might apply differently to women or men is beyond the scope and intent of the article: the relationship of women to Power is not specifically discussed (see Djajadiningrat-Nieuwenhuis 1987:46). The article does draw some clear linkages between male sexual potency and spiritual potency, however, and the examples cited of Powerful figures are all male.

Later studies of Javanese gender relations have been more explicit in revealing the male-centered focus of the ideology of spiritual potency. In particular, several authors have noted that, according to the rhetoric of spiritual potency, women find it much harder than men to harness the self-control and mental discipline needed to acquire spiritual power. Ascetic exercise, which Anderson identifies as one of the primary means of acquiring Power, is said to be especially difficult (although not impossible) for women. In Hatley's words, "Though women may perform ascetic exercise, it is not considered usual for them to do so. Thus they are seen as incapable of refined controlled speech and of the emotional control that is the outward reflection of accumulated spiritual strength" (Hatley 1990:182). This view is shared by other scholars, such as Madelon Djajadiningrat-Nieuwenhuis, who writes, "According to the Javanese idea of the woman's role, she is more bound to her social and material context and consequently less suited for asceticism, which after all means distancing oneself from one's social environment. Only in very exceptional cases can women muster sufficient kekuwatan batin (mental strength) to acquire Power" (Djajadiningrat-Nieuwenhuis 1987:47; see also C. Geertz 1960:329).

Whether or not women actually do engage in ascetic practice is an issue to which I shall return presently. What *is* clear, however, is that women rarely make the extreme effort that men do to suppress strong affect and emotion, or to present an ever cool, refined demeanor to others. Hence it is less common for them to adhere to the codes of outward behavior that are portrayed by the dominant ideologies as reflective of high status and an inner spiritual strength.

When visiting a marketplace in Solo, I witnessed an especially amusing bout of bargaining between two experienced traders that brought home to me the difference between women's and men's styles of interaction, especially where self-control and refinement are concerned. One of the traders, Bu (Mrs.) Sita, was a friendly woman, quite successful in business, who had owned a stall in the market for a number of years. The other trader was a self-assured woman who wanted to buy a quantity of batik cloth wholesale from Bu Sita to sell again elsewhere. The pace of their bargaining was fast and furious, and the language used by the women, all low (*kasar*) Javanese, was rough, their tone almost a growl. The buyer was pointing out imperfections in the cloth and making low offers, while the seller, Bu Sita, kept refusing, insisting on a higher price. The bargaining became more and more intense, and the two of them seemed to be getting angrier and angrier with each other, to the point where I was beginning to wonder if they would actually come to blows. All of a sudden, before I knew what was happening, they both broke into broad grins, slapped each other on the arm jovially, and the sale was made, with sounds of disgust and exasperation, obviously exaggerated, coming from the buyer as she looked at the prices on the receipt that Bu Sita was writing for her. They chuckled together, chatted amicably and inquired about each other's families, the tone of their conversation changing dramatically from what it had been just moments earlier. It was only at that point that I realized the women were old friends who had been doing business together for years.

Two Javanese men would have been much less apt to put on such a display. Even a semblance of a strong emotion like anger would be construed as a lack of control, threatening their status as well as their friendship. Many Javanese men in Solo—even those of the trading class, remarkably enough—are reluctant to bargain at all. Although they often claim disdain for the marketplace and dislike of its *kasar* atmosphere (in keeping with the ideology of spiritual potency), it appears that what they fear most is the possibility of losing the image of self-control, equanimity, and disinterest in personal gain that is so important for maintaining men's status. They therefore avoid the marketplace, where it is especially hard to maintain linguistic propriety and an image of perpetual composure. The majority of Javanese men are more than happy to leave the business of buying and selling to their wives (cf. Siegel 1986).

Sudden shifts in language and behavior are quite common in the marketplace, and in women's interactions more generally. As women, the traders that I observed had the flexibility to switch stylistic registers abruptly without fearing loss of face or loss of friendship, although the sharp swings that sometimes characterize women's speech and behavior are also seen by the dominant representations as indicating their inability to master their emotions and behavioral style. Keeler (1990) observes that women's lability in style is considered by some Javanese as a sign that women are by their very nature lacking in self-control. Dominated by their impulses and emotions, their behavior is never fully predictable.[13] This broad categorization of women, he adds, has negative implications for their social status. Building on Anderson's earlier argument, which ties refinement to spiritual potency and status, Keeler suggests that these generalizations about women's lack of self-control ultimately point to their lack of spiritual potency and consequent lower status relative to men.

The Javanese ideological declaration that men are better able than women to control themselves also dovetails well with Islamic gender ideologies. These pan-Islamic conceptions of male and female nature, which are found in Indonesia and Malaysia as well as in the Middle East and elsewhere in the Islamic world, portray men as innately more capable than women of controlling their base passions and instincts, *nafsu*.[14] Although men as well as women have natural desires that threaten to overcome them, it is believed that men have greater rationality and reason, *akal*, which enables them to suppress those desires and to hold fast to the guidance of the Qur'an (see, e.g., Siegel 1969; Rosen 1984; Abu-Lughod 1986; Mernissi 1987; Ong 1987, 1990; Peletz, this volume). Women are said to be more emotional, sexual, and irrational than men by nature; hence they must be carefully controlled by men so that they do not lead the latter astray from the proper path, thereby wreaking havoc on the social and religious order. Although I did not encounter this explicitly Islamic interpretation of human nature during the course of my research in Solo (where the majority of the population, although professing adherence to Islam, heavily mixes Islamic beliefs and practices with those of Javanese origin, often making it difficult and perhaps irrelevant to distinguish clearly between "Javanese" and "Islamic"), I would conjecture that it has been incorporated into the Javanese ideologies that associate women with irrationality and emotionality and men with self-control and a superior capacity for reason.

These two sets of gender ideologies, Javanese and Islamic, present an unproblematic image of men as potent, self-controlled, and in possession of the higher mental and spiritual faculties that allow them to maintain order in their own lives and in the social and supernatural world. Women, on the other hand, are depicted as spiritually impotent, less rational than men, and lacking in self-control. Such categorical statements about the nature of the sexes are well in keeping with an ideological system that places men at the center of the social, moral, and symbolic order. This ideological system has been generated and reinforced not only by the values of the Javanese *priyayi* elite, as mentioned earlier, but also by the patriarchal tendencies of Dutch colonial rule (in which male dominance was taken for granted in both political and domestic life, and which itself had a marked influence on the development of nineteenth- and twentiethcentury *priyayi* rhetoric), of Islamic doctrine, and of the postcolonial Indonesian state.

Almost everyone I knew in Java, men and women alike, paid lip service to the notion that the father is the head of the household, and therefore deserving of deferential behavior from every other member of the family. Men also dominate the political order, from the community level up to the national level, and tend to serve as the representatives of their households in matters concerning the local and state bureaucracies. It is hardly surprising, then, to find gender stereotypes that associate women with low-status behavior—capriciousness, lack of control, emotionality—and men with the positive, high-status qualities of behavioral stability and self-discipline.

A CONTRARY VIEW: THE DANGER OF MEN'S DESIRE

I stress the *ideological* nature of these constructs, however, because in many situations, one finds an entirely different conceptualization of human nature in Java. This alternative, sometimes submerged view is also formulaic, but it contradicts the dominant ideological premise that to be male is to have greater self-control, whereas to be female is to be lacking in self-control. According to this vision of male and female nature, *men* find it much more difficult to restrain their innate passions and desires (*nafsu* or *hawa nafsu*) than do women. While both men and women are subject to the sometimes overwhelming influence of their own desires, it is women, not men, who can better control themselves. Although this idea is expressed more openly and more often by women than by men, as one might expect, it is *not* a view held exclusively by women, for men, too, often make statements or engage in actions that support this belief. I would argue, in fact, that this conception of the nature of the sexes underlies key roles that men and women play in the household, and that it forms the basis for their practices in other spheres of social life.

By underscoring this alternate understanding of gender and self-control, I do not intend to offer it as a "female countercultural" model that undermines male views. Nor do I propose that this is the "true" Javanese model, to be accorded absolute primacy over competing models, be they Islamic, *priyayi*, or other. Rather, this is a view of human nature that is invoked in specific contexts by males as well as females, devout Muslims and non-Muslims, *priyayi* and non-*priyayi*. To the extent that it contradicts the dominant gender ideologies, it may be seen as counterhegemonic (see Peletz, this volume), yet its proponents include people who in other situations would uphold the dominant ideology of male potency without hesitation. Even to characterize this contradiction as a conflict between ideology and practice, or between thought and action (Gramsci 1957) misses the mark, because both these conflicting representations of gender and self-control are verbalized as axiomatic truths *and* expressed implicitly in people's actions. The key to understanding these contradictory views of gender is to see them as alternative paradigms that can be called upon to legitimate and to interpret the actions of males and females in different contexts. In formal discourse, the hegemonic view of male potency and self-control is more likely to be emphasized, while the view that men have less self-control than women often comes to the fore in casual discourse where there is less at stake ideologically.

Because ethnographers have highlighted the dominant model for so long, in the remainder of this essay I will focus on the subordinate perspective in order to demonstrate its significance for understanding gender relations. To start, it is important to look at the way the concept of desire, *nafsu*, is figured in a specifically Javanese sense. Many Javanese believe that to experience desire is normal to the human condition, but to be governed by it is dangerous, not only to the individual, but also to the family and to society. Here, one should distinguish between ordinary desires, and those that are excessive and therefore potentially disturbing both to an individual's internal equilibrium and to the social relationships in which he or she participates. *Nafsu* connotes ardent longing or passionate desire which, if left uncontrolled, causes people to behave in an unbalanced, irrational, or socially unacceptable manner.

Nafsu may take many forms, but the most powerful, and therefore potentially most dangerous, desires are those for sex and money—lust and greed, which are often seen as intrinsically related. Many Javanese men and women seem to take it as a given that men have an innately greater desire for sex than women, and that this desire is extremely difficult for them to suppress. Although this notion seems to run counter to both Javanese and Islamic ideologies that hold males to have greater control of their instincts and emotions than females, I encountered it often enough to be convinced that it was not just the idiosyncratic opinion of a few individuals. The degree to which it actually contradicts the ideology of male potency is debatable, however, since it reaffirms male sexual potency—a concomitant of male spiritual potency (see Anderson 1972)—even as it challenges men's ability to master their passions.

In relation to economic practices, this alternative view of the inherent differences between women and men leads people in Solo to conclude that women are naturally better suited to managing household finances, the family firm, or the marketplace. But what is the connection between controlling money and controlling one's passions? The words of one unusually candid Javanese man in his seventies summed it up: "Women make better traders and entrepreneurs than men, because men have greater lust (*syahwat*) than women. Men can never hold onto money for long, because if you give them money, they'll spend it on getting women. Give 'em enough money, and they'll have more than one wife, either out in the open or on the sly.[15] Men have greater desires than women (*nafsuné niku, gedhé wong lanang*). It's always men who spend money on women, who 'buy' women. Who ever heard of a woman buying a man?" A female textile merchant made a similar remark: "When men get hold of money, they use it to take another wife, or to gamble." Yet another woman commented, "You can tell if a man is keeping a woman on the side—eventually he gets found out because he's spending money too quickly." A man's lust requires money, I was told, because few women will sleep with a man illicitly unless they can derive some financial benefit from it. Moreover, men's natural proclivity to give in to their desires, it is said, leads them to squander money in the process; they will stop at nothing to find satisfaction for their passions.

One often hears lower-class women in particular, such as household servants or batik workers, complain about the financial drain that their husbands' sexual indulgence, gambling, and general irresponsibility and lack of consideration for the family's welfare create for them and their children. Stories of husbands who abandon their wives and children to run off with other women are everyday fare, but many women feel that this is preferable to having a husband who stays around and continues to sap the family's already strained resources, without contributing anything in return.

Inem, a village woman who worked as a housekeeper for a family in Solo, often grumbled about the problems that her husband's womanizing caused for her and her two children. Not untypically, it was Inem, not her husband, who supported the family; her husband only worked about one month in ten, she figured, but he continued to come to her for money when he needed it. He spent most of his time with another woman in a nearby village, only making an appearance at home once every week or so. Fed up with the situation, Inem asked her husband for a divorce, but he refused, as did the local village authorities, who had the final say in the matter. She told me that she would have been happy to divorce him, and would not want to marry again. She already had two children, lived close to her mother, and got along well with her mother-in-law, with whom she and her children shared a house. What did she need a husband for? She was better off without one, she said. That way, she could devote herself and her limited money exclusively to her two children.

The "official" view that has been emphasized in the ethnographic litera-ture is that men are too concerned with their prestige to bother themselves with petty and demeaning monetary matters. They turn their wages over to their wives and leave all the marketing to their wives as well, because they consider financial affairs to be beneath their dignity. This is consistent with the ideology of male potency, for undue concern with financial gain is considered to be detrimental to an individual's spiritual power and social standing. However, the alternative view, that men cannot hold onto money because they cannot control their desires, suggests that the accepted "offi-cial" line is not sufficient to explain why women take charge of financial affairs while men tend to avoid them. The alternative view of men's lack of control relative to women's is invoked often enough to take on an authority of its own, encouraging as well as explaining certain types of behavior for men and women.

Although anecdotes and warnings about men's lack of self-control fre-quently focus on their lust, men are also accused of (and admit their own guilt over) uncontrolled gambling, extravagant consumption, and other spendthrift practices. However, since lust is considered one of the most potent forms of *nafsu* it seems to stand as a figure for all forms of desire, representing the power of base passions over the will to be self-disciplined. Money tempts men to various forms of profligacy, but lust serves as the ultimate symbol of human—especially male—weakness. Money is thus seen as the gateway to the fulfillment of desire, and sex comes to represent all desires that money can fulfill, which may explain why discussions of men's inability to handle money so commonly refer to their lustfulness. The de-sire for money and the things that money can buy is thought to exert a powerful influence on both women and men, but women are expected (by women and men alike) to be able to keep their desire under control for the sake of the family. While such self-discipline is an ideal for men as well, it is widely believed that a man's passion-ridden nature sorely taxes his ability to exercise restraint, which becomes, of course, a self-fulfilling prophecy. While this flies in the face of the ideology of superior male self-control, it is worth noting that many men appear to take a perverse pride in the unquenchable lust and "naughtiness" of those of their sex—suggesting, once again, that the positive associations of sexual potency and of generally "manly" behavior offset any shame that might accompany their inability to exercise self-control.

A friend related the story of a young village man who had made off with all the gold jewelry that his wife, who was expecting a child, had borrowed from his mother to wear for a ritual ceremony (*mitoni*) that is held during a woman's first pregnancy. Several months after abandoning his wife and unborn child, he showed up destitute on a relative's doorstep in the city, having spent all the money from the sale of the jewelry, everyone assumed, on gambling and prostitutes. His parents came to pick him up and brought him back to the village, where he resumed life in their home with his wife and new baby. The young man, who had never had much money of his own, had been unable to overcome the temptation that was presented when he suddenly had access to a considerable amount of wealth, in the form of his mother's jewelry. However, it is not too surprising that his parents and wife were willing to accept their prodigal son and husband back into their home, since his behavior, although certainly reproachable, was in keeping with common Javanese beliefs about male nature. From infancy on, males are expected to be "naughty" (*nakal*), and the attainment of adult status does nothing to change this expectation (see H. Geertz 1961).

Women's control over their own desires serves to compensate for men's lack of control (as the alternative representation has it), and by so doing preserves the assets that should properly be used to ensure the family's security. It is the wife's responsibility to do her utmost to make sure that her husband's desires do not drain the family's resources, while also doing everything in her means to *increase* those resources, thereby contributing to the improvement of her family's social status. By taking charge of the family's financial affairs and keeping her husband away from matters of money, the wife prevents her husband from squandering the family's wealth. She also protects her husband's dignity and status, which by association (since he is considered to be the main representative of the family) protects her own status and that of her children.

In accepting control of the family's finances, a woman is entrusted, in a sense, with her husband's desires, his *nafsu*. In other words, she must control not only her *own* passions, but also, to whatever extent possible, those of her husband. Women realize that there are limits to how far they can restrain their husbands' desires, but by controlling the family purse, they do what they can to keep in check a major source of temptation: money.

Just as women conserve material resources for the family by restraining desire, they also conserve spiritual resources through a similar, but more intensive, form of self-discipline. Although several authors have reported that few women engage in ascetic practices, my own research in Solo did not support this finding. Many people told me that when a child is sick, or is taking exams in school, it is the child's mother, not the father, who fasts, gets up to pray in the middle of the night, and deprives herself of sleep (all considered forms of asceticism) in order to help her child. I repeatedly encountered women who fasted—sometimes twice a week—or engaged in other ascetic practices on a regular basis, primarily, they said, for the bene-fit of their children and future descendants. In fact, several women told me point-blank that many men, in contrast to women, do not have the strength of will to carry out ascetic practices, contradicting the ethno-graphic commonplace that asceticism is predominantly a male undertak-ing in Java.[16]

The ability to control *nafsu* is considered integral to conserving money for the family and to the production of the more abstract benefits that accrue through ascetic exercise. Although men as well as women engage in ascetic practices, men's asceticism seems usually to be directed toward the fulfillment of *personal* goals, whereas women's ascetic practices are typi-cally carried out on behalf of their families. This is not to say that men take no interest in the welfare of their children. However, women believe that they have a naturally stronger bond with their offspring than their hus-bands do, which leads them to take the burden of securing their descen-dants' futures more heavily on their own shoulders. Most men appear to be more than willing to turn this responsibility over to their wives. Moreover, it is generally believed that if men cannot sufficiently curb their ordinary desires to accumulate material wealth for the family, they can scarcely be expected to exert the additional self-control required to engage in asceti-cism on their children's behalf.

Men's tendency to avoid the marketplace, which scholars have often attributed to their deep concern with prestige and spiritual potency, can also be understood in terms of this alternative model of gender and self-control. As a prime site for the accumulation of money and the acquisition of commodities, the marketplace seems to incite desire and at the same time advertise the potential for its satisfaction. The priority of an economic logic of commodity exchange in the marketplace, moreover, leads to a partial breakdown of the boundaries that conventionally order and circum-scribe social relations in Java, thereby creating a situation in which the social mechanisms for the suppression of desire are weak. Women believe they are better able than men to restrain themselves from giving in to the desires of the marketplace, and many men seem, whether tacitly or explicitly, to concur. Hence, the Solonese say that the market is a woman's world, *donyané wong wédok*. Most women *and* men believe that, aside from concerns of prestige, Javanese men are ill suited to trading in the marketplace because they lack the self-discipline needed to bring money home at the end of the day instead of squandering it.

In the large textile market that I frequented in Solo, few Javanese men were to be found, either as consumers or traders (there were, I should mention, plenty of men of Chinese and Arab descent among the traders; the rules for Javanese men do not hold for members of other ethnic groups). One notable exception, however, was a Javanese transvestite (*banci*) who ran one of the largest rotating cooperative credit associations (*arisan*) among the traders in the market.[17] Every day Pak (Mr.) Hardjo (some people called him *Bu* Hardjo because of his inclination to cross-dress) went around the market collecting money from participating traders, and he was responsible for picking the winners of that day's pot and distributing their shares to them. This was a job that the traders felt required tremendous self-control, because handling several million *rupiah* (well over a thousand dollars) each day was a source of temptation that even those of the strongest character might find difficult to resist. My sense was that as far as the women traders were concerned, Pak Hardjo's ambiguous gender made him an acceptable person to fill the role of *arisan* coordinator (from what I could tell, all the other *arisan* managers in the market were women), whereas a "straight" man would have been distrusted. His femaleness suggested trustworthiness, a self-discipline of which an unambiguously gendered male would not have been assumed capable. By taking on the mannerisms and clothing of a woman, Pak Hardjo also acquired the reputation that women have for being able to control their desires.

THE DANGER OF AUTONOMOUS WOMEN

The relationships between gender, desire, and economic practice are further complicated by the ambivalence with which women's self-control, and their control over money, is viewed. On the one hand, women are considered to be ever mindful of their families and less lustful than men, which keeps them in control of their desires. These are some of the factors which are said to make them "naturally" better traders than men. On the other hand, the more money a woman controls, the more autonomous she is, and an autonomous woman is always somewhat suspect. Self-control over one's desires is evaluated positively in Java, but a woman who is not subject to any *man's* control is potentially threatening to the male-dominated social order. Widows and divorcées, for example, are frequently the objects of gossip and suspicion for their sexual activities because they are no longer under the supervision or control of fathers or husbands (cf. Ong 1987:89).

The connections between economic independence and sexual license are often made explicit, as in the following passage from an Indonesian newspaper article entitled "Hunting for Satisfaction: Sex among the Ranks of Javanese Women":

> At 8:30 in the morning, Hartini, 27, a tall, slender, beautiful woman, steps supplely. Her hips sway, fully confident. "There's a diamond deal in Tawang-mangu," she remarks as she says goodbye to her husband and children and makes for the Mazda 323 Trendynamic that's ready to go.
>
> The metallic black Mazda hits the road without a moment's hesitation. And, at a plush villa, the car comes to a stop. Soon the attractive woman who was driving it gets out, and, as if quite at home, enters the villa. A man with the air of a big shot, who appears to have been waiting for some time, greets her, "Hello dear."
>
> How intimately this man takes Ms. Hartini by the shoulder. And, as if by plan, they jokingly go into a bedroom. Ah . . . must a diamond deal take place inside a closed room between two human beings of different sex?
>
> The above illustration is one incident that was recorded during a field study conducted for almost a year among women traders between the ages of 25–40, in one center of trade in Solo.
>
> The conclusions from that study were truly startling: "The higher the degree of a woman trader's economic independence, the greater her degree of sexual freedom." Might there be something amiss in the study, for instance, that the respondents were chosen incorrectly? [18]

This "field study" merely seemed to confirm rumors about female market traders that were already rife in Solo. There were stories, for instance, that some traders participated in a magical practice that required having sexual relations with someone other than their own spouse as a means of ensuring success in business. Others said that a few of the traders were actually prostitutes or madams who used their market stalls in order to find clients from among out-of-town male traders or customers, especially when sales of textiles and other goods were slow. It was said of market women that their "sarongs are loose" (*tapihé kendho*)—in other words, that they "come off easily" (*gampang dicopot*). In short, women traders had a reputation in the wider society for being willing to sell more than just their wares. One man recounted an anecdote to illustrate the allure of female traders in Solo, a city already infamous for its *femmes fatales:* "A man was on his way to Solo from another city, when he ran into a friend. When his friend found out where he was going, he said that *he* would like to go along, too, so that he could visit the market in Solo. 'I'll go to a batik trader there, and ask to see all her goods,' said the man. 'After she's laid out the last sarong in stock for me, I'll ask her for the *very* last one—the one she's wearing.' "

To say that "sexual freedom" for Solonese market women is the norm would clearly be an exaggeration. Like most stereotypes, this one was clearly blown out of proportion. What is significant, however, is the extent to which such generalizations prevail, and their implications for understanding the logics of gender in Java. These stories suggest that the marketplace, a domain controlled by women, is also a place where women cannot be controlled by men. But can market women control *themselves?* At first glance, stories about the "looseness" of women traders seem to contradict the notion that women have more control over their desires than men, making them better suited to handling money. For if it is indeed the case that the women who have the most dealings with money are also perceived as being the most widely involved in illicit sexual affairs, then it would appear that there is no clear connection between the control of money and the control of desire.

I should point out, however, that I never heard anyone in Solo attribute women's engagement in extramarital affairs to their uncontrollable desires. Sometimes it was attributed to women's dissatisfaction or boredom with their husbands, the wish to "get even" with husbands who had been unfaithful, or even the "need for recreation." More commonly, though, women's infidelity was imputed to economic need or ambition; for instance, a way to compensate for a slow period in the market. As I mentioned earlier, there was a general belief that few women would be willing to have adulterous relations were there not some financial gain to be had in the bargain. When a neighbor told me that a married woman with children she knew was driven by economic hardship to seek out liaisons with men, for example, I asked her if she was sure that the woman was being paid by the men she was seeing. "Well, if they didn't give her money, do you think she'd do it? Of course not," my neighbor answered matter-of-factly. Since a double standard in Javanese society makes it less acceptable for women to engage in extramarital relations than men, it is felt that most women will not take part in such activities lightly.[19]

Prevalent ideas about the dissimilar natures of men and women often lead people to conclude that whereas men are driven by their concupiscence to seek out extramarital relationships, women are more apt to be motivated by other factors, especially concern for the family's financial welfare. Women may be the objects of *men's* sexual desire, but they are not thought likely to succumb to their *own* sexual desires. This notion contradicts the idea that men are ruled by reason and women by their passions, but it should not be taken at face value, for it, too, constitutes a prescription for, rather than a description of, reality. I stress the formulaic nature of both the dominant and alternative conceptions of gender and self-control lest one or the other be taken as a statement of "fact" or "practice." Nonetheless, it should be kept in mind that these normative prescriptions often *do* have a real effect on individuals' everyday practices and their reactions to the behavior of others. In my observation, the belief that women have more self-control than men in matters of sex and money leads women and men to have very different expectations of themselves and of each other, and frequently to fulfill those expectations through particular modes of action.

Despite the definitiveness with which categorical assertions about gender and self-control are made, the stories about the sexual activities of market traders point to the underlying *ambivalence* with which the notion of self-control itself is viewed in Java. When a man controls his desires, it is commonly believed, he makes himself potent. When he lets his self-control lapse, he is a danger to the family. When a woman controls *her* desires, she accumulates economic and spiritual value for the family, more than personal potency. But a woman with too much control over her own person, it appears, is considered a threat to society. The woman merchant occupies an especially ambiguous position in Javanese society. She is thought better able than a man to suppress her own desires, but she is also seen as manipulating the desires of others toward her own ends. At home, she is entrusted with the safekeeping of her husband's desires and the welfare of her family, yet her success in business depends on her capacity to arouse the desires of her customers, to make them willing to spend money. It is this ambiguity that is reflected in the stories about the "sexual freedom" of women traders. Their "danger" lies in their ability to control their own passions, but to awaken those of others.

CONCLUSIONS

Aihwa Ong has noted that gender is a "potentially contradictory configuration of meaning that codes alternative structures of morality, control, and power" (Ong 1990:422). In this paper, I have attempted to demonstrate that Javanese discourses and practices of gender embody contradictory representations that sometimes confound the ideological association of males with a higher degree of self-control, potency, and morality than females. Why is this important? It is important, I propose, because the dominant ideologies of male potency serve to legitimate male control over women and over the society more broadly. By throwing these ideologies into question, the Javanese "cultural" insistence on male superiority and control is also brought into question. For too long the ethnography of Java has reproduced the rhetoric of male potency without discussing its alternatives. By failing to give adequate expression to contradictory representations of gender, these studies have implicitly taken men's claims to superior status and power as unshakable facts of Javanese culture, which, I am arguing here, they are not.

A one-sided approach to the relationships between gender, self-control, and potency, then, obscures the ambiguities, paradoxes, and multiple layers of meaning that attach to ideas about maleness and femaleness in Java. Although describing and analyzing the impact of dominant gender ideologies is worthwhile, to grant them too central a position in analysis may obscure subtler but equally important ways that people think and talk about gender. Furthermore, it is clear that both men *and* women in Java make pronouncements and engage in practices that support as well as contradict the dominant ideologies of spiritual potency and self-control. As I stated earlier, to assume that any of the viewpoints offered here represents "the male point of view" or "the female point of view," would be incorrect (cf. Yanagisako and Collier 1987), even if one perspective seems to privilege men over women (or vice versa), or is voiced more often by men or women.

Javanese women give tacit approval to ideologies of superior male potency and status by deferring to their husbands in both private and public contexts, and by helping them to avoid situations in which their prestige might be compromised (see Keeler 1990 for a nice illustration of this point). At the same time, women freely express the opinion that most men have uncontrollable passions and childlike dispositions which prevent them from acting in the best interests of their families. Women, they add, must rely on their own superior strength of will in order to compensate for their husbands' lack of control. Many Javanese men also admit openly that members of their sex are less capable than women of controlling their base desires (especially lust), even while they make categorical statements about women's inability to manage their emotions and behavior. In formal or public interactions, where male dominance and prestige tend to be highlighted, men attempt to project an image of equanimity and total self-mastery, but in private, they may give rein to their passions, thus fulfilling other cultural expectations for male behavior. Conversely, in public situations Javanese women sometimes appear cheerfully unconcerned with conveying a dignified, self-controlled image (though they are every bit as capable as men of assuming an air of refinement when the situation requires it), but at home they take the injunction to be self-controlled utterly seriously in order to accumulate economic and spiritual resources for themselves and their families.

We need not seek to reconcile these conflicting images of female and male nature and behavior. All cultural systems embody such contradictions and ambiguities, and to try to resolve or to ignore the contradictions gives priority to our own desire for order rather than to the realities of complex social phenomena. Although ethnographers of Java have recognized the marked discrepancies that exist between patently ideological formulations and actual day-to-day practices (see Keeler 1990; Hatley 1990), some of the alternative perspectives on gender have remained largely unexplored. My intention has been to bring to light some of these less prominently articulated, but nonetheless significant, views of gender relations in Javanese society. I am here advocating what Gayatri Spivak refers to as "an espousal of, and an attention to, marginality—a suspicion that what is at the center often hides a repression" (Spivak 1987:104). By paying too much attention to the ideologies of the center, one runs the risk of relegating to the margins of scholarly inquiry perspectives that have already been suppressed because of their subordinate status, but which are still crucial to an understanding of social relations and cultural logics.

Even when ideology seems to be borne out by practice—as, for instance, when Javanese men avoid the marketplace, claiming that they do so because of their disinterest in petty material matters that are best left to women—there may be more going on than meets the eye. Attention to peripheral discourses may reveal fundamental views of women's and men's natures that bypass or reconfigure the idioms of potency and prestige. In this case, as I have shown, an alternative perspective is that men stay clear of the marketplace because they cannot control their desires to the degree that women can. To be sure, both the dominant and alternative views are highly conventionalized, and should not be taken to explain in themselves why market trade tends to be marked as women's, not men's, work. A deeper understanding of why men in parts of Java shun the marketplace, and why women do not, would have to take into account, among other factors, the historical developments that have shaped Java's social, political, and economic landscape, and not just the modern-day cultural pronouncements that attempt to explain or to justify the end products of those developments.[20]

Nevertheless, to the extent that women's and men's interpretations of gender guide and give meaning to their social actions, they deserve attention. The key is not to give so much weight to one set of interpretations that one overlooks others because they are not voiced as formally or as insistently. As Jane Flax writes, advocating a rapprochement between feminist and postmodernist theoretical approaches, "Perhaps reality can have 'a' structure only from the falsely universalizing perspective of the dominant group. That is, only to the extent that one person or group can dominate the whole will reality appear to be governed by one set of rules or be constituted by one privileged set of social relations" (Flax 1990:49). The "rules" that are frequently invoked for Javanese society only represent "reality" as it exists within the limited framework of a particular ideological system—one that grants superior status to men and their domains of activity.

Writing about traditional ideological conceptions of gender in Java, Barbara Hatley comments: "Women's economic activities outside the home, in market trade particularly, are seen as an extension of the natural female household concern with money matters. The association of women with money brings more disparagement than esteem, as men complain of their wives' tightfistedness and rather contemptuously attribute to women a *jiwa dagang*, 'soul of a trader' " (Hatley 1990:182). From this perspective, women's transactions of money and goods inevitably detract from their prestige and lead to their devalued position in Javanese society. But another possibility should be considered. Outside the dominant ideologies, women's dealings with money can be viewed in a different, more positive light: as a means by which they domesticate the antisocial forces of desire so as to ensure the prosperity and status of their families. By accumulating wealth and investing it in the material and social welfare of the family, they generate prestige for their husbands, their children, and, of course, themselves (cf. Djajadiningrat-Nieuwenhuis 1987). Men and women alike directly or indirectly acknowledge the importance of women's economic activities in this regard. *Both* sexes are invested in generating status for themselves and for their families, and their roles in this endeavor are complementary. The common assumption that Javanese women are relatively indifferent to matters of status and prestige, then, is misguided, a result of paying undue attention to ideologies that privilege men and their activities.

This suggests that focusing on "prestige systems" as a diagnostic of gender relations (Ortner and Whitehead 1981) may lead to an analysis that is both too narrow and too ideological if one does not take into account the inherent complexities embodied in the notion of prestige itself. For example, Shelly Errington has proposed that in island Southeast Asia,

> differences between people, including men and women, are often attributed to the activities the people in question engage in or the spiritual power they exhibit or fail to exhibit. If we want to understand gender there, we . . . must understand local ideas of power and prestige; the next step . . . is to ask how people defined as male, female, or something else are mapped onto, as it were, the prestige and power systems (S. Errington 1990:58).

I would caution, however, that "the prestige and power system" may represent, in Flax's words, "the falsely universalizing perspective of the dominant group," which, while defining a certain structure of reality, may *not* represent the entire range of cultural discourses or actual practices in a given society. Sherry Ortner and Harriet Whitehead (1981) observe that almost all prestige systems accord males superior status to females. Should we, then, accept at face value the hegemonic constructs that privilege males, without investigating the possibility that there might be competing ideas that do not always assume female inferiority?

In a recent essay, Ortner (1989–90) has reevaluated her own earlier model of prestige systems, now recognizing the limitations of approaches to prestige that do not consider the multiple logics and conflicting practices of power and prestige that are inevitably at play. Avoiding totalizing models of prestige systems, she observes, can lead to a very different picture of gender and status—one that may call into question the universality and absoluteness of male dominance. Bearing these issues in mind, I maintain that the ideology of spiritual power does not underlie all notions of prestige and hierarchy in Java, nor does it define all aspects of gender; it is a dominant, but not an exhaustive, cultural model. Furthermore, in response to Shelly Errington's statement above, I would add that the notion that males and females can be "mapped onto" a prestige and power system seems to presuppose the unitary nature of such a system, as a rigid grid that allocates fixed coordinates for males and females. Social systems, and ideas about gender, are far more complex than such a "mapping on" would permit. As prevalent as ideologies of spiritual power and prestige are in Java, they only represent one facet of the social and cultural dynamic. Even though women are allotted an inferior position in the "official" Javanese model of prestige and potency, this model, it turns out, is not the sole indicator of cultural value, nor of the respective positions of women and men in the social order.

As Sylvia Yanagisako and Jane Collier point out, the concept of a "male prestige system" rests on the assumption of an encompassing (superior) male sphere and an encompassed (subordinate) female sphere, the latter generally identified as the domestic sphere (1987:28). In Java, the ideologies of the center do tend to identify women with the "mundane" matters of running the household and child rearing; even their activities as traders in the very public domain of the marketplace are seen, as Hatley mentions, as extensions of their "natural" female household concern with matters of money. Since the dominant ideologies often devalue as unprestigious those activities that are associated with what we might refer to as "the domestic sphere" (in particular, the household and the family), as well as those that involve transactions of money and commodities, one might easily assume that women and their activities are uniformly considered to be of low status.

What I have proposed here is an alternative configuration of gender relations and of women's association with the household: one which grants women the role, at least in some contexts, of domesticator (of men, money, and desire, among other things) rather than domesticated, and which sees women's activities as central to the production of the family's status in the wider society. Seen from this angle, neither the household nor women's spheres of activity more broadly should be seen as subordinate domains: they are, rather, crucially important sites of cultural production and social reproduction in their own right.

Yet the linkage between women and "the domestic," I wish to emphasize, is by no means absolute. Since many Javanese women work outside the home, in the marketplace and elsewhere, they move easily between the household and the public domain (cf. Djajadiningrat-Nieuwenhuis 1987:45). In the case of Javanese merchants, it is women's freedom to move between the home and the public sphere—in particular, their willingness to expose themselves to the desires of the marketplace while controlling their own desires—that enables them to accumulate wealth for the family. Even in their forays outside the conjugal bond, women are thought to keep the best interests of their families in mind; they thus retain their status as domesticators. Whereas men's extramarital sexual activity is associated with uncontrolled desire and the dispersion of family resources, female sexuality remains conceptually bound to economic accumulation and to the production of status for the family. A shift away from the ideologies of the center reveals that women do not only participate tangentially in the status systems of men—they themselves play a central role in defining and reproducing the status hierarchies of Javanese society.

NOTES

A shorter version of this paper, entitled "Sex and the Marketplace, or: Why Javanese Men Can't Control Themselves," was presented at the Ninth Annual Berkeley Conference on Southeast Asia Studies, February 29, 1992, at the University of California, Berkeley. I am grateful to two anonymous readers as well as to the following people for their comments on this paper and earlier versions of this work: Benedict Anderson, Nancy Florida, Paschalis Laksono, Aihwa Ong, Michael Peletz, Vicente Rafael, P. Steven Sangren, Saya Shiraishi, Takashi Shiraishi, James Siegel, Budi Susanto, G. G. Weix, and Astri Wright. In formulating the ideas presented here, I have also benefited from many conversations with Leslie Morris, Ward Keeler, and Tinuk Yampolsky.

The research on which this article is based was conducted in Solo, Central Java, Indonesia, from February 1986 to August 1988. It was funded by a Social Science Research Council Dissertation Research Grant, a Fulbright-Hays Dissertation Research Fellowship, and a Woodrow Wilson Research Grant in Women's Studies. Research was carried out under the auspices of the Indonesian Institute of Sciences (LIPI) and the Cultural Studies Center of Gadjah Mada University, under the directorship of Professor Umar Kayam.

1. The Javanese language is structured around a remarkably complex system of language levels that indicate the relative status of interlocutors and the degrees of formality and politeness that they wish to express. A fluent command of the full range of speech levels is usually considered by Javanese people to be a sign of high status, good breeding, and personal refinement. For detailed explanations of the workings of the Javanese language and its place in social life, see C. Geertz 1960; Keeler 1984; Siegel 1986; J. Errington 1988.

2. See Peletz, this volume, for an insightful discussion of hegemonic and counterhegemonic representations of gender in Malay society. See also Ortner 1989–90 on the subject of gender hegemonies more broadly.

3. Some Javanese grooms seem to fear this possible outcome. One man described to me a wedding he had attended where the groom had ducked out of the way when the bride threw her betel. Then, grasping his chance, he took careful aim at his wife-to-be and flung his betel at her as hard as he could.

4. The nuclear family is the basic unit of kinship in Java, and a "typical" household is often thought of as consisting of a husband, wife, and their unmarried children. However, other arrangements are also very common. Many households contain only a woman and her children; in other cases, a household may include other relatives or nonkin from outside the nuclear family. For further discussion of Javanese household arrangements, see H. Geertz 1961; Hart 1986.

5. Some strict Muslims prefer to follow Islamic rules of inheritance, whereby a brother receives two shares for every one share that his sister receives. Although the majority of the Javanese population professes at least nominal adherence to Islam, my impression in Solo was that more people preferred to follow the prescription of "Javanese custom" (*adat Jawa*), i.e., equal inheritance for males and females, than that of "Islamic law" (*hukum Islam*), which some people felt was unfair to women.

6. Although the city of Solo, the site of my research, does have a reputation in Java for having especially independent women who contribute more than their share to the family financially, the pattern of women contributing substantially to their households' incomes is certainly not limited to this city alone.

7. I stress that this is the case among the *Javanese,* because many traders of other ethnic groups—Chinese, Arab, Indian, and other indigenous Indonesian groups, such as the Minangkabau—are men. As trade in Java has for centuries (particularly since colonization) been in the hands of non-Javanese as well as Javanese people, it is important to make this qualification. In inland Central Java, where the court cities of Solo and Yogyakarta are located, male traders are relatively scarce among the ethnic Javanese. In other parts of the island, they are found more commonly. On the north coast of Java, for instance, where Islam has had a more pervasive influence on people's lifestyles and where long-distance trade has been carried on for many centuries, more Javanese men participate in trade than in the inland regions. For further discussion of the ethnic division of trade in Java and the dominance of women traders among ethnic Javanese, see Alexander and Alexander 1991, and Brenner 1991a and 1991b.

8. Collecting and caring for songbirds of various types is a favorite hobby of members of the traditional *priyayi* aristocracy, primarily males. Many non-*priyayi* men, usually men of means, also devote their leisure time, and often considerable sums of money, to the cultivation of birds.

9. The Javanese term *dradjad* (*derajat* in Indonesian) can be glossed as "status." However, numerous other terms are used to refer to status in its different aspects.

10. These stereotypes remain in place even in the face of evidence to the contrary. Many ethnic Chinese in Solo actually do have an excellent command of Javanese language and etiquette, but they tend to be pointed to by Javanese as "excep-

tions to the rule." In general, ethnic Chinese in Java speak Indonesian (the national language, which has relatively few status indicators) or low Javanese on a day-to-day basis, but many have also learned high or refined (*alus*) Javanese and speak it with their Javanese acquaintances or customers.

11. On the definition and cultural significance of the term *kasar* and its polar opposite *alus*, see C. Geertz 1960.

12. For a specific analysis of gender differences with regard to speech styles in Java, see Smith-Hefner 1988: 535–54.

13. Keeler points out quite appropriately that women are certainly as capable as men of speaking and behaving in a refined and dignified manner when they choose to do so, and women who do behave in a consistently refined manner are accorded due respect. But the relative lack of constraints on women's speech compared to men's permits them to use a wider range of styles in various contexts, and it is this latitude that leads to the stereotypes about women's "lack of control" over their speech. For further discussion of the interplay of speech, gender, and potency, see Keeler 1990.

14. The term *nafsu* (a term of Arabic origin) or *hawa nafsu*, is used in Javanese as well as Malay and Indonesian. In *The Rope of God* (1969), James Siegel shows that the Islamic concept of *hawa nafsu* (human beings' instinctive nature, their passions and desires) and its opposite, *akal* (also derived from Arabic), reason or rationality, form the basis for conceptualizing both internal experience and social relations among the Acehnese of North Sumatra, Indonesia. Although all human beings have the capacity to control their *hawa nafsu* with *akal*, which is developed and guided through prayer and religious practice, Acehnese men believe that they possess more *akal* than women, giving them greater self-control and a moral superiority legitimated by God. This paradigm of human nature appears to accord with mainstream Muslim gender ideologies, according to Rosen (1984), who found these ideas to be widespread in Morocco. Similar ideas are also found among Bedouins of Egypt (Abu-Lughod 1986), Malays (Ong 1987, 1990), and other Muslim populations, such as the Mombasa Swahili (Swartz 1991). For a discussion of the influence of this ideology among Malays of Negeri Sembilan, as well as an alternative representation that is commonly expressed among the same population, see Peletz, this volume.

15. Under Indonesian and Islamic law, Muslim men may have up to four wives at the same time, although polygyny is officially discouraged by the government.

16. Whether Solo represents the norm or an exception to the general rule in this sense is a question that deserves further investigation.

17. For a description of the *arisan* in Java, see C. Geertz 1962.

18. "Memburu Kepuasan: Seks di Kalangan Wanita Jawa." *Wawasan*, April 3, 1988, p. 1.

19. Hildred Geertz found during her fieldwork in the 1950s that adultery was widespread among the Javanese, but carried little moral weight. She observes that, "each partner is constantly on the watch to catch the other in a misstep, and both are also looking out for a chance for an illicit affair—although women are less likely either to have such a chance or to take advantage of it after they have children" (1961:128).

20. A discussion of the historical factors that shaped the gendered and ethnic

division of trade in Java is beyond the scope of the present paper, though these are discussed in Brenner 1991a and 1991b, and in Alexander and Alexander 1991. Further exploration of why men avoid the marketplace would also involve consideration of the broader ethnographic setting, and the fact that women rather than men dominate the marketplace not only in Java, but also in many other parts of Indonesia and Southeast Asia. The prevalence of women traders throughout Southeast Asia does not invalidate or make irrelevant specifically Javanese understandings of this gendered division of labor, however, for in each region the meanings of trade, money, and gender are interpreted within the framework of local histories and cultural constructions.

REFERENCES

Abu-Lughod, Lila. 1986. *Veiled Sentiments: Honor and Poetry in a Bedouin Society.* Berkeley: University of California Press.
Alexander, Jennifer, and Paul Alexander. 1991. "Protecting Peasants from Capitalism: The Subordination of Javanese Traders by the Colonial State." *Comparative Studies in Society and History* 33(2):370–394.
Anderson, Benedict R. O'G. 1972. "The Idea of Power in Javanese Culture." In C. Holt, B. Anderson, and J. Siegel, eds., *Culture and Politics in Indonesia,* pp. 1–69. Ithaca: Cornell University Press.
———. 1990. "Further Adventures of Charisma." In *Language and Power: Exploring Political Cultures in Indonesia,* pp. 78–93. Ithaca: Cornell University Press.
Atmowiloto, Arswendo. 1986. *Canting.* Jakarta: PT Gramedia Press.
Brenner, Suzanne A. 1991a. "Competing Hierarchies: Javanese Merchants and the *Priyayi* Elite in Solo, Central Java." *Indonesia* 52:55–83.
———. 1991b. "Domesticating the Market: History, Culture, and Economy in a Javanese Merchant Community." Ph.D. diss. Cornell University.
Deventer, C. Th. van. 1904. *Overzicht van den Economischen Toestand der Inlandsche Bevolking van Java en Madoera.* The Hague: Martinus Nijhoff.
De Wit, Augusta. [1912] 1984. *Java: Facts and Fancies.* Singapore: Oxford University Press.
Djajadiningrat-Nieuwenhuis, Madelon. 1987. "Ibuism and Priyayization: Path to Power?" In Elsbeth Locher-Scholten and Anke Niehof, eds., *Indonesian Women in Focus,* pp. 43–51. Dordrecht: Foris Publications.
Errington, J. Joseph. 1984. "Self and Self-Conduct among the Traditional Javanese." *American Ethnologist* 11:275–290.
———. 1988. *Structure and Style in Javanese: A Semiotic View of Linguistic Etiquette.* Philadelphia: University of Pennsylvania Press.
Errington, Shelly. 1990. "Recasting Sex, Gender, and Power: A Theoretical and Regional Overview." In Jane M. Atkinson and Shelly Errington, eds., *Power and Difference: Gender in Island Southeast Asia,* pp. 1–58. Stanford: Stanford University Press.
Flax, Jane. 1990. "Postmodernism and Gender Relations in Feminist Theory." In Linda Nicholson, ed., *Feminism/Postmodernism,* pp. 39–62. New York: Routledge.

Geertz, Clifford. 1960. *The Religion of Java.* Chicago: University of Chicago Press.

———. 1962. "The Rotating Credit Association: A 'Middle Rung' in Development." *Economic Development and Cultural Change* 10(3):241–263.

Geertz, Hildred. 1961. *The Javanese Family: A Study of Kinship and Socialization.* Glencoe, Ill.: Free Press.

Gramsci, Antonio. 1957. *The Modern Prince and Other Writings.* Trans. Louis Marks. New York: International Publishers.

Hart, Gillian. 1986. *Power, Labor, and Livelihood: Processes of Change in Rural Java.* Berkeley: University of California Press.

Hatley, Barbara. 1990. "Theatrical Imagery and Gender Ideology in Java." In Jane M. Atkinson and Shelly Errington, eds., *Power and Difference: Gender in Island Southeast Asia,* pp. 177–207. Stanford: Stanford University Press.

Jay, Robert. 1969. *Javanese Villagers: Social Relations in Rural Modjokuto.* Cambridge, Mass.: MIT Press.

Keeler, Ward. 1984. *Javanese: A Cultural Approach.* Monographs in International Studies, Southeast Asia Series, no. 69. Athens, Ohio: Ohio University.

———. 1987. *Javanese Shadow Plays, Javanese Selves.* Princeton: Princeton University Press.

———. 1990. "Speaking of Gender in Java." In Jane M. Atkinson and Shelly Errington, eds., *Power and Difference: Gender in Island Southeast Asia,* pp. 127–152. Stanford: Stanford University Press.

Koentjaraningrat. 1985. *Javanese Culture.* Singapore: Oxford University Press.

Mernissi, Fatima. 1987. *Beyond the Veil: Male-Female Dynamics in Modern Muslim Society.* Rev. ed. Bloomington: Indiana University Press.

Ong, Aihwa. 1987. *Spirits of Resistance and Capitalist Discipline: Factory Women in Malaysia.* Albany: SUNY Press.

———. 1990. "Japanese Factories, Malay Workers: Class and Sexual Metaphors in West Malaysia." In Jane M. Atkinson and Shelly Errington, eds., *Power and Difference: Gender in Island Southeast Asia,* pp. 385–422. Stanford: Stanford University Press.

Ortner, Sherry. 1989–90. "Gender Hegemonies." *Cultural Critique* 14:35–80.

Ortner, Sherry, and Harriet Whitehead. 1981. "Introduction: Accounting for Sexual Meanings." In Sherry Ortner and Harriet Whitehead, eds., *Sexual Meanings: The Cultural Construction of Gender and Sexuality,* pp. 1–27. Cambridge: Cambridge University Press.

Papanek, Hanna, and Laurel Schwede. 1988. "Women Are Good with Money: Earning and Managing in an Indonesian City." In D. Dwyer and J. Bruce, eds., *A Home Divided: Women and Income in the Third World,* pp. 71–98. Stanford: Stanford University Press.

Raffles, Thomas Stamford. [1817] 1965. *The History of Java.* 2 vols. Kuala Lumpur: Oxford University Press.

Rosen, Lawrence. 1984. *Bargaining for Reality: The Construction of Social Relations in a Muslim Community.* Chicago: University of Chicago Press.

Siegel, James T. 1969. *The Rope of God.* Berkeley: University of California Press.

———. 1986. *Solo in the New Order: Language and Hierarchy in an Indonesian City.* Princeton: Princeton University Press.

Smith-Hefner, Nancy J. 1988. "Women and Politeness: The Javanese Example." *Language in Society* 17:535–554.

Spivak, Gayatri Chakravorty. 1987. "Explanation and Culture: Marginalia." In *In Other Worlds: Essays in Cultural Politics*, pp. 103–117. New York: Routledge.

Stoler, Ann L. 1977. "Class Structure and Female Autonomy in Rural Java." *Signs* 3(1):74–89.

Sutherland, Heather. 1979. *The Making of a Bureaucratic Elite*. ASAA Southeast Asia publications series. Singapore: Heinemann.

Swartz, Marc J. 1991. *The Way the World Is: Cultural Processes and Social Relations among the Mombasa Swahili*. Berkeley: University of California Press.

Tsing, Anna L. 1990. "Gender and Performance in Meratus Dispute Settlement." In Jane Atkinson and Shelly Errington, eds., *Power and Difference: Gender in Island Southeast Asia*, pp. 95–125. Stanford: Stanford University Press.

Yanagisako, Sylvia, and Jane Collier. 1987. "Toward a Unified Analysis of Gender and Kinship." In Jane Collier and Sylvia Yanagisako, eds., *Gender and Kinship: Essays toward a Unified Analysis*, pp. 14–50. Stanford: Stanford University Press.

TWO

Narrating Herself:
Power and Gender in a Minangkabau
Woman's Tale of Conflict

Jennifer Krier

Jennifer Krier's essay deals with constructions of power and identity in a Minangkabau woman's narrative of conflict. The ethnographic setting for this essay is the frequently studied but still little understood Minangkabau of West Sumatra, who are "staunchly" Islamic but who also constitute the largest matrilineal society in the world. The Minangkabau have been the subject of numerous studies to date, but for the most part gender has not been accorded central analytic priority. (The pioneering work of Nancy Tanner [1974, 1982] constitutes an important, albeit partial, exception; see also Sanday [1990]). Krier demonstrates that the democratic and egalitarian ideology of Minangkabau adat *("tradition," "custom," "customary law")— which allows women and low-ranked lineage members equal voice in lineage decision-making—has the practical effect of legitimizing gendered and other structures of social hierarchy. Her carefully crafted description and interpretation of a locally framed narrative points up the constraints operative on women (and, in slightly different ways, on all other subalterns) relegated to the margins of formal politics; it also illustrates how female subalterns empower themselves by engaging in protracted verbal and other forms of resistance, and why such resistance is typically of limited scope and force. A central tenet of Minangkabau culture—and, as we have seen, of that of Javanese and many other Southeast Asians—is that infrequent and carefully moderated speech, and, in the extreme case, silence, is a sign of spiritual power or potency, and that "excessive," unmoderated speech indicates spiritual powerlessness or impotence. The irony here is that while the very construction and narration of this tale of conflict is an act of resistance, it is at the same time a telling example of how resistance (the subaltern's speech) feeds into continued subjugation and disempowerment by reproducing some of the very same legitimating and other conceptual structures undergirding the differential distribution of power and prestige in the first place. Highlighting the ways women are disadvantaged in a matrilineal society, Krier's material concerning the unresolved, ambivalent outcomes of female resistance and the cultural ambivalence associated with women's real and imagined sexual and other embodied powers provides a nice complement to Brenner's data from Java, and also resonates deeply with material presented in many of the other essays in this volume.*

The women were sitting in the kitchen, ladling rice and curry into bowls for the titled male elders in the lineage.[1] They had donned sarongs and head-coverings by the time the men had arrived. "They are our elders," the women told me, "you must dress respectfully and honor them." So the women served the men fancy food, setting down the plates and glasses where the elders directed, while the big room of the house—women's space in daily life—slowly filled up with men and cigarette smoke and serious talk about the ritual that needed to be planned.

Back in the kitchen, a different kind of talk was going on. The hostess did not approve of the plans taking shape in the next room. "I hate the *ninik-mamak* (male elders)," she scowled. "All they do is cause trouble." While I was surprised at the hostility she expressed toward the people she was also so careful to honor, the other women commiserated in the same vein. One woman told a long story about why she never summoned her *panghulu*, or male lineage elder, anymore: "He is clever at talking about *adat*, but only at talking. He doesn't know how to do *adat*."[2] Another older woman scowled: "Why are you so stupid? Don't you know that all you have to do is disagree with their decision, and then that's the end of it?"

Criticism of male elders held a prominent place in women's informal talk or "gossip"—and often took shape as formal complaints in lineage meetings—in the village hamlet of Sidiam in West Sumatra, Indonesia, where I conducted my fieldwork. While men occasionally criticized the way the village elders did their business as well, I was struck by the subversive messages in women's complex tales of struggle with male lineage elders over ritual preparations, the pawning of rice fields, or property claims. These stories, or "dispute narratives" as I name them here, narrate experiences of oppression at the hands of elders through riveting scenes of women engaging in direct and often violent forms of resistance—such as cursing, threatening, and fighting—to male figures of authority.

Part of the purpose of this paper is to examine how women use narrative to subvert the culturally revered authority of male elders and to establish themselves as political subjects. This examination of "dispute narratives" as "narratives of resistance" fits with the work of other anthropologists who have examined how narrative performances function as "political tools" that anonymously undermine existing power relations (Scott 1985, 1990; Abu-Lughod 1990) or empower the active subject to claim particular relations to authority (Herzfeld 1985: Stewart 1909).[3] Scholars working in Southeast Asia, moreover, have shown that a commanding verbal performance is crucial to the exercise of power on both local and state levels, and that ideals of gender symmetry are betrayed by high-status men's monopoly over public speech (Tsing 1990; Keeler 1990; Kuipers 1990). Thus Anna Tsing asserts that "the performance standards necessary to create political centrality in Meratus forums privilege male talents" and that women, "less assertive than men, become the audience for male stars" (1990:98). In contrast to the rhetorically disadvantaged women of Meratus, Kalimantan, Minangkabau women can be powerful speakers who articulate and press their rights in commanding public forms in addition to spreading insidious, "behind-the-scenes" gossip. Themes of resistance are expressed both explicitly, in narrative action, and implicitly, through narrative strategies such as code-switching and heteroglossia.

Nevertheless, I am also interested in drawing out what "dispute narratives" can tell us about male domination in addition to "women's power" or resistance in Minangkabau society. In this approach I explore Lila Abu-Lughod's observation that "in the rich and sometimes contradictory details of resistance the complex workings of social power can be traced" (1990:42). Focusing on one "dispute narrative" in particular, I will discuss how a woman's self-aggrandizing story of daring resistance to male village elders highlights codes of male domination that are strengthened, as much as they are challenged, by this tale. In the end I will argue that among the Minangkabau speech is used not so much to "enact" power but to protest inequality and subvert distinction, and that compelling narrative performances, public rhetorical posing, and even ritual speech-making are activities that demonstrate relative powerlessness.

GENDER, STRATIFICATION, AND THE STATE
IN MINANGKABAU POWER RELATIONS

Unlike women in other parts of Indonesia, who have little room for speech in the male-dominated discourses of their societies, Minangkabau women are *not* silent. Women's right to a voice is insured by Minangkabau traditional law and custom (*adat*), which promotes egalitarian and democratic codes for the regulation of social relations throughout the local polity or *nagari*.[4] In the next section of this paper, I argue that democratic principles describe the ideology, rather than the practice, of Minangkabau *adat*. In practice, Minangkabau *adat* defines social hierarchy and reinforces relations of inequality.

The egalitarian ideology of Minangkabau *adat* defines the *nagari* polity as a democratic confederation of matrilineages which band together as a result of mutual needs for intermarriage and companionship. According to Sidiam legend, the *nagari* founders descended from four exogamous matriclans (*suku*); these clans remain the most inclusive corporate groups and are the "stems" (*batang*) from which the smallest lineage descent groups or *kaum* originate. *Suku* members share little more than a common "name" and a prohibition to marry each other, but *kaum* members jointly share inherited rights to lineage property (*pusako*) and lineage titles (*soko*). Inter-*kaum* and inter-*suku* decision making is governed by discussion (*musyuwarah*) and consensus (*mufakat*) in a council made up of titled elders (*panghulu*) representing each and every *kaum* in the village.[5] In this way, *adat* proscribes equal legal representation for all.[6]

Egalitarian ideals structure relations within the *kaum* as well. Decisions about the allocation and administration of property and titles are based on *kaum*-wide consensus in which all adult members vote. Moreover, the tenets of matrilineal descent dictate a "complementary" allocation of *kaum* resources to men and women. Women, as the wardens of inalienable *kaum* property (*harto pusako tinggi*) such as houses, fishponds, agricultural fields and ritual regalia, have primary use-rights over these resources.[7] Living in the *kaum* houses (*rumah adat*) and often in charge of cultivating *kaum* rice fields, senior women—respectfully referred to as "womb mother" (*bundo kanduang*)—are conceptualized as the stable centers of *kaum* socioeconomic affairs as well as the source of descent group continuity.

Men, on the other hand, are mobile, moving away from the homes of their mothers in pursuit of marriage and wealth. After marriage, a man's contributions to lineage resources—his male labor power and his status-bearing bloodline (which I will discuss further below)—are redirected from his mother's *kaum* to that of his wife and children. Unable to maintain a central role in the economic sphere of their mothers' households, men assume a different kind of lineage role: authority. As *mamak* (the term for mother's brother) men are acknowledged as the "official" administrators of the affairs of their sisters and sisters' children, and appear as formal figureheads in negotiations over the planning of a ritual (*baralek adat*), the pawning of ancestral rice fields (*gadai sawah harto pusako*), or the transmission of a lineage title (*batagak panghulu*). Men elected to inherit a *kaum* title (*gala soko*)—a right bestowed only upon men—acquire judicial authority that encompasses the whole *kaum*. Yet titles do not grant men autocratic political control. The relations between *kaum* women (*bundo kanduang*), *mamak*, and titled men (*panghulu*) are democratic ones in which consensus is the rule and conflict is resolved through negotiation at the *adat* council.

Male elders in Sidiam often told me that the *panghulu* of a lineage has no "power" (*ndak ado bakuaso*) but serves only as a "symbol" (*simbol*). A *panghulu* is the symbol of *kaum* identity, for people indicate their *kaum* affiliation by naming their *panghulu* (his title rather than his given name); a *panghulu* is also the symbol or the name that unifies *kaum* property that, over time, is held by many individuals. *Kaum*-owned plots of land, houses, and graveyards are said to "belong" to the title (though the man bearing the title may not exert control over *kaum* land).[8]

The fact that even Sidiam villagers say that men's positions of lineage authority balance women's control of lineage property ("men get titles because women get everything else," they often joke) explains why previous anthropologists have stressed gender complementarity and egalitarian relations in Minangkabau local politics.[9] I argue that notions of gender inequality, rather than complementarity, dictate the divided allocation of lineage property and lineage authority, and that women's economic advantages do not automatically offset men's political advantages. Indeed, local representations of gender and sexuality delineate explicit and differentially evaluated distinctions between men and women.

In part, these differences are based on Muslim ideas of gender asymmetry. While descent practices make women the "source" of lineage continuity, Muslim doctrine asserts that men are the "source" of women, for Eve (Hawa) was created from Adam's rib. According to Muslim gender ideology, women are both physically and mentally less complete than men. Thus, men mature at a slower pace than women, villagers say, because men must hone their physical strength and mental power (*akal*) so much more extensively than their more simply constructed female counterparts. Women achieve adulthood early, before they master their passions and base desires (*nafsu*). They never acquire the mental fortitude necessary to act as fair and reasonable judges. Moreover, women are inferior spiritual leaders, for they are periodically prohibited from religious worship during "impure" states such as menstruation and childbirth. The practice of limiting lineage titles and positions of authority to men, therefore, is compellingly explained by an Islamic logic of male superiority.

The logic of male superiority, however, is also rooted in the ideology of Minangkabau descent. According to Minangkabau beliefs about conception, it is the father's sperm which determines the essential character (*sifat*) and status (*pangkat*) of a child. Parents search for husbands who have "good seed" (*bibit nan baiek*) or "white blood" (*darah putieh*) to wed their daughters, and often pay large amounts of money to the parents of the prospective bridegroom in order to secure the match.[10] Adult lineage members attach a high degree of importance to their "patrilineal pedigree."[11] Paternal genealogies (*ranji bako*) are particularly important for men, since only men whose fathers have "good seed" may be elected to inherit a title from their mother's brother.[12]

The logic of male superiority has political effects beyond the realm of gender relations, for notions of relative superiority underpin relations between lineages as well as those between men and women. Men are the vehicles through which social rank is made manifest, but ultimately social rank is traced back to *kaum* origins. Not all men are equal because not all *kaum* are equal. *Kaum* are ranked according to whether their first founders were original settlers (*urang asli*) or newcomers to Sidiam (*urang datang*). Only descendants of *urang asli kaum* bear titles, which signify the enduring "white blood" or "good semen" of kingly ancestors. Newcomer *kaum* are given "commoner" status and rights to low-quality residence and agricultural land at the periphery of the *nagari* territory. Denied the right to inherit titles, they are adopted as low-status "nephews below the knee" (*kemenakan di bahwa lutuik*) of titled, aristocratic lineages.

Though they never openly speak of status differences and usually pay lip service to the democratic ideals of Minangkabau *adat*, most Sidiam villagers are very concerned to either protect or raise the status of their lineage. Many land disputes have status claims at their heart, as people try to lay claim to titles by establishing rights to land "held" by a particular title. Unlike other parts of West Sumatra, where titles are no longer used because title-bestowing rituals (*batagak panghulu*) are considered a costly extravagance and title-bearing duties a nuisance, in Sidiam titles are always and immediately conferred because "titles are a sign of status."

The disputes that erupted during my fieldwork in Sidiam had a distinctive gender pattern: women with use-rights over land struggled with titled men who claimed residual rights to the same property. Though gender appears to be the major cleavage in these disputes, *kaum* status is the real concern. Using different legal strategies that reflect the different ways that matrilineal descent empowers them, men and women from competing *kaum* branches fight it out in claims for lineage, rather than individual, power.

Indigenous definitions of status and authority are still highly valued in local and national politics. The national government recognizes the *nagari adat* council as the appropriate legal forum for disgruntled villagers to voice competing claims to land or to challenge their *panghulu's* allocation of property.[13] But in recognizing the *nagari adat* council and granting it autonomy, the national government has simultaneously redefined it. Under government administration, only panghulu are recognized as official decision-makers on the council. This is a significant modification of *adat* stipulations that untitled elders (*ninik-mamak*), including religious scholars (*ulama*), intellectuals (*cerdik pandai*) and senior women (*bundo kanduang*) also participate in *nagari*-wide decisions. Heightening the status of the *panghulu* office and marginalizing informal positions of influence, the Indonesian state participates in legitimizing—perhaps even strengthens—practices of gender and social hierarchy while advertising a democratic ideology.

Minangkabau *adat* prescriptions hold that men and women, commoners and aristocrats, all have the right to state an opinion and pursue legal settlement. Yet this institutionalization of democratic ideology masks a social system that silently elevates titled men over all other people. Land disputes constitute one of the major arenas in which the hierarchical underpinnings of Minangkabau *adat* are laid bare and where negotiations over status and power take place. In the next section of this paper, I will show how powerful appeals to democratic rights, like the narrative I discuss below, demonstrate a subject's unprivileged position in a social order where the powerful need not say anything at all.

DISPUTE NARRATIVES

In Sidiam, there is no such term as "dispute narrative." Disputes are termed *pakaro,* law suits are called *singketo,* and the meetings in which these issues are properly, formally discussed are called *kaum* meeting (*sapokat*) or village meeting (*rapat balai*). Discussions of disputes outside the formal context of lineage or village meetings are thought of as gossip (*mangunjiangkan urang*) or slander (*cema'i*). Far from being recognized as a distinct form of narrative, these stories are discounted. Their plots detailing the incompetence or unfairness of male elders, in addition to their themes of corruption, betrayal and resistance, contradict and subvert Minangkabau ideals of political democracy, lineage unity, and gender harmony. Nevertheless, the pervasiveness of these stories of conflict—particularly among women—along with their similarity in structure and content, warrants attention as a discrete narrative form.[14]

"Dispute narratives" are often first articulated in formal male contexts. If disputes cannot be settled within the *kaum* by the *kaum panghulu,* they are brought before the *panghulu* who is the head of the entire clan *(rajo suku)* or even to the village council. Women claimants are suddenly put in the position of making their defense to an all-male "jury." In presenting her case to *kaum* or village elders, a woman seeks to reconstruct relationships, transactions and events in vivid and believable detail so that a decision will be made in her favor. Though women in Minangkabau are not trained in formal oratory—a skill required only of men elected to *kaum* or religious offices (*panghulu, ulama*)—fully adult women are expected to know *adat* prescriptions and be able to present their knowledge in male-oriented public settings, even though their daily activities or conversations seldom demand this kind of skill. In the formal and legalistic contexts of dispute settlement, women mimic the verbal styles of their male elders, using esoteric *adat* terms and high-status forms of address.

Having presented a particular "formal" defense, women often repeat their stories outside the council in the informal and lively setting of women's gossip sessions. Such informal presentations of a dispute are particularly characteristic of women defendants. Prohibited from the formal authority roles and political alliances of men, women strategically engage in public and performative politicking. Exchanging news by the roadside as they travel to market, murmuring in darkened back rooms as they cook, or chatting in the shade of a bamboo hut in the rice field, women share their stories with predominantly female audiences. Here, in colloquial speech full of spontaneous exclamations and everyday expressions, they talk about disputes or conflicts (*pakaro*) in rapid sentences and nasal voices that contrast markedly with the smooth and even tones they use in formal contexts.

Shared in such a way, women's dispute "defenses" become subversive "narratives." Despite the homogeneous nature of informal dispute narrative audiences, men recognize that such stories are not simply the airing of grievances or the unloading of emotional burdens. They are intentional, pragmatic acts, designed to slander the enemy and to elicit sympathy and garner support from listeners. Men often warn their women relatives not to participate in these slanderous gossip sessions, for such talk can spread rumor and poisonous retribution around the village.

Most women found both positive and negative reasons for including me in the audience for their dispute narrative. The family with which I lived was wealthy and one of the most active in moneylending in the village. I was also close to the former village head (*wali nagari*) and his family, who continue to be important players in village politics. Perhaps villagers saw me as a conveyor of favorable reports to these families, and told me tales they hoped would reach other ears. On the other hand, the suddenly hushed conversations, bland interviews, and contradictory information I sometimes encountered indicated that villagers saw me as a potentially dangerous "informant" as well. In truth, the dispute narratives I was "allowed" to overhear were all delivered by women with whom I had close and (relatively) trusting relationships.

The best story I heard in the dispute narrative genre, the most colorful and outrageous (but which also contained elements common to other tales), was Mak Nia's story about the day her titled lineage elder came to evict her from her house. The first time I heard Mak Nia talk about this event I was sitting with my foster mother, Tek Lisa, and her neighbor, Mak Linar, in a nearly empty coffee shop in the middle of the afternoon. We were discussing Tek Lisa's recent troubles in her lawsuit with her mother's brother when Mak Nia arrived to buy a snack at the shop. Hearing our conversation, Mak Nia made several comments questioning the fairness and integrity of Tek Lisa's elders and attempting to instruct Tek Lisa in the handling of her dispute. "You mustn't heed your elders," Mak Nia said, "they are corrupt and greedy, and they just want your money." She then proceeded to tell us how she had formed these views, in an abbreviated version of the dispute narrative I present below. To me it seemed clear that Mak Nia, widely regarded as a sly gossip, was seeking an alliance with the wealthy Tek Lisa, who treated her with cool mistrust. However, Mak Nia's story made Tek Lisa uncomfortable, and Mak Nia was hurriedly hushed when men started to arrive at the coffee shop. Later, when I asked Tek Lisa to repeat Mak Nia's story to me, she refused, telling me that women were not allowed to berate their elders the way Mak Nia had. "Go ask Mak Nia yourself," she told me, "she's very clever and articulate (*pandai bicara*)."[15]

So I did. Showing up at Mak Nia's house one day with tape recorder in hand, I asked her to tell me the whole history of her conflict with Dt. (Datuk) Hitam, her *kaum panghulu*.[16] I cannot relate her entire story here, but the section of narrative I present below was told to me in one long stream and illustrates the crucial scenes of conflict, all of which revolve around the fact that Dt. Hitam, who was from a different branch of the *kaum*, assumed the *kaum*'s ancestral title (*soko*) without Mak Nia's consent. Then, on the basis of this title, he tried to deny Mak Nia's claim to high status, thereby depriving her of her right to inherit the holdings of an extinct high-status *kaum*.

The story that Mak Nia told me at her house reports traumatic events after the fact and seems marked by poetic embellishment or even outright fantasizing. Indeed, Dt. Hitam never even mentioned this episode with Mak Nia to me. Village records do not recount the dispute either; they only document a dispute between Dt. Hitam and Mak Nia's mother's brother, which was finally settled outside the village by the nationally administered provincial court. When I asked the village head of Sidiam about Mak Nia's story, he just chuckled and told me that she had made it up because she was so mad that Dt. Hitam had won the dispute with her mother's brother. But in this paper I am not as concerned with what actually happened in the dispute, as with how Mak Nia represented what happened and what this representation tells us about gender and power in Minangkabau society. Let us now discuss Mak Nia's story, which I present below in three episodes of narrative action that are characteristic of the dispute narrative genre and which I name the testimonial, the confrontation, and the gender reversal.[17]

The Testimonial

An important aspect of Mak Nia's story is her description of how she had come to inherit the disputed land in the first place:

> a promise was made . . .
> because my neighbor didn't have any family,
> he had only a brother.
> It was discussed in a meeting with the lineage elders in the council hall,
> and a letter was made.

"When [the neighbor] and his brother die, the land falls to Erni [Mak Nia's
   mother's sister];
that which will fall to her is a house, a plot of house land, coconut trees, a
   fishpond, rice fields."
That's what the letter said, and it was signed by all the elders.

The beginning of Mak Nia's narrative has a "testimonial" quality typical of
dispute narratives, which usually restate details about the development and
settlement of a dispute. All the extended versions of dispute narratives that
I heard included these "objective" statements of legal rights, in which the
author recapitulated details about who she had inherited certain plots of
land from and why she had the right to such land. Here, Mak Nia argues
that her mother's sister was entrusted with the inheritance of an extinct
kaum. One of the most common types of land dispute arises upon the death
of a person, like Mak Nia's neighbor, who held ancestral land, but had no
direct lineal descendants. On the occasion of her neighbor's death, Mak
Nia and her *kaum* members were presented with an excellent opportunity
to increase their *kaum* holdings by making a claim to the lineage land and
title of the deceased.[18] Here, Mak Nia backed this claim by testifying that
a will had been made that allocated all her neighbor's holdings to her
mother's sister. By repeating the course of the original lawsuit, Mak Nia
continued to buttress her position as rightful heir.

The testimonial is a particularly important strategy for women involved
in legal disputes, for women are never able to make residual claims to land
on the basis of a title, as a panghulu is able to do. Rather, often basing
their claims on real and constructed kinship relations, they must try to
protect their rights by telling stories that are designed to keep social connections and legal arrangements clear and elicit the sympathy and support
of the listener. Thus women actively engaged in disputes will tell their testi-
monials/stories to as many people as possible in order to establish the
"truth" of their stance.

The Confrontation

In addition to the "testimonial," another feature of the dispute narrative is
what may be called the "confrontation." The heart of Mak Nia's story
pulsed around three scenes of betrayal and confrontation that arose when
Dt. Hitam denied Mak Nia's right to the land. She told it like this:

He took [the land]
because he won the title of *panghulu*.
He took all of it, he asked to be allowed by the police.
"[This] land cannot be yours anymore," he said.
"So what about this letter? This will?" I said.
"There isn't one of those, that one is not right—

so say [the elders], that this letter is not legitimate."
Of course if they authorize it, there is nothing to do anymore.
[The will] was revised, because he won the title of *panghulu.* . . .

He brought that, that policeman here.
When he arrived here he told me not to be in this house here,
to surrender to Tek Erni's house [her neighbor].
"Don't stay here, go to Padang Keduduk.
That is her place, she lives there, because she is a commoner," Dt. Hitam said.
He said we were commoners, Jenni! To that policeman!
He was brave alright,
because he had that policeman.
The one to stand up to him was only me, Jenni . . .
[my lineage relatives] felt only fear,
all the more difficult to endure because we are poor people.
"You will evacuate this house now," the policeman said.
I said, "What is the problem, this is my house," I said.
"This is the one that is the commoner," I said.
"He's no aristocrat," I said.
"You're clever at talking up the policeman," I said to Hitam.
"You cause me to do this!"
I pulled up my sarong (*buka kain*).
"Do you want this?" I said to him.
The policeman argued with me.
"Why did you say that, pull up your sarong in front of us?" he said.
"Later you will be brought to the police office and arrested there for three
     months."
"Three years, what do I care," I said.
"I'm being soiled (*dicema'i*), I'm being trampled under people's feet.
You're clever at pointed words," I said.
Then I felt hate (*bonci*).
"You're (*ang*) clever at talking, yeah, talking to me.
I am being trampled under people's feet."
I pulled up my sarong—they didn't want to look at me anymore.
Father [her husband] here was shivering with fright in the house,
Father didn't want to watch.
Father was afraid of the policeman.
I pulled up my sarong—go ahead and ask people here.
Because of that I was fined,
because I exposed myself to a *panghulu.*
What kind of era are people [living in], Jenni?
No one would look at me . . .
and not just for one or two days, more like a hundred days. . . .
That one, he asked me to bring him an offering.
He told me to cut a chicken.
I said [to the village elders], "Which one is right? Just look, because I am
     in the village,

that one is behind the bamboo grove" [outside the village boundary, on land settled by low-status lineages].
. . . the other lineage elders from my clan fined me.
They supported Dt. Hitam.
"I'm the *panghulu,*" I said, "I'm the *panghulu.*"
I didn't pay the fine.

In this scene, Mak Nia shows how her legal status as a landholder is easily betrayed as a result of the greedy intentions of title-holding men. This theme of betrayal—usually by one's own male relatives or lineage elders—is pervasive in the dispute narrative genre. Here, by positioning herself as the victim of unjust treatment by her elders, Mak Nia attempts to morally justify the telling of her subversive tale.

In this part of the narrative, Mak Nia draws out the betrayal theme as she talks about her unfair oppression as a "poor" lineage member by an influential and corrupt elder. She describes three separate scenes of how she was "trampled" upon by Dt. Hitam. First, Dt. Hitam discredits her inheritance and denies the validity of her will; then, he comes to her house and orders her to flee; finally, he insists she pay him a fine. While Dt. Hitam is always portrayed as being empowered by his collusion with other men of authority, ("the elders say the letter is not legitimate," "he was brave alright; he had that policeman," "the lineage elders from my clan supported Dt. Hitam"), Mak Nia is powerless in her alienation ("the one to stand up to him was only me," "Father was shivering in the house," "No one would look at me"). She draws attention to the differences in their ability to mobilize people to support their respective causes, the explicit reason for this difference being that she and her relatives are "poor people" with limited financial or political resources to refute Dt. Hitam's claim that they are "commoners," that is, descendants of a low-status lineage. We will see later that the subtext here is that Mak Nia's limited resources can also be accounted for by the fact that she is a woman with no formal authority or political clout.

Not having powerful or influential people to defend her, Mak Nia nevertheless resists Dt. Hitam's claims with a confrontational defense of rightful ownership: "What about the will?" in Confrontation #1, "This is my house," in Confrontation #2, "I am the one in the village," in Confrontation #3. But Mak Nia also resorts to a more radical form of confrontation when she hauls up her sarong to expose herself to her *panghulu.* While on the one hand this act conveys the sense of extreme degradation and violation Mak Nia felt, on the other hand it is an offensive and humiliating attack, an attempt to return the defilement Mak Nia is experiencing. Sidiam villagers, after all, believe that exposure to a woman's genitalia is both polluting and bewitching. In walking over a man's food, a woman can entrance a man, render him socially useless, make him a slave to her house. Thus, Mak Nia's cry, "Do you want this?" is not only a shriek of humiliation; it is also a threat. The threat of female sexuality, which is invested with almost supernatural danger, is a serious crime. For this, not only does the policeman threaten to throw her in jail, but the whole village ostracizes her ("no one would look at me") and the elders call her to the council hall to pay a fine.

The Gender Reversal

Repeating the battle cry, "Do you want this?" a second time in the following part of her narrative, Mak Nia transforms the "occult" threat of female genitals into the hot danger of a knife, the traditional weapon of the lineage elders. Having been called to the village council and ordered to pay a fine, Mak Nia buttresses her claim that "I'm the *panghulu*" with the following actions, and alerts us to a third kind of moment often recounted in dispute narratives, one we might call the "gender reversal":

> I pulled out a knife.
> "Do you want this?" I said, to all the elders.
> "Come outside," I said.
> "I'll wait outside; he'll be given his debt," I said.
> He didn't do it.
> He was afraid, Jenni.
> The village council uses rules but . . .
> After that, nothing. I did not pay the fine.

Here, Mak Nia resists persecution by male elders by posturing as a threatening male herself. Such postures were adopted in a number of different ways in the dispute narratives I heard. While Mak Nia claimed a male title and voice of male authority, other women also claimed male emotion such as bravery (*berani*), heat and anger (*naik darah, paneh*), male action (fighting, arguing, brandishing weapons), and male possessions (knives and other weapons).

In this section, not only does Mak Nia try on the forceful voice and powerful actions of a man, but in challenging Dt. Hitam in front of all the other village elders, she also condemns his dishonest use of this male power. The trials of her own individual repression are revamped into a more general confrontation that challenges the legitimacy of men's authority and women's lack of it. In telling the entire story to me, and in indicating her awareness of the village eye (her repeated instruction to "go ahead and ask people"), Mak Nia made her social critique public. The publicly performative nature of her confrontation, however, is characteristic of women's, not men's, strategizing. Men criticize the village elders too, but quietly, in private conversation. Rather than speaking out or enacting direct resistance, men make subtle moves along the established paths of power. A decision from the village elders can be gently overturned with a stern letter obtained from the district head (*camat*); a *panghulu*'s or village elder's loyalty may be bought by gifts of money or property; an enemy might be intimidated with the threat of police or government intervention. Men usually enhance their influence or authority by crafting covert alliances with other empowered men.

While Mak Nia's struggle with Dt. Hitam was never explicitly posited as a "woman's" struggle with a "man," a closer look at Mak Nia's resistance will give us some insight into the oppressive codes of privileged manhood operating under the veneer of gender equality in Minangkabau society.

FROM THE POWER OF WOMEN'S RESISTANCE TO THE RESILIENCE OF MEN'S POWER

In the three scenes of narrative action that we have examined above, Mak Nia illustrates various forms of female resistance to male authority. With her testimonial in the first scene of resistance, Mak Nia lays out the legal basis of her dispute and positions herself as rightfully entitled to property on the basis of *adat* law. Her resistance is not explicitly gendered but is staged as a defense of the poor against the rich and powerful. Nevertheless, her claims to land and status on the basis of the will are easily displaced by Dt. Hitam's gendered claim to a lineage title. Bearing a title, Dt. Hitam's high status is clear, and he needs only to slander Mak Nia's status to assert his own claim to the land. He is further empowered by his seat on the village council, which links him to a network of powerful men who can be "persuaded" (or bribed) to support him. Mak Nia suggests that his political influence extends into the supra-*nagari,* supra-*adat* plane too, for he finds an ally in the government-appointed policeman who represents an outside authority.

While Mak Nia resists Dt. Hitam's claims by recourse to Minangkabau law, ultimately this action reveals the way the law in practice privileges titled men. For Mak Nia shows that all the material resources that are supposed to empower Minangkabau women are useless when confronted with the power men exercise through their political resources. Conflating the explicit text of the oppression of the poor with the implicit text of the oppression of women, Mak Nia's subversive message is that the egalitarian ideals of *adat* law, which claim to democratically settle all disputes, in fact defend neither the rights of the "poor" nor those of women. In the end, being poor and being a woman are the same thing; women are always essentially poor, always low status, because men, in roles of titled authority, can seize their resources and destroy their status. Moreover, *adat* law's failure to protect the rights of women is furthered by the state, which identifies the *panghulu* as the formal figure of authority over the less formally designated roles of untitled male and female elders (see Blackwood, this volume).

In the scenes of confrontation, the gendered nature of Mak Nia's resistance is made more explicit. Refusing her *panghulu*'s demands, Mak Nia resists with the "female" weapons at her disposal—first her inheritance, next her polluting and bewitching genitalia. On an immediate level, Mak Nia's behavior amounts to a brazen disregard for moral codes stating that women be cool (*dingin*) in their emotional disposition, soft (*lunak*) and unopinionated in character, and shy (*malu*) in their social and physical deportment. But it is precisely because she perceives that ideological codes of gender and equality are being broken that she commits such outrageous acts.

These scenes of confrontation also uncover the negative connotations attached to female sexuality. The disturbing image of the desperate woman catching up her sarong to expose herself to her lineage elder, while crying out "I'm being soiled (*awak dicema'i*)," invokes multiple readings of the polluting effects of female sexuality. With this image Mak Nia suggests both that her female sexual identity makes her "dirty" and that it can be "used" to "dirty" others. Exposing her genitalia in an offensive act of resistance, Mak Nia also exposes an ideology which regards female sexuality as shameful and dangerous and something best left covered up.

Mak Nia's act of self-exposure also foreshadows the next scene, in which she reverses her strategy and presents herself as a man with male weapons. According to local interpretation, dreams of nakedness or undressing signify a release from pressure or an act of liberation. Casting off her female identity as she frees herself from confining clothes, Mak Nia invents a new voice for herself, a knife-wielding voice, a voice that denies a fixed gender identity, a voice that commands, "I'm the *panghulu*, I'm the *panghulu!*" In the end, it is this voice that is victorious, for as Mak Nia says, she did not pay the fine.

Nevertheless, Mak Nia's act of "reversal," in which she abandons the strategies of "female" resistance and replaces them with threats invoking male power, makes the differently loaded symbolism of male and female sexuality even more explicit. The knife Mak Nia waves in the lineage council is an apt symbol of male gender identity. Given as gifts to teachers of specialized knowledge (*dukun* or *guru*), to high-status bridegrooms, or to newly elected *panghulu*, knives symbolize spiritual potency (*daulat*), wisdom (*akal*), and pure blood (*keturunan baiek*)—all qualities passed on by males at conception. The knife, which contains a burning energy, also invokes the heat (*paneh*) of male sexuality. Like female sexuality, male sexuality is dangerous and threatening, and should be repressed. Young men are barely able to constrain their energy and sexual drive, but adult men learn, through mental reasoning (*akal*) rather than physical maturation, to keep their sexuality and heat dormant. Male sexuality, like a knife, lies sheathed and hidden, and is withdrawn by an act of will when necessary or appropriate. Thus Mak Nia's knife threat, more than a physical act of intimidation, may be seen as an attempt to appropriate the male virtues of divine reason, high status and controlled energy that are also the essential ingredients in Minangkabau power relations. But in fact, her very acts signify the loss of control and unmitigated passion associated with *nafsu.*

In her narrative moves, Mak Nia seeks various strategies of empowerment, from arguing the tenets of democratic *adat* law, to pressing her individual right to material resources, to flinging dangerous and subversive sexual insult, to appropriating a male title. Assuming new voices as she assumes new postures of resistance, Mak Nia insists on a many-layered "reading" of her experience. As an author, Mak Nia exhibits verbal finesse and flair, adopting no less than four narrative voices and changing dialects and terms of address as she assumes different characters.[19]

There is a certain freedom and force in Mak Nia's ability to shift voices and identities. Obviously, she is not constrained by the moral codes that determine that she should be soft-spoken and cool-headed. Other anthropologists working in Indonesia argue that it is *men* who are constrained by formal verbal codes, and that women's lower social status allows them to participate more actively in spontaneous behind-the-scenes discourses (Keeler 1990; Kuipers 1990). But while Mak Nia's narrative exhibits a "freedom of style," it is also deliberately and elaborately constructed. Mak Nia's narrative of resistance does not simply represent "verbal play." Rather, it is a political act designed to convince potential allies and to demonstrate her insistence on assuming an active role in lineage politics.

Committing a series of outrageous acts—"talking back" to a policeman, exposing herself to a lineage elder, brandishing a knife in the village council—Mak Nia describes herself in a series of scenes that radically depart from normal descriptions of female decorum. To her own mind, however, the story does not represent a complaint or a radical discourse, but rather a model for self-representation that she feels is well within cultural boundaries and in fact recalls a truer ideology. "In the old days," she told me, "before the elders made a decision, they would ask the opinion of the senior women (*bundo kanduang*) first." In this society, where women have politically recognized and culturally legitimate voices, Mak Nia thinks of her story as a lesson in how to stand up for oneself. "When I was a little girl," she told me, "my mother taught me I had a right to speak (*hak suaro*) and that I should say what I think. I always think those elders are wrong and I just tell them so. I'm not afraid of them." She makes a claim to traditional rights and the kinds of influence that have been lost in the present.[20]

Mak Nia comes across as a rebellious, melodramatic, almost hysterical woman, but I have tried in this paper to explain how this persona is produced through political, rather than psychological, effects. Her dramatic and offbeat story is that of a marginalized person. Though some villagers claimed that Mak Nia had fabricated her story, no one ever said that she was crazy (*gila*) or stupid (*bodoh*). Rather they said that she was clever (*cerdik; pandai*). Whether or not they believed the story to be true, villagers acknowledged its subversive daring. Women, in particular, used Mak Nia's story as a point of reference for their own disputes and dispute narratives. "I'm articulate (*pandai bicara*), like Mak Nia," said one woman who was aggressively pursuing a land dispute; "I won't contest the claim (*mabanta*), because I'm not brave like Mak Nia," said Tek Lisa, who opted for financial settlement rather than overt conflict with her *panghulu*.

POWER AND TALK IN MINANGKABAU

In this paper I have examined how a woman seeks to define herself through story and narrative within a society where verbal arts—"discussion" and "consensus" in particular—are important political activities. Minangkabau *adat* prescriptions do not distinguish between men and women in terms of the right to state an opinion or pursue legal settlement. Nor are women excluded from other verbal realms such as recreational poetry, casting spells, or reciting Qur'anic prayers. Minangkabau women are not supposed to be silent.

But in Minangkabau society, silence can be a sign of prestige and superior knowledge. Many kinds of talk, such as ritual speech-making or the casting of spells, are performed only on certain occasions and according to specific prescriptions. The performance must be paid for with auspicious gifts such as sweet bananas, a small knife, and incense—gifts that keep malevolent spirits (*jinn*) at bay and insure that the performer will not forget his words or lose his knowledge (*hilang akal*) to jealous competitors. The very highest-ranked *panghulu* in the village, who trace their descent to the founding ancestors of Minangkabau society, abstain altogether from speech in village meetings or ritual events, for their knowledge is too valuable to be verbalized.[21] Lower-status *panghulu* speak for them, delivering austere, simple and poetic speeches in lowered tones that are often hard to hear.

Other anthropologists have noted the empowering effects of silence in societies that value verbal expertise. Michael Herzfeld suggests that Greek women strategically use silence to ironically subvert, or "creatively deform their submission" to, swaggering, bragging performances of male dominance (1991:80). Whereas in Greece silence and submission represent the passive-aggressive strategies of society's underdogs, in Indonesia, some scholars argue, muteness and inaction are the ultimate expressions of power. According to Benedict Anderson, the Javanese idea of power fundamentally departs from Western political theory in its emphasis on the accumulation and concentration, rather than the exercise or use, of power. Within this model, forceful and dramatic acts of "self-aggrandizement" indicate self-deprivation, diffusion, and loss of concentration of power (Anderson 1972:8–9).[22]

Scholars have shown that formal, spare and emotionless verbal styles are considered the most potent and authoritative, and command the largest audiences, in various Indonesian societies.[23] Typically used by men, these speech styles demonstrate rationality (Siegel 1978), historical centrality (Kuipers 1990), high status (Keeler 1990), and political skill (Tsing 1990). Women's speech, on the other hand, is locally considered emotional (Kuipers 1990), silly (Keeler 1990), or unfocused (Tsing 1990). While women's unrestrained speaking patterns allow them greater freedom of expression than men, they underscore women's peripheral social and political position.

In Minangkabau dispute settlement, the use of speech is an index of one's powerlessness, for the *panghulu* and his immediate relatives need not speak at all. The *panghulu* title speaks for itself, a manifestation of pure origins, high status, and landholding rights. Where peripheral lineage members seek to prove connections and trace descent, the *panghulu*'s genealogy is clear. He has the unvoiced advantage.

Mak Nia's references to village ostracism ("No one would look at me, and not just for one or two days, more like a hundred days") and her lingering reputation as an untrustworthy gossip indicate the limits of her vocal glory. Her public shows of bravery and violence and her assumption of male face were coarse performances that were neither admired nor respected. In the eyes of Sidiam villagers, Mak Nia's behavior represented the unfortunate and irrational extremes to which a woman will be pushed in order to protect her rights and status.

CONCLUSION

Part of what makes "dispute narratives" like Mak Nia's such compelling pieces of ethnographic data is that they convey the complexity and flux of Minangkabau women's experience. Alternatively threatening and hysterical, powerful and desperate, Mak Nia assumed a variety of voices and social postures that conjure a shifting "poetics" of womanhood rather than an "essential" female identity. Talking her way betwixt and between fixed identities, Mak Nia addressed Dt. Hitam in guises he just could not answer.[24]

Ultimately, Mak Nia was victorious in throwing off her fine and maintaining the rights to her house. But she achieved these effects only by operating outside the main arenas of power and negotiation. Unable to mobilize the help of neighbors, other lineal relations, or outside authority figures like the policeman, she discarded discriminatory *adat* legal prescriptions to seek alternative paths of empowerment. Simultaneously exposing and reversing practices of male domination in her embellished narrative, she "enacted" unconventional modes of resistance—threatening female sexuality and claiming male authority—under the subterfuge of an emotional, *nafsu*-laden "feminine" performance.[25]

Mak Nia's final posture of resistance as a knife-wielding, title-proclaiming man highlights the codes of male superiority that oppress women in this matrilineal society. The most powerful statement Mak Nia could make was a claim of male identity, a claim that necessitates the casting off of female identity in "a tragic dispossession of the self" (Lanser 1991:618). In Mak Nia's imagination, resistance only went so far; she desired to appropriate, rather than overthrow, modes of power that privilege men.[26]

Ironically, with her method of resistance—her use of a subversive and forceful narrative—Mak Nia publicly performed her powerlessness. Her big political act was just a story, a story that was unheard, dismissed, or laughed at for its very loudness. While feminists have argued that claiming a public voice is the first step in gaining equal power with men, I have suggested that Mak Nia's evocative vocalness demonstrates her marginalization and her inability to protect her resources with the silent prestige of a *panghulu*.

NOTES

1. This paper is based on sixteen months of field research I conducted in West Sumatra during 1990–91. The research was generously funded by Fulbright Institute of International Education and Harvard Teschemacher grants. I would like to acknowledge the invaluable contributions of Stanley Tambiah, Mary Steedly, Kenneth George, Michael Peletz, and Lindsay French. Thanks are also due to my husband, Rob Cosinuke, for his patience and clear-sightedness.

2. *Adat* refers to the traditional system of custom and law and is highly codified among the Minangkabau. Kinship and descent patterns, property relations, ritual practices, dispute settlement and local, pre-state government, as well as social etiquette, are all said to be governed by the rules of *adat*. For a good discussion of *adat* in relation to other legal systems, such as Islam, colonialism, and the state, see Taufik Abdullah 1966, 1972; and F. Benda-Beckmann 1979.

3. For an excellent comparative discussion of women's uses of both speech and silence in performative political strategizing, see Gal 1991.

4. In 1983 the National Republic of Indonesia designated the Minangkabau *nagari* as a "traditional legal social unit" (*kesatuan masyarakat hukum adat*). On the basis of Area Regulation #13, the *nagari* is no longer recognized as the local unit of state-administered government in West Sumatra, but functions only to "oversee issues pertaining to *adat* law and *adat* custom" (*Peraturan Daerah* #13, 1983).

5. In Sidiam there are sixty surviving lineage titles, representing sixty *kaum*.

6. For more information on Minangkabau legal reasoning and legal settlement in various dispute forums, see Keebet von Benda-Beckmann 1984. Clifford Geertz also discusses Minangkabau legal reasoning in his essay "Local Knowledge: Fact and Law in Comparative Perspective" (1983).

7. Sidiam villagers often used the phrase *bundo kanduang nan punyo kunci lumbuang* (the senior woman holds the key to the rice barn) or *bundo kanduang nan punyo kunci lamari* (the senior woman holds the key to the cupboards [where gold and ritual regalia are kept]) to refer to the fact that use-rights to lineage properties are usually in the hands of lineage women (see also Blackwood, this volume).

8. While a *panghulu* may assume temporary residual control over ancestral property (*harto pusako*) where there are misunderstandings over ownership or breaches of traditional law (*adat*), ideally these rights should be redistributed to needy lineage members (for the most part women). The allocation of use-rights is decided in lineagewide meetings and again decisions are made on the basis of consensus. In the past, a portion of every lineage's ancestral property was allocated for the exclusive use of the *panghulu* (*sawah kagadangan*), but in Sidiam, many of these plots have already been pawned off. For more details about Minangkabau property rights, see F. Benda-Beckmann 1979.

9. For such interpretations of Minangkabau gender relations, see Ng 1987; Pak 1986; Prindiville 1985; Tanner 1974; and Tanner and Thomas 1985.

10. In Sidiam, "groomprice" payments as high as 5,000,000 *rupiah* have been recorded. Ok-Kyung Pak (1986) discusses the payment of "groomprice" to parents of prospective bridegrooms among Minangkabau villagers in Biaro. She suggests that groomprice payments indicate that it is men rather than women that are exchanged between social groups in Minangkabau. Moreover, she demonstrates that lineage women usually arrange and exchange marriage payments. In this way she contests Levi-Straussian arguments that privilege men as the ultimate directors of social relations as a result of their exchange of women in marriage. However, it is problematic to read Minangkabau "exchange of men" as an illustration of the power of Minangkabau women over men (in effect, reversing the logic of Levi-Strauss's argument), for as Pak points out, the payment of groomprice for high-status men illustrates "the ideology of male ascendancy" that underlies matrilineal descent (Pak 1986:223–254). Michael Peletz also discusses marriage as "the exchange of men" in nineteenth-century Malaysia, but he does *not* suggest that "women were accorded more formal authority, prerogatives, or cultural value than men" (1987:465).

11. Ok-Kyung Pak, following de Josselin de Jong, has discussed the significance of paternal genealogies in Minangkabau kinship. The term "patrilineal pedigree" is hers.

12. Minangkabau status is not completely consonant with lineage identity. That is, while a Minangkabau mother and child share the same lineage identity, they do not necessarily share the same status (*pangkat*). A child whose father has low status (i.e., is *urang datang*, on which see below) will also have low status, even if his/her mother belongs to a lineage whose founders were original settlers (*urang asli*). This "hidden status" is investigated when male children are nominated to inherit lineage titles from their matrilineal "uncles."

13. In Area Regulation #13 for the Province of West Sumatra, the National

Republic of Indonesia names the local *adat* council (KAN) as the body which functions to "to pass judgement on issues pertaining to property wealth of the *nagari* society according to *adat* law, in the ways of the *adat* court of justice, which also deals with lawsuits and disputes over *adat* matters" (*Himpunan Surat Keputusan* 1986:3).

14. Other work on Minangkabau narrative forms focus on epic story-telling (Phillips 1981; Johns 1958) and ritual speech-making (F. Errington 1984)—narrative practices usually performed by men. Little attention has been given to informal speech genres, such as gossip and joking, or to narrative genres performed by women. My own fieldwork revealed that women are prominent participants in semi-public gossip and joking sessions, whereas men consider free and public talk an "indulgence" and are consequently more tight-lipped (see also Keeler 1990, for similar observations in Java). Narrative forms particular to women (which are never performed by men), such as funeral chanting (*marotak*) and the recreational exchange of short verses (*bajoden*), are considered sinful or sacrilegious, especially when performed during Islamic holidays.

15. Dispute narratives are strategically performed for particular audiences, people the narrator considers allies. Sometimes these audiences do include men. However, the dramatic style and subversive content of dispute narratives marks them as a type of demeaning and troublesome "gossip" that Sidiam villagers associate with women, who are thought to be more self-indulgent and less able to control their impulses than men. Unless one is prepared to defend the narrator of the dispute narrative, one's social reputation is best-served by avoiding the story altogether.

16. "Datuk" is the honorific used with *panghulu* titles, and is similar to "Lord." "Hitam" is a title, not a name.

17. Most of the dispute narratives that I heard in Sidiam were characterized by these three themes. Stories about conflict with male elders always began with an account of the rightful moral position of the woman (the testimonial); they always contained scenes of dramatic conflict in which they questioned the immoral behavior of their elder (the confrontation); and they always asserted claims to male authority or knowledge by presenting women who acted like men (the gender reversal). I do not know of any other Minangkabau textual traditions marked by these themes. For an interesting discussion about Karo Batak stories of women posing as men, see Steedly 1993.

18. When a *kaum* becomes extinct because there are no more descendants, usually the *kaum* property reverts to the residual control of a neighboring *panghulu*, that is, the head of a closely related *kaum*. Unless someone else can put forward a legitimate claim to the property (as Mak Nia tries to do in her narrative), the *panghulu* has the right to consider it as his own. When he dies the property will become the inheritance of the whole kaum (*harto pusako tinggi*), but while he lives the *panghulu* may consider it his individually acquired property (*harto pusako rendah*) over which he alone has use-rights.

19. For example, she begins by narrating the story in Indonesian. "He brought that policeman here," she says in the careful Indonesian of her narrative voice. Then she assumes Hitam's voice, which addresses both her own persona—"don't stay here"—and the policeman—"that is her place, because she is a commoner"—verbally capturing the sense of intense intimidation as she is trapped between the

two men. Switching to the narrative voice again, she addresses me directly—"He said we were commoners, Jenni." After that she assumes the voice of the policeman, and then she has her own voice not as the narrator but as a character in the story she is telling. As she hurls insults at Dt. Hitam within the story, she switches to the Minangkabau dialect. "You're clever at talking up the policeman," she says, using the crassest and most insulting form of "you" (*ang*) to address her *panghulu*.

20. Susan Lanser writes of women's narratives, "Women's language becomes not simply a vehicle for constructing a more legitimate (masculine, powerful) voice, but the voice through which the more global judgement of patriarchal practices is exercised" (1991:619).

21. The highest ranked *panghulu* in a village are called *rajo suku*. In Sidiam there is one *rajo suku* title in three of the four matriclans (*suku*). These titles descend from ancestors who were not only original settlers, but who traced their descent back to Pagarruyung, the original courtly settlement of the Minangkabau in West Sumatra. For more information on Pagarruyung and early Minangkabau history, see Dobbin 1983:60–71.

22. Christopher Miller makes related arguments about the power of silence and the deprecating nature of speech in African society (1990).

23. Several articles in Atkinson and Errington's *Power and Difference* (1990) make this point (see articles by S. Errington, Kuipers, Keeler, and Tsing).

24. Kathleen Stewart makes a similar interpretation of Appalachian women's narratives, which should not be understood as "an 'expression' of essential female identity" but instead represent "back-talk" which "fragments and externalizes any assumed feminine character, exposing the multivocal, contested social meanings that bring the categories of gender to attention in the first place" (1990:45).

25. Susan Lanser makes similar points in examining women's narratives in the European literary tradition. She writes, "Beneath the 'feminine' voice of self-effacement and emotionality, then, lies the 'masculine' voice of authority that the writer cannot inscribe openly. . . . The 'feminine style' [is] a caricature donned to mask a surer voice in the process of communicating to a woman under the watchful eyes of a man. But this also means that the powerless form called 'women's language' is revealed as a potentially subversive—hence powerful—tool" (1991:617).

26. Like women's possession by spirits on the shopfloors of Malaysian factories (Ong 1987), Mak Nia's narration of the dispute tale reveals "performative contradictions" (Turner 1983). That is, her dramatic recounting of her conflict with Dt. Hitam and other village elders is an act of defiance and resistance, yet her behavior within the narrative also supports official understandings of the differential distribution of power and prestige in this society.

REFERENCES

Abdullah, Taufik. 1966. "Adat and Islam: An Examination of Conflict in Minangkabau." *Indonesia* 2:1–24.

———. 1972. "Modernization in the Minangkabau World: West Sumatra in the Early Decades of the Twentieth Century." In C. Holt, B. Anderson, and J. Siegel, eds., *Culture and Politics in Indonesia*, pp. 197–245. Ithaca: Cornell University Press.

Abu-Lughod, Lila. 1986. *Veiled Sentiments: Honor and Poetry in a Bedouin Society.* Berkeley: University of California Press.

———. 1990. "The Romance of Resistance: Tracing Transformations of Power through Bedouin Women." *American Ethnologist* 17(1):41–55.

Anderson, Benedict R. O'G. 1972. "The Idea of Power in Javanese Culture." In C. Holt, B. Anderson, and J. Siegel, eds., *Culture and Politics in Indonesia*, pp. 1–69. Ithaca: Cornell University Press.

Benda-Beckmann, Franz von. 1979. *Property in Social Continuity: Continuity and Change in the Maintenance of Property Relationships through Time in Minangkabau, West Sumatra.* The Hague: Martinus Nijhoff.

Benda-Beckmann, Keebet von. 1984. *The Broken Stairways to Consensus: Village Justice and State Courts in Minangkabau.* Dordrecht, Holland/Cinnamonson, N.J.: Foris Publications.

Dobbin, Christine. 1983. *Islamic Revivalism in a Changing Peasant Economy: Central Sumatra, 1784–1847.* London: Curzon Press.

Errington, Frederick. 1984. *Manners and Meaning in West Sumatra: The Social Context of Consciousness.* New Haven: Yale University Press.

Errington, Shelly. 1990. "Recasting Sex, Gender, and Power: A Theoretical and Regional Overview." In Jane M. Atkinson and Shelly Errington, eds., *Power and Difference: Gender in Island Southeast Asia*, pp. 1–58. Stanford: Stanford University Press.

Gal, Susan. 1991. "Between Speech and Silence: The Problematics of Research on Language and Gender." In Micaela di Leonardo, ed., *Gender at the Crossroads of Knowledge: Feminist Anthropology in the Postmodern Era*, pp. 175–203. Berkeley: University of California Press.

Geertz, Clifford. 1983. *Local Knowledge: Further Essays in Interpretive Anthropology.* New York: Basic Books.

Herzfeld, Michael. 1985. *The Poetics of Manhood.* Princeton: Princeton University Press.

———. 1991. "Silence, Submission and Subversion: Toward a Poetics of Womanhood." In Peter Loizos and Evthymios Papataxiarchis, eds., *Contested Identities: Gender and Kinship in Modern Greece*, pp. 79–97. Princeton: Princeton University Press.

Himpunan Surat Keputnsan, Instruksi dan Surat Edaran Gubernur Kepala Daerah Tingkat I Sumatera Barat Sebagai Peraturan Pelaksanaan Perda Dropinsi Daerah Tingkat I Sumatera Barat Nomor 13, 1983. Dihumpun oleh Biro Bina Pemerintahan Desa, Kantor Gubernur KDH Tk. 1 Sumbar 1986.

Johns, A. H., ed. and trans., 1958. *Rantjak Dilabueh, A Minangkabau Kaba; A Specimen of the Traditional Literature of Central Sumatra.* Ithaca: Cornell University, Southeast Asia Program.

Josselin de Jong, P. E. de. 1952. *Minangkabau and Negeri Sembilan: Socio-Political Structure in Indonesia.* Leiden: Eduard Ijdo N. V.

Kahn, Joel S. 1980. *Minangkabau Social Formations.* Cambridge: Cambridge University Press.

Keeler, Ward. 1990. "Speaking of Gender in Java." In Jane M. Atkinson and Shelly Errington, eds., *Power and Difference: Gender in Island Southeast Asia*, pp. 127–152. Stanford: Stanford University Press.

Kuipers, Joel C. 1990. "Talking About Troubles: Gender Differences in Weyewa Ritual Speech Use." In Jane M. Atkinson and Shelly Errington, eds., *Power and Difference: Gender in Island Southeast Asia*, pp. 153–176. Stanford: Stanford University Press.

Lanser, Susan S. 1991. "Towards a Feminist Narratology." In R. R. Warhol and D. P. Herndl, eds., *Feminisms: An Anthology of Literary Theory and Criticism*, pp. 610–629. New Brunswick: Rutgers University Press.

Miller, Christopher L. 1990. *Theories of Africans: Francophone Literature in Anthropology in Africa*. Chicago: University of Chicago Press.

Ng, Cecilia. 1987. "The Weaving of Prestige: Village Women's Representation of the Social Categories of Minangkabau Society." Ph. D. diss., Australian National University.

Ong, Aihwa. 1987. *Spirits of Resistance and Capitalist Discipline: Factory Women in Malaysia*. Albany: SUNY Press.

Pak, Ok-Kyung. 1986. "Lowering the High, Raising the Low: The Gender, Alliance and Property Relations in a Minangkabau Peasant Community of West Sumatra, Indonesia." Ph.D. diss., Université Laval.

Peletz, Michael G. 1987. "The Exchange of Men in 19th-Century Negeri Sembilan (Malaya)." *American Ethnologist* 14(3):449–469.

Phillips, Nigel. 1981. *Sijobang: Sung Narrative Poetry of West Sumatra*. Cambridge: Cambridge University Press.

Prindiville, Joanne. 1985. "Mother, Mother's Brother, and Modernization: The Problems and Prospects of Minangkabau Matriliny in a Changing World." In Lynn Thomas and Franz von Benda-Beckmann, eds., *Change and Continuity in Minangkabau: Local, Regional, and Historical Perspectives on West Sumatra*, pp. 29–43. Monographs in International Studies, Southeast Asia Series, no. 71. Athens, Ohio: Ohio University.

Scott, James C. 1985. *Weapons of the Weak: Everyday Forms of Peasant Resistance*. New Haven: Yale University Press.

———. 1990. *Domination and the Arts of Resistance: Hidden Transcripts*. New Haven: Yale University Press.

Siegel, James T. 1978. "Curing Rites, Dreams, and Domestic Politics in a Sumatran Society." *Glyph* 3:18–31.

Steedly, Mary Margeret. 1993. *Hanging Without a Rope: Narrative Experience in Colonial and Post-Colonial Karoland*. Princeton: Princeton University Press.

Stewart, Kathleen Claire. 1990. "Backtalking the Wilderness: 'Appalachian En-genderings'." In Faye Ginsburg and Anna Tsing, eds., *Uncertain Terms: Negotiating Gender in American Culture*, pp. 43–56. Boston: Beacon Press.

Tanner, Nancy. 1974. "Matrifocality in Indonesia and Africa and Among Black Americans." In M. Rosaldo and L. Lamphere, eds., *Women, Culture and Society*, pp. 129–156. Palo Alto: Stanford University Press.

Tanner, Nancy, and Lynn Thomas. 1985. "Rethinking Matriliny: Decision-Making and Sex Roles in Minangkabau." In Lynn Thomas and Franz von Benda-Beckmann, eds. *Change and Continuity in Minangkabau: Local, Regional, and Historical*

Perspectives on West Sumatra, pp. 45–71. Monopraphs in International Studies, Southeast Asia Series, no. 71. Athens, Ohio: Ohio University.

Tsing, Anna. 1990. "Gender and Performance in Meratus Dispute Settlement." In Jane M. Atkinson and Shelly Errington, eds., *Power and Difference: Gender in Island Southeast Asia,* pp. 95–125. Stanford: Stanford University Press.

Turner, Denys. 1983. *Marxism and Christianity.* Totowa: Barnes and Noble Books.

THREE

Neither Reasonable nor Responsible: Contrasting Representations of Masculinity in a Malay Society

Michael G. Peletz

Michael Peletz focuses on contrasting representations of masculinity among Malays living in the state of Negeri Sembilan, Malaysia. His essay thus complements Brenner's insofar as it concerns masculinity and deals at length with local understandings and representations of "reason" and "passion" and the larger conceptual schema in which these phenomena are embedded. Peletz's main concerns, however, are to delineate the various everyday contexts in which what he refers to as "practical" representations of masculinity—which tend to depict men as neither reasonable nor responsible and which are thus in many (but not all) respects an inversion of official (hegemonic) representations of masculinity—are culturally salient; and, beyond that, to analyze the factors responsible for their (re)production and somewhat skewed distribution among contemporary villagers. His historically oriented discussion of the scope, force, and reproduction of these largely counterhegemonic representations of masculinity is particularly concerned with the ways in which various aspects of colonial policies and state-sponsored capitalism both contributed to class differentiation and undercut and otherwise transformed "traditional" kinship roles, especially those of husband, father, and brother. Peletz shows that poor men (unlike wealthy men) are largely unable to live up to the "elder brotherly" norms that have long informed the father's role; and that these marginal men's "poor showings" in such roles feed into stereotypic (and largely negative) views of both fathers and men as a whole. In the process he illustrates the mutually determined and profoundly ambivalent nature of gender and kinship, the need to reassess the "arelational" notion of masculinity enshrined in much of the literature on women and gender (e.g. Chodorow 1978, 1989; Ortner and Whitehead 1981a), as well as the importance of factoring class variables into analyses of gender (and kinship). The concluding sections of his essay, which focus on variables that constrain (or, alternatively, promote) the elaboration of oppositional discourses (and strategies of resistance) address some of these themes from a slightly different set of perspectives and also shed important light on the changing political context of Islam in contemporary Malaysia. In addition, Peletz advances the argument that symbols, idioms, and entire ideologies bearing on gender are rarely if ever simply "about" gender. Because they are also "about" kinship, human nature, and sociality, as well as relations of equality and hierarchy, inclusion and exclusion, and the like, we must be prepared to cast our conceptual and analytic nets as broadly as possible, and, in any event, must resist efforts to treat gender as an analytically discrete, isolateable domain of inequality or difference.

For much of the twentieth century, kinship was, as Collier and Yanagisako (1987a:1) recently put it, "the central focus of ethnographies and . . . the privileged site for theoretical debates about the character of social structure." This is clear from even a cursory perusal of classic texts by Lowie, Murdock, Goodenough, Schneider, and other American anthropologists. It is even more obvious when one reexamines the Great Books associated with the likes of Radcliffe-Brown, Evans-Pritchard, Gluckman, Fortes, Leach, Levi-Strauss, and others working within the British or French traditions. To illustrate the point with a concrete example, we might consider the landmark collection of essays published in 1961 by Edmund Leach, under the title *Rethinking Anthropology*. Five of the six essays in this widely acclaimed volume focus on kinship terminology, rules of descent and inheritance, cross-cousin marriage, and affinal exchange. The title Leach selected for his book, however, was *not* rethinking *kinship and marriage*, but rather, as I have already noted, rethinking *anthropology*. The choice of this more encompassing title was not an attempt by Leach to claim a broader relevance for his work than the work itself actually merited. On the contrary, the choice of the broad title fit well with the intellectual climate of the times, which is to say that the study of kinship occupied a position of centrality in the field of anthropology during the fifties and sixties, and during much of the twentieth century more generally.

In recent decades, however, and since the mid- to late-1970s in particular, there have been two important changes in the status, scope, and constitution of kinship studies. First, and certainly most obviously, theories and debates about what were once taken to be the basic building blocks of kinship no longer occupy their long privileged position of centrality within the discourse of anthropology. This change, which is clear from recent reviews of the field of anthropology by Ortner (1984), Marcus and Fischer (1986), Fischer (1991), and others (see, for example, Myers 1992:4), has occurred partly because of the critical rethinking of basic concepts and assumptions in the traditional study of kinship by Leach, Needham, Schneider, and other scholars beginning in the early 1960s. More broadly, this shift reflects the waning of structural-functionalism as a guiding paradigm, as well as the feeling that the study of kinship and other traditional subfields—economic anthropology, political anthropology, and the anthropology of religion, for example—cannot be pursued in the isolated terms of what are ultimately functionally-defined institutional domains (Collier and Yanagisako 1987a:1–3).

A second change that has occurred in the study of kinship since the mid- to late-1970s is equally important, but frequently overlooked, particularly by those who persist in viewing anthropology in terms of the conventionally defined subfields. I refer to the fact that the study of kinship has been reconstituted and partially subsumed under other (admittedly problematic and contested) rubrics such as legal anthropology, political anthropology, feminist anthropology, and structural or social history.[1] In some ways most exciting is the scholarship produced by feminist anthropologists such as Rubin (1975), Weiner (1976, 1992), Ortner and Whitehead (1981b), Strathern (1987, 1988, 1992), and Collier (1988). Feminist anthropologists have infused new enthusiasm into the (reconstituted) field of kinship, and have contributed to a most promising resurgence in this area of research. This is especially apparent with the publication in 1987 of Collier and Yanagisako's edited volume, *Gender and Kinship: Essays toward a Unified Analysis,* the primary objective of which is, to quote the editors, "to revitalize the study of kinship and to situate gender at the theoretical core of anthropology by calling into question the boundary between these two fields" (Collier and Yanagisako 1987a:1; see also Ginsburg and Tsing 1990; Loizos and Papataxiarchis 1991; Kelly 1993).

This essay provides an example of one of the ways in which the study of kinship has been reconstituted. It is informed by recent dialogues in the study of kinship and gender, though like many of the dialogues in question it also speaks to more general issues of social and cultural theory. The essay has four objectives. First, to illustrate the basic outlines of my position that kinship and gender are most profitably understood as mutually determined, and in relation to everyday social process and the broader realities of political economy and historical change (cf. Yanagisako and Collier 1987). Second, to point up the value of an earlier approach to the study of gender that helped inspire this position, namely Ortner and Whitehead's (1981a) thesis that cultural constructions of gender (and sexuality) are best understood when they are viewed as inextricably enmeshed both with structures of production and exchange, and with the more encompassing systems of prestige to which these structures are keyed. Third, to suggest that the explanatory power of Ortner and Whitehead's approach, though far-reaching, is somewhat compromised because the analytic framework underlying it is insufficiently attuned to contradictory representations of gender and takes for granted certain critical issues, such as masculinity, that should be (along with femininity) at the center of analysis. And fourth, to advance the argument that feminist anthropologists and others dealing with gender and kinship (and related matters) need to take more seriously cultural constructions of maleness, which continue to suffer from the "taken-for-granted syndrome."[2] As Judith Shapiro (1979:269) remarked of feminist anthropology in the late 1970s, "The research focus is on women; . . . much of the recent cross-cultural research is not only about women, but by women, and in some sense, for women; . . . the social and cultural dimensions of maleness are often dealt with implicitly rather than explicitly."[3] Much of contemporary feminist anthropology also concentrates entirely on women (as opposed to gender) and takes constructions of masculinity for granted.[4] This despite the admonitions of Rosaldo (1980, [1983] 1987), Strathern (1988), and others (e.g., Ortner in her more recent [1983, 1989–1990] work), who have made it increasingly clear that a singular focus on the voices or experiences of women—especially one that fails to examine how these voices and experiences articulate with those of men and with encompassing structures of power and prestige—runs the risk of essentializing "woman," and otherwise hindering the realization of feminists' intellectual and political agendas.

In connection with these latter issues I might emphasize that analytic concerns with maleness (which should not be confused with masculine or masculinist perspectives) are of value not simply because they yield interesting ethnographic data on the contingent, internally dissonant, and ambivalence-laden construction of masculinity while also enhancing our understanding of the dialectically-related domain of femininity.[5] More importantly, these concerns help bring into especially sharp focus the merits—indeed, the necessity—of describing and analyzing gender in relation to other forms of difference and inequality (class, race, etc.) that are in a very basic sense both constituting and constitutive of masculinity and femininity alike. As such, they help underscore the point that the segregation and compartmentalization of gender as a distinctive subject of study "in and of itself" is altogether untenable. The strong version of this position is that gender "in and of itself" is ultimately a "nonsubject" in much the same sense that Schneider (1984) has argued with respect to conventional studies of kinship as an isolable, analytically discrete domain (see Collier and Yanagisako 1987b; Kelly 1993).

The historical and ethnographic material presented here concerns Malays residing in the state of Negeri Sembilan, Malaysia, and is based on twenty months of fieldwork and archival research undertaken from 1978 to 1980, and an additional nine months of fieldwork carried out from 1987 to 1988. The material is organized into four sections. The first provides information relevant to the ethnographic context and analytic framework, and includes brief remarks on Bourdieu's (1977) distinction between "official" and "practical" kinship, which I draw upon and employ in modified form, as well as an equally brief demonstration of the value of such distinctions for an understanding of marriage and funerary rituals, affinal exchange, and kinship and gender generally. The second focuses on the key components of the systems of prestige/stigma[6] and moral evaluation (the concepts of "reason" and "passion") most commonly deployed in Negeri Sembilan to represent similarities and especially differences between males and females. The third deals with contasting representations of gender. In this section of the essay I first describe the ways in which the concepts of "reason" and "passion" are articulated in official representations of gender. I then show how they are articulated in practical representations of gender, after which I proceed to a discussion of the scope, force, and reproduction of practical representations of masculinity. The fourth (and last) section of the essay examines some of the comparative and theoretical implications of the Negeri Sembilan material. My main concerns here are the following: to demonstrate the need to deconstruct the ("arelational") concept of masculinity enshrined in the comparative and theoretical literature on gender (see, for example, Ortner and Whitehead 1981a; Chodorow 1978, 1989); to illustrate how certain (practical) representations of masculinity simultaneously encode and mask local perspectives on class that are otherwise typically unmarked in discourse concerning gender and social relations as a whole; and, more generally, to emphasize the importance both of analyzing gender in relation to other forms of difference and inequality, and of addressing the frequently contradictory entailments of ideology.

ETHNOGRAPHIC CONTEXT AND CONCEPTUAL FRAMEWORK

Negeri Sembilan is one of eleven states in the Malay Peninsula (West Malaysia). Its population is ethnically diverse (as is true of the Peninsula as a whole), and is usually discussed in terms of three major ethnic categories: Malays, who comprise roughly 46 percent of the population, and Chinese and Indians who (along with Others) constitute the other 54 percent (Government of Malaysia 1983).[7] The Malays of Negeri Sembilan have much in common with Malays elsewhere in the Peninsula, but they also differ in various ways. As for the most basic commonalities, all Malays speak a common language, identify with the Shafi'i branch of Sunni Islam, and order various aspects of their social relations in accordance with a body of cultural codes glossed *adat*, a concept which encompasses "tradition," "custom," and "customary law." While the *adat* concept is a strongly marked symbol of basic similarities among all Malays, it also symbolizes locally salient (but analytically overdrawn) contrasts, for there are two major variants of *adat* in the Peninsula. The first, referred to as *adat perpatih*, is predominant in Negeri Sembilan and has long been associated with a social structure having descent units of matrilineal design, which reflects the Minangkabau (Sumatran) origin of the area's first permanent settlers. The second, known as *adat temenggong*, prevails in all other regions of the Malay Peninsula and has long been linked with a social structure that is usually characterized as "bilateral" (or "cognatic").

The Malays of Negeri Sembilan are invariably treated in the literature as a "special class" of Malays that cannot be accommodated by general statements or models that are meant to apply to the ("bilateral") Malays living in other parts of the Peninsula. Elsewhere I have argued that the contrasts between Negeri Sembilan and other Malays are greatly overdrawn, and that the underlying commonalities merit far more analytic attention than they have received thus far (Peletz 1994, 1995; see also Peletz 1988). Suffice it to say here that "descent-focused" comparisons and contrasts of Malay societies typically gloss over the strong emphases on matrifocality, matrifiliation, and matrilaterality characteristic of all Malay systems of social relations. They also tend to lose sight of the importance in all such systems of siblingship, which is a "core" or "key" symbol in Ortner's (1973) sense; i.e., it is an object or focus of marked cultural interest and cultural elaboration, which provides both a "source of categories for conceptualizing the order of the world" and a model for human conduct (Ortner 1973:1339–1340). Comparisons and contrasts of Malay societies that focus on descent do, moreover, give short shrift to basic similarities in all Malay societies with respect to constructions of prestige, personhood, and gender. I might note, finally, that Negeri Sembilan Malays view themselves as "thoroughly Malay," and do not regard or refer to themselves as "Minangkabau(s)" or "Minangkabau Malay(s)," though in most contexts they do acknowledge and are generally proud of their Minangkabau ancestry.

Dealing with gender in Negeri Sembilan is a rather elusive enterprise. In most social and cultural contexts gender is of relatively little concern and does not constitute a highly salient marker of social activities or cultural knowledge. There is, for example, a relative deemphasis of gender in forms of address, other features of kinship terminology, and linguistic conventions generally; in the sexual division of labor (which emphasizes reciprocity, complementarity, and the interchangeability of men and women); and in myriad ritual activities. And there are no men's houses, menstrual huts, or other extreme forms of seclusion or segregation, though it is true that prayer houses, mosques, and coffee shops are to some degree regarded as essentially male domains. Particularly significant as well, in many contexts villagers contend that males and females are fundamentally the same in terms of their temperaments, personalities, and *hati* ("livers"), and of equal status (*pangkat, taraff*), despite their different, though complementary, roles.

Negeri Sembilan's gender ideology has much in common with gender ideologies in Sumatra, Java, Bali, and other areas of Southeast Asia (see

Atkinson and Errington 1990; Ong 1989; and Ong and Peletz, this volume) insofar as it tends, overall, to deemphasize gender and sexuality, and to highlight sameness, equality, and complementarity between the sexes. We should not assume, however, as Clifford Geertz (1973) sometimes does with respect to Bali, that we are dealing with a society that is gender-neutral or ungendered, or, to use Geertz's term, "unisex."[8] Characterizations along the latter lines are highly problematic, especially since—much like Margaret Mead's pioneering (1935) work on gender in New Guinea—they conflate the distinction between etic and emic perspectives, and are otherwise insufficiently attuned to local experiences, understandings, and representations of the similarities and differences between males and females.

In short, despite the overall deemphasis of gender and gender differences in Negeri Sembilan, there are certain areas in which gender differences are culturally elaborated. More generally, Negeri Sembilan's gender ideology contains a good number of inconsistencies, paradoxes, and contradictions, as of course do ideologies everywhere. This became clear to me when I began exploring the symbols and meanings of local (Arabic origin) concepts such as *akal* and *nafsu*, which denote "reason" ("rationality," "intelligence," etc.) and "passion" ("desire," "animality," "lust"), respectively. These are key symbols in many domains of Malay culture—and among Muslims in Aceh, Java, and elsewhere in Southeast Asia and beyond—,[9] and they are frequently invoked in discussions of the similarities and differences between males and females. That these symbols are deployed to convey a sense of gender difference in contextually variable and ultimately contradictory ways will be clear once we examine some of the contrasts (and commonalities) between "official" representations of gender on the one hand, and what I refer to as "practical" representations on the other. Before turning to such matters it will be useful to briefly clarify the terminological and analytic distinction employed here, and to illustrate its relevance for an understanding of selected aspects of marriage and funerary rituals and affinal exchange.

Official and Practical Kinship

To help make sense of the contradictory representations of gender (and kinship) I encountered in Negeri Sembilan I draw upon and employ a modified version of Pierre Bourdieu's (1977:33–38) distinction between "official" and "practical" kinship, which I find heuristically valuable, though ultimately somewhat simplistic (as noted below). The term "official kinship" refers to "official representations" of kinship and social structure that "serve the function of ordering the social world and of legitimating that order" (Bourdieu 1977:34). Official kinship is "explicitly codified in

... quasi-juridical formalism" (Bourdieu 1977:35), and is, at least with respect to kinship as a whole, "hegemonic" in Raymond Williams's (1977) sense of the term. "Practical kinship," on the other hand, denotes the uses and representations of kinship in everyday practical situations which are more oriented toward "getting things done" than to formal representations of kinship and social structure (though I would emphasize that they, too, have important legitimating functions).[10] In many societies the distinction between official and practical kinship is highlighted in the institution of marriage. As Bourdieu (1977:34–35) notes, "marriage provides a good opportunity for observing what . . . separates official kinship, single and immutable, defined . . . by the norms of genealogical protocol, from practical kinship, whose boundaries and definitions are as many and as varied as its users and the occasions on which it is used." To paraphrase: it is practical kin—"utility men," in Bourdieu's terms—who do much of the actual work in arranging marriages; it is official kin—"leading actors," in Bourdieu's terms—who publicly celebrate and validate them.

Bourdieu's distinction between official and practical kinship is useful for my purposes, but it is insufficiently precise both for Negeri Sembilan and for many (perhaps most) other societies. This is partly because official kinship is rarely if ever "single," with all that this implies in terms of being monolithic, internally undifferentiated, and free of contradiction. It is, moreover, essential to appreciate that in some cases—such as those of the Merina (Bloch 1987) and the Andaman Islanders (Ortner 1989–90)— there are three or more contrasting sets of representations bearing on the culturally interlocked domain of gender (to which domain the distinction may be applied), not simply the two that are suggested by Bourdieu's terminological and analytic distinction. To this we need add three other important qualifications. First, contrasting representations bearing on kinship, gender, etc., may be invoked—and contested—in all kinds of different contexts (practical and official alike). Second, the majority of (if not all) such representations may be thoroughly grounded in practice, though differently so (e.g., in different contexts and domains, to different degrees, in different ways, with different effects). And third, all may speak to "partial truths," the more general point being that cultures—or, to be more precise, elements of ideological formations—"get things right" (are truly illuminating) in some contexts, but are "wrong" or "false" (profoundly distorting or mystifying) in others.

Caveats such as these should be borne in mind throughout the ensuing discussion. So, too, should the more basic and in some ways far more important point that distinctions of the sort proposed by Bourdieu, which have deep roots in Marxist contributions to theories of ideology, are not intended to effect "an ontological carving of the world down the middle"

(Eagleton 1991:83 ff.), but rather to highlight the existence and entailments of the different perspectives, discourses, and registers that invariably comprise any given ideological formation. There are, of course, other conceptual and analytic frameworks available for handling polyvocality and multiplicity of the latter sort, but they, too, have their limitations and need not concern us here.[11]

Marriage, Funerary Rituals, and Affinal Exchange

The modified distinction between official and practical kinship that is proposed here is especially relevant to an understanding of marriage and funerary rituals in nineteenth-century Negeri Sembilan.[12] These rituals are of interest not only because they shed valuable light on how people in the nineteenth century represented their systems of kinship and gender. They also illuminate highly significant ("on-the-ground") dynamics of the nineteenth-century systems, the historical reproduction and transformation of which are crucial for an understanding of kinship and gender at present.

In nineteenth-century Negeri Sembilan, official representations of kinship, gender, and affinal exchange were particularly evident on the first day of formal wedding ceremonies. This day served as the occasion for lavish feasting as well as the ritual presentation of "marriage gold" (*mas kawin*) from the clan chief of the groom to the clan chief of the bride. The latter ritual not only validated the bond between husband and wife and the linkage between their respective descent units. It also highlighted clan chiefs, and men more generally, as "leading actors," effectively denying the role, in arranging and maintaining marriage and affinal relations, of untitled males and women as a whole.

The same day served as the occasion for the specifically Islamic dimension of the wedding, which also symbolized official views of kinship, gender, and affinal exchange. This ritual called for the presence of a local mosque official, the bride's Islamic guardian (or *wali*), the groom, and a few male onlookers as witnesses. It focused on the mosque official's recitation of the "marriage service" (*khutbah nikah*) and symbolized, but did not actually effect, a transfer of legal responsibility and control over the bride from her Islamic guardian—usually her father but in any case a male—to her husband. This ritual represented the system of affinal alliance as composed of descent units linked to one another through exchanges of rights over women. As such, it typically entailed a *mis*representation of the practice of affinal exchange and social reproduction generally. In most cases (i.e., with the notable exception of titled men occupying the highest offices in the land) the practice of marriage and affinal exchange did not really center on a father relinquishing rights and obligations with respect to his daughter and doing so in favor of his daughter's husband; rather, it focused on a mother's transfer of claims and responsibilities over her son to the son's wife and the latter's immediate kin. I will return to this point later on.

Most other elements of marriage rituals served to foreground practical views of kinship, gender, and affinal exchange, many of which were clearly contradictory to official representations of these same aspects, insofar as they emphasized not only that men—as opposed to women—were being exchanged, but also that they were being exchanged by groups of women, not by other men. Thus, the second day of wedding festivities witnessed the groom's relatives traveling to the bride's home bearing gifts of food, along with a lavish feast sponsored by the bride's mother. Subsequent to the feast, the groom formally entered the bride's mother's home, laden with gifts of food along with a bundle of clothes and other personal possessions, which symbolized the severance of residential ties with his mother, sisters, and other close kin. Once inside, he was welcomed by his in-laws and formally accepted into their household. Other ritualized introductions typically stretched over the course of the following week or two. One such series of introductions involved visits by the bridal couple to various households inhabited by the groom's kin. Not surprisingly, these were glossed *mengulang jejak,* which refers to the groom's going over, or retracing, his footsteps for the very last time.

Many of these same practical representations of kinship, gender, and affinal exchange were highlighted in funerary rituals. In the event of the husband's death, for example, the widow financed the burial as well as the principal funerary rituals and feasts, all of which occurred in her village. Particularly noteworthy is the ritualized exchange which took place during the final feast in the funerary cycle, and which consisted of a pair of pants, a coat, a sleeping mat, and a pillow; in short, the very same items the husband had brought with him when he began living among his wife's relatives and simultaneously severed residential ties with his own kin. It is especially significant that these items passed from the widow to her mother-in-law. The design of the transfer symbolized both the end of the daughter-in-law's relationship with her former husband, and a return to the mother-in-law of the son that she had in effect "given away" in marriage. Moreover, just as this ritual depicted the principal exchanges in the formation of conjugal and affinal bonds as centering on transfers of rights over males, so too did it portray such exchanges as entailing transfers between women, who were thus represented as trafficking in men, or rights over them.

The rituals following the dissolution of the conjugal bond owing to the wife's death conveyed generally similar messages. In a word, they highlighted the peripheral and "guest" status of the widower among his affines, underscoring that he could only remain among them if his children indicated a desire to have him stay.

These practical representations of kinship, gender, and affinal exchange were largely congruent with everyday practice in the nineteenth century. In practice, the nineteenth-century system centered on the exchange among localized descent units of rights over grooms (rather than brides), such that males (rather than females) served as the connective elements in the nexus of affinal exchange and alliance.[13] Elsewhere I have developed this argument (see Peletz 1987a, 1995), pointing out (among other things) that the exchanges in question focused on rights over men's labor power and productivity; and that data from nineteenth-century Negeri Sembilan pose serious problems both for Lévi-Strauss, Leach, and others who assume that the exchange of women is a universal in systems of affinal alliance, and for those (e.g., Collier 1988) who have adopted the general lines of the Lévi-Straussian position that women's secondary status vis-à-vis men is invariably grounded in systems of kinship and marriage. (See Kelly 1993 for an extensive review and critique of such positions.) Suffice it to emphasize here that with the notable exception of the highest-ranking political leaders (e.g., district chiefs or *Undang*), married men came under the day-to-day authority and social control of their affines, even though they maintained contact with their matrilineal kin and aided them economically and otherwise. We might underscore too that conjugal acquisitions (*carian laki-bini*) such as houses and land were not divisible upon divorce or the dissolution of a marriage through death. This despite the fact that a man may have devoted a great deal of labor and capital to the construction of a house for his wife, and may also have expended considerable labor in transforming acreage in his wife's village into plots suitable for residence or (wet-rice) agriculture. As explained elsewhere (Peletz 1987a, 1995), rights over such property remained under the control of his wife (or her surviving kin), and typically devolved upon her daughters, who thus stood as the provisional proprietors of these newly created "ancestral" holdings (*harta pesaka*).

These circumstances help account for the references in the nineteenth- and early-twentieth-century literature to men "becoming members of" their wives' clans upon marriage (see, for example, Newbold 1839, 2:123; Parr and Mackray 1910:84, 85; Wilkinson [1911] 1976:316; Taylor [1929] 1970 cited in Winstedt 1934:78). They also help clarify the meaning of numerous "customary sayings" or aphorisms (*perbilangan*) discussed in the literature (see Peletz 1988; see also Hale 1898:57; Parr and Mackray 1910:87, 116–117; Caldecott 1918:36–37), one of which may be translated as follows:

The married man must go, when he is bid,
And halt, when he is forbid.
When we receive a man as bridegroom,
If he is strong, he shall be our champion;
If a fool, he will be ordered about
To invite guests distant and collect guests near;
Clever and we'll invite his counsel;
Learned and we'll ask his prayers;
Rich and we'll use his gold.
If lame, he shall scare chicken;
If blind, he shall pound the mortar;
If deaf, he shall fire our salutes. . . .
A bridegroom among his wife's relations
Is like a cucumber among durian fruit;
If he rolls against them, he is hurt;
And he is hurt, if they roll against him.

                    Caldecott 1918:36–37

It is clearly beyond the scope of the present discussion to examine continuity and change in kinship and gender relations or ritual activities from the nineteenth century to the present, though I do address some of the relevant issues later in the essay.[14] The main point to emphasize here is that while the systems of marriage and affinal exchange—and the de facto exchange of men in particular—are no longer *jurally elaborated* as they were in the nineteenth century, they are in many (but certainly not all) respects still *experienced* and *represented* in terms of the sort outlined above, especially by men. This is strikingly evident both from the comments of married men (and women) concerning divorce and their marriage experiences generally, and from the ways in which women (and to a lesser extent men) understand and represent maleness or masculinity. Such dynamics (to which I return) are essential to keep in mind insofar as they have helped motivate and sustain certain (practical) views of men (and women) which are very different from official representations of masculinity (and femininity).

In the next section of this essay I focus on the cultural framework in terms of which male and female similarities and differences are most often represented in contemporary Negeri Sembilan. After elucidating some of the meanings of the key signs of this framework (the concepts of "reason" and "passion"), I turn to a brief consideration of the articulation of these signs and meanings in official representations of gender. This is followed by an examination of their articulation in practical representations of gender, and a discussion of the scope, force, and reproduction of practical views of masculinity.

THE SYMBOLS AND MEANINGS OF "REASON" AND "PASSION"

The Concept of Nafsu ("Passion")

Nafsu is an Arabic-origin term (*nafs* in Arabic) that is widely used both among Malays and most other Muslims in the Malay-Indonesian archipelago (e.g., Acehnese, Minangkabau, Javanese), and among most Muslims (Moroccans, Yemeni, Bedouin, etc.) elsewhere in the world, as well.[15] It is translated in contemporary Malay dictionaries as "passion," "desire," "lust," "want," "longing," and so forth, which is in keeping with its uses both in the field site of Bogang[16] and in other Muslim communities. In many (and perhaps all) Muslim communities, the term *nafsu* (hereafter "passion") frequently carries derogatory connotations, especially when it is applied to humans. In many (but not all) Muslim communities, moreover, one finds an entrenched, highly elaborated belief that "passion" is more pronounced among women (and females generally) than among men (males). The latter point will be addressed below. First, however, we need to contextualize such beliefs by examining villagers' general understandings and representations of "passion" and the ways they relate to local understandings and representations of "reason" (*akal*). As will be apparent in due course, "passion" and "reason" are not simply symbols "of" or "about" gender. They also inform village thought about the essence and dynamics of human nature, social relations, and the world at large, all of which is to say that they are central to the local ontology.

In the Malay view of things, God created the universe and all of its features and inhabitants. In accordance with God's will, "passion" is present in humans and other animals, spirits, and all other living creatures. The presence of "passion" in humans, and in the universe generally, dates from the time of Adam, who, after seeing two doves, asked God to make him a companion or mate. God obliged Adam, and made Hawah (Eve) from one of Adam's ribs. God proceeded to instruct Adam and Hawah not to eat the fruit of a certain tree (a pomegranate tree in some local variants of the myth, an unspecified tree in others). But Adam and Hawah were tempted by the devil to eat the fruit, and they did so, which action resulted in their being driven from Heaven. A piece of the fruit lodged in Adam's throat, and to this day men have "Adam's apples" (*halkum*), which serve as embodied reminders of Adam's transgression. Portions of the apple appeared as breasts (*dada, buah dada*) in Hawah, and to this day women have prominent breasts, which, like men's "Adam's apples," signify both Adam and Hawah's sins and humankind's "passion."

The moral of this myth of genesis is not only that those who disobey God receive divine punishment, but also—and more relevant here—that sensual and other gratification necessarily entails both the indulgence of desire and ipso facto the absence of restraint. Restraint and control of the inner self are strongly marked moral virtues, the attainment of which brings prestige. Conversely, the absence of restraint indicates a lack of virtue and gives rise to stigma.

This system of moral evaluation helps explain villagers' marked ambivalence about the satisfaction of basic (biophysiological) human requirements. On the one hand, villagers do of course recognize that human beings require food, drink, air, shelter, and the like if they are to survive and thrive; and they are well aware that sexual activity is necessary for procreation, and for the reproduction of society and culture. On the other hand, villagers view the satisfaction of these basic human requirements with marked ambivalence since their satisfaction is associated with the absence of restraint. People look down upon individuals who are felt to be overly concerned with food, eating, and drinking, even though this is one of two domains in which relative indulgence is permitted, even enjoined (the other is illness, real or imagined). (Individuals who fail to fast during the month of Ramadan are especially stigmatized and are liable to criminal prosecution if they break the fast in public.) And they talk about such behavior in terms of the preponderance, if only temporary or context-specific, of "passion" relative to "reason," which is seen as unsightly, unbecoming, morally offensive, and, at least in some contexts, as seriously sinful (cf. Newbold 1839, 2:353).

More generally, when villagers speak of gossiping, desiring material possessions, being especially (or overly) interested in sex, they often mention "passion"; they are, moreover, quick to link "passion" with the devil and evil spirits and demons of various kinds who tempt them with sinful behavior. As a male elder put it when we were discussing the origins of the universe and related matters: "This 'passion,' it's the devil. You want to eat a lot, drink a lot, that's all the devil, Satan. You want to buy clothes, buy a house, make your house all beautiful, that's the same: Satan, the devil. These are worldly matters; in the Afterlife they don't exist."

Negative attitudes toward the absence of restraint are well illustrated in villagers' views concerning food prohibitions and ethnic groups who appear (to villagers) not to observe any such prohibitions, such as the seminomadic non-Muslim aborigines (*orang asli;* literally "original people") living in the hilly, forested regions behind the village. The aborigines eat the meat of wild boar, which, like all other pork, is forbidden to Muslims, and which is highest on the list of prohibited foods as far as Malays are concerned. The consumption of pork is in fact seen by Malays as thoroughly revolting, far more so than the consumption of snake, dog, lizard, and cockroach, which the aborigines are also said to enjoy.[17] Because the aborigines eat wild boar, they are assumed not to have any food prohibitions. And because they have no food prohibitions, they "have no religion, only beliefs and superstitions" (*tak ada agama, kepercayaan saja*). More broadly, since the aborigines have no religion, they have no culture (*sopan, kesopo-nan; budaya, kebudayaan*), which, in the local view, is what distinguishes human beings (*manusia*) from "mere animals" (*binatang saja*). Indeed, when villagers speak of aborigines, they frequently comment that the aborigines are "like animals" (*macam binatang*). Some carry this association even further, suggesting that the aborigines are not simply "like animals," but that they really *are* animals, created from "grime" (*daki*) (cf. Newbold 1839, 2:106).

The idea that the aborigines exercise no restraint when it comes to eating pork and are for this reason uncultured and subhuman resonates both with villagers' negative views on other "races" (Chinese, Indians, and "white people" [*orang putih*]) whose behavior—especially with respect to eating, drinking, gambling, and sex—is seen as relatively unrestrained, and with their views of fellow Malays whose behavior is deemed inappropriate and/or aesthetically offensive. The exercise (or absence) of restraint thus serves as an important ethnic marker as well as an index of virtue (or its absence) within Malay communities. In cases of seriously offensive behavior on the part of Malays, the offender is sometimes said to be *kurang ajar*, a literal translation of which is "less than fully taught"—a very serious charge. Violations of incest prohibitions certainly fall into this category, and are sometimes likened to "chickens eating their own flesh" (*macam ayam makan daging sendiri*), which draws a parallel between individuals who mate with their own kind (e.g., members of the same lineage or clan), and domesticated chickens that consume the scraps of cooked food thrown out for them, which frequently include the flesh or meat of their own relatives. The explicit metaphoric link between incest and cannibalism—both of which are construed as quintessentially subhuman—would have certainly delighted Freud ([1913] 1950).[18]

Persons whose comportment is seriously offensive are thus said to be improperly socialized and therefore to stand somewhere between the rule-governed realm of humans, where socialization involves the learning and internalization of moral codes, and the world of animals, which is governed by "passion" rather than moral codes or rules. Socialization is in fact seen as a process entailing the gradual curtailment or control of "passion" through the imposition of man-made (but ultimately divinely inspired) codes and rules embodied in Islam and *adat*. The socialization process, and culture generally, thus "work on" the raw material of "passion," which, as noted above, is directly and inextricably associated with the world of animals and nature, and with the relatively if not altogether uncultured ("natural") behavior of other "races."

Before proceeding to a discussion of "reason" I should stress that there are some crucial differences between Malay understandings and representations of "passion" on the one hand, and those reported for culturally similar groups such as the Acehnese (who reside in northern Sumatra) on the other. We have already seen that in Malay culture "passion" is experienced and construed in predominantly negative terms, as indexing a lack of restraint, hence weakness, animality, etc. This is true for Acehnese as well, though Acehnese sometimes remark that "passion," properly guided by "reason," can be and ideally is channeled into Islamic prayer and chanting as well as other forms of pious and morally virtuous behavior (Siegel 1969). I never encountered remarks or views of the latter sort among Malays, even though there are certain contexts (e.g., weddings and funerary rituals) in which Malays, like Acehnese, engage in Sufistic chanting which sometimes eventuates in a kind of frenzied ecstasy. That Acehnese but not Malays operate with a concept of "passion" that makes explicit provision for its utilization in the fulfillment of religious objectives may reflect the fact that (because of the variegated historical development of Islam in Southeast Asia) Acehnese Islam is more thoroughly infused with Sufistic elements than is Malayan Islam. In any event, the more general point about the absence among Malays of Acehnese/Sufistic constructions of the sort at issue here has also been noted by Malay anthropologists such as Wazir Jahan Karim (1990:36), who recently offered the following (understated) observation: "Sufi thinking that passion can be harnessed to a love for religion and ecstasy over God does not permeate Malay thinking, at least amongst the masses."

The Concept of Akal ("Reason")

Akal is an Arabic-origin concept ('*aql* in Arabic) that is of central importance among Malays and other Muslims in Southeast Asia and beyond. The term denotes "reason," "intelligence," and "rationality," the ability to evaluate alternative courses of action (e.g., display perspective and view things from afar) and render informed judgments, and is widely used in Malay culture in connection with "passion" (and "shame" [*malu*]). As mentioned earlier, it is often said that *akal* (hereafter "reason") distinguishes humans from the rest of the animal world and is our special gift from God; and that "reason" "cooperates" or "works together" both with the *hati* or liver (the seat of emotions) and with *iman* (faith, strong belief or trust in God, resoluteness, sincerity, etc.) to guide the individual along the proper path(s). Villagers also contend that "reason" and "passion" forever struggle against one another within the individual, and that "good behavior" (*budi baik*) is evidence of the preponderance, however temporary or qualified, of "reason" over "passion," just as "bad behavior" (*budi jahat*) reflects the dominance, however short-lived or partial, of "passion" over "reason." "Shame" (*malu*) is relevant here as well, for it, too, acts as a "brake" on "passion" and its expression in social action.

While ("normal," "healthy") human beings are born with the capacity to develop "reason," they do not display or possess it at birth. Rather, in the normal course of things, "reason" "develops" or "expands" (*kembang*) over time, as a consequence of socialization and religious instruction in particular, and is typically manifested in one or another form when a child is seven or eight years old (though this is highly variable), or, as some people put it, when the child begins instruction in the recitation of the Qur'an (*mengaji*). (Children usually begin such instruction at about the time they begin secular education in the national school system, i.e., when they are about six or seven years old.) It is also true that young children and adolescents are often characterized as lacking "reason," but the point of reference here is adults, not (nonhuman) animals.

Diligent observance of Muslim prayer procedure and other religious strictures is one way to help develop one's "reason." Conversely, the cultivation of "reason" through concentration and various types of mental and spiritual exercises entailing studied restraint facilitates proper prayer and other forms of religiously valued and morally virtuous behavior. Compared to children and adolescents, adults tend to have more extensive obligations as Muslims and to take them more seriously. This is one reason why adults are typically regarded as having more "reason" than children and adolescents. Others include their superior ability (relative to children and adolescents) to make informed judgments based on experience in the world; their demonstrated capacity to perform the myriad tasks and activities associated with domestic maintenance, production, and the like; and, more generally, their greater control over their "passion" and their more systematic internalization of—and behavioral adherence to—the moral norms of Malay culture; hence (given the explicit link between being Malay and being human), their stronger commitment to being human.

While the acquisition or development of "reason" is a gradual process, so, too, in many cases at least, is its dissolution or loss in the course of debilitating illness or old age. Individuals afflicted with senility are often said to have "lost" their "reason" and to have reverted to a childlike state in which "reason" is poorly developed or only sporadically manifest. In some instances, senescence seems to be regarded as a "natural" process that is inherent in biological aging, though in others it is attributed to possession by evil spirits harbored by malevolent (human) others.

Various types of severe emotional, psychological, and spiritual disorders (including senility) are sometimes attributed to or regarded as entailing debilitated "reason," but for the most part disorders of this sort are conceptualized in terms of livers and/or "life forces" (*semangat*), not "reason." Thus, a person who exhibits what we might take to be symptoms of extreme anxiety, depression, or obsessive behavior is not usually viewed as having something wrong with his or her "reason" or brain (*otak*), but rather to be suffering an affliction of the liver or life force. Similarly, an individual who is "girl (or boy) crazy" (*gila perempuan* [*gila laki-laki*]), is generally believed to be the victim of human malevolence that "worked on" his or her liver or life force. (Mental retardation and insanity, on the other hand, are seen as disorders of the brain, mind, or "reason.") It is nonetheless true that disturbances of the liver or life force can interfere with one's ability to "reason." In this sense, and in many others discussed earlier, Malays view body and mind as integrally related parts of a single and unified whole, and do not operate with a dualistic mind/body dichotomy of the sort informing Western medicine and Western thought generally.

A final point to stress in this brief overview of local understandings and representations of "reason" is that discourses on "reason" are often framed in terms of heavily value-laden spatial metaphors. Thus certain individuals and classes of people (e.g., adult males) are accorded "long," "broad," "high," or "deep" "reason," just as others (adult females, and children and adolescents of both sexes) are held to be endowed with "reason" that is "short," "narrow," "low," or "shallow." Having "reason" that is "long," "broad," "high," and the like is clearly more valued than having "reason" that is "short," "narrow," "low," and so forth; and the person with "long," "broad" "reason" is accorded more virtue in the hierarchy of prestige (and stigma). All of this is to say that the allocation of "reason" serves to legitimize the distribution of virtue in the latter hierarchy and that "reason" is central to the system of moral evaluation as a whole. I will return to these themes further along.

CONTRASTING REPRESENTATIONS OF GENDER

Official Representations

I already remarked that Malays in Negeri Sembilan and other parts of the Peninsula hold that "passion" is present among all of God's creatures (human and animals alike), and that "reason" is what distinguishes humans from the rest of the animal world. Malays also frequently contend that "passion" and "reason" are present to one degree or another in all humans, but that "passion" is present in greater concentrations (or is more pronounced) among women, whereas "reason" is less so. These latter contentions, which are part of the official discourse on gender, and which are clearly hegemonic (in Raymond Williams's sense of the term), focus on the culturally elaborated perception that women are less controlled and restrained than men insofar as they are more prone to gossiping and desiring material possessions, and are otherwise more closely tied to the "baser" things in life. The arena of sexual relations is the quintessential context, as least (or especially) for men, in which women's stronger "passion" is displayed; for, as some male elders told me, in sexual relations women "still want more" even after their husbands are thoroughly satisfied (have achieved orgasm). This particular contention, which may well derive in part from men's (and women's) limited understandings of the anatomy and physiology of female orgasm, was never conceded by women (more precisely, never came up) in the numerous conversations that I (or my wife) had with them. Nor was the point made by another male elder that "women in hotels" (a reference to prostitutes) can have sex "ten or twenty times in an evening, or even all night long," none of which would be possible for a man.[19] I should emphasize, though, that many women *do* espouse the position that women's "passion" is more pronounced than men's. Virtually all women, moreover, hold that women "need to"—and do in fact—have a stronger sense of "shame" (*malu*) than men since, if they did not, they would be "like wild animals" (*macam haiwan*) and chaos would reign throughout the world.

Malay views of the sort outlined here appear to be of great antiquity. In light of the Arabic origin of the concepts of "reason" and "passion" and of the centrality of these concepts within Islamic discourse, it seems reasonable to assume that such views were introduced into the Peninsula along with "the coming of Islam" beginning around the thirteenth century, and that, because of the subsequent historical development of Islam in the region, they became increasingly prevalent in the centuries that followed.[20] Significantly, the gendered differences encoded in these views not only provided much of the cultural rationale for restricting women's involvement in formal political arenas in Muslim communities in Southeast Asia during the latter part of the period 1450–1800. They also served to delegitimize women's important roles in public communal rituals during this time, thus effecting both a constriction and an overall devaluation of women's ritual activities (Reid 1988; Andaya and Ishii 1992). Gender-skewed political and ritual institutions, in turn, have fostered the reproduction of all such views associated with official representations of gender. So, too, of course, have myriad components of "civil society" including official kinship (which, as we have seen, represents marriage and affinal exchange in terms of men exchanging women), various Islamic institutions (mosque, religious court, etc.), as well as spirit possession and *latah* (a cultural elaboration of the startle reflex involving echolalia, echopraxia, and other forms of "pathomimetic" behavior), both of which predominate among women and are interpreted by women and men alike as evidence of women's greater "animality" and spiritual weakness vis-à-vis men.

These (official) views of the differences between men and women are undoubtedly familiar to many readers, for they are highly congruent with the (official) gender imagery found among Malays elsewhere in the Peninsula, among Acehnese, Javanese and other Muslims in Southeast Asia, and among Muslims in other parts of the Islamic world (though there are some striking contrasts as well, which are keyed to variations in systems of production, exchange, prestige, and personhood). One of the most comprehensive accounts of such imagery comes from Morocco and indicates not only that there is an important developmental dynamic that needs to be considered when assessing Moroccan views of males and females (such views are not static over the life cycle); but also, that in what might be termed "private" or "backstage" contexts (some) Moroccan women contest certain official representations concerning their secondary status and the differences between males and females generally (Dwyer 1978). These significant findings (which are offered as a critique of Ortner's [1974] work on "nature" and "culture") are relevant to Negeri Sembilan as well. In some ways far more interesting, however, are the ways in which gender imagery in Negeri Sembilan differs from what has been reported for Moroccans, other North African groups such as Egyptian Bedouins (Abu-Lughod 1986), and most other societies, including Malays outside Negeri Sembilan. To wit: in Negeri Sembilan there is a highly elaborated alternative discourse, which is in many (but not all) respects an inversion of the official hegemonic discourse that I have outlined here, and which clearly transcends "private," "domestic," and/or "female dominated" contexts. In short, key features of this very public (albeit contextually specific) discourse are espoused by men and women alike.[21]

Practical Representations

The alternative discourse to which I refer is composed of practical representations of gender. In contrast to their official counterparts, these representations are not "explicitly codified in quasi-juridical formalism." Compared with official representations, moreover, they are more thoroughly grounded in the everyday practical situations in which people find themselves. An additional point of contrast (related to the preceding one) is that they are more explicitly oriented to the practical realities of "getting things done"—e.g., managing money and other household resources, taking care of children and other relatives (including the elderly and infirm), maintaining exchange relationships with neighboring households and the members of one's lineage and clan, and in these and other ways ensuring domestic reproduction—than to legitimating the most encompassing structures of power and prestige, though they, too, clearly have legitimating functions. Finally, whereas some practical representations simply differ from, or are largely irrelevant to, official (hegemonic) representations, others constitute subversive challenges to them and are in this sense appropriately characterized as counterhegemonic.

Practical representations of gender portray men as less reasonable (i.e., having less "reason") and less responsible than women both with regard to managing money and other household resources, and in terms of honoring basic social obligations associated with marriage, parenting, and kinship generally. They also depict men as less deserving (and in less need) of subsistence guarantees than women, a point to which I will return in a moment. These representations both derive from, and inform, the ways in which people experience, understand, and represent kinship (particularly marriage and divorce), reciprocity, and social reproduction. And not surprisingly, they permeate everyday discourse concerning the gendered nature of property and inheritance relations, especially why it is that daughters continue to be favored over sons in the inheritance of houses and land, even when the latter are not formally classified as "ancestral"—hence exclusively female—property.

Daughters continue to be favored over sons in the inheritance of houses and land partly because women are believed to require greater subsistence guarantees than men insofar as they are held to be less flexible, resourceful, and adaptive than men, who, it is believed, can eke out a living wherever they find themselves.[22] It is also taken for granted that all women will marry and have children, and that they must have resources to fall back on, particularly since they may not always be able to depend on their husbands. The latter may be involved in temporary out-migration (*merantau*) for many months or years at a stretch, or may simply predecease their wives. Of far greater cultural salience is the issue of desertion and divorce by husbands. Marriage is regarded as a tenuous arrangement (two-thirds of all marriages in Bogang end in divorce), for men's commitments to their wives and children (as well as other kinship and social ties) are seen as provisional, even capricious. In the final analysis, then, women merit greater subsistence guarantees than men not only or even primarily because they are held to be the less flexible, resourceful, and adaptive of the two sexes; but rather, because they must be protected from men, most notably their husbands, but also their brothers and men in other kinship and social roles.[23]

To sum up and elaborate briefly: practical representations of gender portray men as much less reliable and trustworthy than women, and relatively uncommitted to their wives, children, and other relatives. They also depict men as fond of gambling and alcohol,[24] overly inclined to purchase on credit, prone to running up burdensome debts, and thus less restrained—and in certain respects more impassioned (i.e., having more "passion")—than women. In the practical view, moreover, men are "at fault" in most cases of divorce, since, as some of my male informants put it, "they don't follow the rules," are "basically lazy," and "expect to eat for free."

This overview of practical representations of gender is, of necessity, rather sketchy, but it should suffice for the time being. In the next part of the essay I elaborate on some of these representations though my main concern is to situate their (re)production both historically and in relation to the political economy.

The Scope, Force, and Reproduction of Practical Representations of Masculinity

Material presented here and elsewhere (Peletz 1995) indicates that with respect to a wide variety of issues women and men are in general agreement as to the basic similarities and differences between males and females. One important corollary of this is that women appear to accept as valid much of the official discourse on gender, including numerous features of the discourse that portray women (and females generally) in culturally devalued terms. Many women, for example, contend that females have less "reason" than males. And virtually all of them claim that women "need to" (and do in fact) have more "shame" than men since, if they did not, they would be "like animals" and the world would be in chaos. Similarly, women invariably view themselves as having weaker life forces (*semangat*) than men (and thus more likely to be afflicted by spirit possession and *latah*). Noteworthy as well, just as all the women (and men) with whom I discussed the issue claimed that women are more likely than men to be ritually "dirty" and impure, all of them accepted as appropriate that (under normal circumstances) women not be allowed to serve as mosque officials or religious magistrates, or in other positions of public leadership. More broadly, even those women who feel that females are accorded a secondary status in relation to males (not all of them do) do not seem to feel that this is "unfair" or otherwise inappropriate; nor do any men.

There is less agreement between men and women with regard to the hegemonic view that women have more "passion" than men. Based on the twenty informal interviews focusing on such matters that I conducted toward the end of the second period of fieldwork, I found that while most men (8 out of 10 of those interviewed) espouse this view, only about a third (3 out of 10) of the women do. Nearly two-thirds (6 out of 10) claim that men have more "passion" than women, typically citing as evidence that men tend to perform poorly in their roles as husbands and fathers (such that most of the problems in marriage stem from the faults of men); and, more generally, that it is men's greater "passion" that explains why they are far less responsible than women when it comes to taking care of their spouses and children and honoring kinship and other social and moral obligations.

Interestingly, many of the men I spoke with over the course of more than two years of fieldwork also espouse the latter view of men as irresponsible and at fault in most cases of divorce, even though they still maintain that men are less "passionate" than women. A major difference that emerges from a comparison of these aspects of women's and men's views, then, is that in the case of women—about two-thirds of them at any rate— the theme of men's irresponsibility is used to stand the hegemonic view of "passion" (and "reason" and masculinity) on its head. In the case of males, however, this theme does not usually raise serious questions about the legitimacy of the hegemony. This is either because the theme is encompassed within the hegemony in a way that effectively defines it as a nonissue, or because it is segregated from the hegemony in a way that renders it largely irrelevant thereto (and vice versa).

The limited scope of this essay precludes discussion of many important issues raised here, but it is, I think, essential to examine some of the structural factors that have motivated the reproduction of practical representations of masculinity. Such representations—which, as we have seen, include propositions that men are "lazy" and "expect to eat for free," are "at fault" in most cases of divorce, and are, overall, less responsible than women in honoring kinship and other social obligations—are most profitably viewed in relation to (British) colonial and other state strategies which, since the late nineteenth century, have promoted the development of rural capitalism.[25] From the outset, these strategies included policies that effected a break with tradition insofar as they encouraged men to take up commercially valued land in their own names, independently of their sisters, wives, and other female kin. Of comparable if not greater significance, state strategies involved the introduction of highly individualistic forms of proprietorship and inheritance, which undermined many features of the traditional system of property and inheritance relations, and various types of collateral ties, including relationships among (natural and classificatory) siblings. Especially relevant for our purposes is that these changes undercut the economic dimensions of brothers' ties with their sisters and, in the process, helped shift the burden of support for women and children from *brothers* to *husbands*. Phrased in broader terms, responsibilities for the creation of property rights, wealth, and prestige for lineages and clans came to fall increasingly, though not exclusively, on husbands and in-marrying males generally. I will return to this point in a moment.

The new economic opportunies—cash cropping, expanded trading activities, and a limited number of civil service jobs—that were made available to men (and to rural society at large) beginning in the late 1800s were in many (but not all) respects socially divisive and profoundly disruptive. So, too, were the effects of other state economic policies analyzed elsewhere (Peletz 1987b, 1988). Suffice it to say that the period since the late 1800s has witnessed increased household dependence on male cash cropping; declines both in the predominantly female domain of subsistence rice production and in the viability of traditional rural economic institutions in their entirety; and the development of a rather pronounced degree of class differentiation and stratification based largely on differential access to commercially valued land planted in rubber or other cash crops.

These state-sponsored changes fueled the (re)production of practical representations of masculinity in a number of ways, two of which merit brief mention. First, because they entailed the highly inequitable distribution of land and other productive resources, they are directly implicated in the marked disparities that exist in men's abilities to live up to the expectations and demands of their wives and affines. Relatively wealthy men, who constitute a very small minority of the adult male population, can rather easily meet these latter expectations and demands, but the overwhelming majority of adult men cannot. The discrepancy between those who can and do on the one hand, and those who cannot and do not on the other, clearly fuels the view that most men are lazy and irresponsible, and typically "expect to eat for free."

A second, less obvious way in which state-sponsored capitalism helped motivate the (re)production of practical representations of masculinity has to do with the colonial-era restructuring of the roles of brother and husband. I noted earlier that since the late 1800s the responsibility for providing for women and children has been shifting increasingly from brothers to husbands. I need to add here that this shift has not in any way undermined the "elderly brother" (*abang*) norms that seem always to have informed the husband role (i.e., the idea that husbands are supposed to support and protect their wives, and otherwise behave toward them much like elder brothers behave toward younger siblings). On the contrary, elderly brother norms appear to have become more central to the definition of the husband role. They have, at the same time, become increasingly idealized, the more so since many of the moral and material imperatives of brotherhood are no longer put to the test on a daily basis. It merits emphasis, too, that the everyday behavior of men in their roles as husbands is judged not in terms of standards derived from the actual behavior of elder brothers; but rather, in relation to an increasingly lofty and heavily mythologized set of ideals which comprise the fantasy of the perfect elder brother.

Now I would argue that married men have—or at least are perceived to have—a very hard time living up to the elderly brother ideals informing the husband role. This is largely because married men have quite substantial—and in some ways mutually incompatible—moral and material obligations to their relatives, especially the females among them; e.g., their mothers, sisters, and other female matrikin on the one hand, and their wives and female affines on the other. Most relevant here are the heavy affinal demands on married men's labor power and productivity, which reflect

the critically important role of husbands, and of in-marrying males generally, in producing property, wealth, and prestige for their wives' kin groups,
but which frequently exceed married men's productive capacities. These
demands, along with the expectations to which they are keyed, can make
married life very difficult for men (particularly men with little or no productive land), and they often exacerbate tensions in marriage and affinal
relations. Married men who find that they cannot deal realistically with
expectations and pressures from their wives and affines frequently divorce,
or simply abandon their wives along with any children they might have.
This course of action not only feeds into practical views that husbands and
fathers are unreliable and untrustworthy; it also colors practical views of
masculinity as a whole. These latter, practical views serve, in turn, to
counter and moderate official views of males, just as they effectively elevate
practical views of females.

DISCUSSION: NEGERI SEMBILAN IN COMPARATIVE AND THEORETICAL PERSPECTIVE

Deconstructing the ("Arelational") Concept of Masculinity

Negeri Sembilan masculinity (or maleness), far from being a singular, unitary, or otherwise seamless cultural phenomenon, is composed of a number of contradictory representations, many of which are "inveigled in," and
thus best understood as dialectically related to, constructions of adult
men's kinship roles. In fact, the category "male" (*laki-laki, lelaki*) does not
have all that much cultural salience (the same is true of the category "female" [*perempuan*]), though categories such as "brother," "husband," and
"father" (and "sister," "wife," and "mother") clearly do.[26] More generally,
data from Negeri Sembilan indicate that in the practice of everyday life,
certain male relational roles—e.g., husband/father, elder brother—may
well dominate the category of "male," and may also inform the meanings
of all other male relational (and "positional") roles.

Data from Negeri Sembilan have broad comparative and theoretical significance. To sketch out various implications of these data I provide a quick
(and highly selective) overview of some recent developments in Ortner's
thinking about gender, and then turn to a brief discussion of an enduring
theme (the "relational/positional" dichotomy) in the work of Nancy Chodorow, which has informed the thinking of Ortner (and Whitehead),
among many others, and which has, I believe, led to a skewed understanding of some of the differences and similarities in structural definitions of
males and females.

Earlier in this essay I referred in passing to Ortner's (1974; orig. 1972)
argument that women are everywhere held to be "closer to nature" and

"further from culture" than men, and that this conceptual linkage is what explains their universal cultural devaluation (secondary status). This extremely insightful and provocative argument stimulated a great deal of additional research, even though it was highly static and did of course engender much controversy (see, for example, Dwyer 1978; MacCormack and Strathern 1980; Valeri 1990). Some of the criticism, along with largely unrelated developments in social and cultural theory, encouraged Ortner to rethink her overall theoretical orientation. This is readily apparent from the 1981 volume *Sexual Meanings: The Cultural Construction of Gender and Sexuality,* which she coedited with Harriet Whitehead. Both in her essay on "Gender and Sexuality in Hierarchical Societies," and in the introduction to *Sexual Meanings,* which she coauthored with Whitehead, Ortner advocates a processual, dynamic, actor-oriented, practice-theory approach to the study of gender. She suggests, in addition, that the most profitable approach to the study of gender is to examine constructions of gender as inextricably enmeshed both with structures of production and exchange, and with the more encompassing systems of prestige to which these structures are keyed.

I am in broad agreement with this position, as many features of the foregoing analysis would suggest. I also find much of value in Ortner and Whitehead's insights into the ways in which the meanings of "female" and the social standing of women may be "pulled down" by the cultural elaboration of certain kinship roles and their relative hegemony in ideologies of gender. Ortner and Whitehead (1981a:21) point out, for instance, that, cross-culturally, one or another different female relational role—e.g., mother, daughter, sister—". . . tend[s] to dominate the category of 'female' and to color the meanings of all the other female relational roles." For example, in most Islamic, Mediterranean, and Catholic cultures, and of course in the United States, the systems of prestige and moral evaluation are such that the category "female" is strongly shaped by local understandings of "mother" and "wife," which, among other things, focus on sexuality and reproduction and thus effectively situate woman and femaleness "closer to nature" in Ortner's 1974 sense. The same is true for Buddhist cultures in Thailand and beyond, as is evident both from the common ground underlying debates between Kirsch (1982, 1985) and Keyes (1984), and from Ledgerwood's recent (1992) work on Khmer women.

This situation contrasts rather sharply with what one finds in Polynesia. In Polynesia, where kinship and political systems tend to be structured by symbols and idioms of cognatic descent, men build up status and prestige by attracting followers, and do this partly by using kinswomen—especially sisters, but also daughters—as "bait" (to use Ortner's term). Consequently, in many Polynesian societies, the category "female" is greatly colored by local understandings and values of "sisterhood," and is only minimally informed by local notions of "mother" and "wife." This serves to deemphasize women's sexuality, reproductive capacities, and links with "natural functions," and is partly responsible for the fact that Polynesian women are viewed in a more positive light than women in most Islamic, Mediterranean, Catholic, and Buddhist cultures.

I concur with Ortner and Whitehead on many of these points, and am, more generally, deeply indebted to them insofar as their approach helped inspire the analytic framework developed in this essay. At the same time, there are, I believe, certain features of their approach that limit its explanatory power, two of which merit note here. First, their approach to gender ideology (and ideology generally) is a rather totalizing one inasmuch as it focuses almost entirely on official discourse and in these and other ways makes insufficient analytic provision for the existence of the contrasting discourses that inevitably comprise any given ideological formation. I hasten to add, however, that Ortner now recognizes as much, and has gone a long way toward developing an analytic apparatus capable of handling such multiplicity (see Ortner 1989–1990).

A second problem with Ortner and Whitehead's approach, one which Ortner does not address in her most recent work, is that the approach rests on the a priori, unargued assumption that in *all* societies there is a rigid dichotomy between the structural definitions of males and females. More specifically, after Ortner and Whitehead underscore that in all societies females are defined relationally, they go on to claim that there are *no* corresponding patterns in the case of males. In their words, "analogous distinctions among men are *not* critical for masculinity" (Ortner and Whitehead 1981a:21; emphasis added), because men, unlike women, tend to be defined in terms of "positional" ([allegedly] "nonrelational") statuses, such as "hunter," "warrier," "chief," "politician," etc. Such claims, which seem to derive in large part from the work of Nancy Chodorow (about which more in a moment), take for granted important issues, such as masculinity, that should be (along with femininity) at the center of analysis, and they certainly merit reassessment in light of Negeri Sembilan data, as well as data from Aceh and elsewhere, which I do not have space to discuss here.[27] Suffice it to reiterate that, in Negeri Sembilan, the behavior of married men in relation to their wives is judged largely in terms of the behavioral standards that pertain to elder brothers' treatment (nurturance, protection, etc.) of their younger sisters, and that many married men fall short of the "elderly brother" ideal due to their inability to produce sufficient property rights, wealth, and prestige for their wives and their wives' kin. Married men who find that they cannot live up to the expectations of, or otherwise cope with pressures from, their wives and affines, frequently divorce, or simply desert their wives along with any children they might have. This course of action not only informs local (practical) views that husbands and fathers are unreliable, untrustworthy, and motivated by "passion" rather than "reason"; it also colors practical views of masculinity in their entirety. These latter, practical views serve, in turn, to offset and vitiate official views of males, just as they effectively substantiate and promote practical views of females. More generally, these data indicate that in the practice of everyday life, certain male relational roles—e.g., those of elder brother, husband, and father—may not only dominate the category of "male," but may also inform the meanings of all other male relational (and "positional") roles. These same data illustrate that it is not merely the meanings of "female," or the social standing of women, that may be dragged down by the cultural elaboration of relational roles and their relative hegemony in everyday, practical discourses on gender. This can also occur in the case of males, even though males may still come out "on top"—at least in official discourses on kinship and gender, and with respect to the overall distribution of power and prestige.

Ortner and Whitehead's dichotomizing approach to structural definitions of males and females appears to derive largely from Chodorow's feminist reworking of psychoanalytic theory (though it also has deep roots in the pioneering work of Simone de Beauvoir [1949], which also informs Chodorow's thinking on the subject of woman). A brief overview of some of the problems with this dichotomy as it is developed in the highly influential (and in many respects brilliant) work of Chodorow (1978, 1989) may thus be useful here, though I should make clear at the outset that Ortner and Whitehead's position is not burdened with all the cultural and other baggage that Chodorow brings to her analyses.

I cannot do justice to the complexity of Chodorow's extremely insightful arguments concerning the "deep structural" and other implications of the fact that females predominate in all societies in the rearing of infants and young children. I am concerned primarily with the way she frames some of her most general conclusions regarding the implications of such facts for the reproduction of gendered difference, for example, that women are, to use the portmanteau concept, "relationally oriented."[28] One problem in this regard is that Chodorow is inconsistent when it comes to specifying whether the particular male-female contrasts with which she is concerned—e.g., conscious and unconscious emotional needs and capacities to relate to others, conscious and unconscious gender role identifications—involve differences in *degree* versus differences in *kind*. In many places, for example, she argues, quite plausibly in my view, that, compared to women, men have less developed or elaborated relational needs and capacities. Elsewhere she states, also quite plausibly, that men often deny such needs and capacities. In still other places, however, Chodorow advances the implausible argument that men don't have any such needs and capacities. The term "arelational masculinity," which Chodorow employs in some of her most recent writing (see, for example, Chodorow 1989:185), further muddies the issue.

Perhaps most problematic, though, is Chodorow's dubious analytic leap from (a) data concerning conscious and unconscious relational needs and capacities, and conscious and unconscious gender role identifications, to (b) arguments concerning formal cultural or ideological constructions of gender. Chodorow contends, for instance, that in the capitalist world, in other hierarchical, bureaucratically organized societies (the [former] Soviet Union is cited as an example), and, indeed, in *all* societies, men, unlike women, are defined in formal cultural or ideological terms "positionally"— this is, by their positions or roles in the economy or public domain—rather than relationally (i.e., in terms of the domestic domain). But we need to ask here: Who is doing the defining, and in what contexts are the definitions at issue relevant to the ways in which people actually experience, cognize, and represent one another in the practice of everyday life? It seems quite clear that, from the point of view of state-sponsored nationalist ideologies, men in the U.S., the former Soviet Union, Malaysia, and many other places are defined primarily in what Chodorow would refer to as "positional" terms, i.e., as members of particular occupational groups, social classes, and ethnic communities (though I should perhaps emphasize the self-evident point that the meaningfulness of such "positional" identifications is thoroughly relational). But if one looks beyond the elitist top-down perspective and examines the situation either from the bottom up or simply from within the familial contexts, local social fields, and more encompassing (local) communities in which men (and women) act out, experience, and make sense of much of their lives, these types of components and overall definitions of male identity lose much of their salience and are supplanted by relational definitions of the sort ostensibly reserved for women. This is especially true in communities characterized by: (a) relatively little racial, ethnic, religious, class, and occupational diversity; (b) structures of kinship that continue to provide hegemonic frameworks for many domains of society and culture; and, more generally, (c) local ideologies that are in critical respects out of sync with state-sponsored ideologies. To put this last (third) point somewhat differently: "Positional" components and overall definitions of male identity lose much of their salience and are supplanted by relational components and definitions bearing on masculinity in communities in which state-sponsored ideologies are not nearly as hegemonic as they are—or are assumed to be—in Western societies, which is to say, in the vast majority of the contexts in which anthropologists have traditionally studied.

The problem as I see it, then, is that Chodorow and others who adopt her "relational-positional" dichotomy not only impose an overly simplistic "either-or" view on Western data concerning similarities and differences in structural definitions of males and females, which is linked to if not derived from an uncritical distinction between domestic and public domains. They also both overvalorize and overgeneralize from culturally and historically specific state-sponsored constructions of maleness, and, in the process, unwittingly offer up selected elements of a particular variant of a heavily motivated native or folkloric model as an analytic model with purportedly universal applicability.

It is interesting, though not surprising, that the "relational-positional" dichotomy has received very little critical analytic attention to date, and has, for this reason, outlived many of the other dichotomies that informed earlier work on gender and women, such as the (originally formulated) distinctions between public and domestic (or private) domains and "nature" and "culture." Perhaps the main reason for the undeserved longevity of this dichotomy is that constructions of masculinity continue to suffer from what I referred to at the outset of my essay as the "taken-for-granted syndome."

Although the particular dimensions of Chodorow's framework that I have addressed here have received minimal analytic attention to date, recent years have of course witnessed numerous ethnographically grounded critiques of other psychologically oriented universalistic arguments that claim to lay bare either the "essence(s)" of woman or femininity, or the "essence(s)" of male-female contrasts. Stack's recent (1990) work on African Americans, for example, demonstrates quite convincingly that hypotheses of the sort developed by Carol Gilligan (1982)—concerning ostensibly universal contrasts between males and females with respect to the development of moral reasoning—suffer from various ethnocentric biases and are for these and other reasons highly problematic. Firmly-grounded ethnographic analyses of the sort undertaken by Stack are of critical importance if we are to avoid increasingly free-floating and ethereal psychologistic discussions of purportedly universal contrasts (or similarities) between males and females; or, to put it more positively, if we are to advance our understanding of the myriad complexities and nuances of gendered difference (and sameness).

More Deconstruction: Masculinity and Class

To summarize and advance the argument one step further, I contend that Negeri Sembilan masculinity is best understood if it is deconstructed and analyzed in terms of its constituent elements and their interrelations, and that the deconstruction of Negeri Sembilan masculinity calls for a deconstruction and jettisoning of the ("arelational") notion of masculinity enshrined in the comparative and theoretical literature on gender. It remains to emphasize that in Negeri Sembilan practical representations of masculinity simultaneously encode and mask local perspectives on class that are otherwise generally unmarked in discourse concerning gender and social relations on the whole; and that the articulation of variables of gender and class has long been informed by state policies as well as nationalist and transnational discourse bearing on the Malay social body and the Malaysian body politic.

To appreciate the class dimensions of practical views of masculinity we need to bear in mind that while divorce is quite common in Negeri Sembilan, it is by no means equally distributed throughout all segments of society. Specifically, divorce is rampant among the poor and relatively rare among the wealthy (see Peletz 1988, chap. 7). Thus when villagers speak of the prevalence of divorce, and of the fact that many divorces are the fault of "lazy," "irresponsible" men, they are referring, albeit usually unwittingly, to householders, and to the behavior of men in particular, at the bottom rungs of the local class hierarchy. These are the men who are least likely to be able to meet the expectations and demands of their wives and affines, and therefore most apt to experience tensions and other problems of the sort that are aired before the local Islamic magistrate or *kadi*, whose primary job is to try to effect reconciliation and/or insure that women and children receive adequate support from "recalcitrant" husbands.

Further strengthening this interpretation is the fact that the male villager who most emphatically expressed the view that the majority of problems in marriage are caused by the faults (lying, irresponsibility, etc.) of husbands, had served for some twenty-five years as a clerk for the local *kadi*. His experiences in the *kadi*'s office have clearly shaped his views of men. So, too, undoubtedly, has his enviable position in the local prestige hierarchy insofar as he implicitly exempted himself from his generalizations about men being lazy, irresponsible, etc., and was thus making a statement of distinction between most men—"the rabble"—on the one hand, and wealthy, responsible men like himself on the other. Also noteworthy is my adoptive aunt's remark that "All men lie"—later rephrased in somewhat more charitable fashion as "Ninety percent of all men lie"—, which was followed by the comment, "This is what you see all the time at the *kadi*'s office." Here, too, we see a blanket generalization pertaining to *all* men which, though not acknowledged as such, is squarely grounded in perceptions that focus on the actions of men at the bottom of the local class hierarchy.

While stereotypes bearing on the behavior of impoverished men—most notably, their "poor showing" as husbands and fathers—provide most of the raw material for (and are unwittingly pressed into service to support) the view that *all* men are lazy, expect to eat for free, etc., the comportment of other men, including especially that of wealthy men, does on occasion fuel practical representations of masculinity as well. For example, my wealthy (recently widowed) landlord, Haji Baharuddin[29]—a retired schoolteacher and headmaster who draws a handsome pension and undertook the pilgrimage to Mecca (the *haj*) in the mid-1970s—, was frequently mentioned by women when they were discussing the nature of masculinity and casting about for an example to help illustrate their contentions that men have more "passion" than women. A number of women remarked emphatically and somewhat disdainfully that whereas most divorced or widowed women have little interest in remarrying, "even old men like Haji Baharuddin are keen to remarry if they find themselves divorced or widowed." Some of these women went on to disparage his (unsuccessful) attempts to find a new wife, claiming that his flirtatious and "itchy" (*gatal*) behavior (e.g., removing his *haji* cap when he travels outside the village so that he will appear younger and thus more attractive) is highly unbecoming. Perhaps most damning in the eyes of women (and men), however, are the tremendous debts he has incurred both in the village and beyond. Haji Baharuddin's debts are viewed as a consequence of his being consistently irresponsible with money (his own and other people's as well), and overly concerned with splurging at local coffee shops and otherwise attempting to impress upon friends and acquaintances that he is a "man of means." The fact that he has made the *haj* renders these indiscretions and excesses all the more offensive, especially since those who have journeyed to Mecca are invariably expected to behave in a more pious and virtuous fashion than those who have not been fortunate enough to do so.

Class variables impinge upon representations of masculinity in other ways as well, for in terms of the female segment of Bogang's population, practical views of men are most prevalent among the poor and least pronounced among the wealthy. This is not all that surprising, for all things being equal, poor women are much more likely to experience divorce or desertion than wealthy women, and thus have more first-hand experience with "irresponsible men" than do women in wealthy households. Thus, Kak Suzaini, who is one of the most impoverished and marginalized of all village women, has extremely uncharitable views of men, which reflect (among other things) her disheartening and overwhelmingly negative experiences in three different marriages, each of which began "inauspiciously" (under scandalous circumstances), was short-lived, and ended in divorce. The fact that Kak Suzaini has been largely unsuccessful in her repeated court-assisted attempts to obtain financial assistance from the fathers of her (three) children further pains and angers her—and further motivates her animosity toward men—,the more so since her third ex-husband is a man of some means who recently made the pilgrimage to Mecca. My adoptive aunt, who also comes from a very poor household, likewise has very negative views of men, as indicated by her previously noted contention that "All men, or at least ninety percent of them, lie."

Though she herself has never experienced divorce, divorce is by no means a stranger to her household. Her daughter was deserted by her husband when she was five months' pregnant. Making matters worse, he took another (younger) wife without even informing her and proceeded to lie to her about his new relationship when she later confronted him with (circumstantial) evidence of its existence.

Constraints on the Elaboration of Oppositional Discourses

Many practical representations of masculinity are explicitly oppositional and counterhegemonic in that they constitute subversive challenges to their official (hegemonic) counterparts. To say that practical views of masculinity are most pronounced among poor women and least prevalent among wealthy women is thus to point out that wealthy women tend to "buy into" many official/hegemonic representations of gender in a major way, even though a good number of the latter representations portray all women (and much of femininity in its entirety) in culturally devalued terms.[30] For example, Mak Siah and Mak Azlina, who are two of the wealthiest and (in terms of lineage and clan affiliation) highest-ranking women in the village—and clearly the wealthiest and highest ranked of all village women interviewed—, espouse official views of gender to a much greater degree than any of the other village women I spoke with, even though, as just noted, these views depict them (and females on the whole) in largely negative terms. Neither of these women has been divorced (and neither has any divorced children), and they feel that their husbands do highly commendable jobs supporting them and their children and otherwise providing for their households and ensuring domestic reproduction. Compared to other village women, they have relatively little reason (are not strongly "motivated") to question the official discourse on masculinity (and gender generally), particularly since the alternative practical discourse on masculinity, grounded as it is in images of men's poor performance in their roles as husbands (and fathers), does not resonate with their own marital experiences or "lived relations to the world." Women such as Mak Siah and Mak Azlina also have more at stake in expressing (at least tacit or pragmatic) acceptance of the official discourse, or at least rejecting the practical discourse. This is because their overt acceptance, to say nothing of their public articulation, of practical views of masculinity (the only locally available alternative to official views) would effectively align both them and their husbands and households with the women, men, and households associated with the poorest and least prestigious segments of the community. Concerns with validating and ideally enhancing the enviable prestige standing that they and their households enjoy thus militate against their articulation of practical representations of gender and, in the process, help guarantee that, with respect to many aspects of gender, village women do not speak in a single voice.

Circumstances such as these raise important comparative and theoretical issues concerning the myriad moral and material variables that constrain—or, alternatively, promote—the development and elaboration of oppositional discourses and strategies of resistance. Since I discuss such issues elsewhere (Peletz 1995) I will simply note here three sets of variables that have served to constrain the development and elaboration of such discourses. One such variable (alluded to in the preceding paragraph) is the allocation of prestige in terms of households, which tend to be—and, in the case of the wealthy, almost invariably are—composed of men and women alike. (Prestige is also allocated with respect to lineages [and localized clans], but this is less directly relevant here.) The pooling of household resources (including labor) for the purpose of advancing or at least maintaining the prestige standing of one's household vis-à-vis other households both presupposes and promotes day-to-day economic and other cooperation between husband and wife. It also entails husband and wife conceptualizing their needs and strategies with respect to the satisfaction of subsistence concerns and the attainment of prestige—and their place(s) in the world generally—in relation to their household. Bear in mind, too, that the household is the locus of the individual's most intimate and, in many respects, most sustaining and meaningful social interactions. In sum, the primacy of the household in terms of the allocation of prestige, and with respect to economic matters (production, consumption, and exchange) and social identity and emotional sustenance, works against the development and cultural realization of gender-based interest groups, and in these and other ways inhibits the (further) elaboration of oppositional discourses.

A second (related) variable is the historically specific construction of personhood, social adulthood, and adult womanhood especially. In order to be a full-fledged social adult, one must enter into a legitimate marriage (with a socially approved member of the opposite sex), and bear or father (or adopt) children. For women, this involves not only being defined as a particular man's wife (or ex-wife or widow) and the mother of a particular man's children, but also, as noted earlier, a potentially extended (but in some cases very brief) period of economic dependence on (though not necessarily coresidence with) a particular man. The relational components of women's identity that focus on women's roles as wives and mothers have become highly salient over the course of the past century as a consequence of the historic restructuring of femininity that occurred as a result of state-sponsored changes of the sort that effected a realignment of the constituent elements of masculinity. In the case of femininity, the changes have entailed the historical deemphasis of women's roles as daughters (natural and classificatory), sisters, and sisters' daughters, and, as just noted, a foregrounding of their roles as wives and mothers. The factors responsible for such shifts include the economically and politically engendered erosion of a broadly encompassing clanship, and the attendant weakening and contraction of the siblingship undergirding it, as well as the demise of various forms of predominantly female labor exchange associated with the agricultural cycle, which, in former times, drew heavily on women as (natural and classificatory) sisters.

Also clearly relevant is the recent resurgence of Islam, which has been animated and sustained in no small measure by ethnic and class tensions and nationalist and transnational discourse. The doctrines of Islam (like those of Buddhism, Christianity, and the other Great Religions) focus on, and, more importantly, are interpreted locally as focusing on, women's roles as wives and mothers rather than daughters and sisters. More to the point, Malaysia's Islamic resurgence (the *dakwa* movement), which is a largely urban-based, primarily middle-class phenomenon, has highlighted and endeavored to restrict women's sexuality and bodily processes, and has in these and other ways (e.g., through "pro-natalist programs" [Stivens 1987]) emphasized women's roles in biological reproduction along with their other "natural functions." Somewhat paradoxically, the involvement of young Malay women in high-tech factory work in Free Trade Zones and elsewhere since the 1970s has had some of the same ideological effects as the Islamic resurgence, especially since images of factory women, aside from being exceedingly negative, center on their alleged sexual promiscuity (see Ong 1988, 1990, this volume; Ackerman 1991).[31] In short, religious, economic, and attendant developments of the sort noted here have served to define women in relation to men, and as mothers, wives, and sexual (hence "passionate") beings in particular, and have thus effectively promoted official discourses on gender and simultaneously constrained the development and elaboration of oppositional discourses.[32]

A third variable which inhibits the elaboration of oppositional discourses relates to the fact that village men and women alike espouse various features of practical (as well as official) views of masculinity and femininity. This may seem paradoxical and/or tautological, but the paradox and tautalogy, I would argue, are more apparent than real. It is in certain crucial respects much easier to conceive of and develop an oppositional discourse when those against whom it is arrayed or deployed operate with a seamless, rigid, uncompromising, thoroughly self-congratulatory and Other-despising set of assumptions about the way things—and social relations—are and should be. But this is not the case in Negeri Sembilan. In Negeri Sembilan, men's and women's views of gender(ed) difference and sameness are in many respects quite similar: Men and women do, after all, operate with the same overarching framework (of "reason" and "passion") in terms of which gender is experienced, understood, and represented, and even the most extreme contrasts between men's and women's views on gender entail little more than a structural inversion of relationships among the principal signs or signifiers of the framework. More importantly, because many men, especially elite men, espouse views of gender which are far from seamless, uncompromising, thoroughly self-congratulatory or Other (i.e., female)-despising, they effectively preempt charges and help put to rest suspicions on the part of women that they (men) are trafficking in thoroughly distorting or mystifying discourses. For reasons such as these (and others noted earlier) the discourses of men help constrain the elaboration of oppositional discourses on the part of women even though they simultaneously provide legitimate moral space for their existence in the first place. Phrased in broader and more abstract terms: dominant ideological formations both produce and limit the forms, scope, and force of the challenges with which they must invariably contend (see Williams 1977:114; see also Willis 1977; Scott 1985).

Final Remarks

There are, finally, two other sets of issues that merit brief comment. The first relates to Ong's important observations that the sexual promiscuity and dubious morality imputed to young Malay women working in factories in the state of Selangor and elsewhere is, among other things, a register of Malays' profound moral ambivalence about the rapidly changing nature of their "lived relations to the world": most notably, their historically stepped-up involvement in and dependence on the vagaries of the global economy, the transgressions of traditional moral injunctions that such involvement and dependence necessarily entail, and the mystical and other dangers associated with such transgressions (Ong 1988, 1990, this volume). To the extent that female factory workers are among the most exploited members of the Malaysian work force, the denigration of such women, and the heaping upon them of blame for threatening the Malay "imagined community" (Anderson 1983), may be seen as yet another ethnographic example of the distressingly widespread ideological phenomenon known as "blaming the victim." A similar type of victim-blaming ideology infuses practical representations of masculinity in Negeri Sembilan, especially those naturalizing and dehistoricizing representations which attribute to men's "innate" behavior most of the problems in marriage and much of the "fault" in divorce. Interestingly, representations which blame men (male "human nature") in blanket terms for the dissolution of conjugal and familial bonds (and other social ills and threats to the imagined community) are not only thoroughly mute with respect to the specific kinship roles and social classes of men whose behavior (on closer analytic inspection) fuels such representations. They are also blind to the material and other conditions of their own (re)production. They thus divert attention away from the broadly encompassing realities of historical change and contemporary political economy which have engendered land shortages and highly inequitable distributions of wealth, power, and prestige, and which are responsible for a situation in which, as one observer put it (with reference to the state of Kedah), "poverty itself appears to dissolve marriages" (Banks 1983:100). Stated differently, while such representations foreground local cultural views of the indissoluble links between the domains of gender and kinship (and marriage), they simultaneously help bring about (but do not fully effect) a mythical sealing off of such domains from all ravages and other entailments of history and political economy. In these and other ways they effectively define the most serious threats to the imagined community as arising from within the Malay community itself (much like the recently emergent discourses on Malay factory women). This despite the fact that in a good many contexts Malays in Negeri Sembilan and elsewhere are quick to argue that the most fundamental obstacles and dangers to the social and cultural reproduction of the Malay community are posed by non-Malays—Indians and especially Chinese, who, taken together, comprise approximately 43 percent of Malaysia's population—and the state strategies and policies that are responsible both for their existence in Malaysia in the first place and for their economic prosperity relative to Malays.

The second (and final) issue bears on Lévi-Strauss's insightful, oft-quoted ([1949] 1969) remark that "Even before slavery or class domination existed, men built an approach to women that would serve one day to introduce differences among us all."[33] One need not accept this particular (androcentric) formulation of the historical primacy of gender with respect to the development of difference to appreciate that Lévi-Strauss is clearly on to something important here (cf. Bloch 1989:36; Heng and Devan, this volume). That something is that indeterminacies, paradoxes, and contradictions in representations of gender, are, at least potentially, the most profoundly subversive challenges to all ideologies of social order (see March 1984). Such is the case partly because gender differences are among the earliest, least conscious, and most fundamental differences internalized in all societies, though arguably more relevant is that symbols, idioms, and entire ideologies bearing on gender are rarely if ever simply "about" gender. Because they are also "about" kinship, human nature, and sociality—as well as relations of equality/hierarchy, inclusion/exclusion, and the like—challenges to these ideologies necessarily constitute deeply unsettling threats to the most basic categories through which we experience, understand, and represent our selves, intimate (and not so intimate) others, and the universe as a whole. This is perhaps especially so when these ideologies serve to mark and legitimize ethnic and class distinctions, as is clearly the case in Negeri Sembilan and many other societies. In such instances, challenges to ideologies bearing on gender cannot help but raise questions and doubts about the conceptual bases and legitimacy of ethnic and class hierarchies, and the state structures and nationalist discourses that help to sustain them, although the extent to which such questions and doubts are explicitly articulated or culturally realized is of course contextually specific and otherwise highly variable.

In any event, the widely redounding and potentially limitless scope of such ideologies—to say nothing of their psychological, social, and moral force—is more than sufficient reason to strive to ensure that our descriptions and analyses of gender encompass the study of women and men alike, and that they be informed by an understanding of official representations of gender (and kinship) as well as their practical counterparts. More generally, the highly expansive scope and other features of such ideologies should serve as a clear reminder that gender systems are not intelligible as isolates, and are in fact best viewed in light of theoretical perspectives which are conducive to describing and analyzing gender in relation to other forms of difference and inequality as well as everyday social process and the broader realities of political economy and historical change.

NOTES

This is a slightly revised version of an essay that appeared in *Cultural Anthropology* 9(2), 1994.

My analyses draw on fieldwork carried out in the Rembau district of Negeri Sembilan from 1978 to 1980 and 1987 to 1988. The first period of research was supported by the National Science Foundation (under Grant No. BNS-7812499) and the University of Michigan (the Center for South and Southeast Asian Studies and the Rackham School of Graduate Studies); the second was supported by the Fulbright Scholars Program, the Wenner-Gren Foundation for Anthropological Research, and the Picker Fellowship Program at Colgate University. A 1991–92 fellowship from the National Endowment for the Humanities facilitated the writing of this essay, as did a 1992–93 fellowship from the Social Science Research Council. Affiliation with the Department of Anthropology and the Program in Southeast Asian Studies at Cornell University during the tenure of the NEH fellowship was likewise highly beneficial. In addition to thanking these institutions for their support, I would like to acknowledge my debt to Ellen Peletz for assisting me in the research. Some of the material in this essay has been presented in public lectures at various institutions around the country, including the University of California (Berkeley), Cornell University, Harvard University, the University of Wisconsin, and Yale University. Comments received in these contexts were especially helpful. So too were the written comments of Patricia Horvatich, Raymond Kelly, Aihwa Ong, Sherry Ortner, and anonymous reviewers.

1. In the field of legal anthropology, for instance, the past decade or so has witnessed a good deal of innovative and theoretically significant work on kinship by Comaroff and Roberts (1981) and Sally Falk Moore (1986), among others. As for political anthropology, Raymond Kelly's (1985) work on the role of bridewealth in Nuer warfare and expansion merits mention, as do Maurice Bloch's (1989) studies of kinship, ritual, politics, and history among the Merina.

2. The phrase is Gilmore's (1990:1–2).

3. I have rearranged the sequence of the clauses in this quotation (but have not altered the intended meaning).

4. Constructions of the latter sort are also taken for granted by the vast majority of (nonfeminist) anthropologists, sociologists, historians, and others who (unwittingly or otherwise) focus on men or male perspectives.

5. Analytic concerns with maleness can of course lead to the essentialization of masculinity as well (see, for example, Gilmore 1990).

6. The concept of a "prestige/stigma system" is borrowed from Kelly's recent (1993) tour de force on inequality among the Etoro, which makes a number of critically important points: that stigma is the negative reciprocal of prestige; that analytic discussions of "prestige systems" would benefit from greater terminological and conceptual precision (see also Yanagisako and Collier 1987:26–28); and that such systems are more accurately characterized as systems or hierarchies of prestige/stigma. Kelly also distinguishes between systems of the latter sort on the one hand, and systems of moral evaluation on the other. In his words:

> The system of moral evaluation can be defined as the component of the value system that delineates virtues and their opposites (such as generosity and self-aggrandizement). The prestige system [for its part] pertains to the achievable virtues or aspects of virtue that differentiate individuals (as opposed to the virtues or aspects of virtue that are ascribed to a categorical social status). The system of moral evaluation thus provides the basis for two different but interrelated foundations of social inequality: a moral hierarchy, and a prestige system or prestige/stigma system (Kelly 1993:14).

My discussion is informed by Kelly's seminal work, and I should point out that, like Kelly, I sometimes use the term "system(s) of prestige" as a shorthand for "system(s) of prestige/stigma."

7. These percentages are broadly comparable to, but should not be confused with, those pertaining to the population of Malaysia as a whole. Malays comprise roughly 48 percent of the latter population. (Chinese account for about 34 percent, and Indians 9 percent; "Others" make up the rest.) (Government of Malaysia 1983)

8. See Wikan (1990: esp. pp. 67–73) for important perspectives on gender differentiation in Bali.

9. The "keyness" or centrality of these symbols does of course vary from one Muslim society to the next, as do some of their contextually variable meanings and many of their material referents. These symbols are quite central and highly elaborated among Malays, Acehnese, and Moroccans, less so among Javanese and

Minangkabau. Among the Sama of the Philippines, these symbols are "present" but not of central significance, and are minimally elaborated (Horvatich 1992).

10. Bourdieu's distinction between official and practical kinship is in some ways reminiscent of Firth's ([1951] 1963, 1964) distinction between social structure and social organization, though the similarities are actually rather superficial, especially when one stops to consider the very different theoretical rationales for developing the distinctions and the dissimilar uses to which they are put. Since this is not the place to discuss such matters, I would simply note that incisive critiques of Firth's distinction and theoretical orientation are presented by Kelly (1977:280–282) and Bloch (1989:4–5).

11. In the Negeri Sembilan context, for example, one could conceivably speak instead of "official Islamic discourses" on the one hand, and "everyday discourses" on the other. There is some heuristic value in such a distinction, but to my mind it fosters the erroneous impression that "everyday discourses" are somehow "non-Islamic," when in fact the key signs of such discourses ("reason" and "passion") are "thoroughly Islamic" even though they are frequently mapped onto gender difference(s) in a way that constitutes an inversion of the gender realities depicted in "official Islamic discourses." For these and other reasons I employ the modified version of Bourdieu's distinction discussed in the text.

12. All references to "the nineteenth century" are intended to apply to the period 1830–1880. Many aspects of the reconstruction presented in the following pages are applicable to Negeri Sembilan during the post-1880 era and are probably relevant as well to the decades immediately prior to 1830. My decision to focus on the period 1830–1880 is based partly on the limited availability of sources on the pre-1830 era; it also reflects a concern to avoid delineating the impact of British colonialism, which was introduced into some parts of Negeri Sembilan as early as 1874. Some of the local effects of colonial rule (which continued through 1957) are addressed later in the essay. For extensive analysis of such matters as well as complete references for the ensuing discussion, see Peletz (1987a, 1987b, 1988, 1993).

13. This is not to deny the existence of the sexual and other rights over women that men acquired in consequence of their marriages; it is simply to underscore that the bulk, and the most important, of the transactions entailed in marriage and affinal exchange centered on transfers of rights over men. Moreover, none of this is to suggest that we are dealing with some sort of "matriarchal" society. Men monopolized rights to most political offices, and political leaders such as *Undang* stood in many respects "above" the system of marriage and affinal exchange insofar as they were largely immune to the imperatives and constraints of the system in their roles as husbands and in-marrying males. Note also that men monopolized both the means of violence and external exchange, and did, as a group, enjoy more prestige and freedom of movement than women. Contemporary data relevant to some of these issues (e.g., prestige differentials between men and women) are presented in the text, below.

14. For in-depth treatments of such matters, see Peletz (1987b, 1988), Stivens (1985, 1991), and McAllister (1987), and the sources cited in their bibliographies.

15. For discussions of "reason" and "passion" among Malays elsewhere in the

Peninsula, see Kessler (1978:220–232), Laderman (1982:91), Banks (1983:86–87), Massard (1985:72), and Ong (1988:31, 1990:388–390). For relevant material on Muslims elsewhere in Southeast Asia, see Siegel's (1969) pioneering study on Aceh and Brenner's work on Java (this volume), which provides an insightful, much needed reassessment of Javanese notions of self-control. Other pertinent discussions appear in Dwyer (1978) and Rosen (1984), both of which deal with Moroccan material.

16. Bogang is a pseudonym for the village in which I did my fieldwork. It is located in the Rembau district of Negeri Sembilan. Its population in 1980 was 476. By 1988 the population had increased to 503.

17. The Western (non-Muslim) reader might assume that such aversions to eating pork are uniform throughout the Muslim world. Not so: some Javanese Muslims do on occasion eat pork; the Muslim Susu of Senegal claim that the prohibition pertains only to those who do not like pork (James Thayer, personal communication, 1983); and the Sudanese Muslim women studied by Boddy (1989) were not sure if pork was prohibited to them. The intensity of Malay aversions to eating pork has much to do with ethnic antagonism between Malays and Chinese, who, as far as Malays are concerned, eat pork—and lots of it—at virtually every meal.

18. So, too, would the basic cultural premise underlying much of the material presented here, namely that sociality and "civilization" generally are only possible because of the constraining influences of society, which hold in check the individual's instinctive (fundamentally antisocial) impulses. Premises of this sort are enshrined in Freud's later work on religion, e.g., *The Future of an Illusion* ([1927] 1964).

19. The extent to which such views are an index of men's sexual anxiety is both exceedingly difficult to gauge and altogether beyond the scope of the present discussion. I would only note that similar types of views have been documented for Malays in the state of Kelantan, and that the "husband's feelings that he cannot handle his wife's demanding sexual expectations" are given (if only by male informants) as one of the major causes of divorce (Nash 1974:38, cited in Spiro 1977:287, n. 16). Findings such as these, which are not reported for most other societies in Southeast Asia (e.g., Burma, Thailand, Java) have led Spiro (1977:241, n.14) to comment that while "sexual anxiety is of course widespread in South and Southeast Asia [his main frame of reference], . . . Malay men may represent the extreme case."

20. There were, to be sure, crucial structural precedents for these views. Some such precedents were encoded in pre-Islamic notions of *semangat* ("life force") and attendant beliefs concerning men's greater spiritual power or potency vis-à-vis women's. For important perspectives on these and related matters, see Errington (1990) and the sources cited there, and Brenner (this volume).

21. It is beyond the scope of this essay to explain why the alternative discourse in question is far more elaborated in Negeri Sembilan than among Malays elsewhere in the Peninsula. Suffice it to say that attempts to explain such variation would do well to take as their points of departure (a) assessments of similarities and differences in systems of production, exchange, and prestige, and (b) analyses of the variable ways in which the labor power and productivity of men, especially in

their roles as husbands and in-laws, are pressed into service for generating property rights, wealth, and prestige for their wives' kin groups.

22. For a more complete discussion of these matters, see Peletz (1987b, 1988) and Stivens (1985, 1991).

23. Interestingly, even when all children are designated as heirs to their parents' estate, sons and daughters tend to not be included as coheirs with respect to any particular plot of land, or other item of property. This strategy of heirship reflects the assumption and concern that sons might well run up debts, through gambling or otherwise, and thus find themselves compelled to mortgage or sell land or other property held in common with their sisters. Circumstances such as these would bespeak an inversion of proper brotherly behavior insofar as they could easily jeopardize their sisters' subsistence guarantees and force them into inappropriate employment, such as prostitution, to support themselves and their children.

24. Gambling and the consumption of alcoholic beverages are effectively confined to men, but (in cross-cultural perspective) they are not very common among Negeri Sembilan (or other) Malays.

25. The following discussion of colonial policies, social change, and the like is obviously highly attenuated. For more information on these topics in the context of Negeri Sembilan, see Peletz (1987b, 1988, 1993), Stivens (1985, 1987, 1991), and McAllister (1987). See also Ong (1988, 1990, this volume) for important discussions of gender and social change in Malaysia generally.

26. A similar situation obtains among the Ankgola Batak (Rodgers 1990), and is probably quite widespread in Southeast Asia (and elsewhere).

27. I examine Acehnese material elsewhere (Peletz 1995: chapter 7).

28. For a brief discussion of some of the problems with this term, see Fraser and Nicholson (1990:29–31).

29. This is a pseudonym, as are the names of all other individuals presented in the text.

30. For a similar dynamic in the American context, see Martin (1987).

31. This exists despite the broad recognition that female factory workers often make critically important economic contributions to their parents' households, thereby enabling their parents to purchase otherwise unobtainable consumer goods and other emblems of modernity and prestige.

32. This continues despite the fact that these same developments have also fostered the emergence of, and have helped sustain, certain types of oppositional discourses (see Ong 1988, 1990).

33. Cited in Rich (1979:84) and Chodorow (1989:99).

REFERENCES

Abu-Lughod, Lila. 1986. *Veiled Sentiments: Honor and Poetry in a Bedouin Society.* Berkeley: University of California Press.

Ackerman, Susan. 1991. "Dakwah and Minah Karan: Class Formation and Ideological Conflict in Malay Society." *Bijdragen Tot de Taal-, Land-, en Volkenkunde* 147(2/3):193–215.

Andaya, Barbara, and Yoneo Ishii. 1992. "Religious Developments in Southeast Asia, circa 1500–1800." In Nicholas Tarling, ed., *The Cambridge History of Southeast Asia,* pp. 508–571. Cambridge: Cambridge University Press.

Anderson, Benedict R. O'G. 1983. *Imagined Communities: Reflections on the Origin and Spread of Nationalism.* London: Verso.

Atkinson, Jane M., and Shelly Errington, eds. 1990. *Power and Difference: Gender in Island Southeast Asia.* Stanford: Stanford University Press.

Banks, David. 1983. *Malay Kinship.* Philadelphia: ISHI Publications.

Beauvoir, Simone de. 1949. *The Second Sex.* New York: Random House.

Bloch, Maurice. 1987. "Descent and Sources of Contradiction in Representations of Women and Kinship." In Jane Collier and Sylvia Yanagisako, eds., *Gender and Kinship: Essays toward a Unified Analysis,* pp. 324–337. Stanford: Stanford University Press.

———. 1989. *Ritual, History and Power: Selected Papers in Anthropology.* London: Athlone Press.

Boddy, Janice. 1989. *Wombs and Alien Spirits: Women, Men and the Zar Cult in Northern Sudan.* Madison: University of Wisconsin Press.

Bourdieu, Pierre. 1977. *Outline of a Theory of Practice.* Cambridge: Cambridge University Press.

Caldecott, Andrew. 1918. "Jelebu Customary Sayings." *Journal of the Straits Branch of the Royal Asiatic Society* 78:3–41.

Chodorow, Nancy. 1978. *The Reproduction of Mothering: Psychoanalysis and the Sociology of Gender.* Berkeley: University of California Press.

———. 1989. *Feminism and Psychoanalytic Theory.* New Haven: Yale University Press.

Collier, Jane. 1988. *Marriage and Inequality in Classless Societies.* Stanford: Stanford University Press.

Collier, Jane, and Sylvia Yanagisako. 1987a. "Introduction." In Jane Collier and Sylvia Yanagisako, eds., *Gender and Kinship: Essays toward a Unified Analysis,* pp. 1–13. Stanford: Stanford University Press.

———, eds. 1987b. *Gender and Kinship: Essays toward a Unified Analysis.* Stanford: Stanford University Press.

Comaroff, John, and Simon Roberts. 1981. *Rules and Processes: The Cultural Logic of Dispute in an African Context.* Chicago: University of Chicago Press.

Dwyer, Daisy. 1978. *Images and Self-Images: Male and Female in Morocco.* New York: Columbia University Press.

Eagleton, Terry. 1991. *Ideology: An Introduction.* London: Verso.

Errington, Shelly. 1990. "Recasting Sex, Gender, and Power: A Theoretical and Regional Overview." In Jane M. Atkinson and Shelly Errington, eds., *Power and Difference: Gender in Island Southeast Asia,* pp. 1–58. Stanford: Stanford University Press.

Firth, Raymond. [1951] 1963. *Elements of Social Organization.* Boston: Beacon Press.

———. 1964. *Essays on Social Organization and Values.* London: Athlone Press.

Fischer, Michael. 1991. "Anthropology as Cultural Critique: Inserts for the 1990s Cultural Studies of Science, Visual-Virtual Realities, and Post-Trauma Polities." *Cultural Anthropology* 6(4):525–537.

Fraser, Nancy, and Linda J. Nicholson. 1990. "Social Criticism Without Philosophy: An Encounter Between Feminism and Postmodernism." In Linda J. Nicholson, ed., *Feminism/Postmodernism*, pp. 19–38. New York: Routledge.

Freud, Sigmund. [1913] 1950. *Totem and Taboo*. New York: W. W. Norton.

———. [1927] 1964. *The Future of an Illusion*. Garden City: Doubleday.

Geertz, Clifford. 1973. " 'Deep Play': Notes on the Balinese Cockfight." In *The Interpretation of Cultures*, pp. 412–453. New York: Basic Books.

Gilligan, Carol. 1982. *In a Different Voice: Psychological Theory and Women's Development*. Cambridge, Mass.: Harvard University Press.

Gilmore, David. 1990. *Manhood in the Making: Cultural Concepts of Masculinity*. New Haven: Yale University Press.

Ginsburg, Faye, and Anna L. Tsing, eds. 1990. *Uncertain Terms: Negotiating Gender in American Culture*. Boston: Beacon Press.

Government of Malaysia. 1983. *Population and Housing Census of Malaysia, 1980, General Report of the Population Census*. Vol. 2. Kuala Lumpur: Department of Statistics.

Hale, Andrew. 1898. "Folklore and the Menangkabau Code in Negeri Sembilan." *Journal of the Straits Branch of the Royal Asiatic Society* 31:43–61.

Horvatich, Patricia. 1992. "Toward an Understanding of Gender in Southeast Asia." Paper presented at Conference on the Narrative and Practice of Gender in Southeast Asian Cultures, Ninth Annual Berkeley Conference on Southeast Asian Studies, University of California, Berkeley.

Karim, Wazir Jahan. 1990. "Prelude to Madness: The Language of Emotion in Courtship and Early Marriage." In Wazir Jahan Karim, ed., *Emotions of Culture: A Malay Perspective*, pp. 21–63. Singapore: Oxford University Press.

Kelly, Raymond. 1977. *Etoro Social Structure: A Study in Structural Contradiction*. Ann Arbor: University of Michigan Press.

———. 1985. *The Nuer Conquest: The Structure and Development of an Expansionist System*. Ann Arbor: University of Michigan Press.

———. 1993. *Constructing Inequality: The Fabrication of a Hierarchy of Virtue among the Etoro*. Ann Arbor: University of Michigan Press.

Kessler, Clive S. 1978. *Islam and Politics in a Malay State: Kelantan, 1838–1969*. Ithaca: Cornell University Press.

Keyes, Charles F. 1984. "Mother or Mistress but Never a Monk: Buddhist Notions of Female Gender in Rural Thailand." *American Ethnologist* 11(2):223–241.

Kirsch, Thomas. 1982. "Buddhism, Sex Roles, and the Thai Economy." In Penny Van Esterik, ed., *Women of Southeast Asia*, pp. 16–41. De Kalb, Ill.: Northern Illinois University, Center for Southeast Asian Studies.

———. 1985. "Text and Context: Buddhist Sex Roles/Culture of Gender Revisited." *American Ethnologist* 12(2):302–320.

Laderman, Carol. 1982. "Putting Malay Women in Their Place." In Penny Van Esterik, ed., *Women of Southeast Asia*, pp. 79–99. De Kalb, Ill.: Northern Illinois University, Center for Southeast Asian Studies.

Leach, Edmund. 1961. *Rethinking Anthropology*. London: Athlone Press.

Ledgerwood, Judy. 1992. "Khmer Images of the Perfect Woman: Culture Change and Gender Ideals." Paper presented at Conference on the Narrative and Practice of Gender in Southeast Asian Cultures, Ninth Annual Berkeley Conference on Southeast Asian Studies, University of California, Berkeley.

Levi-Strauss, Claude. [1949] 1969. *The Elementary Structures of Kinship.* Boston: Beacon Press.

Loizos, Peter, and Evthymios Papataxiarchis, eds. 1991. *Contested Identities: Gender and Kinship in Modern Greece.* Princeton: Princeton University Press.

McAllister, Carol. 1987. "Matriliny, Islam and Capitalism: Combined and Uneven Development in the Lives of Negeri Sembilan Women." Ph.D. diss., University of Pittsburgh.

MacCormack, Carol, and Marilyn Strathern, eds. 1980. *Nature, Culture, and Gender.* Cambridge: Cambridge University Press.

March, Kathryn. 1984. "Weaving, Writing and Gender." *Man* 18:729–744.

Marcus, George, and Michael Fischer. 1986. *Anthropology as Cultural Critique: An Experimental Moment in the Human Sciences.* Chicago: University of Chicago Press.

Martin, Emily. 1987. *The Woman in the Body: A Cultural Analysis of Reproduction.* Boston: Beacon Press.

Massard, Josiane. 1985. "The New-Born Malay Child: A Multiple Identity Being." *Journal of the Malaysian Branch of the Royal Asiatic Society* 58(2):71–84.

Mead, Margaret. 1935. *Sex and Temperament in Three Primitive Societies.* New York: William Morrow and Co.

Moore, Sally Falk. 1986. *Social Facts and Fabrications: "Customary Law" on Kilimanjaro, 1880–1980.* Cambridge: Cambridge University Press.

Myers, Fred. 1992. "A Note From the Editor." *Cultural Anthropology* 7(1):3–5.

Nash, Manning. 1974. *Peasant Citizens: Politics, Religion, and Modernization in Kelantan, Malaysia.* Monographs in International Studies, Southeast Asia Series, no. 31. Athens, Ohio: Center for Southeast Asian Studies, Ohio University.

Newbold, T. J. 1839. *Political and Statistical Accounts of the British Settlements in the Straits of Malacca.* 2 vols. London: John Murray.

Ong, Aihwa. 1988. "The Production of Possession: Spirits and the Multinational Corporation in Malaysia." *American Ethnologist* 15(1):28–42.

———. 1989. "Center, Periphery, and Hierarchy: Gender in Southeast Asia." In Sandra Morgen, ed., *Gender in Anthropology: Critical Reviews for Research and Teaching,* pp. 294–312. Washington, D.C.: American Anthropological Association.

———. 1990. "Japanese Factories, Malay Workers: Class and Sexual Metaphors in West Malaysia." In Jane M. Atkinson and Shelly Errington, eds., *Power and Difference: Gender in Island Southeast Asia,* pp. 385–422. Stanford: Stanford University Press.

Ortner, Sherry. 1973. "On Key Symbols." *American Anthropologist* 75(5):1338–1346.

———. 1974. "Is Female to Male as Nature Is to Culture?" In Michelle Rosaldo and Louise Lamphere, eds., *Woman, Culture, and Society,* pp. 56–87. Stanford: Stanford University Press.

———. 1981. "Gender and Sexuality in Hierarchical Societies: The Case of Polynesia and Some Comparative Implications." In Sherry Ortner and Harriet Whitehead, eds., *Sexual Meanings: The Cultural Construction of Gender and Sexuality,* pp. 359–409. Cambridge: Cambridge University Press.

———. 1983. "The Founding of the First Sherpa Nunnery, and the Problem of

'Women' as an Analytic Category." In Vivian Patraka and Louise Tilly, eds., *Feminist Re-Visions: What Has Been and What Might Be,* pp. 98–134. Ann Arbor: University of Michigan, Women's Studies Program.

———. 1984. "Theory in Anthropology since the Sixties." *Comparative Studies in Society and History* 26:126–166.

———. 1989–90. "Gender Hegemonies." *Cultural Critique* 14:35–80.

Ortner, Sherry, and Harriet Whitehead. 1981a. "Introduction." In Sherry Ortner and Harriet Whitehead, eds., *Sexual Meanings: The Cultural Construction of Gender and Sexuality,* pp. 1–27. Cambridge: Cambridge University Press.

———, eds. 1981b. *Sexual Meanings: The Cultural Construction of Gender and Sexuality.* Cambridge: Cambridge University Press.

Parr, C. W. C. and W. H. Mackray. 1910. "Rembau, One of the Nine States: Its History, Constitution, and Customs." *Journal of the Straits Branch of the Royal Asiatic Society* 56:1–157.

Peletz, Michael G. 1987a. "The Exchange of Men in 19th-Century Negeri Sembilan (Malaya)." *American Ethnologist* 14(3):449–469.

———. 1987b. "Female Heirship and the Autonomy of Women in Negeri Sembilan, West Malaysia." In Barry Isaac, ed., *Research in Economic Anthropology,* vol. 8, pp. 61–101. Greenwich, Conn.: JAI Press.

———. 1988. *A Share of the Harvest: Kinship, Property, and Social History among the Malays of Rembau.* Berkeley: University of California Press.

———. 1993. "Sacred Texts and Dangerous Words: The Politics of Law and Cultural Rationalization in Malaysia." *Comparative Studies in Society and History* 35(1):66–109.

———. 1994. "Comparative Perspectives on Kinship and Cultural Identity in Negeri Sembilan." *Sojourn: Journal of Social Issues in Southeast Asia* 9(1):1–53.

———. 1995. *Reason and Passion: Representations of Gender in a Malay Society.* Berkeley: University of California Press.

Reid, Anthony. 1988. *Southeast Asia in the Age of Commerce, 1450–1680.* Vol. 1, *The Lands Below the Winds.* New Haven: Yale University Press.

Rich, Adrienne. 1979. *On Lies, Secrets, and Silence: Selected Prose 1966–1978.* New York: W. W. Norton and Co.

Rodgers, Susan. 1990. "The Symbolic Representation of Women in a Changing Batak Culture." In Jane M. Atkinson and Shelly Errington, eds., *Power and Difference: Gender in Island Southeast Asia,* pp. 307–344. Stanford: Stanford University Press.

Rosaldo, Michelle. 1980. "The Use and Abuse of Anthropology: Reflections on Feminism and Cross-Cultural Understanding." *Signs* 5(3):389–417.

———. [1983] 1987. "Moral/Analytic Dilemmas Posed by the Intersection of Feminism and Social Science." In Paul Rabinow and William Sullivan, eds., *Interpretive Social Science: A Second Look,* pp. 280–301. Berkeley: University of California Press.

Rosen, Lawrence. 1984. *Bargaining for Reality: The Construction of Social Relations in a Muslim Community.* Chicago: University of Chicago Press.

Rubin, Gayle. 1975. "The Traffic in Women: Notes on the 'Political Economy' of Sex." In Rayna Reiter, ed., *Toward an Anthropology of Women,* pp. 157–210. New York: Monthly Review Press.

Schneider, David M. 1984. *A Critique of the Study of Kinship.* Ann Arbor: University of Michigan Press.

Scott, James C. 1985. *Weapons of the Weak: Everyday Forms of Peasant Resistance.* New Haven: Yale University Press.

Shapiro, Judith. 1979. "Cross-Cultural Perspectives on Sexual Differentiation." In Herant Katchadourian, ed., *Human Sexuality: A Comparative and Developmental Perspective,* pp. 269–308. Berkeley: University of California Press.

Siegel, James T. 1969. *The Rope of God.* Berkeley: University of California Press.

Spiro, Melford. 1977. *Kinship and Marriage in Burma: A Cultural and Psychodynamic Analysis.* Berkeley: University of California Press.

Stack, Carol. 1990. "Different Voices, Different Visions: Gender, Culture, and Moral Reasoning." In Faye Ginsburg and Anna L. Tsing, eds., *Uncertain Terms: Negotiating Gender in American Culture,* pp. 19–27. Boston: Beacon Press.

Stivens, Maila. 1985. "The Fate of Women's Land Rights: Gender, Matriliny, and Capitalism in Rembau, Negeri Sembilan, Malaysia." In Haleh Afshar, ed., *Women, Work, and Ideology in the Third World,* pp. 3–36. London: Tavistock.

———. 1987. "Family and State in Malaysian Industrialization: The Case of Rembau, Negeri Sembilan, Malaysia." In Haleh Afshar, ed., *Women, State, and Ideology,* pp. 89–110. Albany: SUNY Press.

———. 1991. "The Evolution of Kinship Relations in Rembau, Negeri Sembilan, Malaysia." In J. Kemp and F. Husken, eds., *Cognation and Social Organization in Southeast Asia,* pp. 71–88. Leiden: Koninklijk Instituut voor Taal-, Land-, en Volkenkunde.

Strathern, Marilyn. 1988. *The Gender of the Gift: Problems with Women and Problems with Society in Melanesia.* Berkeley: University of California Press.

———. 1992. *Reproducing the Future: Anthropology, Kinship, and the New Reproductive Technologies.* New York: Routledge.

———. ed. 1987. *Dealing with Inequality: Analyzing Gender Relations in Melanesia and Beyond.* Cambridge: Cambridge University Press.

Taylor, E. N. [1929] 1970. "The Customary Law of Rembau." In M. B. Hooker, ed., *Readings in Malay Adat Laws,* pp. 109–151. Singapore: Singapore University Press.

Valeri, Valerio. 1990. "Both Nature and Culture: Reflections on Menstrual and Parturitional Taboos in Huaulu (Seram)." In Jane M. Atkinson and Shelly Errington, eds., *Power and Difference: Gender in Island Southeast Asia,* pp. 235–272. Stanford: Stanford University Press.

Weiner, Annette. 1976. *Women of Value, Men of Renown: New Perspectives in Trobriand Exchange.* Austin: University of Texas Press.

———. 1992. *Inalienable Possessions: The Paradox of Keeping While Giving.* Berkeley: University of California Press.

Wikan, Unni. 1990. *Managing Turbulent Hearts: A Balinese Formula for Living.* Chicago: University of Chicago Press.

Wilkinson, R. J. [1911] 1976. "Notes on the Negri Sembilan." In R. J. Wilkinson, ed., *Papers on Malay Subjects,* pp. 277–321. Kuala Lumpur: Oxford University Press.

Williams, Raymond. 1977. *Marxism and Literature.* Oxford: Oxford University Press.

Willis, Paul. 1977. *Learning to Labor: How Working Class Kids Get Working Class Jobs.* New York: Columbia University Press.

Winstedt, R. O. 1934. "Negri Sembilan: The History, Polity, and Beliefs of the Nine States." *Journal of the Malayan Branch of the Royal Asiatic Society* 12(3):35–114.

Yanagisako, Sylvia, and Jane Collier. 1987. "Toward a Unified Analysis of Gender and Kinship." In Jane Collier and Sylvia Yanagisako, eds., *Gender and Kinship: Essays toward a Unified Analysis*, pp. 14–50. Stanford: Stanford University Press.

FOUR

Senior Women, Model Mothers, and Dutiful Wives: Managing Gender Contradictions in a Minangkabau Village

Evelyn Blackwood

Evelyn Blackwood's essay on the Minangkabau complements Peletz's work on Malays and all of the other essays that follow in that it deals with the ways in which various types of gender meanings are subverted and partially transformed by state policies as well as nationalist (and transnational) discourse. Blackwood addresses the ways in which the Indonesian government has created new gender categories through what she refers to as the "discourse of the domestic," though her larger concern is the contradictory relationship between "traditional," homegrown representations of gender on the one hand, and gender representations emanating from contemporary Indonesian state policies and programs (both secular and religious) on the other. Blackwood analyzes some of the ways in which state-sponsored development projects and attendant programs geared toward modernizasi *and Islamic reform have the potential to eclipse local understandings of gender, and of women in particular. She also demonstrates that both local and state-derived representations of women are frequently contested in local village councils and ceremonial deliberations bearing on marriage, property, and the like (see also Krier, this volume), which thus become a key site for negotiating and reworking representations of gender and power. Blackwood shows how both the activities and the composition of the councils, as well as the ceremonial deliberations at issue, need to be viewed in relation to the broadly encompassing realities of history and political economy. These realities include the political and economic agendas and strategies of the Suharto regime, and the ascendancy, both locally and in Indonesia generally, of Western-oriented development experts and bureaucrats whose cultural and professional baggage often includes Indonesian variations on the theme of what Nancy Tanner has referred to as "Anglo-American Momism."*

More generally, Blackwood illustrates not only how government experts and other agents of capitalist development and moral advance contravene local understandings of kinship and gender by treating men, rather than women, as household heads;

but also how, in the process of doing so, they undermine the "taken-for-grantedness" of Minangkabau kinship and gender. Thus, despite the continued existence into the present of contradictory discourses on gender, the fact remains that Minangkabau women are increasingly defined in national discourses and, to a lesser extent, in their local spin-offs as wives, mothers, and bearers of future citizens, rather than in terms of kinship or other social roles that portray them as full social beings endowed with autonomy, social control, and prestige in their own right.

While the anthropological discourse on postmodernism and late capitalism appraises the postmodern condition, postcolonial nations are impressing old paradigms on the bodies of their new citizens. Much as their colonial predecessors did, these new nations have developed a core of agents, activities and institutions that direct the formation of group and individual identities, which in turn coalesce into a national identity. In the process of state building, diverse ethnic groups are homogenized into national citizens through pronouncements concerning the acceptable styles and images of life (Foster 1991; Williams 1989). New nations not only redefine ethnicity in producing national identities, but also slot female and male bodies into new gender categories.

It is the process of producing gendered citizens and the responses of those citizens that I will examine in this paper. Foucault (1979, 1980) showed how state apparatuses and technologies of power constitute the body through discursive practices that legitimize and consolidate the power of the state. Although his analysis is crucial to understanding state power, the major limitation of Foucault's work is that his "bodies" are non-gendered. Stoler (1985, 1991) resolved this problem in her important work on the Dutch colonial construction of racial and gender categories, noting that the colonizers created attributes of male and female that legitimated their domination. Ong's (1987, 1990, 1991) work on Malaysian factory women takes this line of thinking one step further, showing how Japanese corporate practices in Malaysia shape and promote a certain image of women. Following on her work, I argue that postcolonial states actively create (or reconstruct) and promote formulations of gender compatible with the perceived needs of development. Rather than simply arising from the dictates of capitalism or the structures of preexisting inequalities and patriarchies, definitions of womanhood are consciously forged through state ideologies.

To promote the unity and stability of the state, and to encourage development, postcolonial state ideologies and practices actively encourage women to situate themselves in the home. In Indonesia, for instance, the state glorifies women as moral guardians and domestic managers in an effort to support the ideology of women as "national reproducers" (Robinson 1989). Men categorized as "providers" and "protectors" are held up as manly, authoritarian leaders (Langenberg 1986). The emphasis on women's domesticity in Indonesia, at least in the New Order era after 1965, is fueled in large part by the practices and theories of development economics, which is a product of the historical and social conditions of Europe and America. In European and American capitalist, class-based societies, "true" womanhood became associated with the domesticity of home and family (Foster 1991). Under the influence of this ideology, development economists have relegated everything within the household to the private (domestic) and noneconomic sphere, thus ignoring gender differences in the economic sphere (Papanek 1984; Folbre 1986). With the importation of development economics into postcolonial states by development experts and scholars, the domestic/public paradigm continues to live on in the postcolonial context.

Though the separation of public and private has long since been abandoned as a meaningful paradigm for gender by many feminists (Yanagisako and Collier 1987; Yanagisako 1987), new nations are reproducing and recreating the domestic domain. In Indonesia, in addition to state efforts to identify women with the domestic domain, mainstream Islamic discourse on womanhood portrays women as wives and mothers above all else. Although there are several divergent interpretations of Islam in Indonesia (as well as regional variations), the discourse of modernist Islamic scholars dominant in national Indonesian publications reinforces the state ideology of womanhood. These two discourses reconstruct the domestic sphere in a way that produces new gendered identities for Indonesian citizens.[1]

What happens when indigenous gender meanings are confronted with a national and Islamic ideology of domesticity? My answer to this question is based on information drawn from the period in postcolonial Indonesia after 1965 when Suharto became president and instituted the New Order. I focus on the reception and interpretation of state and Islamic gender ideologies by one of the larger ethnic groups in Indonesia, the Minangkabau of West Sumatra. Under the New Order, the Indonesian state imposed new meanings on village space through a range of programs and policies directed at, among other things, agriculture, social welfare, family planning, census taking, and religious activities. The discourse and practice of gender in the Minangkabau rice-farming community where I did my fieldwork conflicts with state and Islamic constructions of women's domesticity. Given these conflicts, how do Minangkabau women, who are at the same time Muslim, understand and negotiate these discourses of domesticity?

The Minangkabau living in West Sumatra number approximately 3.8 million. An equally large number live in other parts of Indonesia and the world and are called *perantau* (migrants) by the Minangkabau. They are the largest matrilineal group in the world and one that is devoutly Muslim. Identified with the Sunni branch of Islam, the Minangkabau have been centrally involved in debates between the traditionalist and modernist schools of Islam (Abdullah 1971; Dobbin 1983). Islam in West Sumatra today is part of the everyday life of the Minangkabau, who generally see no conflict between *adat* (the system of customs, beliefs and laws) and Islam (see also Krier, this volume, for further discussion of the meaning of *adat*). Although historically contradictions between Islam and *adat* have led to conflicts in West Sumatra (Dobbin 1983; Whalley 1993), the two have come to be mutually constructed in such a way that it is fruitless to draw sharp theoretical distinctions between them. (For further discussion of this point, see Delaney 1991; Horvatich 1992.) In Whalley's excellent study of Islam in West Sumatra, she relates the following: "The Minang are fond of stating that *adat* and Islam follow complementary paths in an inseparable unity.. . . Today, the Minang resolve that Islam and *adat* should stand side by side." This belief is articulated in the "oft-quoted Minangkabau aphorism: *Adat* sits side by side with Islamic law and Islamic law sits side by side with the Qur'an" (Whalley 1993:22).[2] In the village where I worked Minangkabau consider their daily and ceremonial lives to be congruent with the principles of Islam, as do Southeast Asian Muslims in general (Ellen 1983:65). Local Minangkabau understandings of Islam, however, differ somewhat from the national Islamic discourse that is interwoven with the state model of gender.

The Minangkabau are predominantly rural agriculturalists but, as producers of surplus rice and active participants in circular migration *(merantau)*, they are well aware of nationalist and capitalist discourses. The village of Taram where I worked is located in the province of Lima Puluh Kota ("Fifty Cities"), one of the original three provinces that form the core of the Minangkabau world.[3] During my fieldwork, Taram was a stronghold of *adat*, as well as a major producer of rice for the market. In 1989, it had a population of approximately 6,800; I focused on one hamlet of 650 people, which I call Tanjung Batang. The question of the discourse and practice of gender in this one village is complex. As I will show, at one level state and Islamic representations of women resonate with the Minangkabau conception of women as mothers. At a deeper level, however, these representations contradict Minangkabau conceptions of gender because they attempt to confine women to the home and "domestic" concerns.

REPRESENTING GENDER

The study of gender in matrilineal societies has been dominated by androcentric analyses of kinship, inheritance and marriage. This approach failed to represent accurately the relations between men and women. The prevailing scholarly belief about the Minangkabau has long been that men, as *penghulu* or titled males (usually translated as headmen or lineage chiefs), held the power in lineage and village affairs (Josselin de Jong 1952; Maretin 1961; Schrieke 1955). Schneider and Gough (1961) enshrined the perception—following those before them—that males invariably have jural authority in matrilineal societies. Even recent work such as Kato's repeats the standard view of Minangkabau society that "in the traditional Minangkabau *nagari* [village], the *penghulu* was the richest, most knowledgeable, most powerful, both politically and judicially, and most prestigious person" (1982:65). Kato based his opinion on readings of earlier works and interviews with village headmen and titled men, who, as I show later, were quite willing to substantiate the prevailing view of male authority.

Interspersed in this formidable array of scholarly opinion concerning the importance of men and male-male relationships (i.e., father-son, uncle-nephew), there were occasional odd notes that contradicted accepted conclusions. Willinck, for example, asserted that "the oldest common ancestress . . . actually stood above the *mamak* [mother's brother]" (quoted in F. Benda-Beckmann 1979:84). Nancy Tanner, in her groundbreaking study of the day-to-day workings of Minangkabau families, was the first to explicitly state that "within the household, the senior woman is likely to control the balance of power" (1971:18). Spurred by the misinformation on Minangkabau women in the older texts, anthropologists have recently laid to rest many misperceptions regarding Minangkabau women.[4] Their work has consistently illuminated the "centrality" of women in Minangkabau households and disputed Schneider and Gough's model of matriliny, showing that women have authority in matrilineal kinship relations and economic matters (Ng 1987; Pak 1986; Prindiville 1985; Sanday 1990; Schwede 1991; Tanner and Thomas 1985).

These anthropologists have also shown that Minangkabau gender imagery provides ample evidence to support the centrality and importance of women. The Minangkabau image of womanhood, as found in Minangkabau drama and literature, is of a woman simultaneously strong, nurturant and wise (Tanner 1971:40). In two frequently-cited oral stories *(tambo)*, Minangkabau women as mothers exhibit "motherly wisdom, initiative, assertiveness, stability, integrity, and practicality" (Tanner and Thomas 1985:67; also Schwede 1991). In this literature women are called "Woman-as-Queen-Mother" and "Mother-as-Senior-Woman" (Tanner and Thomas 1985). Further, in Minangkabau proverbs women are metaphorically referred to as Center Pillar of the Big House [the lineage house] and Holder of the Key to the Chest [lineage property]. These designations "reflect [women's] pivotal economic roles and spacially *[sic]* central position" (Prindiville 1981:28; see also Pak 1986; Schwede 1991).[5]

Despite this affirmation of women's position, the notion of centrality, or even matrifocality (which can be interpreted in any number of ways) yields little information regarding the workings of gender, by which I mean the practices and discourses that enact gender. "Centrality" tells us nothing about the relations of power between women and men, or between differently ranked groups of kin. As I show in this essay, Minangkabau women's power extends beyond the confines of household and subsistence activities. Women hold power through their control of lineage land and client kin, and through their knowledge and control of *adat* and social practice.

The problem of formulating an adequate theory of women's power is not unique to discussions of the Minangkabau. Some scholars state that most Southeast Asian societies give women "high status" (Van Esterik 1982), but the actual meaning of such a statement is not always clear. Errington argues that despite women's social and economic equality in island Southeast Asia, women as a group show a "relative lack of power and prestige" (1990:40). Still other scholars, who have looked beyond gender symbolism to the practice of gender, argue that women's contribution to the household and economy creates female autonomy and social power, as did Stoler (1977) in one of the early articles to consider women's power in Javanese society. Likewise, Peletz argues that in nineteenth-century Negeri Sembilan women exercised considerable autonomy and control over the affairs of their households and compounds, and that female elders emerged "as the de facto loci of authority" within the lineage or its household (1987:453). Carrying this thought further, Peletz (this volume) suggests that although official structures such as rituals typically highlight clan chiefs and men as leading actors, in practice women control some property and exchange men. Consequently the official view of gender differs from practical representations grounded in everyday situations (Peletz, this volume). Ong (this volume) also shows the discrepancies between women's actions and the representation of women articulated in official gender ideology in Malaysia. This line of analysis is very suggestive because it highlights the contradictions between official representations and practical power.

Such analysis can be carried even further in cases where multiple gender ideologies, none of which are dominant, support a range of interpretations about gender. In the following sections I focus on the multiple gender ideologies encoded in *adat,* Islam, and state discourses to gain a clearer understanding of Minangkabau gender. This focus takes its insight from Bourdieu's (1977) model of *habitus,* which he defines as the principles (or practices) for the generation of structures that are themselves the product of past practices. *Habitus* produces a commonsense world of shared understandings "immediately intelligible and foreseeable, and hence taken for granted" (Bourdieu 1977:80). It is this sense of culture being taken for granted that I wish to emphasize with regard to gender relations. In addition to seeking gender in contested realms and discourses, we must attend to the level at which assumptions about gender are naturalized and become the foundation for perception and practice. I argue that there is a taken-for-grantedness about Minangkabau gender, based on *adat* ideology and rules of inheritance, that gives continued validity to women's control over household and kin. This perspective provides another way to understand the seeming paradox that although women have power in practice it is not always articulated in ideology.

MINANGKABAU MATRILINY AND GENDER

To understand Minangkabau gender, I will outline the local experiences, perceptions and representations that constitute the core of Minangkabau discourse and practice of gender.[6] Kinship relations constitute the core of Minangkabau culture and set the framework for Minangkabau conceptions of gender. Descent and inheritance are organized matrilineally. Inheritance passes from mother to daughters; the matrilineal line is the enduring possessor of ancestral property.

Each matriline constitutes a sublineage, usually an extended family of three to four generations living in a lineage house (*rumah gadang*) (or more recently in several matrilocally situated houses), holding land and title in common and related to a known, living ancestress. Approximately one hundred and fifty sublineages (*kaum*) make up the lowest level of kinship in Taram, above which are twenty-four lineages (*payung*), and at the highest level seven named clans (*suku*). These kin groups form the dominant sociopolitical units in the village. The members of individual *kaum*— mother, mother's sisters and brothers, and all offspring through the maternal line—work closely together in economic and ceremonial matters. For instance, while I was in Taram, the elder daughter of a landowning family managed their rice fields for herself and her mother and sometimes for her sister when the latter was busy with other matters. A married elite man told me that he had given his sister some land that he had used for several years after turning it from uncultivated land into rice fields. Another man helped build a kitchen behind the lineage house in which his sister, his niece and her children resided. In this way *kaum* members serve the interests of their *kaum* and ensure its continued viability in the village. The *kaum* forms the basic building block of the village. The social and political hierarchy of the village is based on the ranking of *kaum*, lineages and clans.

In the hierarchy of rank, the descendants of the original settlers of Taram comprise the elite lineages of the village. Elites have rights to land and lineage houses and are vested with authority in lineage and village affairs. This system of rank and authority is laid out in *adat*, which is controlled by the elites. A number of lower-ranked families are attached to the hundred and fifty elite lineages. These lower-ranked families are either newcomers to Taram who have been adopted into the elite clans as client families, or servant families who are descendants of slaves brought by the elite clans to Taram. Since elite families control the land, both client and servant families are dependent on the elites for access to land.

The senior woman of the sublineage (*kaum*) is called *Bundo Kanduang* (womb mother, elder or wise woman), a general term applied to any senior woman.[7] As an elder, a senior woman has wide-ranging power over those in her sublineage (or her lineage, if she is of the high-ranking elite), whether they are her offspring or adopted kin. I was told that as *Bundo Kanduang,* a senior woman "gives advice to the children and guides them in the proper way." This image resonates with the Islamic ideal of woman who, as mother, is educator and guide to her children. The Minangkabau interpretation of this ideal, however, does not limit a mother's responsibility to the guidance of children who are still young. The Minangkabau woman's control over her "children" extends throughout their lives. As one elite woman told me, "A senior woman has to know *adat,* her genealogy and her family land (*harta pusaka*) so she can manage the affairs of her kin group wisely." Along with her brother (*mamak*), the senior woman uses her knowledge to handle the affairs of her own children, her extended kin, and client families.

As senior women guide their children, so young women and men are taught to respect the advice of their maternal kin. Later access to their mothers' rice lands may depend on their ability to cooperate with their mothers. Unmarried daughters are expected to be chaste, decorous and modest, as is proper for young Muslim women. Unmarried sons are expected to help their families by providing labor or earnings. Minangkabau folktales encourage this behavior by recounting the deeds of irresponsible young men who only made good when they listened to the advice of their mothers (Johns 1958). As the junior woman in the household, a young married woman is taught to think for herself and to protect the interests of her kin group. One elite woman told me that her married daughter, who was twenty-seven, did not understand things well enough yet to make decisions alone; she needed to learn from her elders. It is as a maturing person that a woman assumes control of herself and her household and begins to take a dominant place in lineage and interlineage affairs. (See also Whalley 1991.)

A man who holds the family title, the titular male or *penghulu*, represents the sublineage (or lineage or clan, depending on his rank) in matters outside the lineage. All collective action within the lineage requires the consensus of the members of the group, both male and female (see Prindiville 1981; K. Benda-Beckmann 1984). Because of this requirement, titled males do not have independent authority within the lineage. The opinions of senior men and women hold more weight than younger members because it is customary for younger people to defer to the wisdom of the older generation. Senior individuals can shape the consensual process or prevent others from making a decision. Ultimately, the senior woman holds greater influence than the senior man because no decision will be made without her agreement. Further, as several woman told me, the senior woman alone decides on the disposition of land after her death.

Regarding the question of authority, a male consultant told me: "For problems within the sublineage, people talk to the senior woman first. If she can, and the problem isn't too large, but is confined to the *kampung* [residential area in which a group of related kin live], the senior woman (*ibu*) can resolve the problem herself without calling in the mother's brother (*mamak*). If the issue is beyond the *kampung*, the *mamak* has to be told about it." Because of the dependence on group consensus, even the *adat* council, a council of high-ranking *penghulu* that decides village-level disputes, does not have the power to make arbitrary decisions or pass down edicts (see Blackwood 1993). Most disputes take months to resolve. During this time, titled males are forced to hold private discussions with the men and women of their lineages so that a public consensus may be reached (K. Benda-Beckmann 1984:53–55). Thus, these *penghulu* constitute an administrative body that executes collective decisions (Pak 1986:276).

A *penghulu* acts in the interests of his matrilineage. By building up his and his sisters' matrilineage he builds up his own standing. Likewise, by taking action that weakens his sister's power or undermines her control of land he ultimately weakens his own base of power. In Taram I did not hear of any cases where titled men directly opposed the interests of women who were members of the same sublineage. On the other hand, differences in rank between client and elite families often led to inequalities of power and access to land. In disputes between lower- and higher-ranked families, women and men of lower-ranked families are both disadvantaged.[8]

The control of lineage rice land is one of the critical elements constituting women's power in Minangkabau society. Although land officially belongs to the sublineage as a whole and cannot be alienated without group consent, effective control of the land resides with the senior woman of the sublineage. It is she who controls the use and disposition of rice land and of the products of that land. She works the rice fields herself with the assistance of kin or hired labor, or leases it to sharecroppers. She decides when and how much of her rice land to give to her daughters, or how much to let her sons use. As each daughter marries, she gives her a small piece of rice land to use for her own needs. If a daughter wants to pawn some of the land her mother has given her, she must first get her mother's permission and inform the *penghulu* (the titled male) before taking action. Only at the mother's death do daughters attain full rights in land.

A son may be granted use-rights to rice land for his lifetime, usually after he is married. He and his wife then work the land as a sharecropping team, half of the produce going to his wife and half to his mother. At his death, or at the death of his children, the land returns to his mother or sisters. The *penghulu,* usually the mother's uncle or brother, has one piece of land that belongs to him as bearer of the hereditary title. He uses it to defray the expenses of his position, but should the title not be passed on at his death, this land will revert to his sisters. A man has control of rice fields only when there are no female heirs remaining in his lineage. He can then pass the land on to other close kin within the matrilineage, or to his children, or sell it to client kin.

A senior woman may lease surplus land to land-poor kin or client kin. Newcomers to the village can be assured of continued access to that land by adoption into the lineage of the landowner as client kin. The Minangkabau practice of adopting newcomers into their lineages establishes binding ties between the sharecropper and landowner, among other social benefits. In return for access to land and the services (advice, guidance) of the elite lineage at ceremonial events hosted by clients, client families provide labor and assist at ceremonies hosted by their elite kin. These ties create a network of social relations that extends the control of the senior woman beyond her own kinfolk to client kin and other laborers.

Since farmers started double cropping in the 1970s, rice has become a predominantly cash rather than subsistence crop.[9] Women sell their rice on the market and use the income to provide for their households and to finance ceremonial activities associated with kinship affairs. The husband's income is used to pay for his children's schooling; if he has additional income beyond his wife's needs, it may be used to help his mother and matrikin. Some women use surplus income to buy gold jewelry, which is both an investment and a means to display one's wealth (see also Whalley 1993). Others have started business ventures in rice production as merchants and mill owners.

Women's dominance in rice production and involvement in business is underscored in local discourse. Men in the village agreed that women control rice production. One male informant justified women's economic activities by saying that becoming a miller or merchant was a "natural" extension of a woman's control of lineage rice land. Islamic scholars who argue for women's rights also point out that, according to the Qur'an, women have the right to own and administer property and to conduct business (Salyo 1985:18–19). In a private Islamic boarding school founded by Rahmah El Yunusiyyah, a Minangkabau woman, this Qur'anic interpretation is manifest in an educational program in which Minangkabau girls learn the tenets of Islam while being prepared for success in the world (see Whalley 1991; Rasyad 1985; Vreede de Steurs 1960).

Another element of women's power over kin and clients can be seen in the domain of ceremonial *adat*. Through their position as lineage elders and *adat* experts, senior women and men control interlineage and village affairs. The lineages are frequently involved in deliberations and preparations for major ceremonies, which form the core of village social relations. Particularly in the case of marriage, many delicate negotiations must take place. Before each ceremony, formal deliberations are conducted to determine the proper *adat* to be used. In the deliberations I witnessed, a titled man led the discussion but asked the senior woman what she had decided about certain matters. According to Dt. (Datuk) Rajo, my primary male consultant, "The senior woman has more responsibilities than the senior man in matters of ceremonies and their negotiations. She is responsible for certain decisions made concerning ceremonies, such as for marriages or deaths. As with the division of labor in the rice field, senior women (*Bundo Kanduang*) and senior men (*ninik-mamak*) each have their own responsibilities."

The preparation and handling of ceremonies is divided into "women's business" and "men's business," according to Dt. Rajo. Women make the critical arrangements with affines, manage and oversee the event, and cook and serve food to female guests who arrive throughout the day bearing trays of food. Men build temporary structures, oversee and conduct the men's part of the ritual and exchange ritual speeches. As Prindiville noted, "men exchange words while women exchange food" (1981:29). The food trays brought by women are prominently displayed on special platforms and are the subject of much discussion. As the men exchange artful speeches punctuated with proverbs and maxims intended to assert the importance of their own lineages, the women contest and assert allegiances and identities through their food exchange.

In productive as well as social relations, the power of a senior elite woman extends beyond her own kin group to include client kin and other laborers. She regulates family land use, property allocation and crop disposition, and thus is empowered to make claims to dependents' labor. Senior women control the activities of their client families, even those who may have surpassed them in wealth and land, thereby setting limits to the status client families can achieve (see Blackwood 1991). This power is the realization of structures of kinship and *adat*. I suggest that the enactment of these structures generates the *habitus*, the structured dispositions, that form the core of Minangkabau gender. In Taram women's control over land and kin, their management of ceremonies and clients, and their claims to the labor of their offspring, all transmit a knowledge and experience of gender that becomes part of a commonsense world in which women's power is fundamental. Women are the meaning and symbol of kin and house, the controllers of land, and the holders of the key to lineage property. Everyone knows that the person who holds the key gets to use it. Women's power does not exist only at the level of practice, although, because it is so commonsensical and taken for granted, it is not readily articulated in daily discourse. Hence it becomes invisible, at least to outsiders. Nevertheless, women's power is legitimated in *adat* ideology and discourse and constitutes one of the core principles of a Minangkabau ideology of gender.

DISCOURSE OF THE DOMESTIC

Turning now to the state ideology of gender, I will examine the way the Indonesian state has forged an ideology of womanhood through its agents, programs and development plans. The Indonesian state was formed in 1945 from a Dutch-created territory that contained at least three thousand ethnic groups. With Suharto's rise to power and the establishment of the New Order in 1965–66, the Indonesian state began to consistently emphasize development based upon integration into the world capitalist economy. Since that period the state has predominated in the exercise of social control, the management of the means of production, the distribution of resources, and cultural production (Langenberg 1986). Further, the rulers of the new state have consciously built up a substantial ideological structure to "[keep] the Indonesian people together as one nation" (KOWANI 1980) and to legitimate their considerable power and authority.

To hasten the transition from an agricultural to an industrial nation, the Indonesian state formulated new economic policies and programs and an ideology aimed at creating an Indonesian citizen in step with the "modern" world. Through its national development plan (REPELITA), it encouraged all Indonesians to be responsible for and participate in national development. Although state planners acknowledged women's importance to development, they insisted that women's primary contribution lay in their roles as wives and mothers (Manderson 1980). State policies enforced this vision of womanhood as supportive wife and nurturing mother. According to the state directive that forms the ideological core of all state programs geared to women's "needs," a woman has five major duties: to be a loyal supporter to her husband; to be caretaker of the household; to produce future generations; to raise her children properly; and to be a good citizen (see Sullivan 1983:148).

Statements by high state officials (among others, the Minister for Education and Culture, the wife of the Minister for Religious Affairs, the Minister for Social Welfare) reiterated the importance of women's domestic duties. In a speech to wives of state officials, Mrs. Tien Suharto, wife of the president, declared: "A harmonious and orderly household is a great contribution to the smooth running of development efforts. . . . It is the duty of the wife to see to it that her household is in order so that when her husband comes home from a busy day he will find peace and harmony at home. The children, too, will be happier and healthier" (quoted in Manderson 1980:83). This statement emphasizes the separation of a domestic sphere from a public sphere where the husband operates. It asserts that women have primary responsibility for the domestic sphere.

These policies were developed by Indonesian officials, many of whom were trained in Western universities (see Reeve 1985:282; MacAndrews 1986) where, as I mentioned earlier, the belief in a domestic/public split and the male as head of household is the backbone of development economics. Colonial Dutch policies and practices also played a significant role in shaping the Indonesian housewife, as do contemporary Westernized images of women presented in the media and women's magazines (see, for example, Lutz 1992). My focus in this section, however, is on the impact of New Order programs and policies. The use of the domestic/public paradigm in New Order policy-making resulted in the development of state programs that conceptualized no role for women other than a domestic one. These programs fostered the belief that women's economic activities were either supplemental to their husbands' income or a threat to the proper fulfillment of their wifely and motherly roles (Grijns 1992; Sullivan 1989).

State programs instituted for women after 1966 implemented the reconstructed view of womanhood by focusing solely on women's familial connections. Dharma Wanita, instituted in 1974, is the organization of wives of civil servants. (Dharma Pertiwi is the organization for wives of members of the armed forces.) All wives are expected to participate; even if a woman is herself a civil servant, she must participate in Dharma Wanita in accordance with the rank of her husband, whether or not it is lower than her own. This group is organized exclusively around domestic issues and any "political" content is carefully excluded. As this group grew, earlier women's organizations active in the struggle for Indonesian independence and for women's rights began to disappear or were reoriented to follow the new state directives for women (Wieringa 1985).

Another women's organization, PKK (*Pembinaan Kesejahteraan Keluarga,* Family Welfare Organization), established in 1973, has had the most far-reaching effect. PKK is a voluntary organization and the main channel used by the state to reach women at the grass-roots level (Royal Netherlands Embassy 1987). PKK's leaders are wives of state officials. These women hold office according to the ranks of their husbands and are not elected or remunerated for their duties. In fact, their participation is considered voluntary, although they are under heavy pressure to take on these duties as good wives. Both PKK and Dharma Wanita are strictly controlled by the state and follow its dictates regarding their structure and programs; their members are kept busy organizing cooking and etiquette demonstrations, sewing and flower arrangement courses, family planning, and health and nutritional programs.

In its efforts to manage its citizens, Indonesia has also established bureaucratic regulations that promote a more subtle identification of women with a domestic sphere. According to state law, all households must be registered with the village administrative office and all household heads must be male, unless there is no adult male in the household. On household registration forms there are spaces to list household head (*kepala keluarga*), wife (*isteri*), and children (*anak-anak*), a system that in effect predetermines the relative positions of the married couple. A similar method was employed in a state-sponsored birth control program that I observed in Taram. In this program every household in the village was given a placard to put on their front door. Each placard was printed with the words "household head" and "wife" followed by the names of the resident spouses, the total number in the household, and type of birth control practiced by that family. While this tactic was used to encourage participation in the birth control program, it also reinforced in people's minds a distinction between household head and wife. Through such record-keeping and registration practices, the state produces hierarchically gendered identities for its citizens.

Likewise, the discourse of the domestic shapes Indonesian agricultural policy around the needs of men. Because men are defined in public policy as providers, women's labor and productivity "outside" the home are not considered critical to development strategies. This perspective led to the creation of agricultural programs geared solely toward male farmers. As late as the mid-1980s, none of the existing agricultural projects in Indonesia addressed women (Colfer et al., n.d.). State agricultural extension programs, such as BIMAS (Mass Guidance Project), which sought to encourage and facilitate the farmer in applying new farming techniques (Tinker and Walker 1973; Rieffel 1969), were aimed solely at men. In West Sumatra, state agricultural extension programs were introduced to Minangkabau farmers through meetings between agricultural extension officers and male elders (*ninik-mamak*) and male religious leaders (*ulama*) of villages (Esmara 1974). A cooperative farm program set up in 1967 in Taram had 57 members, of which only 14 were women (25 percent). Although all these women owned and/or managed farmland, half of them were listed as housewives, and only 4 were listed as farmers.[10] Thus, despite the prominence of women in farming, men benefited more directly from state farm assistance.

I have presented only a brief summary of some of the relevant New

Order programs that affect women in Indonesia. Each of these policies reflects and carries out the state discourse of domesticity, which encourages women to identify themselves with their households and spouses to the exclusion of any other identity. Although such programs contribute to the well-being of Indonesian families, they do not adequately represent and support women's activities as producers. Rather, they are responsible for narrowing the playing field on which women can legitimately operate.

ISLAM AND WOMEN AS MOTHERS AND WIVES

With nearly 90 percent of Indonesia's citizens registered as Muslim, Islamic views on womanhood have a strong influence on state policy, particularly in the creation of the domestic discourse. In 1973 the political influence of Muslim parties was curtailed when the New Order merged the four existing Muslim parties into one secular party. On the other hand, the state required all citizens to profess an officially recognized religion, instituted mandatory religious instruction in school, and supported mosques by allowing development funds to be used for mosque-construction projects. Together with the influence of a worldwide Islamic reformist movement, these actions have resulted in a resurgence of Islamic practices during the 1980s in both rural and urban areas (Hefner 1987; Thomas 1988). Indonesian Muslim groups report an increase in the number of study groups, mosques and people going on the pilgrimage to Mecca. Along with this resurgence has come renewed debate on the status of women in Islam.

Nationally recognized Islamic leaders in Indonesia assert that women's primary duties are to be wives and mothers, although there are variations on this discourse (see, for example, Whalley 1993). This Islamic model of womanhood corresponds to and validates the model set forth by the Indonesian state. In an article on the status of women in Islam, an Indonesian Muslim scholar and intellectual of the modernist school of Islam stated, "Man is suited to face the hard struggles of life on account of his stronger physique. Woman is suited to bring up the children because of the preponderance of the quality of love in her. [W]hile the duty of breadwinning must be generally left to the man[,] the duty of the management of the home and the bringing up of the children belongs to the women" (Raliby 1985:36). Further, in the Qur'an, the man is said to be the ruler of the people of his house and the woman the ruler of the house of her husband (Raliby 1985). The Indonesian Marriage Law of 1974 follows this Islamic tenet quite closely, stating that "the husband is the head of the family and the wife is the mother of the household" (Salyo 1985:20).

While Islamic beliefs have influenced state policy, Islamic scholars have accommodated and helped to shore up the state ideology regarding women. Some Indonesian Muslim women highly placed in government and leaders of women's organizations find no contradiction between development directives for women and the Islamic emphasis on wifely duties. In an article on "Woman and Career in Islam," the author, an Indonesian businesswoman, states, "[T]he main duties of women are . . . family affairs, including the children's education matters. [O]ther duties, such as social and professional roles, are additional depending upon the condition of respective families" (Pramono 1990:73). According to this interpretation, a woman should first attend to her domestic duties and then work in the community, a clear echo of the state directive that women should first educate their children and provide their husbands moral support.

Although certain Indonesian Muslim intellectuals point out that the Qur'an supports women's right to work and earn their own incomes, much of the discussion concerning women focuses on their household obligations. In Muslim magazines, columns entitled "Family and Marriage" are specifically oriented toward women (e.g., *Kiblat,* an Indonesian weekly magazine). Support for women's careers "outside the household" is double-edged, that is, it is contingent on their ability to manage an orderly home (Pramono 1990). Although some Muslim women argue that women should be free to be persons (Djamas 1985), the dominant Islamic discourse defines women by their marital status. It strengthens the state view that women's lives are domestic, centered around husbands and children, while giving men personhood in a larger world outside the home.

CONTRADICTORY GENDER IDEOLOGIES

Having outlined the articulation of state and Islamic discourses of domesticity at the national level, I will examine in this section the ways in which these discourses permeate local Minangkabau society as well as Minangkabau responses to them. State and Islamic ideologies underwrite a different identity for women than that legitimated in village *adat*. Minangkabau women have access to national discourses via religious programming on state television, through the magazines sold at local markets, and through their participation in state-sponsored projects. Through such diverse avenues, Minangkabau women in Taram are confronted daily with the problems of being good citizens, good Muslims and good elders. Within this multiplicity of discourses, there are no neat dividing lines by which women can articulate one identity over another; the ideologies and practices of the state, Islam and the Minangkabau interpenetrate.

In its development efforts, the Indonesian state has appropriated various cultural symbols from its many ethnic groups as a way to bolster the appeal of its programs (see Bowen [1986] on the state ideological use of the term *gotong royong*). In West Sumatra, the state has appropriated the Minangkabau term for mother, *Bundo Kanduang,* in its campaign to educate women regarding their duties as mothers. The state's "model mother" (*ibu teladan*) program gives awards to women who are exemplars of proper motherhood. The honor of being *ibu teladan* goes to women who have provided their children a responsible upbringing (health, education, and nutrition). In West Sumatra women who win this award are called *Bundo Kanduang*. By giving this title to Minangkabau women who are good homemakers and child rearers, the state implicitly promotes the slippage of *Bundo Kanduang* from lineage elder to domestic wife. It is not a woman's leadership or management of her kin group that is rewarded, but fulfillment of certain tasks labeled "domestic" by the state. Thus, women's vision of themselves as *Bundo Kanduang* is overwritten by an alternate vision of *Bundo Kanduang* promulgated by the state.

The definition of household head as male further obscures people's understanding of women's relationship to their own households. As I noted earlier, in the village registry and on the doors of each house, the resident male is identified as household head. Only households of divorced or widowed women are marked as headed by women. Some people take down the signs, not because of any resistance to state intrusion or rejection of state labels, but because, as one divorced woman told me, she was embarrassed to be listed as household head. When I asked people to identify the household head in their family, using the Indonesian term *kepala keluarga* (the Minangkabau do not have the same term in their language), almost everyone responded with the name of the husband or male in-law.

By defining households as male-headed and confined to the individual conjugal unit (by its emphasis on the marital relationship of household head and wife), state bureaucratic regulations give substance to a new form of household. These regulations serve to create a "domestic" space that is headed by a husband and distinct from any larger kin grouping. State categories of "household" and "household head" in effect contradict the much more encompassing Minangkabau understanding of family, which they experience as the dynamic nexus of social, economic and kinship relations controlled by female and male lineage elders.

The effect of the contradiction between state and Minangkabau categories can be seen in the response of a young elite man to my question, "Who is the head of household [in your house]?" He replied, his mother and her husband. This young man's mother, Bu Fitriani, is *Bundo Kanduang* of her clan (highest-ranking woman of the clan). His answer highlights his problem in sorting out the proper response for household head because, although he does name his stepfather, he also includes his mother as household head. As the highest-ranking woman in her clan, his mother has considerable power within her clan and household, and is not to be left out of an answer simply because state categories do not include women as household heads.

Bu Fitriani, now in her fifties, is the oldest surviving member of her family. Her sublineage includes her own six children and her deceased older sister's two sons. One of her nephews, age twenty-nine, bears the family title. Fitriani controls all the rice land belonging to her sublineage, including that allocated to her titled nephew, Dt. Sango. When one of her married sons asked for land, she refused, saying that there was not enough for everyone. All her children had to get her permission before they could marry. Fitriani has four client families attached to her sublineage plus a number of other sublineages who come under her and her family's influence. If there is a problem with her client kin, she is called upon to handle it. If there is a problem within her lineage, the *penghulu* are consulted along with Fitriani. Fitriani explained to me that she makes the decisions concerning the proper conduct of ritual ceremonies, including the program, the drinks, and food. Another senior woman of the same lineage told me, "Fitriani is the *pucuk* ["tip of a shoot," a term used for the highest-ranking person], she makes the decisions. I just go along with whatever she wants. If I don't go to a ceremony, Fitriani will ask me why I didn't attend."

Although not all lineage members agreed that Fitriani was the most knowledgeable person, they did not question her power as highest-ranking female elder. This acceptance of her power as lineage elder reflects a commonsense understanding of Fitriani. She is the controller of house and land, the wielder of lineage power; people disagree with her at the risk of serious consequences. It is this perception of his mother that made it impossible for the son to simply name his stepfather as the head of Fitriani's household. His stepfather is a guest in his mother's house, not the figure of household head that the state label invokes.

Senior women readily told me other stories of the power of high-ranking women. I asked one senior woman about her responsibilities as lineage elder. She said, "When a person dies, the family will come and ask, when will I attend, when should the person be buried, what should relatives take to the family, and I will tell them. For marriages, [I tell them] when it will be, what type of clothes they should wear, and what should be slaughtered. For circumcision, [I tell them] what to provide, what extent of ceremony can be carried out. If someone wants a divorce, I will talk to the wife so it won't happen." While I was talking to a *penghulu* one day at his house, a woman came to the door seeking his mother-in-law, a tiny woman in her seventies. (The *penghulu* was, after all, living in his wife's house.) The two women talked for ten minutes about the arrangements for the woman's son's wedding. I asked the *penghulu* why this woman had sought out his mother-in-law to discuss these matters. He said, "She is the commander (*komandan*)." His use of the term *komandan* was unusual. It emphasized the control senior women have over others below them in the lineage. He told me that as senior woman, his mother-in-law had to be informed and must give her consent to any decision made by women who were members of the client lineage. In the examples shown here, women's power, substantiated through *adat,* forms part of people's commonsense understanding of gender relations.

This understanding of women's power conflicts with the state model of womanhood, producing disparities in the way different people represent gender. Despite women's power within the lineage, the majority of men and women who answered my question about household head gave the name of the resident male. Younger women uniformly named their husbands. On the other hand, several older high-ranking women, Fitriani included, named themselves as household heads. To try to resolve the disparities, I posed a slightly different question, one that avoided use of the term *kepala keluarga.* I asked, who holds authority (*yang berwewenang*) in the sublineage (the group that has land in common, often coequal with household). More than half the people responded with the name of their *penghulu* (56 percent), while the remainder (44 percent) named the senior woman and the *penghulu* or the senior woman alone as the ones who held authority in the sublineage.[11] When I asked people whom they would go to for the resolution of disputes or for advice within their family (sublineage), the percentage of those who said they would consult the *penghulu* dropped from 56 to 35.[12] For respondents from elite lineages, that percentage dropped even lower, to 24. Thus, when people were given a specific context in which an elder must be consulted, such as finding a marriage partner, deciding to pawn land, resolving a quarrel, or conducting a ceremony, they named the senior woman.

The tendency of the majority of people to name a man as household head, I would argue, has more to do with providing the expected answer than with actual relations within the household. *Kepala keluarga* is, after all, an Indonesian term and not a cultural category for the Minangkabau. Given a category that does not fit with Minangkabau practice, people are willing to pay lip service to state ideology, but in so doing they are not necessarily representing Minangkabau household relations. The range of responses I received suggests that the commonsense understanding of gender continues to shape people's perceptions; there is no one dominant or official representation of authority within the village.

The disparities in the way people represent power are not only due to state gender ideology. Another reason people readily articulate men's power and misrepresent women's is because men's power has been consistently underwritten by Dutch colonial practices. Dutch colonial authorities in West Sumatra assumed that the titled male was the lineage chief and traditional authority of the Minangkabau (Kahn 1976; Sanday 1990). Their writings make no mention of the equivalent position of the senior woman. The Dutch plan of control in Indonesia was to bolster local authority figures so that they could carry out colonial policies. The Dutch installed the highest-ranking *penghulu* as village head in each village and used other *penghulu* as assistants to the chief. They also bolstered male authority through the establishment of a court system in which only a male lineage head could represent a lineage in disputes; a woman could not represent herself (K. Benda-Beckmann 1984:56). The result of these impositions on Minangkabau society was a curtailment of women's participation in areas identified by the Dutch as political or civic.

These historical processes continued under Indonesian rule and helped to validate male *adat* experts who represented men as authorities. *Lembaga Kerapatan Adat Alam Minangkabau* (LKAAM [Association of *Adat* Councils of the Minangkabau World]) was formed in 1970 by a group of educated, urban *penghulu*, many of whom held state office, for the purpose of preserving and disseminating information about Minangkabau *adat*. Many Minangkabau consider this organization to be the official authority on Minangkabau *adat*. Because LKAAM is organized under state auspices, however, its publications go to considerable lengths to align *adat* principles with the State's Five Principles (*Pancasila*, the guiding principles for the state and development) and other state directives.[13] Consequently, their publications highlight male leadership duties and characteristics, while emphasizing women's child rearing and household management responsibilities (see, for example, LKAAM 1987). This gender representation resonates more closely with the state's ideology of women's domesticity than with the body of *adat* that legitimizes senior women's power in Minangkabau villages. As an ideology of male *adat* experts, this discourse is strongest in the urban areas of West Sumatra, particularly in Padang, the West Sumatran capital. It travels to the villages when the educated or *perantau* (migrants) return home.

In the villages, educated men and *perantau* tend to reproduce the "expert" version of Minangkabau gender, emphasizing the prominence of men in decision making while remaining silent about women's power. I made the following notes about a conversation with a man from an elite lineage. This man was in his forties and was usually away on construction projects, coming home about once every six months. I asked him what his responsibilities were toward his matrilineage.

> He said if he is at home, he attends *baralek* [ceremonial feasts], and the deliberations beforehand. He said men's role is heavy (*berat*) during deliberations. I asked what they have to do. He said men have to make the decisions. They decide how many goats to slaughter, how much rice to cook. When I questioned this and said, "Aren't the women the ones who know about cooking?" he said, "Yes, they decide how much to make and the men tell them if they should make more." I said, "Don't people make decisions together?" He said, "Yes, everything is decided together" (*bersama-sama*). (Fieldnotes 7/29/90)

In his representation of gender relations, men take center stage in handling lineage affairs and making decisions. Despite his agreement that everything is done by consensus, he describes women in a way that suggests they follow men's orders. His statement was typical of the way this particular group of men emphasize their own importance and construe gender in general.

Male *adat* experts, such as those in LKAAM, produce knowledge about *adat* that emphasizes male dominance, asserting the primacy of titled men in decision making and authority within the lineage. They thereby marginalize female elders (*Bundo Kanduang*) and underscore the state ideology of domesticity. Even though Minangkabau urban male intellectuals are otherwise proud to define their culture as a "matriarchate," women are excluded from their discourse (Sanday 1990:163). The absence of representations of women as lineage elders and leaders in the literature and discourse of urban male *adat* experts buttresses an impression that only men are *adat* experts and leaders within the Minangkabau community. This discourse substantiates men's power and has some influence in everyday life, but because it is urban- rather than village-based, it has not undermined the legitimacy of women's power.

Educated urban Minangkabau women are not silent in this discourse. A Minangkabau woman, who is a district official in the Department of Education and Culture (*Tingkat* II), told me that Minangkabau women have power and control in their households and lineages. Such educated women argue for increased political activity among women and try to counter what they see as a tendency toward the "Indonesianization" of Minangkabau women (Thaib 1987). Following LKAAM by several years (1974), a group of these women set up their own organization parallel to but separate from LKAAM, which they call Bundo Kanduang. Its goal is to promote the education and prosperity of Minangkabau women. This group is not as well recognized or as influential as LKAAM.

Within these gender discourses in West Sumatra runs an equally strong text drawn from Islamic scholars. People have access to national Islamic discourse through commercially produced cassettes, televised sermons and publications of nationally-known Islamic scholars. Many Minangkabau women in Taram talk about themselves in terms that reflect this national discourse.[14] Some of the women in the village interpreted Islamic teachings about husband/wife relations to mean that a wife is not supposed to leave her house without her husband's permission, unless it is related to household affairs—to go to the market, for instance. While such a custom may be more applicable to young married women, even older women firmly in control of their households insisted that they needed their husband's permission to go out. If the husband is home, the wife should be there too, I was told. This perception of the husband's control led one divorced woman to tell me that she was actually happy not to have a husband around because she could come and go as she pleased. Another woman told me that, according to Islam, a good wife must submit to the wishes of her husband, unless he is being unreasonable.[15] Such statements suggest a correspondence between their interpretation of the husband/wife relation and their own lives. But viewed in the larger context of Minangkabau gender relations, where women own their own households, land and businesses, and their husbands provide assistance, these statements seem ambiguous at best.

Women also discuss work in ways that situate it within the house, another reflection of state and Islamic ideologies and the discourse of male *adat* experts. Some women, particularly those who are well-to-do, claim that they are simply housewives. This situation may have more to do with their wealth and desire to be thought of as nonworking middle-class women than with their actual belief in the ideology of domesticity. Women who were otherwise busy farmers or active in community affairs declared to me that it was more important to stay home and take care of the children. Several women overseers told me that they were housewives (*ibu rumah tangga*) despite the fact that they managed their own rice fields. Two women mill owners were quick to say that it was their husbands who ran the business and not they. One mill owner, who is no longer actively involved with the mill business, told me she preferred to "stay home" and take care of her family. "There is plenty of work [housework] to be done at home," she said. A woman rice merchant told me her husband does all the work, but when I pressed her about her business, she revealed that she was the one who buys the rice at harvest from her clients and has it brought to the mill, while her husband handles the processing and sale of rice at the mill. In their conversations with me, elite, well-to-do women were intent on proving that they fulfilled the housewife role. Their statements suggest that the categories of "household," "domestic," and "work" are becoming synonymous for women, particularly those more educated and familiar with state models of gender and media representations of women.

Although these women prefer to accentuate their domesticity in line with other models of gender, the prevalence of this discourse has not led to any considerable shift within household relations. In actual practice, the husband continues to be peripheral to his wife's house and has no authority over her productive activities or her activities within her lineage. Most husbands in the hamlet of Tanjung Batang in Taram move to their wives' residences at marriage (91 out of 116 households). The few cases of male-headed or joint households in that hamlet consisted largely of families who were newcomers to the village or wives who had moved to their husbands' houses because their own families were very poor. As young wives in their mothers' households, women are busy following the orders of their mothers, not their husbands. One newlywed in the village garnered considerable sympathy from her neighbors because she was always running errands for her mother and taking care of several younger siblings while her mother worked in her rice fields.[16] A husband is an honored guest in his wife's house. His children belong to his wife's kin group and he is an outsider in all affairs within her matrilineage.[17] Women handle lineage affairs, including the affairs of their children, together with their brothers or other male relatives. As one of my male consultants told me, his children are, after all, someone else's nieces and nephews (*kamanakan orang punya*).

A husband is expected to contribute to the family income but has no control over his wife's property or her income from that property. Women provide for their own households by farming their lineage rice land or through other income-earning activities. Many husbands and wives work together on their rice lands but even income from land worked jointly belongs to the wife to run her household or invest as she sees fit. One older elite woman laughingly told me that she gives her husband cigarette money in payment for his labor on her rice fields. Even if the couple builds their own house together, it is legally considered the woman's property. At divorce a husband leaves behind his contributions to his wife's household and returns to his mother's house. In Taram the husband's position in the household contradicts both state and Islamic ideology concerning his role as household head and provider. Consequently, Minangkabau practices and perceptions underscore women's power in a way that counters alternative discourses, allowing for multiple interpretations of gender.

PKK AND VILLAGE ADMINISTRATION

The state-imposed village administration is the final site in which I will explore the contradictions of gender in West Sumatra. Village administration brings state directives and programs into direct daily contact with the villagers. The frequent meetings of the various administrative committees (social welfare, security, development) add another cadence to the rounds of ceremonial and agricultural events in the village.

State-imposed village projects, particularly PKK (Family Welfare Organization), have had considerable bearing on women's views of themselves. As mentioned earlier, PKK is a voluntary organization and is the main channel used by the state to reach women at the grass-roots level (Royal Netherlands Embassy 1987). Although only high-ranking or wealthy women are elected to village administrative offices, PKK, which is quite successful in Taram, reaches out to large numbers of women. Many of the younger women from elite and client lineages attend PKK activities; its leadership is composed of elite women in their forties and fifties. How do these women manage the contradictory meanings of gender within PKK and the village administration?

PKK in Taram conducts the typical social-cultural programs required by the state, hosting events such as cooking contests and cosmetics classes (which promote cosmetics that most women cannot afford). Because PKK-mandated activities are not always in keeping with the needs of women in the village, however, these women have taken the initiative to organize other activities for their members. PKK has purchased a large quantity of dishes, glassware, and pots that are lent out for a small fee to families for use at ceremonies. Its members volunteer to help with food preparation and service at ceremonies, helping to spread the burden of ceremonies beyond the immediate kin. Through its involvement in ceremonial affairs, PKK in Taram has turned the domestic policies of the state to broader purpose, creating new practices that incorporate both state directives and *adat*. Because PKK blurs the distinction between "domestic" and kinship affairs, the "wife" category takes a back seat to other meanings of Minangkabau womanhood.

The situation with the village administration is more problematic for women. The Village Law of 1979 created the current structure for village governance. It established a village council (LMD, Lembaga Musyawarah Desa) that handles village operations, and a village security council (LKMD, Lembaga Ketahanan Masyarakat Desa) that advises the village head on development activities and coordinates all state activities at the village level (Sinaga 1985; MacAndrews 1986). This structure is designed to integrate village society more closely with the state "by linking it systematically into a coordinated and elaborate scheme for national development" (Watson 1987:57).

Village council members are chosen from the leading influential and educated village members. Most come from the ranks of male *adat* leaders but some council members are wealthy farmers, business people, or civil servants (*orang besar,* big person). Consequently, villagers now make the distinction between *adat* leaders (*pemuka adat*) whose leadership is based on *adat* principles, and community leaders (*pemuka desa*), prominent and respected members of the village but without high rank in the kinship hierarchy. The prominence of community leaders suggests that new status categories have become salient in the village, though these categories are still closely linked to *adat* and the kinship hierarchy.

Younger, educated women (mostly in their forties), who are either *adat* leaders or *orang besar,* make up over 40 percent of the twenty-eight-member village security council (LKMD). One woman was elected to the nine-member LMD. Because state directives require PKK participation on the village council, most women are members of the village council through their participation in PKK (at an LKMD meeting, eleven out of the twelve women attending were members of PKK). As PKK representatives, these women are directed to handle issues of family welfare. Thus, PKK leaders face a contradiction between their broader authority as community and *adat* leaders and the limited nature of their responsibility as PKK leaders.

Another ideological slippage that has occurred in women's participation in village administration concerns the role of older women, that is, women of the generation born in the 1920s and 1930s. Older women from elite lineages are lineage elders and represent the power of women in lineage affairs, but they also are thought to be too old-fashioned to participate in village administration.[18] According to state propaganda, modern Indonesians should exhibit a new "rational and dynamic way of thinking," not the traditional way of the village (Sullivan 1983:168). Older women always wear sarongs and cover their hair with a scarf whereas younger women wear skirts and blouses. Many older women have had only three years of elementary school—all the education that was available for most children at that time—and are not fluent in the national language. Unlike them, many women in their twenties, thirties, and forties received a high school education and some are college-educated; many have lived in urban areas for some length of time and are more accepting of nationalist values. Older women are said to hold certain beliefs that younger, educated women feel are outmoded. For instance, I was told that women of the older generation would not feel comfortable sitting on chairs in the Village Office, or being in the same room as their daughters' husbands at village council meetings. Thus, whereas the older generation of women ruled by virtue of their position as lineage heads in accordance with *adat* principles, in village administration only the younger generation of women serve.

At the village council meetings I attended, the men, many of whom were members of the *adat* council, were more outspoken than the women. The two groups sat in sex-segregated fashion, men on one side and women on the other nearer the door. The meeting was chaired by the male village head. During the meeting one or two women occasionally voiced an opinion but most of their talking was carried out in whispers among themselves. Of the men, three or four out of the eleven present did most of the talking while the others sat quietly. No formal votes were taken, and if no strong disagreement was expressed, the meeting moved on. Although this council is part of the state system, the seating arrangement and decision-making procedures incorporated Minangkabau practices, thus reflecting an interweaving of state bureaucratic methods with Minangkabau *adat*.

Nurani's Story

The contradictory meaning of gender is embodied in the person of Nurani, the one woman elected to the village council (LMD). Nurani is in her early forties, divorced with two children, one attending university and the other now a civil servant; Nurani completed a high school education. She is a member of an elite lineage and takes her social responsibilities as an elite woman seriously. She frequently participates in ceremonies in the village, representing her sublineage as senior woman (her mother is in her seventies), knows *adat,* prays faithfully, fasts and pays the tithe. Nurani's family is well-to-do, possessing numerous rice fields that Nurani ably manages for her mother and younger sisters. The profit from Nurani's own rice fields enabled her to become a rice merchant. Many of the village's wealthy elite are her clients, including the village head and his sister, who are constantly in debt to her and forced to sell most of their rice to her at harvest to pay it off.

Nurani has become a big person (*orang besar*) in the eyes of village folk. She is considered a modern farmer (*tani moderen*) because of her success in adopting new farming technology in her rice fields. The rice she grows has a reputation of high quality among rice buyers. She is also said to be rich by most others but herself. Nurani is very active in civic activities within Taram. Because of her contributions to the community, her success as a businesswoman and the respect she has in the community, she was appointed to the village council.

Nurani is the only woman on the village council who does not represent PKK, even though she is a PKK member. Before council meetings, she discusses the matter at hand with other women from PKK so they can agree on a position. The head of LKMD, who is also Nurani's business partner, frequently comes to Nurani's house to discuss both business and village council matters with her. At council meetings she sits attentively with the women, participates in low-voiced discussion with them, and of the women is the most outspoken. Of her participation in discussion, Nurani says she does not need to speak up if she agrees with the men's statements; her presence alone is important.

Nurani's style in village council meetings invokes the style of lineage deliberations where men make the formal speeches and women interject their opinions only when they disagree. Much of Nurani's political work is done in private discussions with other women or with the head of LKMD, the same pattern used by titled men to settle disputes. Nurani is not silenced in these meetings by male authority, rather she follows the Minangkabau pattern for public deliberations, a pattern that allots the formal speaking role to men but demands consensus among all members.

How does she feel about her position? Nurani complains that it is too much work for her to be on the council. She told me she does not have time for council work because of her responsibilities as a business woman and single mother. The meetings are always late in the evening, she says, and she should be home taking care of her daughter (who is twenty-two years old). Although she was elected to this position because of her status as a well-to-do, educated, elite business woman, her statements to me conveyed the sense that it was more important for her to be a good mother first.

Nurani's attitude expresses some of the contradictions of womanhood she faces. Her ambivalence about operating in a domain that has been defined as public and male speaks to the tensions created by contradictory state, Islamic and Minangkabau ideologies of gender. She was, in fact, embarrassed to be called head of household. On the other hand, she is a powerful woman in the village, and a recognized leader whose opinions are respected in council matters. Even though she represents herself in accordance with the ideology of domesticity, she expresses the power of Minangkabau lineage elders. Although she—and other women like her—may find it difficult to articulate the significance of their leadership at the village level, their positions as village and *adat* leaders bridge multiple ideologies of gender, providing the opportunity to reshape notions of women's power.

CONCLUSION

Geared to national development, Indonesian state policies, programs, and agencies form, in Foucault's words, "the apparatus and technologies of power" that reconstruct categories of gender for its citizens. While privileging males as producers and protectors, the Indonesian state consigns women to "domestic" reproduction. In an attempt to create a modern family compatible with the needs of nationhood and capitalist development, the agents of the state ideologically transform Indonesian women from productive actors into model housewives. This state discourse is bolstered by the practice and theory of development economics and the Islamic discourse on womanhood and is underwritten in West Sumatra by the discourse of urban male *adat* experts.

Despite the dominance of these discourses, I do not grant them hegemonic or official status as the shapers of gender because of the continuing power of gender ideology and practice legitimated in *adat*. Rather, I suggest that there are multiple interpretations of gender available to women in West Sumatra. As Bourdieu states, the range of these discourses enables "agents to generate an infinity of practices adapted to endlessly changing situations . . ." (1977:16). In the Minangkabau situation, contradictions between the state's development-driven construction of gender, Islamic discourse and Minangkabau gender ideology create disparities in people's representation of gender. The resulting conflicts may pull women toward the domestic model created for them by the state, particularly well-to-do women who are not highly placed in the kinship hierarchy. In their every-day speech in Taram these women may pay lip service to state models of gender by speaking of themselves as housewives, while representing men as decision makers. They may even downplay the extent of their own power, particularly in situations where state practices legitimate male authority, as in the village and *adat* councils, or where Muslim practices call for their acknowledgement of the husband's primacy.

At the same time, women continue to wield significant power within the village. The representations and practices of *adat* in Taram encode a gender ideology that powerfully defines women as heads of lineages and controllers of land. Women's power, because it is naturalized, is not readily discussed. But senior women act on their taken-for-granted power to control their own households and rice land as well as the affairs of their subordinate kin. State structures are present in the village but they are not all-pervasive. The core of village life continues to be centered around the ceremonial and kinship relations in which women's power is most evident, reinforcing cultural perceptions that keep women from being marginalized despite ideologies legitimating men's power.

Minangkabau women operate within a number of alternative discourses, none of which are exclusive. Their actions cannot be construed as a subversive challenge nor resistance to dominant ideologies because their power is legitimated in village discourse and substantiated by *adat*. In their efforts to manage their identities in the village, women may emphasize in turn idioms of modernity or religion or *adat*, or they may play up their rank, wealth or standing within the community. The use of these discourses is highly contextualized and variable, the result of differences in power, rank and wealth. Ultimately, the multiplicity of discourses fosters subtle shifts in social identity, gender and power as rural elite women seek new constructions that mediate among alternative ideologies.

Although I emphasize the strength of local ideologies, I also maintain that in the process of nation building, states actively create homogeneous categories of male and female bodies. In the postcolonial period, these bodies are fit into reworked models of the public/domestic that often ignore the realities of household and gender relations. How these new categories of gender are received depends in large part on the particular historical and social circumstances in which people are located. As the Minangkabau case shows, the power of state and Islamic ideologies to redefine gender is mediated by the cultural *habitus* and presence of strong alternative discourses. Although the Indonesian state has the power to create and instill new definitions and identities for its citizens, the Minangkabau rework these definitions within their ideologies of gender and rank, kinship and matriliny.

NOTES

This paper is based on field research conducted in West Sumatra for sixteen months in 1989 and 1990, with the assistance of funds from the Department of Anthropology, Stanford University. A 1992–93 predoctoral fellowship at the East-West Center in Honolulu, Hawaii, was very beneficial to me in developing my ideas for this paper. I would like to express my great appreciation to the following people for their insightful comments on various drafts of this paper: Patricia Horvatich, Michael Peletz, Aihwa Ong, Jane Collier, Deb Amory, Sue Reinhold, Geoffrey White, Joel Streicker, and Gigi Weix.

1. I do not mean to suggest that these are the only factors creating a "new" definition of womanhood. The Dutch also had a prominent role in constructing certain notions of womanhood in the colonial period prior to Indonesian independence. Dutch influence as well as Javanese notions of gender and power may be formative in the current construction of gender, which is thereby not necessarily "new" but revised. Consideration of these factors, however, is beyond the scope of this paper.

2. Whalley does distinguish between *adat* and Islam in her work. In my discussion I do not try to separately determine the impact of *adat* or Islam on any particular set of behaviors or norms, as the Minangkabau in Taram do not make such distinctions. They told me, for instance, that any ceremony they hold is both Islamic and Minangkabau.

3. I have chosen to use the actual name of the village where I worked. It was the site of an earlier study (Bachtiar 1967) in which the name of the village was used, and is already known to the government officials from whom I received permission for this study. The names of the hamlets and people in the village have been changed, however, to protect their privacy.

4. For instance, as Pak (1986) points out, the marriage system is not an exchange of women, as suggested by Josselin de Jong (1952), but an exchange of men (see also Peletz [1987] for the culturally similar case of Negeri Sembilan, the region in Malaysia settled by Minangkabau).

5. The Minangkabau terms are: *Limpapeh Rumah nan Gadang, Umbun Puruak Pegangan Kunci* (Rajo Penghulu 1978:21).

6. My interpretation of Minangkabau gender is based on fieldwork in one village in West Sumatra and may not be consistent with findings in other areas. West Sumatra has distinct regional cultural variations, more notably between rural and urban areas, but also among villages in different provinces and with different land resources. Taram in 1989 had an adequate land base to support its population and did not suffer from excessive out-migration (19 percent). The local population, in particular elite women, had firm control of rice land.

7. According to a Minangkabau scholar, the meaning of *Bundo Kanduang* extends beyond its translation as "womb mother" to the broader sense of "elder" and "wise woman" (Sjamsir Syarif 1993. Personal communication.) I use the terms "senior woman" and "female elder" interchangeably in this essay to refer to female heads of *kaum*s and lineages.

8. For instance, in land disputes such as that described by Krier (this volume), the opinions and claims made by a titled male will have greater weight in disputes than those of a family or individual with no claim to title (such as Mak Nia whose claim to land was the promise made by a "neighbor"). The advantage of the titled male does not necessarily signify male dominance, as Krier suggests; it may attest to the importance of rank and descent in land disputes. The power of a *penghulu* is further limited by the fact that he controls or disposes of land only when there are no remaining members of his sublineage. Analyses of gender and power in Minangkabau society need to take into account the complexities of rank and identity as well as gender. (For further discussion of this point, see Blackwood 1993).

9. Women have been using their rice harvest as a source of cash for at least forty years, however. Older women told me they used to sell small amounts of husked rice in the market when they needed cash.

10. Several state programs and offices have belatedly directed their efforts toward strengthening women's economic position (Sjahrir 1985; Royal Netherlands Embassy 1987; KOWANI 1980), but the primacy of women's domestic role remains a continuing theme.

11. The people interviewed lived in the hamlet of Tanjung Batang and represented a range of households, including all three ranks and all household incomes (poor to wealthy). For this question, total respondents numbered 16, of which 12 were women and 4 men. One of the men (Fitriani's nephew) and one-half of the women named a woman or both men and women as the authorities in the sublineage.

12. Of the 29 respondents to this question, 20 were women and 9 were men. Twelve of the women and 2 of the men (both *penghulu*) stated that they would go to the senior woman first. Although the responses to my questions varied across gender, rank and age, the majority of women tended to identify a senior woman as the person they would consult first while men predominantly identified the *penghulu*.

13. The state declared in 1982 that all state-sponsored policies, programs and "mass organizations" must reflect the *Pancasila* in their purposes (Morfit 1986).

14. In some parts of Southeast Asia, men are thought to possess *akal*, or reason, in greater degree than women, while women are said to have greater passion, or *nafsu*, than men. Although in such areas these terms are quite central to notions of gender (see Peletz, this volume, for Malaysia), the same is not the case in all parts of West Sumatra. Whalley (1993) does not mention these terms in her in-depth study of Islam at one of the Islamic centers for women in West Sumatra. Nor did I hear reference to them in conversations in Taram. In fact, Minangkabau folklore suggests an opposite interpretation. Minangkabau stories of the mythical female figure *Bundo Kanduang* describe her as a wise woman (Tanner 1971), which resonates with the meaning of *akal*. In general women in the village where I worked were not represented as less wise than men. In fact, several female consultants credited men with less ability to control their passions (*nafsu*) than women. Young men especially were said to be irresponsible. These women claimed that men are unable to go without sex but women have more restraint. This difference in Islamic

representations of gender points to the variability within Islamic discourses and across regions.

15. Whalley (1993) argues that urban middle-class Minangkabau women are creating their own version of Islam and modernity, one in which women have a right to a career and to positions of public leadership. Her argument is based on a study of urban women educated at *Diniyah Putri*, a private Islamic boarding school for girls. The difference between her interpretation and mine may reflect the differences between urban women and rural women, whose access to the writings and speeches of Islamic scholars may be limited to those in the media. Whalley does note, however, that even the *Diniyah* ideal emphasizes a woman's role as wife and mother (1993:20).

16. In such a situation a young woman might find it very useful to argue that as a good Muslim wife, she must follow her husband on *merantau*. Such threats can be used to loosen her mother's control over her.

17. Peletz (1987), who draws the same conclusion for the similar case of nineteenth-century Negeri Sembilan, states that the husband actually had fewer rights in his wife than the wife had in her husband.

18. The distinction in age also holds for men. Younger men serve on the council rather than senior men.

REFERENCES

Abdullah, Taufik. 1971. *Schools and Politics: The Kaum Muda Movement in West Sumatra (1927–1933)*. Modern Indonesia Project. Ithaca: Cornell University.

Bachtiar, Harsja W. 1967. *"Negeri* Taram: A Minangkabau Village Community." In Koentjaraningrat, ed., *Villages in Indonesia*, pp. 348–385. Ithaca: Cornell University Press.

Benda-Beckmann, Franz von. 1979. *Property in Social Continuity: Continuity and Change in the Maintenance of Property Relationships through Time in Minangkabau, West Sumatra*. The Hague: Martinus Nijhoff.

Benda-Beckmann, Keebet von. 1984. *The Broken Stairways to Consensus: Village Justice and State Courts in Minangkabau*. Cinnamonson, N.J.: Foris Publications.

Blackwood, Evelyn. 1991. "The Marriage of the Miller's Daughter: Politics of Identity in a Minangkabau Village." Paper presented at the Ninetieth Annual Meeting of the American Anthropological Association, Chicago.

———. 1993. "The Politics of Daily Life: Gender, Kinship and Identity in a Minangkabau Village, West Sumatra, Indonesia." Ph.D. diss., Stanford University.

Bourdieu, Pierre. 1977. *Outline of a Theory of Practice*. Cambridge: Cambridge University Press.

Bowen, John. 1986. "On the Political Construction of Tradition: *Gotong Royong* in Indonesia." *Journal of Asian Studies* 45(3):545–561.

Colfer, Carol J., Veronica Kasmini, Atin Kurdiana, and Russell Yost. n.d. "Time Allocation Studies: A Methodology for Food Production Systems." Unpublished ms. Honolulu: University of Hawaii and Center for Soils Research.

Delaney, Carol. 1991. *The Seed and the Soil: Gender and Cosmology in Turkish Village Society*. Berkeley: University of California Press.

Djamas, Nurhayati. 1985. "Women in the Eyes of Islam." *Mizan* 2(2):22–28.

Dobbin, Christine. 1983. *Islamic Revivalism in a Changing Peasant Economy: Central Sumatra, 1784–1847*. London: Curzon Press.

Ellen, Roy F. 1983. "Social Theory, Ethnography and the Understanding of Practical Islam in South-East Asia." In M. B. Hooker, ed., *Islam in Southeast Asia*, pp. 50–91. Leiden: E. J. Brill.

Errington, Shelly. 1990. "Recasting Sex, Gender, and Power: A Theoretical and Regional Overview." In Jane Atkinson and Shelly Errington, eds., *Power and Difference: Gender in Island Southeast Asia*, pp. 1–58. Stanford: Stanford University Press.

Esmara, Hendra. 1974. *The Economic Development of West Sumatra: Collected Papers*. Padang: Andalas University and Provincial Development Planning Agency, West Sumatra.

Folbre, Nancy. 1986. "Cleaning House: New Perspectives on Households and Economic Development." *Journal of Development Economics* 22:5–40.

Foster, Robert J. 1991. "Making National Cultures in the Global Ecumene." *Annual Review of Anthropology* 20:235–60.

Foucault, Michel. 1979. *Discipline and Punish: The Birth of the Prison*. New York: Vintage Books.

———. 1980. *Power/Knowledge: Selected Interviews and Other Writings, 1972–1977*. New York: Pantheon Books.

Grijns, Mies. 1992. "Tea-pickers in West Java as Mothers and Workers: Female Work and Women's Jobs." In Elsbeth Locher-Scholten and Anke Niehof, eds., *Indonesian Women in Focus: Past and Present Notions*, pp. 104–119. Leiden: Koninklijk Instituut Voor Taal-, Land-, en Volkenkunde.

Hefner, Robert W. 1987. "Islamizing Java? Religion and Politics in Rural East Java." *Journal of Asian Studies* 46(3):533–554.

Horvatich, Patricia. 1992. "Mosques, Misunderstandings, and the True Islam: Muslim Discourses in Tawi-Tawi, Philippines." Ph.D. diss., Stanford University.

Johns, A. H., ed. and trans. 1958. *Rantjak Dilabueh, A Minangkabau Kaba: A Specimen of the Traditional Literature of Central Sumatra*. Ithaca: Cornell University, Southeast Asia Program.

Josselin de Jong, P. E. de. 1952. *Minangkabau and Negri Sembilan: Socio-Political Structure in Indonesia*. Leiden: Eduard Ijdo N. V.

Kahn, J. S. 1976. " 'Tradition,' Matriliny and Change among the Minangkabau of Indonesia." *Bijdragen tot de Taal-, Land- en Volkenkunde* 132:45–95.

Kato, Tsuyoshi. 1982. *Matriliny and Migration: Evolving Minangkabau Traditions in Indonesia*. Ithaca: Cornell University Press.

KOWANI. 1980. *The Role of Women in Development: The Indonesian Experience*. Jakarta: KOWANI.

Langenberg, Michael van. 1986. "Analysing Indonesia's New Order State: A Keywords Approach." *Review of Indonesian and Malaysian Affairs* 20(2):1–47.

LKAAM (Lembaga Kerapatan Adat Alam Minangkabau). 1987. *Pelajaran Adat Minangkabau (Sejarah dan Budaya)* (A Study in Minangkabau *Adat* [History and Culture]). Padang: LKAAM.

Lutz, Nancy. 1992. "Constructing the 'Modern' Indonesian Woman." Paper presented at the Conference on the Narrative and Practice of Gender in Southeast Asian Cultures, Ninth Annual Berkeley Conference on Southeast Asian Studies, University of California, Berkeley.

MacAndrews, Colin, ed. 1986. *Central Government and Local Development in Indonesia.* Singapore: Oxford University Press.

Manderson, Lenore. 1980. "Rights and Responsibilities, Power and Privilege: Women's Role in Contemporary Indonesia." In *Kartini Centenary: Indonesian Women Then and Now,* pp. 69–92. Melbourne: Monash University.

Maretin, J. 1961. "Disappearance of Matriclan Survivals in Minangkabau Family and Marriage Relations." *Bijdragen tot de Taal-, Land-, en Volkenkunde* 117:168–195.

Morfit, Michael. 1986. "*Pancasila* Orthodoxy." In Colin MacAndrews, ed., *Central Government and Local Development in Indonesia,* pp. 42–55. Singapore: Oxford University Press.

Ng, Cecilia. 1987. "The Weaving of Prestige: Village Women's Representations of the Social Categories of Minangkabau Society." Ph.D. diss., Australian National University.

Ong, Aihwa. 1987. *Spirits of Resistance and Capitalist Discipline: Factory Women in Malaysia.* Albany: SUNY Press.

———. 1990. "State versus Islam: Malay Families, Women's Bodies, and the Body Politic in Malaysia." *American Ethnologist* 17(2):258–276.

———. 1991. "The Gender and Labor Politics of Postmodernity." *Annual Review of Anthropology* 20:279–309.

Pak, Ok-Kyung. 1986. "Lowering the High, Raising the Low: The Gender, Alliance and Property Relations in a Minangkabau Peasant Community of West Sumatra, Indonesia." Ph.D. diss., Université Laval.

Papanek, Hanna. 1984. "Women-in-development and Women's Studies: Agenda for the Future." Working Paper no. 55. East Lansing: Michigan State University.

Peletz, Michael G. 1987. "The Exchange of Men in 19th-Century Negeri Sembilan (Malaya)." *American Ethnologist* 14(3):449–469.

Pramono, Dewi Motik. 1990. "Woman and Career in Islam." *Mizan* 3(1):72–75.

Prindiville, Joanne. 1981. "The Image and Role of Minangkabau Women." In G. Hainsworth, ed., *Southeast Asia: Women, Changing Social Structure and Cultural Continuity,* pp. 26–33. Ottowa: University of Ottowa Press.

———. 1985. "Mother, Mother's Brother and Modernization: The Problems and Prospects of Minangkabau Matriliny in a Changing World." In Lynn Thomas and Franz von Benda-Beckmann, eds., *Change and Continuity in Minangkabau: Local, Regional, and Historical Perspectives on West Sumatra,* pp. 29–43. Monographs in International Studies, Southeast Asia Series, no. 71. Athens, Ohio: Ohio University.

Rajo Penghulu, H. Idrus Hakimy Dt. 1978. *Pokok-Pokok Pengetahuan Adat Alam Minangkabau.* Bandung: Remadja Karya CV.

Raliby, Osman. 1985. "The Position of Women in Islam." *Mizan* 2(2):29–37.

Rasyad, Aminuddin. 1985. "Rahmah El Yunusiyyah—Educational Pioneer for Girls." *Mizan* 2(2):48–63.

Reeve, David. 1985. *Golkar of Indonesia: An Alternative to the Party System.* Singapore: Oxford University Press.

Rieffel, Alexis. 1969. "The BIMAS Program for Self-sufficiency in Rice Production." *Indonesia* 8:103–134.

Robinson, Kathryn M. 1989. "Choosing Contraception: Cultural Change and the Indonesian Family Planning Programme." In Paul Alexander, ed., *Creating Indonesian Cultures*, pp. 21–38. Sydney: Oceania Publications.

Royal Netherlands Embassy. 1987. *Women and Development in Indonesia.* Jakarta: Development Cooperation Department.

Salyo, Suwarni. 1985. "Islamic Influences on the Lives of Women in Indonesia." *Mizan* 2(2):15–21.

Sanday, Peggy Reeves. 1990. "Androcentric and Matrifocal Gender Representations in Minangkabau Ideology." In Peggy R. Sanday and Ruth G. Goodenough, eds., *Beyond the Second Sex: New Directions in the Anthropology of Gender*, pp. 139–168. Philadelphia: University of Pennsylvania Press.

Schneider, David, and Kathleen Gough, eds. 1961. *Matrilineal Kinship.* Berkeley: University of California Press.

Schrieke, B. 1955. *Indonesian Sociological Studies: Selected Writings of B. Schrieke*, Part One. The Hague: W. van Hoeve, Ltd.

Schwede, Laurel Kathleen. 1991. "Family Strategies of Labor Allocation and Decision-making in a Matrilineal, Islamic Society: The Minangkabau of West Sumatra, Indonesia." Ph.D. diss., Cornell University.

Sinaga, S. M. 1985. *Himpunan Peraturan Pemerintahan Desa & Kelurahan.* Jakarta: PT. Bhuana Pancakarsa.

Sjahrir, Kartini. 1985. "Wanita: Beberapa Catatan Antropologis." (Women: Some Anthropological Notes) *Prisma* 10:3–15.

Stoler, Ann L. 1977. "Class Structure and Female Autonomy in Rural Java. *Signs* 3(1):74–89.

———. 1985. *Capitalism and Confrontation in Sumatra's Plantation Belt, 1870–1979.* New Haven: Yale University Press.

———. 1991. "Carnal Knowledge and Imperial Power: Gender, Race and Morality in Colonial Asia." In Micaela di Leonardo, ed., *Gender at the Crossroads of Knowledge: Feminist Anthropology in the Postmodern Era*, pp. 51–101. Berkeley: University of California Press.

Sullivan, Norma. 1983. "Indonesian Women in Development: State Theory and Urban Kampung Practice." In Lenore Manderson, ed., *Women's Work and Women's Roles: Economics and Everyday Life in Indonesia, Malaysia and Singapore*, pp. 147–171. Canberra: Australian National University.

———. 1989. "The Hidden Economy and Kampung Women." In Paul Alexander, ed., *Creating Indonesian Cultures*, pp. 75–90. Sydney: Oceania Publications.

Tanner, Nancy. 1971. "Minangkabau Disputes." Ph.D. diss., University of California, Berkeley.

Tanner, Nancy, and Lynn Thomas. 1985. "Rethinking Matriliny: Decision-Making and Sex Roles in Minangkabau." In Lynn Thomas and Franz von Benda-Beckmann, eds., *Change and Continuity in Minangkabau: Local, Regional, and Historical Perspectives on West Sumatra*, pp. 45–71. Monographs in International Studies, Southeast Asia Series, no. 71. Athens, Ohio: Ohio University.

Thaib, Raudha. 1987. "Sisi lain wanita Minangkabau." (Another Side of Minangkabau Women.) *Limbago* 2, *Tahun* 2:12–13.

Thomas, R. Murray. 1988. "The Islamic Revival and Indonesian Education." *Asian Survey* 28(9):897–915.

Tinker, Irene, and Millidge Walker. 1973. "Planning for Regional Development in Indonesia." *Asian Survey* 13(12):1102–1120.

Van Esterik, Penny, ed. 1982. *Women of Southeast Asia.* Monograph Series on Southeast Asia, Occasional Paper no. 9. Dekalb, Ill.: Northern Illinois University, Center for Southeast Asian Studies.

Vreede de Steurs, Cora. 1960. *The Indonesian Woman: Struggles and Achievements.* The Hague: Mouton.

Watson, C. W. 1987. *State and Society in Indonesia: Three Papers.* Occasional Paper no. 8. Canterbury: University of Kent, Centre for South-East Asian Studies.

Whalley, Lucy A. 1991. "Who Wears the Veil? The Politics of Women's Dress in West Sumatra, Indonesia." Paper presented at the Ninetieth Annual Meeting of the American Anthropological Association, Chicago.

———. 1993. "Virtuous Women, Productive Citizens: Negotiating Tradition, Islam, and Modernity in Minangkabau, Indonesia." Ph.D. diss., University of Illinois, Urbana-Champaign.

Wieringa, Saskia. 1985. "The Perfumed Nightmare: Some Notes on the Indonesian Women's Movement." Working Papers. The Hague: Institute of Social Studies.

Williams, Brackette. 1989. "A Class Act: Anthropology and the Race to Nation across Ethnic Terrain." *Annual Review of Anthropology* 18:401–444.

Yanagisako, Sylvia. 1987. "Mixed Metaphors: Native and Anthropological Models of Gender and Kinship Domains." In Jane Collier and Sylvia Yanagisako, eds., *Gender and Kinship: Essays toward a Unified Analysis*, pp. 86–118. Stanford: Stanford University Press.

Yanagisako, Sylvia, and Jane Collier. 1987. "Toward a Unified Analysis of Gender and Kinship." In Jane Collier and Sylvia Yanagisako, eds., *Gender and Kinship: Essays toward a Unified Analysis*, pp. 14–50. Stanford: Stanford University Press.

FIVE

State Versus Islam:
Malay Families, Women's Bodies, and the Body Politic in Malaysia

Aihwa Ong

Aihwa Ong examines the contradictory social effects and other consequences of recent developments in state policies and Islamic revivalism in Malaysia, and is especially interested in understanding the origins and implications of the different models of Malay womanhood, family, and kinship that both undergird and infuse Malay(sian) nationalist discourses. Ong argues that the analytically distinct discourses produced in recent years by state agencies and representatives on the one hand and Islamic revivalists on the other are radically divergent in many respects but nonetheless have in common certain overriding (and overdetermined) concerns. These include concerns to control female reproductive roles and thus maintain (or rework) race, class, and religious boundaries between social groups. Ong notes that the discourses of the Islamic resurgents depict Malay Muslim women as both the bearers of racial difference and the embodied markers of boundaries that ideally guard against the intrusions of other races. The state, in competition with Islamic resurgents for Malay constituents, produced a counternarrative celebrating motherhood and fecundity as patriotic contributions to the expanding national economy. Some university-educated women initially resisted, but many soon succumbed to the moral imperatives that defined them as upholders of (invented) traditions, religion, and racial purity. By participating in the creation of a specific Malay Muslim community, they clearly gained a new sense of family and of racial and national belonging.

Ong's analysis reveals how state policies and Islamic resurgence have incited and intensified concerns and ambivalence about female sex, space, and actions, and, more generally, how competing knowledge-power schemes deployed to patrol the borders between races and classes have affected women in different classes in different ways. Partly because the crisis of national identity and attendant moral uncertainty is most pronounced among the middle classes, educated women have tended to embrace the Islamic resurgence and have come to negotiate, in their words and bodily presentations, the changing meanings of resurgent Islam in Malaysian nationalism.

After nearly a decade of struggle between Islamic prosletyzing and official Islam, the country has settled down to a low-key nationalism, a climate that enables female professionals to renegotiate their status within Islam, by reworking local views that women have more "passion" and less "reason" than men (see Brenner and Peletz, this volume). Ong's more general conclusions are that social constructions of gender are always class-specific in both their origins and their effects; and that emergent middle classes seeking to conserve their economic, political, and cultural resources find in religion (if not Islam, then Christianity or other Great Religions) "important sources of rival nationalist ideologies in modernizing societies."

I n the summer of 1990, on my annual visit to Malaysia, I noticed that many young Malay women had traded in their black Islamic robes (*hijab*) for pastel colored ones, and that their headcloths (*mini-telekung*) were now embroidered with flowers. The effect was rather like seeing a black and white film in color. In the late 1970s and early 1980s, when Malaysian campuses were the hotbeds of Islamic resurgence, female students shrouded in black robes and veils sometimes appeared like phalanxes of Allah's soldiers. Now university women were dressed in *hijab* outfits that had been transformed by color and more subtle touches in cut, style, and decoration. As they walked around campus, many attracted the eyes of young men, who were sometimes rewarded with subdued giggles and responsive glances. The Islamic resurgence of the 1970s, emerging in its black female garb and fiery criticism of Western consumerism, official corruption, and the spiritual hollowness of modern life, had settled down as a normalized cultural practice in which people carried on the daily affairs of life of an affluent, developing country.

Competing images of the Malay woman and family are key elements in the social construction of modern Malaysian society. This chapter discusses the social effects of state policies and Islamic resurgence from the 1980s to the early 1990s, as they both negotiated different models of Malay womanhood and kinship. By seeking out the contrasting logic and tropes of official and resurgent discourses, my interpretation differs from other studies of the secular Malaysian state and the Islamic resurgence. Scholars have examined the impact of state intervention on Malay class differentiation (Jomo 1988; Scott 1985; Shamsul 1986; Wong 1988) while viewing the Islamic resurgence as an antigovernment strategy among the politically marginalized (Kessler 1978, 1980; Nagata 1984; Chandra 1986; Hassan 1987). These works on state-peasant relations have focused on the structural reorganization of Malaysian society but have quite misplaced the class emphasis of the Islamic resurgence, and the critical role of gender renegotiation in modern Malay life.

Challenging these views, I argue that the state project and the Islamic resurgence must be seen as competing forms of postcolonial nationalism that fix upon the Malay family and woman as icons of particular forms of modernity. Writing about "imagined communities," Benedict Anderson (1992) focused on the rise of "official nationalisms" led by traditional elites in their struggles against colonial rulers, but he quite neglected the importance of what Partha Chatterjee calls the "narrative of community" that is not domesticated to the requirements of the postcolonial state (1993:238–239). In Malaysia, state-sponsored development expressed a particular vision of modernity that incited an Islam-inspired backlash among the emergent Malay middle classes attempting to secure their interests against state encroachments that challenge male authority. These tensions in the state-Islamic struggle are frequently ignored by scholars accustomed to interpreting Malaysian political culture in terms of peasant politics and electoral struggles (a major exception is Kessler 1978). For instance, *Fragmented Vision* (Kahn and Loh 1993), a volume that claims to explore different visions of postcolonial Malaysian society, remains heavily focused on intra- and interethnic rivalries while giving short shrift to gender relations in the re-envisioning of modern Malaysia. Such a male bias reproduces an orientalist view whereby Asian women, fetishized as sexual objects (mothers, wives, prostitutes) and cheap docile workers, are disregarded as political subjects and icons in the struggle to redefine communal identity (Ong 1993).

Indeed, the political culture of postcolonial societies is often forged in ideological struggles over the concepts of family, gender and race. For instance, in implementing secular, technocratic development projects, modern states routinely zero in on the domestic unit as the object of social policy. In countries as different as early-twentieth-century France (Donzelot 1979), contemporary Singapore (Salaff 1988), and socialist China (Anagnost 1989), the family has been variously defined, manipulated and generally subjected to the regulation of health, educational, and welfare programs. Such disciplinary interventions are an aspect of what Michel Foucault calls "bio-power," or the state management of the population to secure its control, welfare and productivity (1978:141–147). Modern state power is not imposed so much as absorbed into society through the "capillary" actions of the human sciences and social techniques that penetrate the nooks and crannies of everyday life. In Malaysia, the New Economic Policy (introduced in 1972) represented not only the economic modernization of Malay society, but also a social intervention into its very constitution and understanding of itself. Official policies were introduced to re-shape domestic relations, to mark off the domestic from the public, and to sponsor the large-scale entry of young women into mass education and industry.

What have been the cultural effects of this state reconstitution of the

Malay peasantry? James Scott (1985), insisting upon an indefensible demarcation between state hegemony and Malay peasant culture, maintains that "everyday forms of resistance" are an index of peasants' agency protesting economic change in the countryside. While Scott's general observations about peasant resentment may have captured the contrary impulses of village Malaysia, his model of individualistic expressions of free will unmediated by larger solidarities as Muslims and as Malays in Malaysia is highly problematic.[1] As Foucault has pointed out, subjects are materially constituted by power relations and are always part of them. Malay peasants' increasingly dense ties to government programs, party politics and patronage networks cannot be discounted in our understanding of their agency. Thus the question of agency, as reformulated by Marilyn Strathern, goes beyond the independent action of individuals, and must focus on the interests "in terms of which they act"; their aims are "not necessarily . . . independently conceived" (1987:22). Her perspective refines and moves beyond the "active/passive" model often used in discussions of women's agency. Although I will sometimes talk about the independent actions of individual women and men, in this essay I generally conceive of social agency in terms of "how social effects are registered" (Strathern 1987:23) in shifting fields of power. For instance, regardless of the motivations and experiences of individuals, tensions between state policies and the Islamic resurgence have incited and intensified concerns about female sex, spaces, and actions, and these tensions have gone into shaping the changing social order. Knowledge-power schemes imposed by the state, and the counterdisciplinary actions proposed by Islamic revivalists, have affected women in different classes in different ways. In Malaysia, there are different Islamic resurgent groups (Negata 1984), and an Islamic party PAS (Patai Islam Se-Malaysia) enjoys broad peasant support in the rural state of Kelantan (Kessler 1978, 1980). However, the widespread popularity of ABIM (Islamic Youth Movement of Malaysia) among the emergent Malay middle class raises the question as to why university-educated men and women in the 1980s came to identify, in their words and bodily presentation, with the ethos of a resurgent, patriarchal form of Islam.

I will begin by briefly discussing the official racial construction of Malayness, and the ways in which Islam and local customs concerning community, kinship, and gender have shaped an understanding of Malayness in village society. Next, I discuss the state's interventions in Malay peasant society, especially through its family planning policies, its promotion of female out-migration and industrial employment, and its ideology of rural women's duties in "poverty eradiction" campaigns. These changes in Malay society, both in villages and among migrants in the cities, contributed to the rise of a strict form of Islamic culture among young men and women who had benefited directly from government efforts to create a Malay petty bourgeoisie overnight. The next section discusses the ways in which competing state and Islamic resurgent discourses use women as symbols of motherhood, Malay vulnerability, and as boundary markers in their visions of Malaysian modernity. I end by considering the apparently paradoxical problem of educated middle-class women who express their agency by aligning themselves with the patriarchal forces of an alternative Islamic imaginary.

KINSHIP, GENDER, AND COMMUNITY IN MALAY PEASANT SOCIETY

Before British intervention in the late nineteenth century, Malays were defined not by race but by their allegiance to sultans in the Malay Peninsula (Milner 1982). Colonial administrators were the first to legally differentiate the sultans' subjects from non-Malay immigrants in racial terms: a Malay was "a person belonging to any Malay race who habitually speaks the Malay language . . . and professes the Muslim religion."[2] This racial and behavioral definition was broad enough to embrace immigrants from the Malay archipelago, who could settle in the Peninsula and receive land grants denied to non-Malays. Thus, "Malays" in contemporary Malaysia, the majority of whom live in the *kampung* (villages), include groups like the Javanese, Bugis, Acehnese, and Minangkabau. Collectively racialized by the colonial state as "Malays," they were categorically opposed to Chinese, Indians and other immigrants to colonial Malaya.

After independence (1957), the UMNO (United Malay National Organization) inherited the practice of defining citizens in racial terms (*bangsa*), distinguishing between Malays, who are all Muslim,[3] and the predominantly non-Muslim Chinese and Indians.[4] Statistics measuring the relative size of the three "races" and providing evidence of their relative poverty and wealth have been a critical part of modern Malaysian politics and racial consciousness. In 1969, racial riots protesting the poverty of Malays, the majority of whom were peasants, forced a rapid adjustment between the state and the races. The UMNO government introduced a New Economic Policy (NEP) designed to "eradicate poverty" and to bring an end to the ethnic identification with economic roles. This policy was to have profound social implications for village Malay culture and domestic politics.

Local conditions and the historical interactions of custom (*adat*) with Islam have shaped Malay beliefs and practices concerning kinship, residence, and property. Although men traditionally enjoyed prerogatives in religion and property, women were neither confined to the household nor totally dependent on men for economic survival. Malay society is often cited as an example of a Muslim society that permitted relatively egalitarian relations between the sexes (Djamour 1959; Firth 1966; Swift 1963; Karim 1992), compared, say, with the rigid gender segregation found in Bangladesh (Kabeer 1988). However, throughout the twentieth century, and more recently under the NEP, forces linked to economic development and the Islamic resurgence have undermined the *adat* emphasis on bilaterality while strengthening Islamic tenets that increase male control in the emerging Malay middle class.

In 1979 and 1980, I conducted fieldwork in Sungai Jawa (a pseudonym), a village in Kuala Langat, in the state of Selangor. Among the villagers, the sexual division of labor and emphasis on bilateral kinship somewhat attenuated the patrilateral bias of Islamic law. Both men and women tapped rubber and tended coffee trees in their holdings. Until the early 1970s, only *kampung* men sought migrant work; a few women, usually divorcées or widows, were compelled to earn wages outside the village as rubber tappers or domestic servants. In recent years, however, population growth and land scarcity have affected gender relations and peasant householding. The *adat* practice of awarding equal land shares to sons and daughters has been superseded by the Islamic Shafi'i law dictating that sons be entitled to claim shares twice those of their sisters. Female-owned plots too small to be farmed separately are now often bought up by brothers. This emphasis on male inheritance has led to a situation in which most farms are the husband's property. In the sections that follow, I will discuss domestic relations in Sungai Jawa in order to show how concepts of kinship, gender, and reproduction have been transformed by state policies and Islamic revivalism.

Malays throughout the Peninsula (excluding the matrilineally-oriented Minangkabau), it has been shown, prefer nuclear households to more complex domestic arrangements (Firth 1966; Laderman 1983). In Sungai Jawa, 80 percent of the 242 households I surveyed were nuclear units. Despite important day-to-day relations between kin and neighbor, the founding of a *rumah tangga*—a "house served by a single staircase"—was considered essential to male adulthood. A married man compelled to reside with his parents would consider his status diminished. An informant noted that Malays would find intolerable the extended households of rural Chinese, in which different generations pool resources and even set up father-son businesses. It was a question of autonomy (he used the English word "independence") and control by the adult male. *Adat* required the father to give his son the property in order to establish a new household upon marriage. Once the head of his own household, a man was free from parental claims on his labor and earnings. A married man working on his father's land would expect to be paid like any other hired help.

Second, independent householding by a man made clear his sexual rights in his wife and authority over his daughters and sons. This fact was brought home to me when I first sought residence in Sungai Jawa. Since I am a Chinese woman, villagers advised me against setting up a separate household. Elsewhere, single female nurses and teachers who wished to live in villages stayed in government quarters, their status and reputation protected. As a researcher, however, I did not have such a clearly specified role or this sort of official supervision. If I were to rent a house on my own, I would be perceived as a woman eminently seduceable by village men. I was kindly invited to lodge with a household, on the condition that I take the role of an adopted daughter, thus dispelling suspicions that I might be a mistress to men in the family. In fact, the Malay expression for living together (*bersama*) implies having a sexual relationship, much as the American expression does.

Strathern points out that gender ideas often operate as an indigenous conceptualization of social cause and effect (1987:24). In the Malay village, gender differentiation was commonly expressed not in terms of biological makeup but in terms of morality. A basic aspect of a man's role was guardianship—of his sisters', wife's, and daughters' virtue. By extension, all village men were responsible for the moral status of all village women. This code of morality was often explained in terms of men's greater rationality and self-control (*akal*) and women's greater susceptibility to animalistic lust (*nafsu*). This notion of moral capacity was also reflected in the concept of procreation, in which the male seed was considered "the active principle" nourished by the womb (Banks 1983:67–68). In accordance with Islamic tradition, Malays considered the children of one man mothered by different women (all bear his name) to be more closely related than the children of one woman fathered by different men. The former relationship was one of clearly defined paternity (*keturunan*), whereas the latter was considered the product of *saudara anjing*, or "dog relations" (Banks 1983:68). (Malays find dogs especially loathsome [*menghina*], and the phrase connotes indiscriminate and impure sexuality on the part of the woman.) However, in practice, *adat* often prevailed over the Islamic law on paternity, by stressing a woman's rights in her children. Thus, children by different fathers were also called "milk siblings" (*adik beradik susu*). In divorce cases, judges often gave women custody of the children, favoring the *adat* emphasis on maternity ("shared breast"). This custom reflected the belief that children, if they so chose, should remain with their mothers. Nevertheless, a man could contest such a settlement by appealing to the Islamic court, and he could even claim as his own all children conceived during the period in which he had provided his wife support. In return for his provision of food, shelter, and clothing, a woman provided for her husband's everyday needs. A man could divorce his wife by simply repudiating (*talak*) her three times, whereas she needed judicial intervention to divorce her husband, on the grounds of his failure to provide support or to consummate the marriage.

Masculinity thus depended to an important degree, though not entirely, on a man's economic power and moral authority over women in his household. The Islamic emphasis on female chastity imposed more rigorous restrictions on unmarried women (called *anak dara,* or virgins) than on unmarried youths, although promiscuity in either sex was criticized. Young girls were required to be bashful and modest, but the Islamic emphasis on *aurat* ("nakedness" that should be covered) did not, until recently, extend to covering girls' hair (an erotic feature), which they wore loose or plaited. Everyday dress consisted of loose-fitting long tunics over sarongs (*baju kurong*). Before the recent wave of out-migration for wage work and higher education, adolescent daughters were expected to stay close to home and to keep a circumspect distance from male kinsmen. An important role of young men was to prevent their sisters from interacting with men, a practice that compromised their virtue.

Adat defined adult womanhood in other ways, but always within the Islamic construction of womens' relation to men. In everyday life, married women could move freely in tending to their cash-crop gardens or engaging in petty trade. They were not, however, supposed to sit in coffee shops or to seek male company. Women were the ones who maintained kin and neighborly relations by sharing resources, information, childcare, and the work of preparing feasts. *Keluarga,* the word often rendered as "family" in English, were open-ended kindred circles maintained by female kin between village households. In their own homes, married women customarily held the purse strings, despite the Islamic emphasis on men's keeping and handling money. Most important, women's special knowledge and skills were used in cooking, childbirth, health care (Laderman 1983), and the intensification of sexual pleasure (Karim 1992).[5] Women's *adat* knowledge included the art of preserving their sexual attractiveness to retain their husbands' interest. Married women wore their hair in buns, but on special occasions they dressed up in close-fitting, semitransparent jackets (*kebaya*) and batik sarongs. A lacy shawl (*selendang*) draped loosely over the head and shoulders could be used as a sunscreen and, occasionally, as a means of flirtation. Emphasizing their sexual charms, married women's clothing was in sharp contrast to the modest attire required of unmarried girls. Because sexually experienced and not legally subordinated to any man, previously married women, whether widows or divorcées (called by the same term, *janda*), were considered both vulnerable and dangerous. *Janda* were frequently suspected of trying to steal husbands. The virginity code and sanctions against adultery permitted sex only between spouses.[6] This did not prevent premarital or extramarital sex, but the Islamic ban on *khalwat* (illicit proximity) made having affairs a risky business.

Just as self-control, and control of his wife's sexuality defined a man's adult status, regulating the activities of unmarried women—virgins and *janda*—defined the collective identity of *kampung* men. In Sungai Jawa, young men, with the implicit backing of Islamic elders, kept a watch on couples carrying on illicit affairs. If "caught wet" (*tangkap basah*) and found to be unmarried, a couple would be compelled to marry as soon as possible. If either party were already married, the man would be beaten as a warning to other would-be adulterers. Sometimes the Islamic court would impose fines or even imprisonment, but villagers preferred to police and punish sexual misconduct themselves, as part of their role in safeguarding morality and protecting the boundaries between Malays and non-Malays (Ong 1990). Thus, youths would be more ferocious in their attacks if the paramour were an outsider or a non-Malay man. For instance, a Chinese man who dated a Malay factory girl was attacked and, according to one of my informants, "left half-dead; he was in a coma for three days." Male protection of female sexuality delineated the boundaries between male and female spaces (cf. Mernissi 1987:xv–xvii), as well as between Muslims and the wider, multiethnic society.

In *kampung* society, then, Islamic law defined a man's identity in terms of his ability to prepare his sons for independent householding, to control the sexuality of his wife and daughters, and to provide all economic support for his household. However, *adat* practices and kindred relations provided women a measure of autonomy and influence in everyday life that prevented a rigid observation of male authority. In recent years, state policies and capitalist relations have created conditions that make the regulation of female sexuality a major issue. The possibilities for interracial liaisons created by the interweaving of Malay and non-Malay worlds have been perceived as a threat to Malay male rights and as a dangerous blurring of boundaries between Muslim and non-Muslim groups. As we shall see, control over female sexuality has been made a focus of the resulting efforts to strengthen male authority, reinforce group boundaries, and ensure the cultural survival of the Malay community undergoing "modernization."

STATE INTERVENTION: MAKING THE MODERN MALAY FAMILY

Under British rule, numerous laws like land tenure enactments presaged the dramatic postcolonial "social engineering" of Malay society brought about by the NEP. Under this program, Malays were now legally defined as *bumiputera* or "sons of the soil."[7] The most important goal of this indigenization program was to correct interethnic economic imbalances by bringing 30 percent of the nation's wealth under *bumiputera* control by 1990.[8] The new state ideology, *Rukunegara,* produced a view of Malaysian modernity in which Malays were to become capitalists, professionals, and workers, a dominant part of the citizenry who, because of their certified status as original natives, had special claims to national wealth. An expansion of state policies to remake the peasantry along these lines gradually increased class differentiation in Malay village society and stimulated the urban migration of young women and men. Such changes in the political economy, class and ethnic formations, including state policies affecting the Malay family, contributed to the growing crisis of the Malay peasantry, which became inseparable from a crisis in Malay cultural identity. *Kampung* notions of kinship, conjugal rights, and gender were increasingly subjected to the operation of state policies.

Capitalist Development and Out-migration

Among the complex effects of the NEP was an improvement in living conditions in the *kampung* coupled with a reduction in the ability of most peasants to support their children by farming. For instance, double-cropping introduced into the Muda region, Malaysia's rice-bowl area, increased class differentiation: as a minority of commercial farmers emerged from a growing class of smallholders, the landless were cut adrift from the tenure system and cast upon the urban economy (Scott 1985:70–77). In Kuala Langat, an expanded state bureaucracy and population pressure on the land also increased class differentiation: well-to-do peasants and civil servants, who had contacts with state and UMNO party officials, benefited more than others did from farm subsidies and loan speculation. In my survey of 242 households, a quarter were landless or owned only their house lot. Sixty-one percent had access to farms under 2.5 acres, a size just adequate for supporting a family of four. About 65 percent of the household heads (mainly men) were working as day laborers or migrant workers, reflecting a movement out of cash cropping into the wage economy. With land fragmentation, rising land costs, and an increasing reliance on wage employment, many village men found themselves unable to pass property on to their children so as to make a *kampung* livelihood. This increasing "crisis of transmission" was first noted by Banks (1983) among Kedah rice peasants. In Sungai Jawa, only a few years later, many fathers did not have enough land left for their sons. In fact, they were beginning to depend on children's wages to augment the household budget.

Meanwhile, welfare policies seemed to prepare *kampung* children for different places in the wider economy. From independence to 1975, development expenditures in rural areas increased about sixfold (Scott 1985:54). In Kuala Langat, a coeducational high school and a free trade zone were set up. The best students were creamed off through nationally certified examinations and sent to urban schools and colleges or to overseas universities on state scholarships. Like *kampung* youth throughout the country, those high school graduates left in Sungai Jawa rejected farming as a way of life. Many youths preferred to remain unemployed, waiting for a plum job as office boy in some government agency. With the NEP, the out-migration of young *kampung* men and, increasingly, women for higher education and wage work became an irreversible process, dramatically changing parent-child and gender relations.

Family Planning

As in many developing countries, family planning in Malaysia was informed by the postwar World Bank prescription of increasing agricultural develop-ment while reducing family size. For instance, in land development schemes Malay settlers were given maternity benefits for only the first three children. Concerned that family policy could be construed as interference in Malay husbands' rights, officials packaged family planning as a "health programme," emphasizing nutrition and well-being while strategically pushing fertility control. Family planning ideology promoted a model based on the Western conjugal family, using the term *keluarga* (kindred) to designate a "nuclear family" made up of a working father, housewife, and dependent children. A pamphlet promoting contraceptives depicted family problems caused by a tired and irritable wife burdened with house-work and childcare. She was portrayed as inadequate to her husband's needs. Village women were urged to take the Pill in order to spare their husbands "inconveniences." But in suggesting that the Pill could improve husband-wife relations, the program was an unwelcome intrusion into an area governed by Islamic law and personal desires.

Not surprisingly, village men actively resisted family planning, using the health services of the "maternity and children's" clinic in Sungai Jawa to attain the highest birthrate in the district. There is little doubt that throughout the country, in fact, "family planning" programs contributed to rising birthrates among Malay villagers: during the 1970s and 1980s, fertility rates rose among Malays but fell among the Chinese and Indians (Hirschman 1986). In Sungai Jawa, a survey of 238 ever-married women (from 242 households) showed that they had given birth to an average of five to six children, a higher rate than in previous decades.

Nevertheless, the ideology of family planning increased tensions be-tween husbands and wives. In Sungai Jawa and, I suspect, most villages, the Pill was the main contraceptive provided by government clinics. Villagers noted that women taking the Pill complained of headaches, a "bloated" appearance, and a lethargy that made them "too lazy to work." Some hus-bands even threatened that if their wives got sick from the Pill, they would be refused help. Male hostility to family planning was so strong that men rejected contraceptives even when they were poor and could barely sup-port large families. A 27-year-old mother of six children under 15 was seven months' pregnant when I met her; she had wanted to go on the Pill after the fourth child but her husband, a laborer, had refused her permission. She said that most women had children because their husbands wished it, even though women themselves did not desire many children (although they did feel some concern about having children for old-age security). In another case, after a woman had had her sixteenth child—delivered by Caesarean—the nurse had suggested family planning. The woman had refused, saying "Allah giveth." Her father and her husband were both devout Muslims.

Family planning challenged *kampung* men's exclusive rights to their wives' sexuality. In addition, the men feared that contraceptives might embolden women to dissent from their husbands' wishes.[9] Villagers and religious leaders often used Islam, citing the hadith (an authorized compilation of the Prophet's words, deeds, and exemplary practices) to criticize family planning as "killing the fetus." In the villagers' daily conversations, the distinctions between miscarriage, abortion, and contraception were often blurred. An *imam* told me that the Qur'an allowed abortion when the mother's health was endangered or the family could not possibly support another child, but, as the above examples illustrate, husbands rejected contraception even in such cases.

Since family planning was considered anti-Islam, those who used contraceptives had reason to conceal their decision. The Sungai Jawa clinic kept records on ninety-seven family planning couples, showing that 70 percent of the husbands were wage workers. Most of the wives were between 14 and 28 years old. I was told that perhaps twenty or more young couples bought their own contraceptives rather than get them free at the clinic. The factory women I interviewed said they did not intend to have more than four children. Young couples who depended mainly or exclusively on wage income had begun to talk about children in terms of "costs." Besides creating more expenses, children required help with their schoolwork so that they could later compete for white-collar jobs. Wage employment and family planning together, thus, produced an adjustment in family relations challenging two key elements of masculinity—a man's control of his wife's sexuality, and his ability to raise children.

Whatever the local effects of the family planning program, most Malays viewed the family planning ideology as ultimately a threat to their national survival. Although teachers and other state servants might have been practicing contraception in private, in public they loudly proclaimed the practice contrary to Islam. A teacher said that he rejected family planning for Malays because it implied that they were incapable of raising as many children as they desired. He hinted that, as *bumiputera,* Malays were promised government preference in scholarships, jobs, business licenses, and credit. Moreover, family planning conflicted in practice with state policies encouraging Malays to have many children as one way of increasing wealth and ensuring the success of the race. Civil servants warned that if contraception were widely adopted, Malays would lose their voting power vis-à-vis the other races. Modern concepts and practices concerning health and sex thus challenged male conjugal rights, their moral authority over women, and Islam. And not only did family planning challenge Islamic culture, but it threatened Malay racial power as well. The recruitment of young women into the labor force offered a further challenge to local norms for regulating female sexuality and social reproduction.

The Deployment of Female Labor in Free Trade Zones

As welfare policy tried to manage the bodily care and reproduction of peasant Malays, social engineering redistributed the younger generations in new locations scattered throughout the wider society. The *Third Malaysia Plan* notes that the general aim of the NEP was to promote the "progressive transformation of the country's racially-compartmentalized economic system into one in which the composition of Malaysian society is visibly reflected in its countryside and towns, farms and factories, shops and offices."[10]

Throughout the 1970s, state intervention in the peasant sector generated a steady influx of Malays into cities, a rising number of them young women. Tens of thousands of female migrants collected in urban free trade zones, working in labor-intensive subsidiaries of transnational corporations (Jamilah 1980). These corporations had established electronics firms, garment factories, and other light manufacturing plants in the special zones, where they were legally required to have a 30 percent *bumiputera* representation in their work force. By the late 1970s, some 80,000 *kampung* girls between the ages of 16 and the mid-twenties had been transformed into industrial laborers (Jamilah 1980). The industrialization strategy, originally focused on creating a male Malay working class, found itself producing an increasingly female industrial force, largely because of the manufacturing demand for cheaper (female) labor.

This army of working daughters introduced another line of division into the Malay household. In Sungai Jawa, the local free trade zone turned village girls into factory operators. Many peasants eagerly sent their daughters off to earn an income to be put toward household expenses. Most working daughters were induced to hand over part of their paychecks, especially when brothers proved reluctant to share their own earnings, were unemployed, or were attending school. Daughters' wages paid for consumer durables and house renovations that broadcast the new wealth of *kampung* families (Ackerman 1984:53). Not unexpectedly, working daughters strengthened the influence of mothers in the household: since it would be shameful for fathers to ask help from daughters, mothers extracted the earnings. Village men found themselves unable to fulfill their duties as fathers and husbands. Some felt humiliated that they depended on daughters' wages and could not keep them at home, their virtue protected (Ackerman 1984:56; Ong 1987:99).

Nationwide, as thousands of peasant girls descended on cities and free trade zones, they came into competition with their male peers. For young men, sisters became an easily tapped source of cash, but as would-be wives working women transgressed the wider arena of male power. So long as unmarried girls were confined to the *kampung* milieu, men's superiority in experience and knowledge could remain unchallenged. Now, young women too were acquiring experience in market situations, situations where they could mingle freely with men. Furthermore, the new class of female workers and college students induced in their male peers a widespread fear of female competition in the changing society.

For the first time in Malay history, a large number of nubile women had the money and social freedom to experiment with a newly awakened sense of self. Many came to define themselves, through work experiences and market choices, as not materially or even morally dependent on parents and kinsmen. Factory women could now save for their weddings, instead of receiving money from their parents, and could therefore choose their own husbands. The increasing number of brides who were wage earners produced a trend toward larger wedding outlays by grooms for feasting and for outfitting the bride and the new household. In Sungai Jawa, many men did not hesitate to emphasize their prestige by spending lavishly. Civil servants had access to government loans for just such expenses. Between 1976 and 1980, wedding payments exceeding M$1,000 (approximately US$500) increased from 17 to 53 percent.[11] These sums were presented in fresh bank notes expertly folded into money trees, a ritual symbolizing masculine power, now subsidized not by fathers but by the government. In the changing *kampung* society, young men and women found themselves dependent on the labor market and the state, rather than on their parents, as they negotiated the path toward adulthood. Young women, however, came to bear special moral burdens for realizing the image of a modern Malay society.

Work Ethics, Women's Duties, and the Modern Family

In the early 1980s, the state introduced a "Look East" policy to enforce discipline in modern institutions. Some observers saw bureaucrats as the focus of this campaign (Mauzy and Milne 1983), but in my view, the object of this discourse has been workers, especially Malay female workers in transnational firms, many Japanese-owned (see also Kua 1983). The prime minister lauded Japanese companies for their "family system," which displayed concern "for the welfare of their employees," and he remarked on the similarity between Japanese and Malaysian "morals and ethics" (Das

1982:38–39). The aim of the policy, an educator explained, was "to urge Muslims to follow the attitude and work ethics of a successful race [the Japanese] as long as it does not contravene Islamic ideals and principles."[12] The presumed "communal spirit" of Japanese enterprises was presented as in keeping with Islamic kinship values.

Whereas health policy pushed a nuclear family ideal, industrial ideology promoted a patrilineal "family welfare" model said to reflect the *keluarga* emphasis on mutual obligations and loyalty. In the Kuala Langat free trade zone, a company motto proclaimed its goal to be

to create one big family,
to train workers,
to increase loyalty to company,
country and fellow workers.

Despite this corporate "philosophy," many factory women felt manipulated and harassed by male supervisors whom they were urged to consider as family elders. To some workers, management was implacably the other ("aliens"): it did not speak their language, was not Muslim, profited from their labor, and sometimes treated them as though they were not "human beings." Among operators, only fellow workers were considered "siblings" (*saudara saudari*). Despite factory-induced competition among operators, workers in the same section would help each other and look out for new recruits, as one would for one's *keluarga*. Such mutual dependence, of course, unintentionally reinforced self-regulation, commitment, and discipline among workers—the goals of the "one big family" ideology.

The "poverty eradication" program also promoted new concepts of female duty, based on the Western notion of family as a privatized unit of obligations and exclusion (cf. Asad 1987). In the Fifth Malaysia Plan, women were seen as key to improving the lot of "low-income households." Rural women were blamed for not being hardworking and for their presumed lack of response to "modern practices" and "new opportunities" for improving the well-being of their families. Officials dictated a series of tasks women could undertake to improve the health and wealth of their families. Peasant mothers were instructed to ignore "customary" practices in preparing their children for "a progressive society"; they were called upon to raise children with values such as "efficiency" and "self-reliance."[13] A government program called KEMAS ("tidy up") instructed village women in home economics and handicrafts. The new housewife requirements echoed the slogan "Clean, Efficient, and Trustworthy," displayed in factories with largely female work forces. The official discourse on the modern family thus defined women's modern roles: as working daughters who could pull their families out of "backwardness" and as housewives (*seri-rumah*) who could inculcate "progressive" values in their children. This privileging of the mother-child relationship reflected the Western family model while ignoring the central role of the Muslim father.

Through various NEP programs, then, the ideology of a modern Malay society unintentionally undermined the source of customary male power. Welfare policies progressively defined a privatized domestic sphere and women's responsibilities in it. This family model seemed to undermine male conjugal and paternity rights while supporting a more assertive role for women at home. Second, the emphasis on *bumiputera* rights greatly raised the expectations of young people without eliminating their sense of uncertainty in the multiethnic society to which they were channeled as students, wage workers, professionals, and unemployed youths. Their cultural dislocation was compounded by the changing sexual division of labor and the new freedoms of daughters, wives, female students, and female workers. Moral confusion over the proper roles of men and women and the boundaries between the public and domestic, Muslim and non-Muslim worlds contributed to a crisis of national identity.

ISLAMIC REVIVALISM: ENGENDERING THE *UMMA*

In Malaysia, Islamic resurgent movements are not historically unprecedented: during the struggle for national independence, Islamic reformists challenged traditional Malay systems (Roff 1967), and in postindependence Malaysia, the major opposition party, PAS (*Partai Islam Se Malaysia*), used Islam to articulate the discontent of poor peasants in the east coast states (Kessler 1978). In the 1970s, diverse Islamic revivalist groups, collectively referred to as the *dakwa* (proselytizing) movement, began to develop among the *kampung*-born and educated Malays who had emerged as a new social force under the NEP.[14]

Here, I will focus on the major group, ABIM (*Angkatan Belia Islam Malaysia* or Islamic Youth Movement of Malaysia), which rose to national prominence through the 1970s, at its height numbering some 30,000 members and innumerable sympathizers. Besides its size, it drew on the largest cohort of young Malays to have benefited from mass literacy. They differed from earlier generations of revivalists in that they emphasized a direct engagement with holy texts (the sunnah, hadith, and Qur'an), bypassing the received wisdom of traditional religious leaders (*ulama*). ABIM members and supporters were mainly young men and women who, hailing from villages like Sungai Jawa, had migrated into cities for wage employment and higher education. Despite the *bumiputera* rhetoric, they had been made aware of the gulf between them and the older Malay elites who had come to power under British tutelage. Students sent on scholarships to universities in London, Cairo, and Islamabad were exposed to the various strands of Islamic resurgence abroad. Upon returning home, many became *dakwa* leaders who railed against the decadent lifestyle of nouveaux-riches Malays, with their pursuit of glittering acquisitions and sensual pleasures and their blithe disregard of Islam (Chandra 1986:70–71). ABIM's leader, Anwar Ibrahim, proclaimed that Islam opposed "development which propagates inequality and which is void of moral and spiritual values" (Anwar 1986:5). Embedded in this critique was a class analysis linking upper-class corruption to the impoverishment of the Malay majority (Kessler 1980). Moreover, the *dakwa* perception that non-Malay communities were more successful in the secular milieu produced fears for Malay survival. Looking back, an ABIM leader said: "After 'May 13' [1969; that is, the racial riots] . . . [i]t was all a question of the survival of the *umma,* of the Malay race. Previously, we [thought] about all these problems outside Islam, when actually we could have solved them through Islam." (Zainah 1987:11)

ABIM's search for an Islamic revivalist identity was an assault on a hegemonic construction of *bumiputera*hood that did not address the cultural problems of Malays living in a secular, multiethnic world. As the above quotation suggests, the recovery of the *umma* (social and religious community) became a central goal in dealing with the breakdown in social boundaries that had traditionally defined Malay group identity. Through *dakwa* activities, ABIM members aimed to awaken a "broader religious consciousness" among Muslims (Nagata 1984:81–82). *Dakwa* attacks on capitalism focused on its spawning choices and practices "based not on divine morality but on sensuality and as such not according to truth and justice" (Mohammad 1981:1046). The "truth" that Islamic revivalists sought was to be found in an *umma* that would infuse the community as well as the government with revitalized Islamic values (Hassan 1987).[15] By insisting on a stricter adherence to the *umma,* the *dakwa* was urging a social system more gender-stratified than existed in Malay society.

Writing about Islamic revivalism in Morocco, Mernissi noted that the *umma,* which recognized Allah as its only leader, resisted the secular power of the modern state when it spread to previously uncontested areas of domestic relations (1987:20–22). The *umma* was "ultimately a society of male citizens who possessed . . . the female half of the population" (Mernissi 1987:169). For Malay revivalists, the *umma* had been unmade by the influx of women into modern schools and offices; a new "sacred architecture" of sexuality (Mernissi 1987:xvi) had to be created, through everyday practices inventing "Islamic" traditions (Hobsbawm 1983) that would redraw boundaries between Malay men and women, Muslims and non-Muslims. Almost overnight, large numbers of university students, young workers, and even professionals began to enact—in prayer, diet, clothing, and social life—religious practices borrowed from Islamic history, Middle Eastern societies, and South Asian cults. Here, I will present two cases which show that attacks on changing gender and domestic relations were central to the *dakwa* construction of the *umma*.

In Sungai Jawa, villagers felt a general anxiety about the ways in which state policies and secularization had weakened male authority over young women. Parents were torn between wanting their daughters to work and being concerned about keeping their status honorable. With independent earnings, women's agency, formerly channeled through legal superiors (parents, husbands), came to express individual interests in consumption and in dating. Factory women took to wearing revealing Western outfits (such as jeans and miniskirts) and bright makeup. This "sarong-to-jeans movement" was seen as a license for permissiveness that overturned *kampung* norms of maidenly decorum. In the factories, nubile women were daily supervised by men, many non-Malays, an arrangement that seemed to mock at Malay male authority. Worse, some working women began to date non-Malay men, breaking village norms of sexual and religious segregation. "It is not a matter of romance, but of social relationships," one worker commented. Women who were unrestrained (*bebas*) by family guidance in relations with men were derided as being no longer Malay (*bukan Melayu*). Villagers viewed this development of an autonomous female agency as a weakening of male control and of the boundaries between Malays and non-Malays (see also Peletz 1993).

The religious response to women's assertiveness was exemplified in a speech given at a village celebration of the Prophet Muhammad's birthday in 1979. A young scholar complained that the modern ills afflicting Malays included drug taking, excessive watching of television, and communism (he mentioned the Soviet invasion of Afghanistan). Islamic societies were weak not because Islam was weak, but because Muslims were weak human beings who succumbed to their baser nature (*nafsu*). He elaborated this theme by saying that women's roles as mothers and wives had to be strengthened according to Islamic tenets. When a student at Al-Azhar, Cairo, he had had the opportunity to observe the great respect children showed their mothers in societies where Islam was an overwhelming force in everyday life. He urged villagers to raise their children with great respect for authority. And, while all Muslims should obey Islamic laws and respect their elders, women should first and foremost serve their husbands. He then raised the vision of factory women "letting themselves" be cheated by men, thus "damaging themselves." Wage work was presented as dishonorable, inducing women to indulge their indiscriminate passions. He continued by saying that a woman's sensual nature was acceptable only if (his hands sculpting the air to suggest a curvaceous body) her sexual allure were reserved for her husband's pleasure. He ended by calling on village women to emulate the Prophet's wife, Katijah.[16] This call for a strengthening of the Malay race required women to adhere to a stricter Islamic version of male authority and of women's roles as mothers and wives.

The use of foreign Islamic practices to validate increased male authority over women was also evident in the middle-class milieu. In the mid-1980s, a Malay socialist named Kassim Ahmad stirred up a hornet's nest by publishing a modest critique of the hadith, the text used in the everyday teachings of *dakwa* members. Exposing various "contradictions" between the hadith and the Qur'an, Kassim Ahmad argued that the latter was the only source of truth for Muslims. For instance, contrary to the Qur'an, the hadith was "anti-women." It prescribed "stoning to death" for adulterers (Kassim 1986:95–96, 101–102) and even claimed that fasting women should submit themselves to their husbands' carnal desires (Kassim 1986:104–105). This challenge galvanized orthodox *ulama* and Islamic revivalists alike into calling for a ban on Kassim Ahmad's book and censuring him in other ways. Although the controversy was mainly phrased in terms of Kassim Ahmad's religious expertise, its very silence over the "contradictions" specified by Kassim Ahmad revealed the depth of popular sentiment about husbands' control of their wives.[17] Public discussions of the case failed to refer to local Malay traditions that do not condone the punitive measures mentioned in the hadith. This controversy in fact provided an opportunity for Islamic revivalists to insist anew that Muslim men should have total authority over women.

In thus defining a new *umma*, ABIM and other *dakwa* groups were inventing practices harking back to a mythic, homogeneous past, while rejecting their Malay-Muslim cultural heritage. This Arabization of Malay society depended in large part on implementing a rigid separation between male public roles and female domestic ones, a concrete realization of the architecture of male rationality (*akal*) and female eroticism (*nafsu*) that went way beyond any arrangement found in indigenous village arrangements where *akal* and *nafsu* are found in both women and men (see Peletz, this volume). A new radical division between Malay men and women, Muslims and non-Muslims, was thus being constructed in public life, primarily by inscribing a religious spatialization of power on women's bodies.

WOMEN'S AGENCY AND THE BODY POLITIC

Draped in dark veils and robes, women are the most potent symbols of Islamic revivalism. Their presence calls into question feminist assumptions that women in Muslim societies would invariably "resist" Islamic resurgent movements (see, for example, Kabeer 1988). In Malaysia, women displayed a range of responses, both to modernization and to Islamic revivalism, that cannot be reduced to "resistance," a term implying only oppositional tactics. Here, I suggest that among Malay women, agency in terms of autonomy or adherence to interests not independently conceived differed according to class. Whereas working-class women were less morally compromised by working, middle-class women were significantly swayed by the spirit of Islamic resurgence in their understanding of femininity.

It would be erroneous to assume that state policies unambiguously provided Malay women with conditions for employment and individual security. Land scarcity, widespread female wage labor, and secularization in many cases reduced men's customary obligation to be the sole supporters of their families where possible. Furthermore, the trend toward female wage employment made all Malay women vulnerable to a reduction or even withdrawal of their husbands' support. At an UMNO Women's meeting, wives of the rural elite complained that government promotion of the "housewife" did not guarantee women economic support. Leaders reminded village women of their responsibilities for the educational success of their children and the preservation of the UMNO heritage for their grandchildren. However, some women noted that men viewed their wives as having rights only in housework and childcare, with no claim on their husbands' salaries. Invoking the Islamic marriage contract, members proposed that mutual respect and intimacy within marriage would be improved if the state could guarantee that "housewives" would be paid an "allowance" drawn from their husbands' salaries. This proposal indicated that even women not caught up in Islamic revivalism felt that social and economic changes made them vulnerable to loss of the male protection provided by Islamic law. Although their demands for payment for housework may seem an echo of Western feminist demands, they were really calling on the government to enforce men's customary role as sole supporters of their families. It is such protests by middle-class women that have resulted in new Islamic family laws for the "protection of women's rights" regarding divorce. For the first time, Islamic judges nationwide have been ordered to regulate their implementation of family laws.[18] For Malays who consider divorce and polygamy male rights, this law must seem to be yet another instance of state inroads on the power vested in men by Islam.

For unmarried women, the impact of modernizing forces has been greater and more disorienting, especially among the first large generation of Malay university women. Many have found refuge in the *dakwa* movement. On the University of Malaya campus, at least 60 percent of the students showed some commitment to *dakwa* in the early 1980s (Zainah 1987:33). Whereas ABIM men wore Western shirts and pants, *dakwa* women put on the *mini-telekung*, a cloth that tightly frames the face and covers the head, hair and chest, considered parts of the *aurat* ("nakedness") that Islam requires women to conceal. This headcloth was usually worn with the customary *baju kurung*. Some women also donned long black robes (*hijab*), socks, gloves, and face-veils, denoting a full purdah (*parda*) historically alien to Malay culture.[19] This representation of the female body may be seen as "subversive *bricolages*" (Comaroff 1985:197–198) combining elements of different traditions to register protest over cultural dislocations linked to colonial and postcolonial domination.

Students walking around in full purdah were a source of irritation to government officials worried that "Arabic" robes would scare off foreign investors. In fact, *dakwa* groups were critical of the kind of cultural colonializing promoted by the market, media, and foreign corporations. A female *dakwa* lecturer assailed working women for adopting the consumerist "feminine false consciousness" promoted by factory culture (Amriah 1989). As a male revivalist remarked, "I feel that secularism is the biggest threat to the Muslim *umma*" (Zainah 1987:76). *Dakwa* groups sought to provide networks and daily support for Malay women disoriented by the consumerism of modern life.

ABIM recruitment of women was not only a resistance to capitalist culture, but also a reorienting of women's agency to rebuild a Malay-Muslim identity. State policies had "liberated" women for campuses and the marketplace, but could not offer protection against new self-doubts and social anxieties among women and men. Released from the guidance and protection of their kin, many young women were compelled to act as "individuals" representing their own interests in the wider society. Furthermore, Malay society for the first time confronted the problem of a large group of unmarried young women, whose unregulated sexuality was seen as symbolic of social disorder (cf. Mernissi 1987:xxiv). Fatna Sabbah argues that Muslim women's entry into the modern economy is often seen as a challenge to men's economic role, the basis of their virility; men thus perceive women's participation in modern public life as a form of "erotic aggression" (Sabbah 1984:17). This reading is highly suggestive for the Malaysian case. The *dakwa* obsession with women's "modesty" in "male" and multiethnic spaces was reflected in their insistence that women cover themselves. Women's bodily containment was key to the envisaged order that would contain those social forces unleashed by state policies and the capitalist economy. The *mini-telekung* and long robes marked off the female body as an enclosed, "pregnant" space, symbolic of the boundaries drawn around Malay society, and the male authority within it.

Such dramatic reversals from their brief exposure to personal liberation were more evident among female university students than among blue-collar women. Campuses were the seats of the most intensive *dakwa* campaigns to cover the female body and maintain sexual and ethnic segregation. Women were discouraged from participating in sports that exposed their naked limbs (Nagata 1984:100). A University of Malaya ban on the *mini-telekung* in lecture halls failed to deter many female students from covering their heads. Even female lecturers who rejected the *dakwa* prescription felt sufficiently intimidated to wear headscarves and avoid Western-style clothing.

The following two examples illustrate the centrality of sexuality to female students' struggles between autonomy and group identity. One student, who favored leotards and disco dancing, was repeatedly chastised by *dakwa* members over a period of two years. One day her boyfriend urged her to don the *mini-telekung* because, he said, it would help him resist her sexual appeal. When she finally complied, *dakwa* women immediately embraced and salaamed to her (Zainah 1987:64–67). In another case, a student confided that when she first came to the university she had worn "miniskirts and low-cut clothes." She had mixed with Chinese students and attended campus "cultural" events, but not religious ones. One day she received a letter, signed "servant of Allah," accusing her of having sinned by befriending Chinese infidels, who would lead her astray. Just for not covering her head, she would burn in hell (Zainah 1987:60). As these cases indicate, ABIM recruits were often women who had tasted individual "freedom" but, subjected to pressure and even outright threats, later found security and acceptance in Islamic revivalism. By donning *dakwa* outfits, they could negotiate the urban milieu without being insulted by men. The *dakwa* robes registered the multiple effects of cultural disorientation, protest, and intimidation, enfolding them in a moral community.

Furthermore, through their *dakwa* outfits, women proclaimed the impossibility of interethnic liaisons or marriages, thereby stemming any potential loss in progeny to the Malay race, who form a small majority in Malaysia.[20] *Dakwa* women have thus asserted Malay singularity against Malaysian multiculturalism, at the same time partaking of the aura cast by the global Islamic efflorescence.

Depeasantization, Middle-Class Women, and Religious Nationalism

The Islamic resurgence and all its trappings quickly became associated with upwardly mobile *kampung* and urban middle-class women, rather than peasant or working-class women. In Sungai Jawa, where most young women were employed in factories, only a handful who managed to enter teachers' colleges and the university wore *dakwa* outfits. Village elders noted that the religious clothing, while admirable, was inappropriate for life in the village. An elder woman explained that her granddaughter, clothed in *mini-telekung* and *hijab,* was dressed in the way of "an educated woman." In contrast, because she herself was a peasant (*tani*), she could sit comfortably in her carelessly tied blouse and sarong.[21] Hardly any factory woman adopted the *dakwa* robes, although many believed that the intensified religious environment provided them protection against sexual and social abuse in the wider society (Ong 1987:181–193). Thus, *dakwa* clothing became a symbol of depeasantization,[22] a process of class mobility whereby successful Malay women explored their gender identity in modern Islamic terms.

For many Malay women, depeasantization and higher education were not to be associated with exploring their sexual selves; rather, a higher social and moral status required rigid constraints on sexual expression. Thus many university-educated women were caught between the demands of individualistic competition in higher education and the job market on the one hand, and their hopes of being married on the other. Indeed, the *dakwa* granddaughter mentioned above, who was in her early twenties, spent her holidays in the village reading British romances, ostensibly to improve her English. Her mother complained anxiously about her lack of suitors, blaming it on her ignorance of the finer aspects of cooking, cleaning, and childcare, the important skills of village wives.

Such tensions are reflected in a university survey of a hundred and fifty female seniors who revealed ambivalence about their new status, stating that they did not believe in competing with men in the labor market. They would only seek jobs which involved serving others—for example, as clerks, teachers, nurses, or doctors (attending to women and children only). The respondents considered occupations that would put them in authority positions over men forbidden by Islam, because to work in such positions would change the status of women vis-à-vis men (Narli 1981:131–133; see also Nagata 1984:74–75). A deep concern among educated women was their postponement of marriage and their fear of being progressively priced out of the marriage market by their academic credentials. By seeking to maintain, rather than challenge, male authority, they would be better assured of finding husbands. They are the ones most likely to don *dakwa* robes that soon became the Malay woman's working uniform, replacing the body-fitting *batik sarung-kebaya* of the days before the Islamic resurgence.

The discourse on Muslim womanhood thus became a countermodel to the government's promotion of working women, the modern family, and the secular "housewife" ideal. These were all seen as threats to male authority at home and in the public sphere. ABIM members insisted that women's first duties were to their husbands and that wives should obey their husbands just as all Muslims should obey Allah. The moral of wives' obedience seemed to be an appropriate ideology for the urban middle class, among whom divorce has lately declined, possibly because of women's fear of the economic and social losses it would entail, but also because of middle-class men's ability to fulfill the economic and moral implications of the husband/father role (Peletz, this volume). Among working-class women, divorce rates remained high (Azizah 1987:109–110; Ong 1990:453–454). The nurturing and self-sacrificing role of women as homebound mothers emphasized in resurgent teachings was more easily realized by middle-class women who did not need to make a living. ABIM members frequently invoked the Qur'anic phrase "paradise lies beneath [our] mothers' feet" (Nagata 1984:100), to celebrate women's primary responsibility for instilling Islamic values in their children. Women were also urged to spread Islamic values among their female friends. In *dakwa* discourse, the redirection of women's agency from labor force to moral force tapped into the deepseated spiritual unease of women aspiring to be upwardly mobile, yet filled with ambivalence about careers and the solitude of modern life.

Thus, although a substantial number of its members were engaged in a genuine spiritual quest, the *dakwa* movement also reflected a discontent with changing gender roles and the declining force of male authority in the new middle-class family. This analysis helps to explain the apparently paradoxical fact that many young women who had benefited from state policies (which opened up educational and employment opportunities to them in the first place) found the *dakwa* call so appealing. In *dakwa* visions, women are all married and fulfilled. As wives and mothers, they play central roles in rebuilding and preserving Malay society as part of the larger Islamic family (Anwar 1986:5). The Islamic resurgence reminds them of their moral duty to construct and nurture a modern Muslim-Malay community imagined by *dakwa* leaders. In the university survey, most of the women interviewed considered themselves to be "first and foremost Muslims," arguing that "nowadays, there is only one tradition—that is, Islamic tradition." They saw Islam as a "more comprehensive value system" than Malay customs, one more fit to guide them in this era of rapid change. Some insisted on being reidentified, saying "I am Muslim rather than Malay" (Narli 1981:132–133). The *dakwa* movement thus constructs a kind of religious nationalism, divested of many attractive features of indigenous Malay culture, that is based on an invented tradition, and the creation of a strict Muslim patriarchal domination in both public and domestic spheres.

OFFICIAL ISLAM'S NEW WOMEN

The powerful Islamic claim on a Malay moral identity and criticisms of modernization caused the state to launch an Islamization campaign of its own in the early 1980s. Its most important move was to co-opt the charismatic ABIM leader Anwar Ibrahim into the government, putting him in charge of youth and sports. In addition, the state set up official Islamic institutions for banking, university education, and missionary programs. More rigorous efforts were made to punish Muslims who broke religious laws forbidding gambling, drinking, and sex out of wedlock (Mauzy and Milne 1983). On television, Islamic programs proliferated, some promoting the image of "ideal mothers" who would put their husbands and children before anything else.

The new religious tone of state programs prepared the stage for a new "family development" policy. A new language linking development, population, and the family articulated the new moral role of Malay women. The government proclaimed a goal of population growth from 14 to 70 million over the next hundred years in order to meet the anticipated labor needs for sustained capitalist development.[23] Although there was widespread skepticism about the possibility of attaining this goal, the new population policy found support even among Malays disaffected with the UMNO regime. The uncharacteristic silence over racial composition led many to believe that population growth would be encouraged only among Malays. The program seemed to allow natural population growth among Malays to be augmented by the largescale immigration of Indonesians who could easily be absorbed into the *bumiputera* category (Clad 1984:109–110). Second, in producing a discourse on "family development" (thus overturning family planning), the state appropriated the *dakwa* themes of defining and empowering Malays in opposition to non-Malays. Despite its technocratic language, the policy explicitly links the success of the Malay family to the strengthening of the body politic. Third, the "pro-natalist" (Stivens 1987) thrust of the message diffused Malay fears of female domination in the labor force while accommodating the *dakwa* insistence on women's primary role as mothers. The prime minister was quoted as saying that women whose husbands could afford it should stay home to raise families of at least five children (Chee 1988:166). Undoubtedly, through such official approval and flattery of middle-class men (who can afford to support nonworking wives), the state regained control over the definition of the domestic domain, earning moral and even Islamic legitimacy in the process. The family development campaign suggested that middle-class women should rethink their options since the pregnant body at home can be even more patriotic than the female body at work. Furthermore, male-dominated Malay families are not incompatible with a growing population and capitalist economy.

Thus, despite differences over the issue of economic development, both resurgent Islam and the secular state have made the image of an Islamic modernity, with its powerful claims on women and their bodies, the key element in their competing visions of Malaysian society. The consequence of such ideological competition between official and religious nationalisms has been the intensification of Malay gender difference, segregation, and inequality. The intersection of hegemonic and counterhegemonic visions was occasioned in large part by an obsession with racial, political, and demographic domination on the one hand, and by an emergent, conservative middle class's need to maintain patriarchal control of the family on the other.

SOFT NATIONALISM AND SISTERS IN ISLAM

By the end of the 1980s, the Islamic resurgence had settled in as a low-key but pervasive part of urban Malay culture. Malay women continued to be conservatively dressed in long robes and *mini-telekung,* but their clothes were now cut in colorful, more glamorous styles. Few chose to drape themselves entirely in black. Growing economic affluence among Malays and increasing economic interdependence with other Asian countries had somewhat routinized the fervor of resurgent Islam and instilled a detachment from Middle East events like the Rushdie affair and the Gulf War. While the Islamic resurgence took more militaristic forms in the Middle East, in Malaysia both official and religious nationalisms became low-key, integrated into the fabric of a rapidly modernizing society in which the domination of the Malays is now well-assured. As inconsistencies between the *dakwa* political body and the physical body of desire and affluence grew, women's outfits reflected an interesting nexus of religious and fashion consciousness.[24] It is not so much that eroticism is breaking through the *dakwa* body, but rather that the body is being remanaged with a lighter hand.

Talking about another invented tradition in Malaysia, Clive S. Kessler (1992) notes the new expressions of loyalty through popular songs and media images celebrating the subject-leader relationship in Malay culture. On television, women again play important iconic roles, but this time, decked out in colorful, stereotypical costumes representing the different ethnic groups, they take turns singing a new patriotic song (*Lagu Setia*). Kessler observes that the song projects patriotism and loyalty as "a kind of falling in love, a voluptuous yearning, a chaste seduction." Loyalty, Kessler argues, is "reimagined and reinvented . . . as something modern, subtle, low-key" (1992:155). In sharp contrast to the forbidding *dakwa* image, this new multiracial female body is seductive, even yielding, tentatively open to outside influences. Such a repackaged "soft" nationalism, whereby politics, religion, culture, and entertainment are interwoven and inseparable, allows the racial body, and by extension the wider imagined community of Malaysia, to engender a limited kind of multiculturalism.[25]

As the Muslim–non-Muslim boundaries became less rigid, the state redirected its ideological energy toward the larger Asian arena. Increasingly, the state faced off challenges not so much from an Islamic resurgence, as from elements in the middle class agitating for the rights of women, political detainees and restive workers. The prime minister became internationally known for his outspoken criticism of the West, and defended his occasional curtailment of civil rights by proclaiming a culturally relative notion of "human rights" in Asian modernity. Anwar Ibrahim, former ABIM leader and the new deputy prime minister, had long set aside his ascetic, firebrand image for expensive batik silks. Perhaps anticipating being the ruler of a rich multiracial country, he speaks cordially of multicultural tolerance among the different races. This muting of racial and religious differences in public discourse also owes something to the fact that Taiwanese Chinese have become the most numerous foreign investors in the country, while the Malaysian government is competing for investments in China. Similarly, the low-key Islamic resurgence has been adjusted to local realities. The *hijab* has even become something of a patriotic fashion that is sometimes adopted by non-Muslim women to proclaim a generalized loyalty and vision of a multicultural Malaysia.

The merging and muting of state and religious nationalisms have created openings for a renegotiation of gender relations. The moral economy of resurgent Islam gave women little choice but to inscribe themselves into a "traditional" subordination, even when that position was itself an invented tradition.[26] Because Malay community, kinship and gender matters are informed by Islamic law, women who may resist their second-class status cannot draw upon civil laws to articulate women's rights. However, the *umma* has nurtured a group of Malay female professionals to invent other Islamic traditions heretofore ignored by male leaders. Calling themselves "Sisters in Islam," they seek to articulate women's rights within Islam by emphasizing the need to interpret the Qur'an and hadith in their proper historical and cultural contexts. They point out that narrowly literal interpretations of Islamic texts like the right to strike one's wife and polygamy may work against the rights of Muslim women in modern times. Through a careful citing of Islam's holy books, the Sisters identify the universal principle that the sexes are equal, "members, one of another."[27] They argue that the Qur'an suggested "a single strike" against the wife to restore marital peace (Verse 4:34) but that this was at a time when violence against women was rampant. Furthermore, they contest the view that polygamy is Islam's answer to "men's allegedly unbridled lust." Instead, they call upon men who abuse polygamy to seek Islamic guidance to change their promiscuous attitude to "one of self-discipline and respect for the opposite sex." Thus, contrary to hegemonic Islamic discourses that oppose male reason to female passion, the Sisters chide men for their lustfulness and lack of discipline: "It is not Islam that oppresses women, but human beings with all their weaknesses who have failed to understand Allah's intentions."[28]

Furthermore, by acting as reasoning Sisters in Islam, they present themselves as siblings arguing on equal terms with men and appealing to their much-vaunted male reason in reinterpreting Allah's will regarding women's status. They also criticize other forms of patriarchal practices said to be required by Islam, like the imposed female dress codes and even speech restrictions, as "mechanisms of control" masquerading as norms promoting feminine modesty. However, the Sisters' strategy unintentionally strengthens the reason-as-to-male versus passion-as-to-female ideology since only by being reasoning sisters can they get respectful male attention concerning the subordination of daughters, wives, and mothers (i.e., kinship statuses in which women's passions are experienced as more threatening). Thus women's rights in Islam are being fought for by a group exuding the chaste aura of learned sisters; the division between reason and passion remains, but now men have to be more mindful of their unruly passions, and women who work with their minds must be cast as sexually unthreatening.[29]

In contrast to the growing negotiations over middle-class Muslim women's rights, the resurgent Islamic party PAS, working among the rural poor, is agitating for greater controls over Muslims, especially over women. Recently, PAS introduced strict Islamic laws (*hudud*) in Kelantan state to punish offences like theft, robbery, apostasy, and unlawful sexual intercourse by stoning, whipping, and amputation. The laws are especially discriminatory against women since a rape victim must produce four male eyewitnesses in her defense. Thus just as the nation's Islamic elites have begun the tentative articulation of women's rights, peasant-based revivalists are seeking to impose a stricter kind of Islam, springing in part from an intensified sense of political marginalization and exclusion from the material benefits of capitalism. In Kuala Lumpur, where Malay middle-class religious fervor is tempered by affluence and cosmopolitanism, there is something surreal in the prime minister declaring that "I don't think we are going to allow them to chop off heads, hands, and feet."[30] The chaste voluptuous body of affluent Malay nationalism faces off the specter of a truncated one representing patriarchal Islam. Thus, the struggle between state nationalism and Islamic radicalism continues in another guise on other sites, rooted in other class, political, and regional dynamics, but still focused on regulating women, who symbolize the varied ways Islam may be deployed to loosen or control the body politic in an unevenly modernized country. Indeed, it appears that the newly "reasonable" resurgent Islam and the newly affluent state are both seeking to regulate not just women's bodies, but ultimately *all* bodies.[31]

CONCLUSIONS

In the postcolonial era, many Third World states have had to contend with communally based narratives expressing particular interests that have been overlooked in nationalist struggles against colonialism. In Southeast Asia, as postcolonial states sponsored changes that uprooted peasants, intervened in the conduct of family relations, and created new urban classes, they also produced nationalist ideologies that rationalize these transformations in technocratic (World Bank) terms. Among groups dislocated by these changes, crises in cultural identity created counterideologies that are obsessively concerned with controlling resources, group boundaries, and articulating belonging in transcendental terms. Women, as symbols and agents of change, have to be brought into line with the new orthodoxies. Other scholars have shown that historically, the emerging middle classes have turned to a religious resurgence to construct patriarchal family orders, and to patrol the boundaries between the domestic and public, insiders and outsiders. It bears remembering that all Great Religions—Islam, Christianity, Hinduism, and Buddhism—are heavily patriarchal, investing substantial weight in women's roles as wives and mothers. Whether the emerging middle classes turn to Christian fundamentalism (e.g., Ryan 1981) or Islamic resurgence in order to conserve their economic, political and cultural resources, they find in religion an important source of competing nationalist ideologies in modernizing societies.

The twists and turns in gender contestations show vividly that gender politics are seldom merely about gender; they represent and crystallize nationwide struggles over a crisis of cultural identity, development, class formation, and the changing kinds of imagined community that are envisioned. The management and self-managing that women's bodies come to represent is in tandem with the larger forces at work in the construction of the body politic. Religious conservatism, almost always symbolized by confining women's agency and space, may eventually give way to looser mechanisms for controlling women's bodily and social movements, and the boundaries of the imagined community. As the middle class gains more security and confidence, women play a greater role in reworking gender inequality and group boundaries within the religious orthodoxy. In places like late-twentieth-century Malaysia, local conditions and complex racial and cultural features have produced a particular form of rivalry between the ideological state and Islamic revivalists, and conditioned the responses of women who both symbolize and negotiate these contestations over women and imagined communities. Rather than seeing the agency of middle-class Malay women in terms of mere resistance or passivity, I have argued that it has been shaped by the intersection of their own self-interests with their group identity, contingent upon the historical changes in Malay society and in Malaysia over the past two decades. By yielding to religious and class forces, and by working to protect the integrity of their bodies, families, and the body politic, women have found new ways of belonging in a changing Malaysia.

NOTES

An earlier and shorter version of this chapter appeared as "State versus Islam: Malay Families, Women's Bodies, and the Body Politic in Malaysia," *American Ethnologist* 17(2):258–276, May 1990. I am particularly grateful to Michael Peletz for his thoughtful and helpful suggestions in this new version.

1. Furthermore, Scott's argument that Malaysian state hegemony stops at the village gates and that peasants' everyday resistances are informed by a Malay village subculture unadulterated by wider politics is problematic for two major reasons. It reveals his misreading of the Gramscian notion of hegemony as an ideological formation which dominates through the creation of false consciousness, and which does not allow for oppositional views (Scott 1985: 316–18). Actually, Gramsci was very critical of the "false consciousness" model, and developed hegemony as an alternative theory of rule by consent (not oppression or mystification), which is an always open-ended process (1971; see also Williams 1977). However, in Scott's view, when Malay peasants challenge hegemonic views of development, they can only do so from a position he artificially defines as outside the realm of state hegemony (Scott 1985: 335–40). He seems to have missed the Gramscian notion of counterhegemony, and its dialectical relationship to hegemonic forms. Thus Scott came to misrepresent social realities in rural Malaysia as a simple dichotomy between a national hegemony and a resistant village subculture. In contrast, other scholars provide a more complex and entangled picture of Malay peasants in their daily lives deeply implicated in the religious, ethnic, and political economic hegemonies prevailing in the country (see Kessler 1978; Shamsul 1986; Ong 1987; Peletz 1995).

2. Federated Malay States Enactment no. 15, 1913.

3. "Malay" in the Malaysian context denotes persons of a Malay-Muslim identity. They are Sunni Muslims at birth. The term "Malay" will be used interchangeably with *bumiputera* (sons of the soil). Since the Malay language does not use suffixes to denote the plural condition, words like *kampung* and *bumiputera* will not be suffixed with an "s."

4. This article deals only with the situation in West (Peninsular) Malaysia. In 1985, there were about 13 million citizens, with Malays making up some 56 percent, Chinese 33 percent and Indians 10 percent of the population (Government of Malaysia 1986:128–129).

5. It is important to stress that the Malay *kampung* women I interviewed saw Islamic beliefs about sexuality in a positive light. For instance, *kampung* women claimed that female circumcision (partial removal of the clitoral hood) increased a woman's sexual pleasure during intercourse (cf. Reid 1988:149). *Kampung* women use different techniques and tonics (*jamu*) to condition their bodies for enhancing erotic pleasure. Sex was considered essential to good health and a normal life and only viewed negatively when indulged in excessively or with an unsuitable partner.

6. Similar attitudes toward female sexuality outside marriage are found in many Asian, Middle East, and Mediterranean societies. See Goddard (1987) who argues

that Neapolitan male control of female sexuality is linked to women's role as the bearers of group identity.

7. See Government of Malaysia (1976:2, 9), and Siddique (1981). In 1970, the Malay share of equity capital was 2.4 percent. The NEP sought to expand that figure by entitling *bumiputera* to equity held in trust by special government agencies. By 1990, *bumiputera* equity still fell short of 30 percent, but the new affluence has made it possible for the government to promote economic growth among the poor in all ethnic communities without holding back wealth accumulation by the *bumiputera* as a whole.

8. Government of Malaysia (1976:86–89).

9. Formerly, Malay women could turn to midwives for covert treatment to prevent childbirth, but traditional midwifery is now officially frowned upon (Laderman 1983:104–105). The modern health system reduces women's role in birth prevention because men have become more directly involved in decision making affecting women's health.

10. Government of Malaysia (1976:9).

11. In the 1960s, wedding payments were in the range of M$100 to M$500. The increase in payments between 1976 and 1980 also reflected a rise in mean age at first marriage—from late adolescence to 22 years for women and 28 years for men.

12. *The New Straits Times*, November 8, 1983, p .2.

13. Government of Malaysia (1986:83–84).

14. The term "Islamic resurgence" is widely used to describe the activities and ideologies of both rural peasant and urban middle-class groups. I focus on the latter here because they were more numerous and had a wider effect on the upper echelons of Malay society. For different interpretations of the causes of the Islamic resurgence, see Lyon (1979), Nagata (1984), Chandra (1986), Kessler (1978, 1980), Mohammad (1981), Muhammad Kamal (1987), and Zainah (1987).

15. The *dakwa* leaders were challenging the legal dualism between religion and government inherited from British colonial rule (see Roff 1967). They wished to expand the scope of Islamic law (*hukum*) to cover areas currently governed by civil and criminal law.

16. He did not mention that Katijah (Ar., Khadija) was many years older than Muhammad and an enterprising business woman in her own right.

17. This rhetorical insistence on the husband's sexual needs ignores the *adat* expectation that husbands and wives will satisfy each other sexually. Good marriages seem to require lively sexual encounters, commonly referred to as "sparring" (*melawan*). A man's inability to please his wife sexually may become the subject of gossip (Karim 1992).

18. *The New Straits Times*, July 14, 1988, p. 2.

19. See Reid (1988:85–90) for a brief historical account of Malay clothing from the fifteenth century onward. The coming of Islam induced otherwise bare-chested Malay women and men to wear loose tunics (*baju*) above their sarongs. However, heavily veiled women "covered from head to foot" were observed only in Makassar (in present-day Indonesia) in the mid-seventeenth century.

20. A. C. Hepburn observes that in societies dominated by a numerically small

majority, the containment of intermarriage is crucial to the maintenance of the existing population structure (1978:4).

21. This grandmother, lounging on her verendah in full view of passersby, sometimes opened her blouse and allowed her three-year-old grandson to play with her breasts. She gave the impression that she pitied her granddaughter who was "having such hard life" as a student and unmarried woman.

22. Soheir Morsy used the word "depeasantization" to describe the Islamic resurgence in Egypt, where out-migration and education have created a new ideology of the discontented upwardly mobile (personal communication).

23. Government of Malaysia (1984:21–22). Demographic projections of the various ways the population can grow to 70 million in a hundred years have been worked out by Jones and Lim (1985), and by Chee (1988:167), who argues that the population policy could legitimize using women as a population reserve.

24. Conflicts between the status body and the physical body are a key theme in Takie Lebra's (1994) highly suggestive essay on the imperial family and body politic in Japan.

25. Prasenjit Duara makes a distinction between an incipient nationality with soft boundaries that allow cultural practices to be shared and adopted between groups, and nationalism with hard boundaries, when selected cultural practices are used to mobilize and define the boundaries of a particular group (1993:20). Here I am using "soft nationalism" in a slightly different way, as one that allows some intermingling of culture at the borders of groups, and as a national identity that can coexist with nationalism identified with fixed boundaries. I also use "soft nationalism" to denote the low-key, media-processed patriotism that has overtaken more strident forms like the Islamic resurgence.

26. It is important to note that this "re-traditionalization" (Williams n.d.) is a mythic invention. One should therefore be cautious of statements about the Malay middle class's reconstruction of Malay identity "through the symbols of a traditional, village-based, feudalistic and patriarchal Malay culture" (Joel Kahn, cited in Kessler 1992:146) when that "culture" is described in such static and extreme terms. See Banks (1983), Ong (1987), and Peletz (1995) for more complex, ethnographically based descriptions of gender relations in different Malay village communities.

27. *Asiaweek*, August 9, 1991, p. 27; see also *Asiaweek*, November 17, 1993, p. 17.

28. Ibid.

29. See Peletz 1995, chapter 5, for an extended and careful discussion of how the reason:passion gender ideology is unevenly embraced by Malay women and men as practical knowledge. See also Peletz 1988 for a discussion of the striking importance of the sibling relationship in Malay society as a channel for familial aid, exchange and mediation, but also as a source of ambivalence and hostility.

30. *South China Morning Post*, November 22, 1993, p. 14.

31. Including the bodies of male transvestites called *pondan/Mak Nyah* (Peletz 1995, chap. 3). I thank Michael Peletz for pointing this out to me.

REFERENCES

Ackerman, Susan. 1984. "The Impact of Industrialization on the Social Role of Rural Malay Women." In Hing Ai Yun, Nik Safiah Karim, and Rokiah Talib, eds., *Women in Malaysia,* pp. 40–70. Petaling Jaya, Malaysia: Pelanduk Publications.

Amriah Buang. 1989. "Development and Factory Women—Negative Perceptions from a Malaysian Source Area." Paper presented at the Commonwealth Geographical Bureau Workshop on Gender and Development. University of Newcastle, April 16–21.

Anagnost, Ann. 1989. "Prosperity and Counterprosperity: The Moral Discourse on Wealth in Post-Mao China." In Arif Dirlik and Maurice Miesner, eds., *Marxism and the Chinese Experience: Issues in Contemporary Chinese Socialism,* pp. 210–234. Armon, N.Y.: M. E. Sharpe.

Anderson, Benedict R. O'G. 1992. *Imagined Communities: Reflections on the Origins of Nationalism.* 2d ed. London: Verso.

Anwar Ibrahim. 1986. "Development, Values and Changing Political Ideas." *Sojourn* 1(1):1–7.

Asad, Talal. 1987. "Conscripts of Western Civilization." Unpublished ms.

Azizah Kassim. 1987. "Women and Divorce among the Urban Malays." In Hing Ai Yun, Nik Safiah Karim, and Rokiah Talib, eds., *Women in Malaysia,* pp. 94–112. Petaling Jaya, Malaysia: Pelanduk Publications.

Banks, David. 1983. *Malay Kinship.* Philadelphia: ISHI Publications.

Chandra Muzaffar. 1986. "Malaysia: Islamic Resurgence and the Question of Development." *Sojourn* 1(1):57–75.

Chatterjee, Partha. 1993. *The Nation and Its Fragments: Colonial and Postcolonial Histories.* Princeton: Princeton University Press.

Chee Heng Leng. 1988. "Babies to Order: Recent Population Policies in Malaysia and Singapore." In Bina Agarwal, ed., *Structures of Patriarchy: The State, the Community, and the Household,* pp. 164–174. London: Zed Books Ltd.

Clad, James. 1984. "The Patchwork Society." *Far Eastern Economic Review* (April 20): 109–110.

Comaroff, Jean. 1985. *Body of Power, Spirit of Resistance: The Culture and History of a South African People.* Chicago: University of Chicago Press.

Das, K. 1982. "Mahathir's 'Restoration.' " *Far Eastern Economic Review* (June 11): 38–39.

———. 1983. "A Shift in the Balance." *Far Eastern Economic Review* (June 2): 42–43.

Djamour, Judith. 1959. *Malay Kinship and Marriage in Singapore.* London: Athlone Press.

Donzelot, Jacques. 1979. *The Policing of Families.* New York: Random House.

Duara, Prasenjit. 1993. "Deconstructing the Chinese Nation." *Australian Journal of Chinese Affairs* 30:1–28.

Federated Malay States Enactment, no. 15. 1913. Ms. *Arkib Negara Malaysia* (National Archives of Malaysia). Petaling Jaya, Malaysia.

Firth, Rosemary. 1966. *Housekeeping among Malay Peasants.* New York: Humanities Press.

Foucault, Michel. 1978. *The History of Sexuality.* Trans. Robert Hurley. Vol. 1, *An Introduction.* New York: Pantheon.

———. 1980. *Power/Knowledge.* Trans. Colin Gordon. New York: Pantheon.

Goddard, Victoria. 1987. "Honor and Shame: The Control of Women's Sexuality and Group Identity in Naples." In Pat Caplan, ed., *The Cultural Construction of Sexuality,* pp. 166–192. New York: Tavistock Publications.

Government of Malaysia. 1976. *Third Malaysia Plan, 1976–1980.* Kuala Lumpur: Government Printing Press.

———. 1984. *Mid-Term Review of the Fourth Malaysia Plan, 1981–1985.* Kuala Lumpur: Government Printing Press.

———. 1986. *Fifth Malaysia Plan, 1986–1990.* Kuala Lumpur: Government Printing Press.

Gramsci, Antonio. 1971. *Selections from the Prison Notebooks of Antonio Gramsci.* Ed. and trans. Quinten Hoare and Geoffrey Nowell Smith. New York: International Publishers.

Hassan, Muhammad Kamal. 1987. "The Response of Muslim Youth Organizations to Political Change: HMI in Indonesia and ABIM in Malaysia." In William R. Roff, ed., *Islam and the Political Economy of Meaning,* pp. 180–196. Berkeley: University of California Press.

Hepburn, A. C. 1978. "Minorities in History." In A. C. Hepburn, ed., *Minorities in History: Papers Read before the Thirtieth Irish Conference of Historians at the New University of Ulster, 1977,* pp. 1–10. London: Edward Arnold.

Hirschman, Charles. 1986. "The Recent Rise in Malay Fertility: A New Trend or a Temporary Lull in a Fertility Transition?" *Demography* 23(2):161–184.

Hobsbawm, Eric. 1983. "Introduction: Inventing Traditions." In Eric Hobsbawm and Terence Ranger, eds., *The Invention of Tradition,* pp. 1–14. New York: Cambridge University Press.

Jamilah Ariffin. 1980. "Industrial Development in Peninsular Malaysia and Rural-Urban Migration of Women Workers: Impact and Implications." *Jurnal Ekonomi Malaysia* 1:41–59.

Jomo K. Sundaram. 1988. *A Question of Class: Capital, the State, and Uneven Development in Malaysia.* New York: Monthly Review Press.

Jones, Gavin, and Lim Lin Lee. 1985. "Scenarios for the Future Population Growth in Malaysia." *Kajian Malaysia* 3(2):1–24.

Kabeer, Naila. 1988. "Subordination and Struggle: Women in Bangladesh." *New Left Review* 168:95–121.

Kahn, Joel S., and Francis K. W. Loh, eds. 1993. *Fragmented Vision: Culture and Politics in Contemporary Malaysia.* Honolulu: University of Hawaii Press.

Karim Wazir Jahan. 1992. *Women and Culture: Between Malay Adat and Islam.* Boulder: Westview Press.

Kassim Ahmad. 1986. *Hadis: Satu Penilailan Semula* (The Hadith: A Reinterpretation). Petaling Jaya, Malaysia: Media Intelek Sdn. Bhd.

Kessler, Clive S. 1978. *Islam and Politics in a Malay State: Kelantan 1838–1969.* Ithaca: Cornell University Press.

———. 1980. "Malaysia: Islamic Revivalism and Political Disaffection in a Divided Society." *Southeast Asia Chronicle* 75:3–11.

———. 1992. "Archaism and Modernity: Contemporary Malay Political Culture."

In Joel S. Kahn and Francis K. W. Loh, eds., *Fragmented Vision: Culture and Politics in Contemporary Malaysia,* pp. 133–157. Honolulu: University of Hawaii Press.

Kua Kia Soong. 1983. "Look East, But Watch for Blemishes." *Far Eastern Economic Review* (March 31): 69–70.

Laderman, Carol. 1983. *Wives and Midwives: Childbirth and Nutrition in Rural Malaysia.* Berkeley: University of California Press.

Lebra, Takie. 1994. "Status Dilemma and the Body Politic in Japan." Paper presented at the Department of Anthropology, University of California, Berkeley, January 28.

Lyon, Margo. 1979. "The Dakwah Movement in Malaysia." *Review of Indonesian and Malaysian Affairs* 13(2):34–45.

Mauzy, Diane K., and R. S. Milne. 1983. "The Mahathir Administration in Malaysia: Discipline through Islam." *Pacific Affairs* 55:617–648.

Mernissi, Fatima. 1987. *Beyond the Veil: Male-Female Dynamics in Modern Muslim Society.* Rev. ed. Bloomington: Indiana University Press.

Milner, A. C. 1982. *Kerajaan: Malay Political Culture on the Eve of Colonial Rule.* Tuscon: University of Arizona Press.

Mohammad Abu Bakar. 1981. "Islamic Revivalism and the Political Process in Malaysia." *Asian Survey* 21:1040–1059.

Nagata, Judith. 1984. *The Reflowering of Malaysian Islam.* Vancouver: University of British Columbia Press.

Narli, Ayse Nilufer. 1981. "Development, Malay Women, and Islam in Malaysia: Emerging Contradictions." *Kajian Malaysia* 2:123–141.

Ong, Aihwa. 1987. *Spirits of Resistance and Capitalist Discipline: Factory Women in Malaysia.* Albany: SUNY Press.

———. 1990. "Japanese Factories, Malay Workers: Class and Sexual Metaphors in West Malaysia." In Jane M. Atkinson and Shelly Errington, eds., *Power and Difference: Gender in Island Southeast Asia,* pp. 385–422, 453–457. Stanford: Stanford University Press.

———. 1995. "Postcolonial Nationalism: Women and Retraditionalization in the Islamic Imaginary, Malaysia." In Connie Sutton, ed., *Feminism, Nationalism, and Militarism.* Arlington: American Anthropological Association.

Peletz, Michael G. 1988. *A Share of the Harvest: Kinship, Property, and Social History among the Malays of Rembau.* Berkeley: University of California Press.

———. 1993. "Sacred Texts and Dangerous Words: The Politics of Law and Cultural Rationalization in Malaysia." *Comparative Studies in Society and History* 35(1):66–109.

———. 1995. *Reason and Passion: Representations of Gender in a Malay Society.* Berkeley: University of California Press.

Reid, Anthony. 1988. *Southeast Asia in the Age of Commerce, 1450–1680.* Vol. 1, *The Lands Below the Winds.* New Haven: Yale University Press.

Roff, William R. 1967. *The Origins of Malay Nationalism.* New Haven: Yale University Press.

Ryan, Mary. 1981. *The Cradle of the Middle Class.* Cambridge: Cambridge University Press.

Sabbah, Fatna A. 1984. *Women in the Muslim Unconscious.* New York: Pergamon Press.

Salaff, Janet W. 1988. *State and Family in Singapore: Restructuring a Developing Society.* Ithaca: Cornell University Press.

Scott, James C. 1985. *Weapons of the Weak: Everyday Forms of Peasant Resistance.* New Haven: Yale University Press.

Shamsul Amri Baharuddin. 1986. *From British to Bumiputera Rule: Local Politics and Rural Development in Peninsular Malaysia.* Singapore: Institute of South East Asian Studies.

Siddique, Sharon. 1981. "Some Aspects of Malay-Muslim Ethnicity in Peninsular Malaysia." *Contemporary Southeast Asia* 3(1):76–87.

Stivens, Maila. 1987. "Family and State in Malaysian Industrialization: The Case of Rembau, Negri Sembilan, Malaysia." In Haleh Afshar, ed., *Women, State, and Ideology,* pp. 89–110. Albany: SUNY Press.

Strathern, Marilyn. 1987. "Introduction." In Marilyn Strathern, ed., *Dealing with Inequality: Analysing Gender Relations in Melanesia and Beyond,* pp. 1–32. Cambridge: Cambridge University Press.

Swift, Michael. 1963. "Men and Women in Malay Society." In Barbara Ward, ed., *Women in the New Asia: The Changing Social Roles of Men and Women in South and Southeast Asia,* pp. 268–286. Paris: UNESCO.

Williams, Brackette F., ed. n.d. *Mannish Women: Retraditionalized Female Gender and the Nationality of Domesticity.* New York: Routledge. Forthcoming.

Williams, Raymond. 1977. *Marxism and Literature.* Oxford: Oxford University Press.

Wong, Diana. 1988. *Peasants in the Making: Malaysia's Green Revolution.* Singapore: Singapore University Press.

Zainah Anwar. 1987. *Islamic Revivalism in Malaysia.* Petaling Jaya, Malaysia: Pelanduk Publications.

SIX

State Fatherhood:
The Politics of Nationalism, Sexuality,
and Race in Singapore

Geraldine Heng and Janadas Devan

Geraldine Heng and Janadas Devan explore how the problematization of mothers in Singapore's state narratives is linked to the wider, largely hidden anxiety over racial and class imbalances. The national "narrative of reproductive crisis" employs various genetic and sociobiological studies to substantiate its claim that highly educated ("graduate") women are failing to produce babies at a sufficiently high rate, compared to poorly educated women who are perceived as reproducing "too freely." Significantly, such "lopsided" female reproductive rates also vary along racial lines, with "graduate women" encoding mainly Chinese women, and "women of no education" mainly Malays and Indians. Thus female sexuality becomes a target of state discipline, as "graduate women" are urged to marry and bear children as a patriotic duty, the realization of which will avert the slide toward economic and broadly social chaos. The problematization of (Chinese) female sexuality entails discourses on (unreproductive) women that focus on their interstitial positioning, just as it feeds into the reproduction of state ideologies refiguring Confucianism. Official narratives depict Western ways (even or especially their Singaporean versions) as a threat to Confucian culture, by inculcating a feminized social body that is (overly) receptive to other cultural influences. A phallic Confucian narrative is thus elaborated to tie the (re)traditionalized Chinese family more closely to state authority, a key feature of which is the defense of cultural continuity and economic success against the "invasion of difference" represented by other "softer" cultures and races. Heng and Devan suggest that by borrowing the categories of the West, the "internalized orientalism" of state narratives participates in a "gendered formation of power" whereby a timeless Confucian paternal essence is defined as embodying the nation, whereas women are "by definition always and already antinational."

Postcolonial governments are inclined, with some predictability, to generate narratives of national crisis, driven perhaps—the generous explanation—to reenact periodically the state's traumatic if also liberating separation from colonial authority, a moment catachrestically founding the nation itself *qua* nation. Typically, however, such narratives of crisis serve more than one category of reassurance: by repeatedly focusing anxiety on the fragility of the new nation, its ostensible vulnerability to every kind of exigency, the state's originating agency is periodically reinvoked and ratified, its access to wideranging instruments of power in the service of national protection continually consolidated. It is a post-Foucauldian truism that they who successfully define and superintend a crisis, furnishing its lexicon and discursive parameters, successfully confirm themselves the owners of power, the administration of crisis operating to revitalize ownership of the instruments of power even as it vindicates the necessity of their use.

If a postcolonial government remains continuously in office for decades beyond its early responsibility for the nation's emergence, as is the case in the Republic of Singapore, the habit of generating narratives of crisis at intervals becomes an entrenched, dependable practice. While the metaphors deployed, causes identified, and culpabilities named in the detection of crisis necessarily undergo migration, accusation by the government of Singapore—whose composite representation is overwhelmingly male, Chinese, and socioeconomically and educationally privileged—has been increasingly directed in recent years to such segments of society as do not give back an image of the state's founding fathers to themselves. Precise adequacy on the part of the citizenry to an ideal standard of nationalism then becomes referenced, metonymically, to the successful if fantasmatic reproduction of an ideal image of its fathers. Crisis is unerringly discovered—threats to the survival and continuity of the nation, failures in nationalism—when a distortion in the replication or scale of a composition deemed ideal is fearfully imagined.

NATIONALISM AND SEXUALITY: IDEOLOGIES OF REPRODUCTION

That an obsession with ideal replication in the register of the imaginary can lend itself to somatic literalization—transformed through acts of state power into a large-scale social project of *biological* reproduction—is the disturbing subtext of one of the most tenacious and formidable of state narratives constructed in Singapore's recent history, with consequences yet proliferating at the time of this article. Hinging precisely on a wishful fantasy of exact self-replication, this narrative of crisis posits, as the essential condition of national survival, the regeneration of the country's population (its heterogenous national body) in such ratios of race and class as would faithfully mirror the population's original composition at the nation's founding moment, retrospectively apotheosized. In an aggressive exposition of paternal distress in August 1983 that ranges authoritatively over such subjects as genetic inheritance and culture, definitions of intelligence, social and economic justice and responsibility, and gender theory, the nation's father of founding fathers, then Prime Minister Lee Kuan Yew, levelled an extraordinary charge against the nation's *mothers,* incipient and actual—accusing them of imperiling the country's future by wilfully distorting patterns of biological reproduction. The disclosure of a reproductive crisis took place, suitably, on the anniversary of the state's birth, during the Prime Minister's annual National Day Rally speech, as part of the celebrations commemorating the country's emergence as a national entity.[1]

The crisis, as formulated by him, received this inflection: highly educated women in Singapore, defined as those with a university degree, were not producing babies in sufficient numbers to secure their self-replacement in the population, either because of a failure to marry, or, having married, a failure to bear more than 1.65 children per married couple, he declared. On the other hand, poorly educated women, defined as those who do not complete the equivalent of an elementary school education (women of "no education" or "no qualifications," as they came to be called), were reproducing too freely, generating 3.5 children each; women with only an elementary education, producing 2.7 children, were also outstripping the "graduate mothers," as the Prime Minister called them.

This was a problem, Lee reasoned, because graduate mothers produced genetically superior offspring, the ability to complete a university education attesting to superior mental faculties, which would be naturally transmitted to offspring through genetic inheritance. Eighty percent of a child's intelligence, Lee explained, citing certain studies in genetics and sociobiology, was predetermined by nature, while nurture accounted for the remaining twenty percent. Within a few generations, the quality of Singapore's population would measurably decline, with a tiny minority of intelligent persons being increasingly swamped by a seething, proliferating mass of the unintelligent, untalented, and genetically inferior: industry would suffer, technology deteriorate, leadership disappear, and Singapore lose its competitive edge in the world. Since his was a tiny country of no natural resources and few advantages other than the talents of its people, if measures were not immediately taken to counteract the downhill slide caused by "lopsided" female reproductive sexuality, a catastrophe of major proportions was imminent a scant few generations down the line.[2]

It would seem that men did not figure prominently in the Prime Minister's dystopian vision because his statistics revealed to him that Singapore women as a rule selected mates of equal or superior academic standing; graduate mothers alone, therefore, could be relied on to guarantee the genetic purity of the tribe. Closer examination of his tables consequently revealed that class and race, however, were the major, suppressed categories of his anxiety, since the women of recalcitrant fertility were by and large Chinese, upper- and middle-class professionals, while those of inordinate reproductive urges and no university degrees comprised, by a stunning coincidence, working-class women of Malay and Indian ethnic origin—members, that is, of Singapore's minority racial groups. The Chinese majority, then 76 percent, was shrinking at the terrifying rate of 7 percent in each generation, even as Malays, a mere 15 percent, were wildly proliferating by 4 percent per generation, and Indians, then 6 percent of the population, by 1 percent. The threat of impending collapse in the social and economic order, for which an unruly, destabilizing, and irresponsible feminine sexuality was held to account, was covertly located at the intersecting registers of race and class. Chaos, in this prophecy of national disaster, was visualized as the random interplay of excess and deficiency among female bodies, which, left unregulated, would produce disabling, ungovernable, and unsafe equations of class and race.[3]

If Lee's articulation of genetic inheritance, culture, education, intelligence, and reproductive sexuality seems inordinately mechanical, his faith in the assumed infallibility (and univocality) of statistics oddly uncritical, and his commitment to the logic of racial and class regulation relentless, it is because he subscribes, without apology, to a projective model of society as an economic and social machine. His stated preference, on the controversial issue of intelligence, for genetic catalogs and theories of determination over such arguments as would consider the interplay of social, psychic, historical, cultural, environmental, *and* genetic forces operating on the human subject (the reductive impatience leading him to extract, from a small-scale study on identical twins by Thomas Bouchard of the University of Minnesota, easy, simplistic axioms and catchphrases on universal essences of human nature, expressed in tidy percentages) merely evinces a concomitant desire for the human organism to function, also, like a machine. The language of eugenics is precisely for Lee a language of efficient automation—a syntax and grammar congenially identical to his own, and to that routinely employed by his ministers and cohorts in public discourse—the appeal of eugenics residing, for him, in its very promise, however fugitive it might seem to others, of state-of-the-art biological replication: a superior technology to guarantee the efficient manufacture of superior-quality babies (the machine of eugenics confirming the body machine).[4]

The investment in mechanical models of human reproduction, social formations, and the body, exposes, of course, the desire for an absolute mastery, the desire that mastery be absolutely possible. Functional machines in everyday life—machines as they are recognized by Lee, and used in Singapore society—are predictable and orderly, blessedly convenient:

malfunctioning ones can be adjusted, faulty components replaced, and the whole made to work again with a minimum of fuss. Most pointedly, a machine presupposes—indeed, requires—an operator, since a machine commonly exists in the first place in order to be operated: relieving all suspicion that full supervisory control may be impossible (exorcising, that is, the specter of desire, instability, and an unconscious from human formations), the trope of the machine comfortingly suggests that what eludes, limits, or obstructs absolute knowability, management, and control, can be routinely evacuated.

The indictment of women, then—working-class and professional, Malay, Indian, and Chinese—inscribes a tacit recognition that feminine reproductive sexuality refuses, and in refusing, undermines the fantasy of the body-machine, a conveniently operable somatic device: thus also undoing, by extension, that other fantasied economy, society as an equally operable contraption. Indeed, the disapproval, simultaneously, of an overly productive and a non(re)productive feminine sexuality registers a suspicion of that sexuality as noneconomic, driven by pleasure: sexuality for its own sake, unproductive of babies, or babies for their own sake, unproductive of social and economic efficiency.[5] That women of minority races should stand accused of a runaway irresponsibility, moreover, neatly conjoins two constituencies of society believed to be most guilty of pursuing the non-economy of pleasure (pleasure as, indeed, noneconomic): the female, and the "soft" Indian/Malay citizen, whose earthy sexuality, putative garrulousness, laziness, emotional indulgence, or other distressingly irrational characteristics conform to reprobate stereotypes of ethnicity and gender that have, in recent years, prominently found their way into public discourse.

In the months that followed his sketch of a future, feminine-instigated apocalypse, controversy of a sort arose around the issue, whose political volatility was at once and slyly undercut, however, by its characterization in the national press and electronic media (which are in Singapore either directly state-owned, state-dominated, or subject to severely restrictive licensing laws) as a "Great Marriage Debate." Its reduction to merely a "debate," and over merely an old, respectable, and comfortably familiar institution, marriage, strategically moved the issue away from any explicit recognition of or engagement with its deeply political, and politically extreme, content. The English-language newspapers would have it, moreover, that the vast majority of their readers were concerned merely to help the Prime Minister accomplish his goal of increased numbers of graduate babies; and since access to popular opinion through media uninflected by state control was, and still remains, unavailable, the character of the public response could only be gauged from what was selected for publication in newspaper letters' columns, or broadcast on state-run radio and television programming.[6]

Even as public discussion began, however (a discussion mercilessly regulated by speeches and pronouncements from government cohorts of every description, all tirelessly repeating and expatiating at length on the Prime Minister's arguments in a concerted drive to overwhelm public opinion), the government moved with characteristic preemptive speed to launch a comprehensive system of incentives and threats, together with major changes of social policy, to bend the population in the direction of the Prime Minister's will. Cash awards of S$10,000 were offered to working-class women, under careful conditions of educational and low-income eligibility, to restrict their childbearing to two children, after which they would "volunteer" themselves for tubal ligation. The scheme was piously tricked out in the language of philanthropic concern and state munificence—one fawning newspaper headline even proclaiming it the "Govt's $10,000 Helping Hand for the Low Income Families" [sic]. At the same time as the formal statement from the Prime Minister's office grandly and unctuously trumpeted its benevolence, maternity charges in public (that is, government-run) hospital wards most frequently used by working-class mothers were increased for those who had already given birth to their state-preferred quota of two children.[7]

To entice graduate women to have more children, on the other hand, generous tax breaks, medical insurance privileges, and admission for their children to the best schools in the country were promised, *inter alia*— prompting legal scholars and others to object that such discriminatory, class-inflected practices were manifestly and blatantly unconstitutional.[8] Changes in school admissions policy to privilege further the privileged were nonetheless implemented, the government countering criticism with a massive disinformation effort which shamelessly sought to persuade the disadvantaged that their children, too, would profit from the new hierarchies ("Non-Graduates Will Also Benefit," one newspaper headline soothingly cajoled the public; another announced, with unremitting cruelty, "More Good News for Non-Graduate Mums: All Primary Schools Are of Fairly Equal Standard").[9] Other transformations in social policy followed— altered entrance criteria to the country's only existing university to favor men over women applicants, since the Prime Minister's statistics had suggested to him that male more than female university graduates tended to marry and have children;[10] a revised family planning program that now urged *all who could afford it* to have at least three children (where its former policy had encouraged the two-child family as the ideal norm for all, equally); and, more recently, the suggestion that certain restrictions may be placed on legalized abortion, freely available in Singapore since 1974[11]—but with their relationship to the priorities advertised in the so-called Great Marriage Debate officially denied, minimized, or simply passing unreported and undiscussed. Among its own employees, the govern-

ment decided to require members of the Civil Service in the higher echelons—Division One officers, who no doubt qualify as intelligent—to submit
detailed personal information on themselves and their families, including
their "marital status, the educational qualifications of their spouses, and
the number of children" they had; and at least one civil servant was sum-
marily selected ("assigned") to undergo an experiment in the use of commercial matchmaking services abroad.[12]

Cabinet ministers began to exhort graduate women to marry and bear
children *as a patriotic duty*. Obediently taking their cue from the government, two (nonfeminist) women's organizations accordingly proposed, in
a disturbing collusion with state patriarchy, that women be *required* to bear
children as a form of National Service—the equivalent, in feminine, biological terms, of the two-and-a-half-year military service compulsorily performed by men for the maintenance of national defense.[13] A sexualized,
separate species of nationalism, in other words, was being advocated for
women: as patriotic duty for men grew out of the barrel of a gun (phallic
nationalism, the wielding of a surrogate technology of the body in national
defense), so would it grow, for women, out of the recesses of the womb
(uterine nationalism, the body *as* a technology of defense wielded by the
nation). Men bearing arms, and women bearing children; maternal and/
as military duty: the still-recent history of Nazi Germany grimly but not
uniquely reminds us that certain narratives of nationalism and dispositions
of state power specifically require the exercise of control over the body,
the track of power on bodies being visited differently according to gender.
The demand that women serve the nation biologically, with their bodies—
that they take on themselves, and submit themselves to, the public reproduction of nationalism in the most private medium possible, forcefully reveals the anxious relationship, in the fantasies obsessing state patriarchy,
between reproducing power and the power to reproduce: the efficacy of
the one being expressly contingent on the containment and subsumption
of the other.[14]

As the Prime Minister himself spoke with ominous nostalgia of the traditional means by which women had been variously coerced into bearing
children in most Asian cultures of the past, the dependence of paternal
power—its assurance of regenerative survival—on the successful con-
scription and discipline of female reproductive sexuality within hierarchical structures dominated by patriarchs, explicitly surfaced. Lee spoke feel-
ingly of the past, when families could enforce the marriage of their
daughters by arranging marriages of convenience without their daughters'
consent.[15] He expressed regret at his government's socialist policies in the
heady days of early postcolonial independence, when women's suffrage
and universal education relinquished to women some control over their
biological destinies.[16] He speculated thoughtfully on the possibility of rein-

troducing polygamy (by which he meant *polygyny* rather than polyandry), outlawed in Singapore since the Women's Charter of 1961, and voiced frank, generous admiration of virile Chinese patriarchs of the past, whose retinues of wives, mistresses, and illegitimate children unquestionably testified, under principles of social Darwinism, to their own, and thus their children's genetic superiority.[17]

Men, it would seem, figured prominently in Lee's dystopian vision after all. Behind the ostensible crisis of maternity and reproduction—too much or too little, never exactly enough—was a crisis of *paternity* and reproduction. A few women suggested, with irony, that if increased numbers of superior children were exclusively at issue, then women ought to be encouraged, nay, urged to have children outside the institution of marriage, with all stigmatization of single mothers and illegitimate offspring removed. Many women, they challenged, did not wish to marry, but wished nonetheless to have children; should not the government in its urgent desire recommend moves toward women-headed families?[18] Recognizing the threat to patriarchal authority vested in the traditional Asian family—after which its own hierarchies and values were after all patterned—the government conspicuously failed to generate enthusiasm for this alternative. A future in which women might conceive and raise children with the support of society, but without the check of a paternal signifier, could not be thought of, even in the name of putative national survival. Addressing as it did the hidden stake in Lee's narrative of crisis, whose undisclosed object of concern was precisely the stable replication of the paternal signifier and its powers, this vision of women-led families struck at the core of state fatherhood itself, the institutional basis on which governmental patriarchy was posited.[19]

The narrative behind Lee's narrative could then be read: a fantasy of self-regenerating fatherhood and patriarchal power, unmitigated, resurgent, and in endless (self-) propagation, inexhaustibly reproducing its own image through the pliant, tractable conduit of female anatomy—incidental, obedient, and sexually suborned female bodily matter. His sentimental indulgence in the saving visions of a reactionary past, selectively idealized, stages that past as the exclusive theater of omnipotent fathers: state fathers, whose creative powers incorporate and subsume the maternal function, as attested by their autonomous birthing of a nation. The subsequent show of protective solicitude over the national offspring then aggressively, if fantasmatically, replays the cherished moment of paternal delivery: by arresting change and difference in the national body, and wishfully transfixing the population in its original composition at birth, a living testimony to the founding moment is made perpetually available, a constantly present reminder; and the fearful threat of material transmogrification—growth, alteration, difference, the transformations wrought by an undisclosed, never-certain future (imagined, conveniently, as issuing from mothers, that displaced, but ever looming, ever returning source of threat and competition)—is simultaneously warded off and disengaged.

Out of that obsession with a past ideologically configured had come, then, the script of a dangerous agenda of racial and class manipulation: the very agenda explicitly renounced by the publicly subscribed goals—democracy, equality, and social justice, regardless of race, gender, creed, or class—on which Lee's government had so prided itself, for which it had won the country freedom from Britain, and by which its public mandate to govern today is still declaratively based. It is as a defense against his fear of the future—a future which finds its representation and threat, for him, in a race-marked, class-inflected, ungovernable female body (so commonly figured as the receptacle of the future that it is the perennial locus of social accusation and experiment)—that Lee's Great Marriage Debate was invented. The past—that ground in which the powers of reproduction and the reproduction of power had seemed miraculously to converge in a self-legitimating moment of plenitude echoing through time—served, in this case, as in the case of so many other nations and nationalisms, as the imaginary treasure-house of a superannuated political fantasy.

NATIONALISM AND RACE: REPRODUCTIONS OF IDEOLOGY

Concurrent with the rhetoric of crisis identifying what might be called the threat from within the nation that inaugurates the "Great Marriage Debate," there has also been over recent years the discovery of a threat from without, a *cultural* crisis of equally disturbing magnitude. Represented as the intensified danger of contamination by the West, this particular crisis has required the formulation of related themes in defense of the social body—the retrieval of a superior, "core" Chinese culture in the name of a fantasmatic "Confucianism"; the promotion of Mandarin, the preferred dialect of the ruling class of imperial China, as the master language of Chineseness; and the concoction of a "national ideology," grounded in a selective refiguration of Confucianism, to promote the interests of the state.

All three themes take shape as urgent national priorities to combat this other, external threat to the survival, prosperity, and identity of the nation: "Western" values, variously depicted as individualism, relativism, and hedonism at worst, or as an unstable pluralism and a needlessly liberal democracy at best.[20] The decadent individualism of the West, cabinet ministers declare, has caused the economic decline of the United States relative to Japan, South Korea, Taiwan, and Singapore, the so-called "four Asian tigers"; concomitantly, these East Asian economies are said to owe their prosperity to their Confucian-based cultures, their "communitarian value system," industry, thrift, and social cohesiveness being attributed to a changeless Confucian *essence* that has been preserved intact through the ages, an essence which not only survives transmission without alteration, but which has made rapid industrial development possible. Taught in Singapore schools since 1982, Confucianism has been offered as an option to Chinese secondary school students, who are encouraged to study it in place of a religion in "moral education" classes. Preceding this initiative by a few years is the "Speak Mandarin" campaign for the preservation of Chineseness: if all Chinese Singaporeans spoke Mandarin, this argument goes, they could communicate without the use of English across dialect boundaries; Chinese values would be disseminated without the dilution and distraction that multiple dialects threaten, and the auditory unity of a common tongue would mitigate the dangers of the West.[21]

Like the script of the "Great Marriage Debate," racial and sexual categories are conjoined in the attribution of value and accusation in the detection of crisis. Prime Minister Lee has often reiterated his conviction that the industrial prominence of East Asian societies over the relatively less developed economies of the Indian subcontinent and Malay archipelago is rooted in the "hard" values of the former over the "soft" cultures of the latter, unapologetically proffering, in simultaneous praise and contempt, figures of phallocentric toughness and gynocentric laxity that are scarcely disguised. Indians, moreover, Lee confidently proclaims, are "naturally contentious"; like women, they are loquacious and theatrical, too indulgent and irresponsible ("soft") to be capable of the social discipline of "hard" Confucian cultures which renders East Asian societies increasingly potent as political powers to challenge the West. Lest one miss the point, Lee has wondered aloud whether Singapore could have achieved its economic and social strides if the population had been composed of an Indian racial majority and a Chinese minority, instead of the other way around. State policies instituted to manipulate female reproductive sexuality in preferred ratios of race and class leave no doubt as to what his government believes the answer to be.[22]

Because almost all Singaporeans under the age of forty speak English today with varying degrees of fluency—93 percent of primary-school-age children are in schools where it is the language of instruction—they are deemed uniquely vulnerable to infection by the West, unlike Japanese, Koreans, and Taiwanese. Encouraged by British colonial policy for over a century, the dominance of English was institutionalized after decolonization by Lee's own government which established it as the preferred language of education and business, and as the *de facto* language of government: a privileged medium of access to Western science and technology which augmented the nation's attractions to multinational capital. In the 1950s and 1960s, when the Malayan Communist Party was influential among the

Chinese-educated in Singapore and Malaya, the policy of both the British colonial administration and the postcolonial governments that succeeded it involved the diminution in social and political status of Chinese education: "left-wing activist," "Communist," and "Chinese-educated" were virtually synonymous, interchangeable terms ("the English-educated," as Lee put it then, "do not riot"). The association of English with progress and economic enfranchisement resulted, by the mid-1970s, in a considerable reduction in the number of Chinese schools, and the closure of the only Chinese-language university in Singapore.

Ironically, thirty years after independence, the very political authority that had institutionalized the language now expresses "doubt about the wisdom of teaching Singaporeans English." "If one went back to Korea, Taiwan, or Hong Kong 100 years from now," Lee speculated in a wistful fantasy of paternal control, "their descendants would be recognizable because what they took in from the West was what their leaders decided to translate into their books, newspapers and t.v. programmes." In Singapore, on the other hand, "we have given everybody a translator in his pocket and all doors are open." In this nightmare vision—the unresisted seduction of a vulnerable, "soft," social body feminized by language ("all doors are open")—Lee saw "a wholesale revision of values, attitudes of good and bad, or role-models and so on."[23] English, once the conduit of rapid economic development that consolidated the power and legitimacy of the new state and its founding fathers, is now a dangerous passage facilitating an invasion of difference that would rupture the continuity of cultural identity, and alter the course of ideal generational propagation.

These changing fantasmatic definitions of threats to the state, requiring sporadic redeployment of valid and invalid identities, languages, and cultures in narratives of history and national survival, reveal, then, the essentialist counters of race and culture as amenable to arbitrary representations, inflected by the interests of state power. Differences *within* cultures and races—and the conflation of these two terms is a necessary gesture in the essentialist discourse of nationalism—are converted into differences *between* cultures and races, into differences that strategically serve to distinguish valid, enabling, or potent cultural identities from those other identities represented as seductive and disabling, subverting the firmness of national purpose. Narratives of history and survival thus deployed in the production of differences support specific formations of power; the past itself becomes a category produced by present causes to legitimate the exigent directives of the state, and is punctually offered as a reusable counter to vindicate genealogies of state dispensation. Each construction of an essential identity requires a reconfiguring of the past: the equation of "Confucian Chineseness" with the interests of the state demands not only the discounting of Singapore history in the 1950s and 1960s, but also a radical retroping of the enabling conditions of economic development and modern nationhood. No longer is an absorption of Western values, liberal democracy, technological organization, and habits of objectivity deemed sine qua non the legitimizing prerequisites of a modern state. That Singapore, like Japan, Korea, and Taiwan, has "arrived" as a developed economy is to be traced instead to the presence in these societies of "core" Confucian virtues—to the efflorescence, as it were, of what has always been there, fully present, denying the perceived absence or lack that instigated the movement toward the West in the immediate postcolonial period. Locating the ideological source of the modern East Asian state in an unchanging Confucian essence allows, moreover, the idealized recuperation of the entire history of Chinese culture as a seamless narrative of continuity and cohesion, suffering neither a fall (as into communism) nor a lack—allows, that is, an ideological fantasy of transgenerational replication, where a signifying essence gendered in a particular modality of authority reproduces itself across history and national boundaries in unobstructed transcendent resurgence. The history of Singapore is then a single moment in the history of Chinese racial culture, written into an integrated script of transnational ideological revitalization.

The mystifications exercised in this figuration of (trans)national ideology should not, however, be read as implying irrationality. The very discovery of Confucianism is articulated by the need to manage, not to resist, an increasingly successful industrial nation. Confucianism accordingly is promoted in Singapore as constitutive of the rational organization of society, and has itself been submitted to stringent inquiry, that it might be systematically delivered as an object of knowledge, a rational and authoritative epistemology. Confucian scholars are hired from abroad (from metropolitan centers such as Harvard and Princeton, among others) to staff an Institute of East Asian Philosophy at the National University of Singapore: they help to formulate the syllabi and design the texts for school courses, sift Confucian tenets consciously for useful emphases and prescriptions, and systematize the propagation of the subject. Bizarre as this programmatic exercise might seem to Western eyes, it merely repeats, in effect, the modalities of producing and using knowledge long assumed in the West by the social sciences, including the discourse Edward Said calls Orientalism. Based on expertise and scholarly systematization, the knowledge produced is then delivered as a rational, objective, disinterested and coherent (philosophical) system, conferring legitimacy on the state which establishes the promise of a truly rational organization of society, even as it enables the state to police the boundaries of permissible discourse through the continued regulation of knowledge. Thus mantled in objectivity and knowledge, the state assumes what Foucault calls its "pastoral" function, subjecting its citizens to a "set of very specific patterns" that totalizes the operation of an apparently benign, implicitly paternal power.[24] In Singapore, the paradigms of economic or corporate management and their protocols of rationality serve at once as the model and chief beneficiary of the state's pastoral power, submitting citizens to a structure of values which best subtends, with minimal fuss and resistance, the efficient working of state corporatism and multinational capital.[25] The location of this structure of values in Confucianism, moreover, and the figuration of Confucianism itself as racial and (trans)national identity, continuous with other East Asian societies and with an organically fecund past, stages the modern state and nationalism as merely the theater where a primordial paternal signifier can gather to itself new instruments of potency, without the irritation of difference to trouble its timeless sway. The description of history as the movement and repetition of the same discovers an aggressive and ruthless absorption of contemporary forms of power: few nations can boast the degree of thoroughness to which the founders of Singapore have carried the paternal logic of the modern state.

The policies of the Singapore government cannot therefore be dismissed as an instance of a peculiarly irrational but unique oriental despotism, for their exercise of power is made possible, in large measure, by the reinscription of *Western* modes of discourse in an Asian context. Represented as an invasive threat to Singapore society from without, Western modalities are in fact already operating as instruments of power for the local production of subjects *within* the nation. The strategic deployment of selective material from contemporary metropolitan disciplines such as genetics and sociobiology (in the fabricated exigency dubbed the "Great Marriage Debate") is one explicit instance of state collusion with Western institutions of power/knowledge. Indeed, the domestication of an economy of power operative and operable as rationality—knowledge as a technique, a circuit, of power—is crucially necessary to the constitution of a "native" center of authority. Though the ultimate horizon of complicity between authoritative knowledges in the metropolitan West and formations of power in the postcolonial state is beyond the scope of this article, a few of the productive effects of this complicity can be briefly described.

The institution of what can be called, for suggestive convenience, an "internalized Orientalism" makes available to *postcolonial* authority the knowledge-power that *colonial* authority wielded over the local population, and permits, in Singapore, an overwhelmingly Western-educated political elite to dictate the qualities that would constitute Chineseness. Internalized orientalism allows the definition of an idealized Chineseness fully consonant with the requirements of a modern market economy, and supplies the mechanism of justification by which qualities deemed undesirable (and projected as forms of racial and sexual accusation) may be contained or excised. Thus simultaneously concerned with replication and containment, internalized orientalism supervises the erasure of the rich cultural resources of dialects spoken over countless generations, and arbitrarily names Mandarin the single repository of core Chinese virtues so as to facilitate cultural dissemination and bring within the possibility of governance a Chineseness that might otherwise have remained, like female reproductive habits, too resistantly diverse and prolific.

Ignoring the materiality of Chinese history, internalized orientalism writes its own narratives of history and nationalism, in service to the state. In the effort to establish congruence between the individual's place in a "natural institution like the family" and the individual's loyalty to an "omnipresent government" (see note 20 above), the Singapore brand of Confucianism suppresses the fact that loyalty to family and clan functioned frequently in Chinese history to subtract from loyalty to the state.[26] State fatherhood specifically requires, of course, the intimate articulation of the traditional family with the modern state, and the ostensible homology of the one to the other, claimed by Singapore Confucianism, facilitates and guarantees the transfer of the paternal signifier *from* the family *to* the state, the metaphor of state as family then rendering "natural" an "omnipotent government."[27]

For all the anti-Western rhetoric that characterizes this detection of crisis, then, internalized orientalism in fact supplies state fatherhood with an efficient mechanism for the processing of Western culture—an apparatus of definition, selection, and control that manipulates the rationalizing power of Western modes of knowledge and organization for the efficient management of local capitalism, even as it sets aside as waste what is deemed seductively decadent and dangerous: in short, it presents the ideal regulative machine to the modern Asian state. Whether it provisions the state with a schematic Confucianist system of knowledge or selected statistics from genetics and sociobiology, internalized orientalism serves a paternal master: a gendered formation of power absorbed in fantasmatic repetition, and seeking a reliable machinery of efficient self-regeneration. Recent discoveries of national crisis—in female reproductive sexuality, and the social insufficiency that must be rectified by Confucianism, Mandarin, and a national ideology—mark significant breaches, or failures of repetition. The narratives of identity, sexuality, history, culture, and nationalism officially issued with their discovery merely reinstate the proper mechanisms of correction.

In the reproductions of ideology contained in these narratives, then, a dream of a timeless paternal essence emerges, splendid, transcendant, immortal.[28] Masking its power in myriad forms, but somehow always managing to reveal itself, this paternal signifier moves across history and national boundaries, harboring within itself a Chinese soul wielding a Western calculus of choice (so the fantasy goes). Triumphantly resurfacing through many ages, countries, and cultures, always appropriating to itself new, and ever puissant forms of contemporary power, it finds that it is checked nonetheless in its primordial play, in one location on the globe, by a troublesome figure of difference. Invariably, that figure is feminine. Whether represented by actual women (as in the "Great Marriage Debate") or "other" races and cultures whose identifying characteristics are implicitly feminized—whether, that is, it is a sexual, or a social, body that haunts and threatens—the figure of threat, auguring economic and social disintegration, dismantling the foundations of culture, undermining, indeed, the very possibility of a recognizable future, is always, and unerringly, feminine. The Great Marriage Debate, and the great cultural crises in Singapore— the threats from within and without—merely reposition an age-old reminder, repeated in the scripts of many nations, many nationalisms:

Women, and all signs of the feminine, are by definition always and already antinational.

NOTES

This chapter was previously published in *Nationalisms and Sexualities,* ed. Andrew Parker et al. (New York: Routledge, 1991).

1. The trope of father and daughter is so commonly invoked in Singapore to express the relationship between the governing political party which won Singapore independence from Britain (the People's Action Party, or PAP), and the nation itself, as to be fully naturalized, passing unremarked. Singapore is never imagined, by its government or citizens, as a "motherland" or "mother country" (identifications reserved exclusively for the ancestral countries of origin of Singapore's various racial groups—India, China, etc.), but rather as a female child, or at best, an adolescent girl or "young lady." A letter to a national newspaper, entitled "Dear PAPa . . . ," and signed by "Singapore, A Young Lady," in the persona of a respectful growing daughter petitioning for greater freedom from her stern father captures the tenor of the relationship perfectly (*The Straits Times* [Singapore], January 5, 1985). (An answering letter, fictitiously from "PAPa," subsequently appeared in the same newspaper.) The psychic economy of the nation prominently circulates between these two gendered positions, tropes of the mother appearing only as counters of facilitation in and reinforcement of the father-daughter dyad.

2. "If we continue to reproduce ourselves in this lopsided way, we will be unable to maintain our present standards. Levels of competence will decline. Our economy will falter, the administration will suffer, and the society will decline. For how can we avoid lowering performance when for every two graduates (with some exaggeration to make the point), in 25 years' time there will be one graduate, and for every two uneducated workers, there will be three?" ("Talent for the Future: Prepared Text of the Prime Minister, Mr. Lee Kuan Yew's Speech at the National Day Rally Last Night," *The Straits Times* [Singapore], August 15, 1983).

3. Lest anyone assume that Lee's articulation of race, class, and gender in the detection of reproductive crisis is unique to Singapore, attention might be drawn to the increasing number of articles in popular U.S. magazines which describe similar discoveries in alarmist, prophetic tones like his—see, e.g., "A Confederacy of Dunces: Are the Best and the Brightest Making Too Few Babies?" in *Newsweek* (May 22, 1989), and R. J. Herrnstein, "IQ and Falling Birthrates" in the *Atlantic Monthly* (May 1989), the latter glossed by the cover headline: "In this issue: Why Are Smart Women Having Fewer Children?" Lee, in the latter article, is admiringly played up as a stalwart example of farsighted and courageous leadership that dares to take measures to rectify envisaged future disaster. Significantly, he is cast in this favorable light with Arthur Balfour, the Prime Minister of Britain who moaned in 1905 that "Everything done towards opening careers to the lower classes did something towards the degeneration of the race." The eugenic nightmare of a representative of British high imperialism is echoed thus across the century—the cadences of alarm, fear, and threat remaining unchanged—by the postcolonial Prime Minister of (a formerly British) Singapore. Nor is Lee's reductive faith in the genetic transmission of intelligence a subscription exclusive now to retrograde third world autocrats. Even as a redoubtable Stephen Jay Gould stirred himself to counter Lee's misuse of scientific arguments ("Singapore's Patrimony [and Matrimony]: The Illogic of Eugenics Knows Neither the Boundaries of Time nor Geography," *Natural History*, May 1984), U.S. genetic determinists Thomas Bouchard, Jon Karlsson, and the seemingly indefatigable William Shockley, lent themselves to eager support of Lee's vision: " 'The Singapore program,' says Shockley, 'is discriminate in a very constructive way. Discrimination is a valuable attribute. Discrimination means the ability to select a better wine from a poorer wine. The word has become degraded. And social engineering? As soon as you've got welfare programs, where you prevent improvident people from having their children starved to death, you are engaged in a form of social engineering. Of genetic engineering even. We have these things going on now, but we're not looking at what effects they have, and that's where the humanitarianism is irresponsible' " (see "The Great Debate over Genes," *Asiaweek*, March 2, 1984).

4. Lee has, on occasion, referred to the people of Singapore as "digits," their inherited attributes as "hardware" to be "programmed" with "software" (ideology, education, culture, etc.). A cohort of his recently suggested, in public, that people "interface" more with one another to increase human communication and understanding. Typically, Lee's National Day Rally speeches (the August 1983 one is no exception) began with a report of the nation's economic progress for the year in a detailed statistical format, the machinery of statistics representing, for him, and for his government, the power of a penultimate, absolute, and unarguable force. That his statistics in this particular instance are not immovable, however, is suggested by curious vagrancies in the figures subsequently cited, with confident authority, by various government individuals in his support (the "1.6" children born to graduate parents sometimes mutating, for instance, into "1.3" or "1.7" children).

5. Thomas Laqueur's contention that feminine pleasure (and in particular the female orgasm) was historically read as essential to the economy of female reproductive sexuality suggests that its functional removal from that economy has specifically marked it as superfluous, irrelevant ("Orgasm, Generation, and the Politics

of Reproductive Biology," in Catherine Gallagher and Thomas Laqueur, eds., *The Making of the Modern Body: Sexuality and Society in the Nineteenth Century* [Berkeley: University of California Press, 1987], pp. 1–41). The pleasurable and the economic are not only read as separate in Singapore today, but inimical (the trope of the machine allowing no role for pleasure, which by its very concession of unusefulness, nonnecessity, and excess disables the fantasies of order and regularity on which a local notion of the economic must depend): indeed, pleasure is tacitly suspected of subverting what would otherwise have been an economic reproductive sexuality, distorting this instead into its opposite, a self-indulgent noneconomy.

6. *The Straits Times,* publishing 31 of the 101 letters it received immediately following the Prime Minister's speech, defended its decision not to publish the remaining 71 letters thus: "Sifting through the pile, one can detect some misunderstanding of Prime Minister Lee Kuan Yew's message. Most of the correspondents did not address their thoughts to the main issue: The better-educated segment of the population should be encouraged to have more children (than what they are having now) to bring about a more balanced reproduction rate. Instead, they interpreted the speech as one more setback for the less intelligent in our society" (A. S. Yeong, "What the Others Said: An Analysis of Unpublished Letters on the PM's National Day Rally Speech," *The Straits Times* [Singapore], August 29, 1983). Among the letters published—no doubt because it was thought acute and useful—was an argument to do away with the right of every adult citizen to an equal vote in national elections: "If, at any stage, there is a threat to progress due to increasing numbers of incompetent people, government may even think of introducing a weightage factor for every vote that comes from a 'qualified' person so that power and administration are kept in the hands of truly competent persons. In a democratic set-up, the principle of 'one person one vote' is fast becoming a menace to society" (G. Rangarajan, "Maintain a Competent Majority," letter to *The Straits Times* [Singapore], August 19, 1983).

7. The statement from the Prime Minister's Office declares, in officialese borrowed from sociology: "Unless we break this low education large family cycle, we will have a small but significant minority of our people permanently trapped in a poverty subculture, whilst the rest of the population will move even further up the economic and social ladder" (Margaret Thomas, "Govt's $10,000 Helping Hand for Low Income Families," *The Sunday Monitor* [Singapore], June 3, 1984). The aim of this money incentive, according to the report, "is to encourage poorly-educated and low-income Singaporeans . . . to stop at two so that their children will have a better chance in life." The writer of this article, driven to notice the coincidence of class and race in the encouragement of this particular group of citizens, nonetheless finds in it an opportunity to play up the dewy-eyed innocence and ingenuous charity of the proposal: "Though it is not spelt out in the statement, a significant proportion of the people caught in the poverty trap are Malays. . . . The relatively disadvantaged position of the Malay community is a matter of concern to both leaders of the community and the Government."

8. The relevant clause in the constitution, article 16(1)(a), reads: "there shall be no discrimination against any citizens of Singapore on the grounds only of religion, race, descent or place of birth . . . in the administration of any educational institution maintained by a public authority and, in particular, the admission of

pupils or students or the payment of fees." Of six unnamed "legal experts" consulted by one newspaper, four agreed that the privileging of certain children over others in the proposed new admissions policy was in direct contravention of this clause (see Siva Arasu, "Unconstitutional? What Legal Experts Say," *The Sunday Times* [Singapore], March 4, 1984). Protests against the scheme were lodged by one government Member of Parliament (Tan Ban Huat, "A Violation of Constitution, Says Dr. Toh," *The Straits Times* [Singapore], February 13, 1984); the lone opposition-party Member then in Parliament (see "House Throws Out Motion by Jeya on Entry Scheme," *The Straits Times* [Singapore], March 14, 1984); the National University of Singapore Students' Union in a petition carrying 3,000 signatures (Hedwig Alfred, "NUS Students' Union Wants to Meet Dr. Tay," *The Straits Times* [Singapore], March 14, 1984); and "500 undergraduates, or nearly 40 per cent" of the student population of the Nanyang Technological Institute ("NTI Students Pen Protest Against Priority Plan: A Class System Would Arise, They Say," *The Sunday Times* [Singapore], February 19, 1984).

9. The Minister of State for Education at the time, Dr. Tay Eng Soon, repeatedly characterized the country's top schools (a description earned on the basis of examination results and the traditional reputation of the institutions) as schools that were merely "popular" as a consequence of public misconception (see "Equal Standard, Equal Chances," and Hedwig Alfred, "More Good News for Non-Grad Mums: All Primary Schools Are of Fairly Equal Standard—Dr. Tay," *The Sunday Times* [Singapore], March 4, 1984). In the midst of public anxiety, resentment, and anger over the proposed changes, the Minister admitted, in an interview with *The Straits Times,* that for all the fuss and trouble, only 200 children were eligible for the new privileges that year (June Tan, "Non-Graduates Will Also Benefit," *The Straits Times* [Singapore], January 24, 1984). Despite Tay's firm assurance in January 1984 that the new policy would be a permanent one, public opinion nevertheless triumphed, and the demise of the scheme was announced in March 1985: "Education Minister Dr. Tony Tan has decided that Singapore can do without the controversial priority scheme which favored the children of graduate mothers but made a whole lot of people angry" (see "Graduate Mum Scheme to Go," *The Straits Times* [Singapore], March 26, 1985).

10. In August 1983, Lee pronounced the larger number of male to female university graduates a source of satisfaction (Bob Ng, "PM: Watch This Trend: Talent Problem Will Worsen When Women Graduates Are No Longer in the Minority," *The Straits Times* [Singapore], August 22, 1983). By October, a change in university admissions policy was announced: "This more-girls-fewer-boys trend was worrying, [the Vice-Chancellor] said, on general principles. Asked if the new policy had anything to do with the Great Marriage Debate—that many women graduates are staying unmarried because a lot of male graduates are marrying less educated women—he said it was unfair to say so. But if [the National University of Singapore] continued to take in more girls than boys, 'the problem of unmarried women graduates will be aggravated' " (June Tan and Abdullah Tarmugi, "NUS Relaxes Rule on Second Language: To Redress Imbalance between Male and Female Undergrads," *The Sunday Times* [Singapore], October 30, 1983).

11. "Whatever the changes, the two-child family will remain the norm, except

that now well-educated parents who have the means to bring up children in a good home are encouraged to have more than two"(June Tan, "New Family Planning Slogan: Message Will Tell Different Things to Different People," *The Straits Times* [Singapore], January 31, 1984). A year later, in 1985, restrictions on abortion began to be publicly discussed (Irene Hoe, "When MPs Shake Their Heads Over Unwed Mums," *The Straits Times* [Singapore], March 17, 1985).

12. The information to be furnished compulsorily was formidably exhaustive: "They must state whether the spouse has a pass degree or is an honors graduate, and if so, which class, the year it was obtained and the name of the college or university. Those with spouses having a pass degree or lower qualifications have to furnish details of the examinations they sat for, the subjects taken, the grades achieved, the name of the school and the year they got their certificates" (see "Officials Asked to Disclose Spouses' Education," *The Straits Times* [Singapore], September 9, 1983, and Teresa Ooi, "Singapore Diplomat Is Asked to Try Out Match-Making Service," *The Straits Times* [Singapore], September 18, 1983).

13. Tsang So-Yin, "The National Service for Women," *The Straits Times* (Singapore), August 17, 1983. Sunday columnist Irene Hoe tartly responded: "if childbirth is indeed national service, the women in the S[ingapore] C[ouncil of] W[omen's] O[rganizations] should be the first to volunteer—before they seek to draft other women" ("The National Service for Women: If Childbirth Is That, These Women Leaders Should Set an Example," *The Sunday Times* [Singapore], August 21, 1983). For the homology between military service and maternal service in cultural representation, see Nancy Huston, "The Matrix of War: Mothers and Heroes," in Susan Rubin Suleiman, ed., *The Female Body in Western Culture* (Cambridge, Mass.: Harvard University Press, 1986), pp. 119–36.

14. Alice Jardine finds "a climate of sustained . . . paranoia" to exist whenever "the *regulation* of the mother's body . . . [serves] as ground for a monolithic, nationalistic ideology" ("Opaque Texts and Transparent Contexts: The Political Difference of Julia Kristeva," in Nancy K. Miller, ed., *Poetics of Gender* [New York: Columbia University Press, 1986], p. 108). Laurie Langbauer suggests that "the mother's confinement during delivery" in the nineteenth century represents an attempted immobilization of a certain fear of feminine regenerative uncontrollability—the physical transfixing of the woman being itself an admission of her "controlling power" of reproduction ("Women in White, Men in Feminism," *Yale Journal of Criticism* 2, 2 [1989], p. 223).

15. "In the old days, matchmakers settled these affairs. . . . I remember, as a young boy, hearing my grandmother talk, and she got my aunt married off. She was already 20 plus . . . and there was a widower with no children. Well educated, highly suitable. The result is a family of five, all of whom made it to university. My cousins. . . . We are caught betwixt and between, from an old world in which these matters are thoroughly considered and carefully investigated and properly arranged, to this new world of hit and miss" ("Talent for the Future").

16. "When we adopted these policies they were manifestly right, enlightened and the way forward to the future. With the advantage of blinding hindsight, educating everybody, yes, absolutely right. Equal employment opportunities, yes, but we shouldn't get our women into jobs where they cannot, at the same time, be

mothers. . . . You just can't be doing a full-time, heavy job like that of a doctor or engineer and run a home and bring up children . . . we must think deep and long on the profound changes we have unwittingly set off" ("Talent for the Future").

17. "Mr. Lee told an audience of university students that polygamy allowed the mentally and physically vibrant to reproduce. He said that in the old society, successful men had more than one wife. Citing the example of former Japanese Prime Minister Kakuei Tanaka as a man who had a wife and a mistress and children by both, he said the more Tanakas there were in Japan, the more dynamic its society would be" (Kong Sook Chin, "Woman MP Questions Notion of Polygamy," *The Sunday Times* [Singapore], December 28, 1986).

18. In a forum conducted by the *Sunday Times,* two women, who went by the pseudonymous names of "Veronica" and "Mrs. Chan," produced the following dialogue: "Mrs. Chan: 'No woman would support polygamy.' Veronica: 'But there are women like me who would love to have children even though we're unmarried.' Mrs. Chan: 'Yes, a lot of women would like that. Our laws should not penalize such women. Those who are professional and financially self-supporting are quite capable of bringing up their children alone. We should encourage single motherhood, allow such interested women to have artificial insemination.' Veronica: 'It needn't be by artificial means.' (Laughter)" (Tan Lian Choo, "Marriage and the Single Girl: The Sunday Times Roundtable," *The Sunday Times* [Singapore], July 20, 1986).

19. Single motherhood appears to make patriarchy of the first-world as much as the third-world variety equally queasy. In a *Newsweek* article (October 31, 1988) on what seems to be a highly successful program of state-supported single motherhood in Sweden (the title of which—"What Price Motherhood? An Out-of-Wedlock Baby Boom in Sweden"—strategically projects an air of doubt and skeptical disapproval), Neil Gilbert, "who heads the Family Welfare Research Group at the University of California at Berkeley," is quoted as saying piously: "If people aren't willing to make commitments . . . you wonder what kind of society you will have down the line."

20. Professor Tu Wei Ming of Harvard University, the government's most prominent Confucian "expert," has offered the view that "democratic institutions . . . are institutions that, if not diametrically opposed to, are at least in basic conflict with *natural* organizations such as family. . . . Some very deep-rooted Confucian-humanistic values are values that need to be fundamentally transformed to be totally compatible with democratic institutions." The newspapers that published the text of Professor Tu's talk glossed it thus: "Democratic institutions are opposed to basic Confucianist ideas like the primacy of the family, an *omnipresent* government, and a preference for a community of trust rather than an adversarial relationship" (emphasis ours). See "When Confucianism Grapples with Democracy," *The Sunday Times* [Singapore], November 27, 1988.

21. Singaporeans are commanded by the most prominent slogan in the campaign to "Speak More Mandarin, Less Dialects" *[sic],* as if Mandarin itself were not a dialect. Mandarin is now referred to as the "mother tongue" of all Chinese, though virtually all Chinese in Singapore, left to themselves, would likely identify their "mother tongues" as Teochew, Hokkien, Cantonese, Hainanese, Shanghainese, Hakka, or some other regional dialect spontaneously used in their family. Their

official "mother tongue," by contrast, has to be acquired through formal education, a large percentage of Chinese schoolchildren proving so inept at it as to require extensive extracurricular private tuition. The government has gone to great lengths, nonetheless, to promote Mandarin, including dubbing Cantonese feature films and soap operas from Hong Kong into Mandarin for Singapore television, and instituting a campaign to discourage taxi drivers—notoriously resistant to government regulation—from speaking in dialect. By the government's own estimate, the measures have been successful; 87 percent of Chinese Singaporeans, it claims, can now speak Mandarin.

22. Recently, in defending a government policy to import up to 100,000 Chinese from Hong Kong to redress declining birth rates among Chinese Singaporeans, Lee repeated the scenario of crisis he sketched in inaugurating the "Great Marriage Debate" in marginally more delicate terms: "Let us just maintain the status quo. And we have to maintain it or there will be a shift in the economy, both the economic performance and the political backdrop which makes that economic performance possible" (see "Hongkongers' Entry Won't Upset Racial Mix," *The Straits Times Weekly Overseas Edition*, August 26, 1989).

23. See N. Balakrishnan, "Pledge of Allegiance: Core Values Touted As an Antidote to Westernisation," *Far Eastern Economic Review* [Hong Kong], February 9, 1989.

24. Michel Foucault, "Afterword: The Subject and Power," in Hubert L. Dreyfus and Paul Rabinow, *Michel Foucault: Beyond Structuralism and Hermeneutics* (Chicago: University of Chicago Press, 1983), pp. 213–14.

25. Significantly, the notion that East Asian industrial powers owe their prosperity to a Confucian essence circulates prominently also in the West, repeated so often in U.S. print and electronic media as to be naturalized as fact. The image of a ruthlessly efficient Confucianist Orient, with a highly commendable "communitarian value system," celebrated in the West chiefly, one suspects, for the purpose of promoting a particular reorganization within Western industrial societies, is shared by the Orient itself to promote a similar agenda: the efficient management of capitalism.

26. For instance, in *The Gates of Heavenly Peace: The Chinese and Their Revolution, 1895–1980* (New York: Viking, 1981), Jonathan Spence quotes a writer who blamed "Chinese faith in the family for having destroyed all possibilities of true patriotism" (340), and cites Lu Xun's contempt for Confucian scholars, the fictionist asserting in a story that these Confucianists had survived through the centuries because they "had never laid down their lives to preserve a government" (122).

27. In 1989, speaking on the problem of escalating emigration from Singapore, the then First Deputy Prime Minister Goh Chok Tong introduced a plaintive inflection of the trope of state as family: "No country is perfect just as no family is perfect. But we do not leave our family because we find it imperfect or our parents difficult" ("The Emigration Problem," *The Straits Times* [Singapore], October 6, 1989).

28. Personal immortality is sometimes claimed by the representatives of paternal essentialism as well. An issue of *Newsweek* (November 19, 1990) quoted Prime Minister Lee as saying, in concern over the future of Singapore: "Even from my sickbed, even if you are going to lower me in my grave and I feel that something is going wrong, I'll get up."

SEVEN

Alternative Filipina Heroines: Contested Tropes in Leftist Feminisms

Jacqueline Siapno

Earlier chapters dealt with efforts to control the images and behavior of women as daughters, wives, and mothers by state apparatuses. In this essay, Jacqueline Siapno raises the question: Why are heroines in Southeast Asian literature considered dangerous by repressive regimes? Following Edward Said and Gayatri Spivak, Siapno addresses the issue of cultural narratives as forms of political resistance that are often eclipsed by imperialist history and male custodians of culture. She argues that recent developments in the Philippines, including, most notably, the institutionalization of martial law, the development of an antidictator movement, and antiforeign resistance, are waged primarily in ideological arenas. She critiques the different representations of cultural conflict in the Philippines by American social scientists, and by Philippine professionals who write in English, including male literary critics and communist leaders. Siapno's analysis of the increasingly intense and high-stakes struggles for the hearts and minds of Filipinos centers on the recovery of indigenous female voices writing in Tagalog. Her more specific goals are to analyze the plot and textual strategies of a novel entitled Dekada '70, *written by Lualhati Bautista, one of the Philippines' most celebrated writers.* Dekada '70 *is widely regarded as the most authoritative historical chronicle of the Martial Law period, and as a powerful feminist text pioneering in its treatment of sexuality, especially the sexuality of women.*

Elaborating on the ways in which class, race, and gender are articulated in this novel, and in the contemporary Philippines generally, Siapno examines the dilemmas and contradictions facing the novel's heroine, Amanda, an upper-middle-class woman who has lost her youth and beauty and has become increasingly irrelevant to her husband and children. Finding herself trapped in—and seeking to transcend—the domesticated roles of wife and mother, she eventually comes to the ambivalence-laden realization that the only way she can express herself is through her (autoerotic) sexuality, particularly since she is morally and otherwise unable to leave her husband

*and accept her daughter-in-law Mara's invitation to join the revolutionary move-
ment and thus renounce the class privileges she has long enjoyed. Amanda's dialogue
with her revolutionary daughter-in-law reveals the dilemmas and contradictions facing many Filipino women, up to and including Cory Aquino. The counterposed
female moralities and class-gender subjectivities presented through Amanda and her
daughter-in-law point to the limitations of liberal, middle-class feminism, which
Bautista appears to condemn, at least in relation to its more radical (revolutionary)
counterparts. Furthermore, the marginalization of the guerilla Mara (and by extension her author Bautista) registers the multiple repression of subaltern women's voices
by the male-centered and Western visions of bourgeois and communist elites alike.*

D*ekada '70* (Decade 1970) is a novel about the political radicalization of the urban middle-class in the antidictatorship movement
in the Philippines in the 1970s. It was written by a woman, Lualhati
Bautista, who grew up in Tondo (one of the worst urban-poor slums in
Manila), was educated in public schools,[1] and began her writing career by
publishing her stories with *Liwayway*[2] magazine. Unlike some contemporary Filipino writers who think and write predominantly in English, Lualhati Bautista chooses to write fiction *only* in the Tagalog language. Her
major works have yet to be translated.[3] The themes she chooses to write
about are always decidedly political. Some of her works were either
banned, censored or confiscated by the Marcos regime.[4] They were
banned because, according to *Veritas*, "Where other writers simply hinted
by using vague metaphors and parallel cases in other countries, Lualhati
Bautista, in a work of supposed 'fiction,' named names, cited actual atroci-
ties and pointed an unerring finger where the blame lies."[5]

In this essay I will look at how Lualhati Bautista's work fits into the ongoing debates about the role of culture in revolutionary organizing in the
Philippines and the attempts by leftist feminists to construct alternative
heroines. Perhaps the most striking parallel in Indonesian literature is Pramoedya Ananta Toer's *Gadis Pantai* (*Girl from the Coast*, 1987), which is also
a construction of a fictional 'ideal' heroine.[6] The story of the feudal lord
(*bendoro*) who chooses a poor woman from a fishing village as his 'trial wife'
(*istri percobaan*), raises issues about class and gender in nineteenth-century
Java, and the hierarchical relationship between the colonial apparatus, the
feudal aristocracy and the people in the fishing village. Although Gadis
Pantai herself is merely a character in fiction, the Indonesian government
finds her so dangerous that they have banned the novel along with all of
Pramoedya's works. As Keith Foulcher says with regard to the Indonesian
state's repressive posture toward Pramoedya Ananta Toer's writings, "The

extreme response of the state, in the form of bans and arrests which have followed in their wake, indicates the seriousness of the ongoing struggle to assert the state's cultural hegemony." (Foulcher 1990:313).

Indeed, the parallels between *Gadis Pantai* and *Dekada '70* as countertexts which break from the dominant discourses of Southeast Asia's most repressive regimes are fascinating. The thoughts and aspirations of Gadis Pantai are very similar to those of Raden Adjeng Kartini.[7] In *Dekada '70*, Bautista has created alternative heroines to the traditional trope of Maria Clara in Jose Rizal's *Noli Me Tangere*, and one could argue, to Corazon Aquino, the "housewife" turned national mother figure. The dominant fictions constructed by the Indonesian and Philippine governments, respectively, on Kartini and Cory as "national mother figures" are contested by the existence of alternative heroines such as Gadis Pantai and Bautista's revolutionary Mara, both of whom dream about seizing and killing the immense, powerful fish which controls the ocean and terrorizes the little fish (*ikan besar yang menguasai samudra dan ikan-ikan kecil*). The *ikan besar* is perhaps a metaphor for a monster, anything of immense size and power, who seeks to reduce all wills to one will. When Gadis Pantai tells her mother, a solid *kampung* woman who believes that poverty and subservience to power is "destiny," her mother warns her to stop having these dreams:

> Silly child! whispered her mother while silencing her. Go to sleep, child, go to sleep. Why do you preoccupy yourself with this fish? An immense fish? Don't ever speak to your father about this *ikan besar;* never again. It is not allowed. Do not make your father's heart small, my child. Each *ikan besar* is danger. And in the ocean who will help him? One could scream for as long as a year. The waves are much stronger than their screams. There are many more *ikan besar* than fishing people. Their teeth are much stronger than your father's spear. Do you understand? (Pramoedya 1987:54)[8]

The irony is that although the fictional heroines speak from the margins (symbolized by Gadis Pantai's origins, *pasisir,* living on the coast) they are perhaps *more* threatening to the existing political order than the supposedly "real" women. I look to fictional narratives to understand contemporary Philippine society because, under repressive regimes which ensure a high degree of censorship and compliance through systematic state terror, "one finds reality in fiction, while that which is often thought of as 'reality' is actually fictive." (*Mengapa kesusasteraan? Jawabnya, karena di dalam yang fiktif ditemukan kenyataan, sedangkan yang sering dianggap 'kenyataan' sebetulnya semata-mata fiksi.*)[9]

Postcolonial critics have written extensively on the way colonized people and those who have been unrepresented, such as women, use narrative fiction to express political resistance and assert the existence of their own history. As Edward Said writes, "The main battle in imperialism is over land, of course; but when it came to who owned the land, who had the right to settle and work on it, who kept it going, who won it back, and who now plans its future—these issues were reflected, *contested,* and even for a time decided in *narrative*" (Edward Said 1993:xiii, emphasis added). In "postcolonial" Philippines (although it can be argued that the Philippines is actually neocolonial in its relationship to the United States), the cutting edge of political theory and analysis is not so much in the writings of social scientists as in the narrative fiction of writers, poets, and artists such as Lualhati Bautista.

In this essay I would like to focus on a work of narrative fiction by a Filipino woman with a feminist perspective. Although social scientists have written extensively on the politicization of the urban middle-class and the social formations that emerged during the Martial Law period,[10] very little attention has been paid to the realm of cultural studies, to newly emergent social values, or to the articulations of female voices. This is largely because most of the primary sources on the cultural renaissance (in literature, theater, film, and popular music) of the 1970s and 1980s are in Tagalog and other Philippine languages, which are inaccessible to scholars without the necessary linguistic skills. The more fundamental problem, however, is that American scholarship on the Philippines has focused mainly upon the modern "nation-state"—and thus upon politics—rather than culture or noetics[11] (i.e., literary and oral traditions). This lack of interest in cultural studies among American social scientists studying the Philippines is not so much a disciplinary as it is an ideological issue, reflecting the lingering colonial arrogance that Filipinos are "people without culture."[12] Renato Rosaldo, in a critical and thought-provoking analysis of American "imperialist nostalgia" for the Philippines, argues that one of the reasons why American social scientists are not interested in already "civilized," Christianized, educated Filipinos who have become citizens of the modern nation-state, is that they have become too transparent for study, too much like "them." Rosaldo observes that "full citizenship and cultural visibility appear to be inversely related. When one increases, the other decreases. Full citizens lack culture, and those most culturally endowed lack full citizenship" (Rosaldo 1989:198). The "imperialist nostalgia" tinged with guilt cannot comprehend a possible continuum between "vanishing primitive" subjects (headhunters, for instance) and the modern, civilized, politicized citizen. Most often one or the other is studied rather than those in between, who actually happen to constitute the majority of the Filipino population.

The scholarship of Reynaldo Ileto, Vicente Rafael and Benedict Kerkvliet, which is more interdisciplinary and less fixated on the "break" between savage headhunters and "civilized" metropolitan citizens, and which looks at sources other than print literature (e.g., the *pasyon,* popular theater, cartoons, and oral traditions) in the study of politics and culture in the Philippines, is an exception to the general trend.[13] Furthermore, these scholars are interested in listening to subaltern voices, and are much more sensitive to a critical analysis of gender issues. This said, however, a feminist and gendered perspective is still very much lacking in the field of Philippine studies. It is important to read and listen to the concealed voices of powerless women, for these voices give a radically different account of political representation, nationalism and other social movements in the Philippines.[14]

Dekada '70 is a profoundly moving work. This paper is an attempt to read it in a way that looks at the participants who are virtually *absent*. By using a reading strategy which includes not only the production but also the consumption (the implied audience) of the text, we may begin to understand the politics of representation in literature. Moreover, I make those marginal participants whose voice is heard merely through interruptions and distractions the central problematic of the text. I hope that other literary critics will begin to analyze the many complex issues on colonialism and language hierarchy which I have left out and begin to recognize Bautista's enormous contribution to feminist literature. This essay is a small contribution toward writing an alternative historiography on cultural resistance in the Philippines, "reading 'plenitude' and 'creativity' where the (colonial) narrative has made us read 'lack' and 'inadequacy'."[15]

SOCIAL AND LINGUISTIC CONTEXT OF *DEKADA '70*

In the seventies, the antidictatorship movement (a diverse coalition of rightist, liberal, and militant organizations) in the Philippines began to be shaped by the vision and creativity of the women's movements (also a very diverse coalition, of women from different classes and with different ideologies). The leftist-oriented groups in the women's movements have radically altered the terms of discourse by incorporating issues that profoundly affect women's lives, e.g., militarization, the debt problem, exploitation of women's labor in the export-processing zones, prostitution and "sex-tourism," mail-order brides, and the abuse of migrant women workers, among others.[16] These issues are discussed mostly in the realm of culture and ideology—in particular, popular theater, film, novels, short stories, and poetry.[17]

When asked about the role of culture in revolutionary organizing and whether or not the Philippine left had anything to learn from Antonio Gramsci, Francisco Nemenzo (one of the leading Marxist theorists in the progressive movement in the Philippines) replied: "Our struggle today is largely a struggle in the realm of ideology. I don't know if you can still talk about the final hegemony of proletarian culture. But my sense is that culture is the critical area of confrontation" (Bello 1992:4). Of course, this is partly in response to the "overemphasis on military work" and the "economistic and reductionist analysis that does not pay enough attention to culture, consciousness and values" (ibid.:4) by the central leadership of the militant leftist groups, i.e., the Communist Party of the Philippines (CPP), the New People's Army (NPA) and the National Democratic Front (NDF).

The Communist Party of the Philippines (CPP) has been described as "the most sophisticated Marxist-Leninist organisation still waging a full-blown armed rebellion anywhere in the world."[18] It was first formed in the 1930s by a trade union leader, but did not fully expand its membership until the early seventies. Before its widely-publicized internal leadership crisis began in 1992, the New People's Army (NPA), the military arm of the Communist Party, had a mass base of 10 million (7 million in the countryside) and a membership of thirty-five thousand cadres. It operated on at least sixty guerrilla fronts covering twelve thousand villages or significant portions of eight hundred municipalities and sixty-three provinces in the Philippines. In Southeast Asia, where communist parties and socialist ideals in general have a history of violent suppression, this expansion is quite extraordinary. It was fueled largely by the antidictatorship movement and by the village-level grassroots organizing orchestrated by the National Democratic Front (NDF). Founded in 1973, the NDF's main function was to bring together workers, peasants, students, women's groups and other progressive people in the urban and rural areas on a national scale.

In the leftist movement the women's groups are a powerful force. They range from workers' organizations for the urban poor (e.g., *Samakana, Kasamahan ng Manggagawang Kababaihan*), to peasant women's organizations (e.g., *Amihan*), women artists and intellectuals (e.g., *Kalayaan*), underground armed women's groups (e.g., *Makibaka*), and a national mass organization *(Gabriela)*. These are the more well-known among more than a hundred grassroots women's organizations in the Philippines today. Together, they are one of the strongest—if not *the* strongest—feminist movement in Southeast Asia.

As mentioned earlier, the arena in which women's voices, consciousness and ideals are expressed and are most visible is in the realm of culture, in particular popular theater and literature. Most of this is in Tagalog, which is much more accessible to a nonliterate audience (at least in the Tagalog-speaking areas) than English. Prior to the seventies, most of the cultural production which dealt with historical and political issues was in English. The seventies and eighties witnessed the emergence of Tagalog as an expression of cultural nationalism and of a counterhegemonic cultural identity, in response to the so-called neocolonialist, universalist, bourgeois literature written in English. Bautista's work is unusual in its articulation of political ideas and historical analysis in a language which the colonizers and their elite collaborators had previously relegated to the kitchen and to the discussion of trivia. In a standard Filipino film, for example, the elite curse in Spanish, speak to each other in English, and give orders to their servants in Tagalog. In *Dekada '70*, Bautista shows the middle-class appropriation of Taglish (a mixture of Tagalog and English) as the characters manoeuver between these two worlds: their political ideas, consciousness and "complicated ideas" are articulated in English, and everything else is in Tagalog. Urban-poor characters like Mara, who have not had the privilege of an English-language education and are not part of an English-speaking social circle, think and speak only in Tagalog.

However, while Tagalog may be seen as a language of resistance to English, the colonizer's language, its appropriation as a nationalist language is not perceived as democratic. Other language groups (such as Cebuanos, Ilokanos and others) feel that their contributions have not been included and represented in the construction of Philippine nationalism, in particular in its literary representations. Disadvantaged Muslim groups in Mindanao, in particular, have strongly articulated this anger against the power of a dominant group striving for cultural and class hegemony in the shaping of a national identity.

Within this language hierarchy, those who speak neither English nor Tagalog—the languages of power—but merely a regional dialect, are even more invisible and voiceless. There is growing interest in regional literatures in languages other than Tagalog, especially amongst educational policy-makers and other bureaucrats who are nervous about separatist movements in the Cordilleras and Mindanao. But this interest seems more like condescending charity to the poor, and unrepresented relatives, than a genuine desire to represent these language groups. On Philippine television, for example, other language groups or dialects are hardly represented, and when they are, it is as a caricature, as the dialects of the unsophisticated masses from the provinces.[19] Usually the "stupid servants" (a common trope) speak these "funny" dialects. It is within this social and linguistic context, then, that I place the feminist and uncompromisingly class-conscious writings of Lualhati Bautista.

CLASS-GENDER SUBJECTIVITY

Male literary critics such as Bienvenido Lumbera (1988) and Edel Garcellano (1987) have praised *Dekada '70* as one of the most authoritative historical chronicles of the Martial Law period, while feminist critics such as Soledad Reyes (1990) have described it as a powerful feminist text pioneering in its treatment of sexuality. Bautista's novel, *Dekada '70*, was so daring that, according to Edel Garcellano, *"it was mistaken for the work of a man"* (1987:30). Garcellano uses the Tagalog verb *"nangahas,"* meaning to act like a snake, to be daring. "To be mistaken for the work of a man" because it was as political as male writing (which, ironically, was meant as a compliment) is quite revealing about Filipino machismo. Women are imagined in opposite extremes as either virgins and martyrs or as *asuangs*. Those who dare to go outside these rigid boundaries are "men." As Marjorie Evasco, another Filipina writer, commented, "I was often told that to be a good writer, one must write as a human being, not as a woman. As if to write as a woman meant that one wasn't writing as a human being" (1985:40). Indeed, one of the most feared women in Philippine belief systems and oral traditions is the *asuang*, a woman with supernatural powers and the ability to assume nonhuman forms.[20]

However, while praising the book, critics have also been highly critical of or confused by the ending, calling it a "weak ending," or a "betrayal." About the novel's protagonist, Amanda Bartolome, Garcellano writes: "Her liberation even from conventional, male-dominated marital relationships comes almost as an afterthought, and collapses like a house built on sand" (1987:35). In this paper I argue that there is a different way of reading *Dekada '70*, a different interpretation of the author's intention in giving the novel this particular ending; that in fact the ending is not at all conventional, weak, out of place, or confusing, but subversive.

Lualhati Bautista is a woman from an urban-poor background. In *Dekada '70* she assumes the voice of the middle-class narrator and protagonist, Amanda Bartolome, who lives in a fancy subdivision in Manila. Amanda Bartolome (a very Spanish-mestiza, elite-sounding name compared to "Lualhati Bautista"), begins her life in the early seventies as a fairly content, apolitical middle-class housewife married to Julian Bartolome, an engineer from a former haciendero family in the north. They have five apathetic teenage sons who lead protected lives in the enclosed walls of their subdivision. Paradoxically, these exclusive, affluent subdivisions are called "villages"—e.g., Dasmarinas Village, Corinthian Village, etc. The disruption of Amanda's harmonious life begins when her eldest son Jules, like thousands of urban middle-class students from the University of the Philippines in the early seventies, joins the New People's Army (NPA). It is through Jules, and through her other sons' experiences outside their subdivision, that Amanda narrates the major political events of the most turbulent decade in contemporary Philippine history—Dekada 1970.

As her children begin to actively participate in the political transformations outside their enclosed subdivision, Amanda feels increasingly left out, and begins to question whether it is sufficient to live contentedly with her material comforts and continue to preserve her traditional family and class values. While her sons begin to get interested in direct confrontation with the Philippine military and institutions of state power, Amanda's anger is more personal, being directed toward marriage as an institution and the oppressive rules and social values to which she has to conform, including the culturally institutionalized *"querida* system."[21] *"Querida"* is a Spanish term of endearment meaning "dear one," "lover," or "beloved." In the Philippines, it is popularly used to mean "mistress." As it is considered scandalous to refer to the mistress by her proper name, she is referred to as "so and so's *querida.* . . ." Perhaps the male counterpart *"querido"* has never been as popular as *querida* in the Filipino cultural vocabulary because it is not common for women to have extramarital affairs. Amanda's husband, Julian, like most Filipino men, has a *querida,* whom she does not find out about until the end of the novel.

The narrator, Amanda Bartolome, is first introduced to us as an apolitical character who is defensive when her children accuse her of political apathy:

> Why should I be guilty? Julian has a wonderful job and he and I and our children are the offspring of influential parents. It is not my fault that the rest of the country is suffering. In fact, I owe no one anything, and will not give any of my children to any cause or movement fighting for change. But the question which keeps coming back to me, ever bigger and deeper is "why." I can understand why workers and the so-called lumpen would join the resistance movement. They will not lose anything except their chains; but that is only true for them. What I cannot understand is the participation of young people like my Jules, to whom a beautiful and prosperous future is guaranteed. (Bautista 1988:125–126)

As *Dekada '70* progresses, Amanda begins slowly to criticize her husband's chauvinism (especially with regard to their sex life) and political conservatism, and becomes increasingly determined to leave him for good, and begin a new life.

In the first chapter, Amanda gives us a critical analysis of her husband's and her own family background and her position within it:

> Julian Bartolome, Sr. is the true scion of an haciendero family from the north with Spanish ancestry. In other words, he has "rich" blood. And feudal . . . where the man is God and the woman merely his follower, who has no right to act on matters concerning business and politics.
>
> The family I come from also has a "say" (*may sinabi*) or is also "affluent"— middle-middle class—but the kind of family which, although it is able to afford privileges and annual vacations, is ruled by a father who believes in educating only the men; who believes that women ought to remain in the house; as though we were created only to service the men; to make children for it and never think of our own development and participation in the world which they believe is exclusively theirs. (1988:20)

In the rigid class structure of Philippine society, there is a difference between the "haciendero family" and the "middle-middle class." By "haciendero family"[22] Bautista means families such as Corazon Cojuangco, owner of Hacienda Luisita in Pampanga, one of the largest sugar plantations in the country, and one of the wealthiest and most powerful families in the Philippines; by "middle-middle class" she means middle-level civil servants, doctors, engineers, nurses, teachers, businessmen, and so on. Thelma Kintanar, a literary critic, likens Amanda to Jose Rizal's Maria Clara in *Noli Me Tangere* and traces Amanda's character to the "Maria Clara tradition" (1990:90). However, while it is true that Amanda's character is greatly influenced by the traditional Maria Clara aesthetics,[23] a perceptive analysis cannot overlook Bautista's critical attempt to pull away from that tradition. Unlike Maria Clara, Amanda will no longer allow herself to be brushed aside by men like Crisostomo Ibarra in what Vicente Rafael has characterized as "the *distraction* that leads to forgetfulness" (1984:125) which keeps him from fulfilling his "important" duties. Indeed, the model for her character may still be the demure Maria Clara but we now have a woman who unashamedly discusses masturbation (Bautista 1988:21). This in itself is not so unusual; there are several modern Filipino novels, short stories and poems,[24] which explicitly discuss sexuality, but these usually involve a young, unmarried, sexually aggressive woman. In *Dekada '70* we have a middle-aged mother discussing eroticism. In traditional Philippine print literature and even in oral traditions, the seductive and sexual female is usually young and unmarried. Widows, being unattached, are also associated with sexual licentiousness, but not middle-aged wives. Mothers like Amanda are not supposed to express sexual desire, only maternal tenderness; and they ought not to be so daring as to openly discuss sex with their husbands or invite them to do so. Women are desirable only as long as they are the object of sexual desire, not their subject. Sexuality is what women satisfy, not express for their own satisfaction.[25]

In the poignant scenes below Amanda gives a picture of marriage as prostitution and sex as "work" (*trabaho*). She challenges Julian to treat her better than a prostitute: to tell her explicitly that he wants sex, or at least to try to seduce her rather than just summoning her (*Umakyat ka na!*) for "service."

Amanda!
And Julian's authoritarian summons suddenly rent the fabric of silence.
It's late, what are you still doing down there?
I've just put some laundry into the washing machine. Why?
At this hour? Come upstairs. Now!
Throughout our long marriage, I've figured out what this cue means. But in all these years, not once did Julian tell me explicitly why he wanted me to go upstairs or why he wanted me to go to our room.
Amanda!

Why? What for? I repeated. This time I wanted to force him to answer me. Julian became impatient.

What do you mean why? Just come upstairs, period! It's late!

I wanted to refuse. I don't want to do it. I'm not in the mood. When I feel like doing it, he's the one who doesn't want to do it. I wanted to escape. The truth is sex with Julian doesn't even matter to me anymore. It doesn't give me pleasure. If one doesn't get pleasure, what's the point of having sex? The truth is after having sex with Julian, I get even more depressed. It makes me think that perhaps it is my sole function in life: to service Julian. (*'Naiisip ko kasi kung 'yon na lang ba talaga ang silbi ko sa buhay: ang magserbisyo kay Julian.*)

What's going on? yelled Julian once more.

Punyeta, did you hear me?

I said, I don't understand why you're calling me. What do you need me for?

I order you to come here, now!

Why, I ask?

Julian is infuriated. Why do you have to ask why?

I finally went upstairs, but by this time, Julian was no longer in the mood. However much I embarrassed him, he never told me why he wanted me to come to his room. (1988:85)

In a powerful scene toward the end of the novel, when Amanda informs Julian that she has decided to leave him, Julian confronts Amanda with the reason for his reluctance and impotence in expressing his sexuality with her:

I tried to accept what you are (what society has socialized you to be). I said to myself—"there is nothing I can do"; there was nothing else I could do with you except the most standard way of *gano'nan* (having sex), as you call it. Because if I tried to do something more exciting, you would be insulted. You would accuse me of treating you like a prostitute. (I opened my mouth to say something but Julian pointed his finger at me, shouting.) Now don't you dare interrupt me! You are so demure and virtuous, aren't you? (Aren't you supposed to be so *mahinhin?*) You are too inhibited. Did you ever think about what I might have felt through all this? Believe me, Amanda, I don't get pleasure from it either. Especially since you act as though it's work (*trabaho*) which you want to finish as quickly as possible. (1988:190)

In the above scene, the reader is forcefully struck by the violence of Julian pointing his finger and shouting at Amanda, *"Now don't you dare interrupt me!"* What makes it even more violent is that it is said in English, which suddenly jumps out at you from the Tagalog text. Reading a novel written and narrated by a woman may have lulled the reader into believing that finally we will hear a woman's voice—uninterrupted—until we are hit with the realization that, on the contrary, this pioneering text is *the* interruption in the long tradition of canonized literature which is mostly dominated by the male voice, articulated in the colonizer's language. This discussion about *kahinhinan* between Julian and Amanda defines the function (*trabaho*) of a wife in a middle-class Catholic household as a virtuous, modest woman who preserves the sanctity of the home by preserving her own. *"Masyado kang mahinhin, di ba?"* "You are so *mahinhin*, aren't you?" (or "Aren't you supposed to be so *mahinhin?*") *Mahinhin* can be translated as demure, virtuous, pious or modest—the representation of the purity of the Virgin Mary, of the noble suffering of Filipina women from Maria Clara to Corazon Aquino who was always portrayed as a pious, faithful, national mother figure.[26] As with the Tagalog word *damdamin* (emotions, to feel) which is related to the Malay-Indonesian word *dendam* (revenge, passion, desire), the Tagalog adjective *mahinhin* (modest, demure, eyes always cast downwards, one who will never laugh too loud with mouth wide open) is also related to the Malay-Indonesian word *menghina* (to humiliate, to insult, to regard as unimportant). It is fascinating that a negative action—*menghina*—has evolved into an adjective for moral virtue—*menghinhin, mahinhin*—which, in the Tagalog context, then became gender-specific. *Mahinhin* is an adjective used to describe passivity and demure behavior, the preservation of moral values, applied only to women. It conjures up the image of a prison for women, bringing to mind Kartini incarcerated at twelve, Maria Clara inhibited by heavy layers of clothes, or the *asuang* who can go in and out of this prison and travel alone, but only by assuming the form of a bat, dog, or some other nonhuman being.

Earlier in the book, Amanda tells the reader that she too wants to "undress" herself of *kahinhinan*—*Gusto ko ring maghubad ng kahinhinan, Julian . . . pero natatakot akong mag-alala ka na baka kung ano nang nangyayari sa akin!* "I too would like to undress myself of *kahinhinan*, Julian . . . but I am afraid you might be alarmed that something weird is happening to me" (1988:23). Amanda would like to change, to be "modern," but is afraid of the social punishment which comes from breaking away from the compulsory tradition of *kahinhinan*, a term closely related to the word *kahinaan*, meaning "weakness" or "powerlessness." Those who seek the freedom to be in control or to express their sexuality are punished with socially ostracizing nicknames such as *'malandi'* ("flirt," the opposite of *mahinhin*) or *kalapating mababa ang lipad* ("pigeon which flies low"). On the other hand, adjectives describing the behavior of men, such as *palikero* (from *paliko-liko*, meaning to turn and turn, not to go straight—to be a playboy), tend to have a more positive, even a complimentary, meaning.

Julian responded that if he had tried to do something sexually more exciting, she would have been insulted. She would have accused him of treating her like a prostitute (*puta*). The paradox is that he treats her like a prostitute *anyway*, demanding sexual service even when Amanda does not want to give such service. A prostitute is someone who gets paid for sexual service, she doesn't desire. The difference between Amanda and a prostitute has to do with the way society sees her, rather than the physical act. Also, a woman who controls her actions (especially her sexuality) is viewed as debased not because she expresses her desires, but because she is the object of male desire. In macho Filipino culture, prostitutes do not really sell *their* sexuality, but the sexuality of their clients back to them.

Our narrator, Amanda Bartolome, mother to five sons, is painfully aware of this powerlessness in a family where her husband makes all the decisions. I quote and translate the excerpt below at length because it is the beginning of Amanda's critical questioning of the silencing of her voice and her desire for a more active life beyond the domesticated role of wife and mother:

> I felt no sense of achievement in the passing of the past ten years . . . Throughout twenty-seven years of being a housewife, I did not fully develop as a person . . . I served merely as witness, to my husband's search for fulfillment of his ambitions, as witness to the growth of my children and the discovery of their strength and worth as men. Throughout this, no one bothered to ask me about my own desires . . .
>
> I see wrinkles beginning to crawl on my face and I am terrified . . . I am turning 50, a few more years and I might turn into an invalid, or perhaps die. I am afraid of the prospect of leaving this world without leaving any mark, without having done anything. People will talk about me at my funeral and say, "She was a wife and mother and nothing else. She did nothing in this world except give birth." I will die without having discovered what other things I might have been able to do, without having others understand fully who, and what, I am. Because I myself do not know who and what I am!
>
> I become increasingly anxious, especially now that I am often alone in the house, as I realize that I am becoming more and more useless and separated from the lives of these men whom I have served and considered to be all of my life . . .
>
> I will die and leave these men . . . that will be the beginning. (1988:181–182)

While this is the anguished voice of a woman who feels that she has "failed" because hers was a life defined only by her connection with her husband and sons, it is also the anxious voice of a woman from a privileged class overwhelmed by the political events in the streets outside the protected walls of her exclusive subdivision. Her eldest son Jules has joined the NPA, her third son Emmanuel has become a journalist who documents government corruption and human rights violations, and her fourth son, Jason, has been brutally "salvaged"[27] by the military. Yet Amanda's changing subjectivity is expressed solely in her individual desire to seek release in sexual expression, to critique the institution of marriage and conservative family values. She does not seek to become an active subject of history directly involved in the seizure of political power. The armed struggle and concrete ideas for revolutionary change are left to Mara.

Amanda attempts to leave, but cannot, because despite her liberal feminist radicalization she is wedded to her class and the consolidation of her class. In her article, "From Rocking the Cradle to Rocking the Boat," Lualhati Bautista argues that "Filipina women writers do not just yearn for a 'Room of their Own' (referring to Virginia Woolf's *A Room of One's Own*, the cult text of European and American feminism). Their room is class struggle—the streets, the demonstrations, the rallies, the picket lines" (1989:55). If the ideal alternative heroine's "room" is class struggle, why then does Bautista create a protagonist who fails to join this class struggle?

THE POOR WRITER AND HER RICH NARRATOR

One of the aims of this essay is to explore the author's control of distance between herself, the narrator, the implied audience, and the *intended* but marginal heroine Mara in the novel. In the preface, Lualhati Bautista responded to queries from her readers as to whether *Dekada '70* was "autobiographical," by clarifying that *she* (the writer) is *not* Amanda (the narrator).

> Several people have asked me whether or not *Dekada '70* is autobiographical, if I am Amanda Bartolome who is the focus of interest in the whole novel. To the extent that I had to reread the novel so that I could see clearly which characteristics Amanda and I had in common that looked similar. We do have some similarities, but these things are just the consequence of the fact that we are both women . . . and both mothers. (1988:5)

The author felt compelled to explain that although she and her narrator shared some similarities (they are both women and both mothers), there is a distance between them which the reader may have missed. The important *implied* difference is class: the author is from working-class Tondo, while Amanda, her narrator, is from an exclusive subdivision in Manila. While Bautista's own values are perhaps closer to Mara's (the intended heroine), she is aware that her implied audience in its subdivisions has to be politicized (first through Amanda's unthreatening, nonviolent character) before it can be receptive to an alternative heroine like Mara. To Bautista's readers, an NPA narrator was still unacceptable in their living rooms. One could argue that in the novel, Mara is a symbol for the NPA which was constituted as a peripheral actor in the official narrative of "people power" in 1986. Yet it is the NPA's/Mara's presence on the margins which causes the urban middle classes in the Philippines to be nervous. Its troubling presence begins to make women like Amanda question their privileges, especially when her own children have begun to join its ranks. According to Benedict Anderson, "One of the most striking features of the last years of the [Marcos] regime was the gradual adoption of a nationalist-Marxist vocabulary by notable sections of the bourgeois intelligentsia, the lower echelons of the Church hierarchy, and the middle class more generally. Only the militant Left appeared to offer some way out" (1988:23). While repressive government censorship under the Marcos regime necessitated the preservation of a liberal middle-class subject in *Dekada '70,* the author also prepares the groundwork for the emergence of an alternative heroine whose presence *haunts* not only the main characters in the text, but more profoundly, the Philippine military and the ruling elite.

One could argue that one of the aims of the novel was to popularize the National Democratic Front (NDF) program to appeal to the urban middle class. We must also remember that in 1982, when *Dekada '70* was first published, government censorship was quite strict, and it would have been very difficult to popularize a novel with an NPA woman as narrator. A few years later, Bautista's implied audience was to play a significant role in the so-called "EDSA Uprising" of 1986 (named after Epifanio De Los Santos Avenue, a major avenue in Metro Manila where the "people power" demonstrations occurred). In the 1980s, the intensification of armed struggle in the countryside and the cultural struggle in the cities caused urban mass protests gradually to increase, involving the participation of an estimated five hundred thousand to two million people. This culminated in the overthrow of Ferdinand Marcos in February 1986.

HOW DO WE CONSTRUCT HEROINES?

Through her gradual radicalization in the seventies, Amanda begins to wonder whether a revolution was really necessary. *Naiisip ko . . . naiisip ko lang naman . . . wala sanang magalit sa 'kin pero naiisip ko . . . na kailangan na nga yata natin ang rebolusyon!* "I'm thinking . . . it's just a thought . . . I hope no one will be angry with me but I keep thinking . . . that perhaps we really do need a revolution!"(1988:163). Halfway through the novel, a different kind of voice is introduced—that of Mara, a laborer in a factory from an urban-poor family, who becomes an NPA guerrilla. Mara marries Jules (Amanda's eldest son who has also joined the NPA) and becomes Amanda's daughter-in-law. Mara's voice is barely articulated in the text. We only hear her voice as brief interruptions on the rare occassions when she suddenly appears at Amanda's house in Manila. Yet on these occasions, it seems that the author's voice and Mara's become one—there is no manipulation of distance between them. Most of the time Mara is in the provinces or living "underground" as an urban guerrilla and is unable to contact her husband Jules, or Amanda.

The urban-rural gap (those who live in Manila and those outside it) in this novel is quite huge—a realistic portrayal of the "urbanness" of the

1986 uprising, which occurred mainly in Manila. The only people who actually go out to the provinces (in this case, Bicol) on an *"exposure trip"* (1988:64; the phrase itself is revealing) are the NPA guerrillas who, predictably, give a very romanticized account of peasant life. Their account implies an audience so distant from rural life that it needs to be "exposed" to it.[28] Indeed, the so-called "First Quarter Storm" generation of activists who joined the NPA in the early 1970s were mostly urban student members of *Kabataang Makabayan* (Nationalist Youth) from the University of the Philippines in Diliman.

In a scene in which Mara discusses revolution with Julian, we see not only how far removed Julian is from the reality of political violence, but that Amanda (who *narrates* the scene) is much closer to understanding it and is much more attracted to Mara's ideology. Here the author is no longer controlling distance or manoeuvering between her implied audience and the censors; she assumes Amanda's voice as a sympathetic narrator but articulates her own aspirations through Mara's. In this scene the author directly *intervenes* to give us a program which tells us how social justice in the Philippines is to be achieved.

Why don't you stay here with Jules until you have the baby? asked Julian. [Mara is pregnant.]

It is not really possible for Jules and myself to live like you. We have committed our lives to the struggle, replied Mara.

But what about your child? S/he also needs a normal life, Mara!

What is "normal"? Mara answered scornfully, state violence against millions of our people?

There you go again . . .

Wala po ng tinatawag na peaceful revolution. There is no such thing as a "peaceful revolution." *Ang pagbabago, ang rebolusyon . . . di po maiiwasang maging madugo. Gaya ng panganganak.* With change, with revolution . . . blood (violence) cannot be avoided. Like childbirth.

Julian nodded slowly, thoughtfully. I was envious as I observed how seriously he listened to her ideas:

But who wants violence? Julian argued. A river of blood is not a pretty sight, iha.

This Mara, she is not afraid to debate with Julian. Not afraid to look him straight in the eye.

Those like you who belong to the ruling class . . . radical change will never begin with you. Even now, especially now, almost all the laws favor foreigners and multinational companies. And your class is complicit in this.

Well dear . . . we have a Ministry of Labor to deal with the grievances of the workers . . . , Julian replied patronizingly.

We also have a total banning of all strikes, Mara calmly replied.

Ya . . . but whenever they strike production comes to a standstill . . .

Striking is the only effective weapon for the workers.

This Mara, she is brilliant, fearless, unflinching. And in my heart, I wished I could be like her. [*At sa loob ng sarili ko, nawi-wish ko na sana'y gaya niya ako.*] (1988:143)

It is striking that in the above passage Mara compares revolution to childbirth. *Wala po ng tinatawag na peaceful revolution.* There is no such thing as a "peaceful revolution." *Ang pagbabago, ang rebolusyon . . . di po maiiwasang maging madugo. Gaya ng panganganak.* With change, with revolution . . . blood (violence) cannot be avoided. Like childbirth." Yet when Mara gave birth to her first child, Rev (for revolution), her husband Jules could not be with her because he had "more important revolutionary duties," as though childbirth was "a distraction that leads to forgetfulness."[29] Mara gave birth alone. It is on this issue, the utilitarian treatment of women, even by the NPA, that Amanda and Bautista voice their strongest condemnation: *Ama ka na, anak mo 'yong ipinanganak . . . at unang anak mo! Nasa'n ka no'ng ipinapanganak siya?* (1988:145) "You are a father now, it is your child which was born . . . and it is your first child! Where were you when he was born?" In the preface to *Dekada '70,* Bautista explains that this repressed anger (*hinanakit,* from the root word *sakit* or pain; also related to the Indonesian word *dendam*) is not so much a mother's as it is a wife's. *Bagama't iyon ay hinanakit hindi ng isang ina kundi ng isang asawa.* This *hinanakit* is even more poignant at a time when the left is facing its worst crisis in its twenty-four-year history. According to Bello, one of the major criticisms against it is its "instrumental view of people—a tendency to evaluate their worth mainly on whether or not they advance or obstruct the Left's class-determined political objectives" (1992:6). *Makibaka,* one of the most militant women's organizations in the Philippines, was founded by Maria Lorena Barros and other NPA women cadres to change what they saw as the trivialization of the gender issue within the NPA. In *Dekada '70* Bautista powerfully articulates the idea that revolution is like childbirth—men, especially those who believe in effecting revolutionary changes, cannot fully give their lives to the former while considering the latter "a distraction" or "an interruption."

DISCUSSION AND CONCLUSION

At the end of the novel, Amanda is determined to leave Julian and begin her own life. When she confronts Julian about a separation, a violent argument ensues. She attempts to leave him and make plans for a new life, but he seduces her by promising to change, telling her that in fact Dekada '70 and the political violence toward his own children have already changed him. She decides to give him another chance and remains in the marriage. The novel ends with Amanda still married to Julian. This is the controversial ending which has been called a betrayal and a cop-out by critics (e.g., Garcellano 1987) who expected a more radical transformation in Amanda's character.

I would argue, however, that were Amanda successfully rebellious, and had she managed to escape from her husband, the impact of Bautista's social criticism would be considerably weakened and the novel would become escapist. An unstoppable progression to complete liberation (just as the grim and determined leaders, mostly male, would have it) would indeed be a romantic-leftist conventional narrative. Indeed, for Amanda, and for most people, there is immanent tension between tradition and change (or militancy). The novel is a realistic portrayal of the unresolved, ambivalent, contradictory positions occupied by Amanda (as privileged housewife) and Mara (as NPA guerrilla), their common ground being that they are both women and mothers, each struggling against different kinds of male domination (Amanda by a hacienda-type husband and Mara by male guerrillas putting "revolution" before women's needs and contributions). As Leonora Angeles argues elsewhere,

> In a sense, the women's movement's assertion of its autonomy in relation to the nationalist movement is parallel to the situation of a wife gaining consciousness about her own oppression within the marital relationship and society. She is trying to assert her independence (read autonomy), individuality and equality with her husband. Like a wife who struggles for freedom and economic independence, women refuse to play "wife to the revolution," or to replicate within the movement the structures of male domination in the larger society. (1989:13)

However, this novel is not just about gender relations, and I cannot end simply with a sympathetic reading of Amanda's difficulties as a woman. The novel is also about class and social formations in the seventies and the conflicts between women from the ruling elite, who had more access to representation and to monopoly of the microphone, and poor women who were either marginalized or virtually unrepresented. Like Amanda, the majority of the leaders of the women's groups come from middle- or upper-middle-class families. Like Amanda, some of them initially became involved in the national democratic movement because of their interest in feminist issues. The excerpt below is a critical self-analysis by middle- and upper-middle-class feminists in Manila about their own complicity in the oppression of urban-poor and peasant women. It is interesting because it reveals the patronizing attitude which the sophisticated, urban leaders of the feminist movement have towards their servants.

> If you look at the leaders of the hundred and twenty or so women's groups in the Philippines, including Gabriela, almost all come from the middle-class or even the upper class. We middle-class feminists are also responsible for

the exploitation and oppression of many lower class women who are rendering us service as housemaids. We are able to engage in the women's movement because we have maids. If they are not around to help us, would we
have the luxury of discussing in a seminar? (De Dios, 1988:30)
    I'd like to share my insight on what Aurora said about maids. I think we
should start with transforming our own attitude toward and treatment of our
maids. Perhaps we can encourage them to study by giving them some free
time in the afternoon when housework isn't heavy. Likewise, in connection
with unifying women and crossing class barriers, I think we should start by
remolding ourselves. (De Dios, 1988:30–31)

Indeed, in Amanda's world, peasant and urban-poor women do not exist, except for what she hears of them from her son's "exposure trips."
Thus, the novel can be read as a satire and a caricature of Amanda's kind
of liberal feminism which tends to be urban-biased and exclusive. Bautista
more or less consciously insults her implied audiences with Amanda's seduction and deception but ultimate inability to leave her (symbolic) marriage to the oligarchy. For the middle- and upper-middle-class liberal subject, "conscientization" means rebelling against patriarchy through sexual
autonomy or individual self-worth and working towards reforms within the
existing order. The author manipulates her implied audience into either
uncritically identifying with Amanda or arrogantly judging her for not being "more revolutionary." It is only toward the end that the reader realizes
(or may never realize), when the author intervenes through Mara's voice,
that in fact Amanda's values—with which the reader was so quick to identify or judge—are a caricature of the values of her own implied audience.
    In 1986, three years after *Dekada '70* was published, an "inexperienced
housewife" with a background somewhat similar to our character Amanda,
became president of the Philippines, in one of the more miraculous events
in Philippine history.[30] As with Amanda, the audience had mistaken hopes
in Cory that she could transcend her class interests and bring about radical
change in land reform and Philippine politics in general. Both Cory and
Amanda, to some extent, were willing participants in the marriage with
the oligarchy, because of their class origins. The difference is that while
Amanda's inability to leave her oppressive marriage can only disappoint
her expectant readers and literary critics, Cory's indecisiveness and complicity with the military and ruling elite cost the lives of thousands of
people.
    Most literary critics who have analyzed *Dekada '70* have focused solely
on Amanda's dominant character without any acknowledgement of Mara's
existence, or of Bautista's more or less conscious attempt to present a new
emergent morality and an alternative heroine.[31] It is interesting that literary critics have uncritically celebrated Amanda, a character they are able
to recognize and identify with, while Mara is constituted as nearly absent

in the text. Perhaps it is appropriate to ask the question, "Can the subaltern speak?"[32] when the representation by literary critics of the dominant voices (which justify and legitimize elite rule) turns into self-representation and the preservation of their own class. It is not really in their interest to make sense of the inchoate, garbled, distracting, militant voices of urban-poor women, members of the NPA, or peasant women.[33] In a confrontation with Julian and Amanda, Mara condemns them and the class they represent: *Ang mga kabilang sa naghaharing uri . . . hindi sila kailanman pagmumulan ng tunay na pagbabago* (1988:140). "Those who belong to the ruling class . . . radical change will never begin with them." But why does Bautista herself relegate Mara's voice to the margins and make Amanda's the dominant narrative voice? This is the problem that a non-elite feminist writer from Tondo faces when trying to write for an implied audience and publishers who may not accept her work—unless it flatters *their class* and puts *them* at the forefront, unless "*they* are assured of a primary role in the fulfilment of the end towards which history moves" (Ileto: 136, emphasis added).

It is Mara, the NPA guerrilla, whom Bautista provides as the proper heroine, the proper representative of the ideals of a "real" revolution. This is powerfully articulated at the end of the novel, when Bautista reappropriates the Philippine national anthem in order to give it her own semantic meaning:

Aming ligaya,
na pag may mang-aapi,
Ang *pumatay* nang dahil
sa 'yo!

Hindi ang mamatay . . . ang pumatay! Sapagka't ang sambayanan ay di na martir kundi rebelde! (1988:220)

It is with joy
that if someone tries to oppress you,
we shall *kill*
for you.

Not to die (*ang mamatay*) . . . but to kill (*ang pumatay*)! Because the people are no longer martyrs but rebels!

The above version is indeed a powerful subversion of the official anthem. The original national anthem, which is sung in public ceremonies, ends with *Ang mamatay ng dahil sa 'yo!* ("We shall die for you.") However, during the seventies, when this song was sung in leftist demonstrations, the verb *mamatay* (to die for) was radically changed to *pumatay* (to kill). In this act of cultural resistance, those who are unrepresented appropriate the official discourse of the government in order to subsequently deploy it to serve their own semantic ends. If the national community (*sambayanan*) was previously portrayed as passive, women as members of this community were doubly so. Within the standard rhetoric of nationalism, the most dominant trope contested by feminists is the image of the "woman martyr."

> The silently suffering martyr is one of the most dominant images projected by women characters in early Philippine literature written in English. As mother, wife, lover, sister, or daughter, she is molded after the image of the ideal woman: the Virgin Mother who suffers in silence and denies her wounds for the sake of love. (Evasco, 1985:44)

Breaking from the dominant discourse of patriarchal nationalism, Bautista is bored with the trope of martyred women and shrinking violets in Philippine literature. She constructs an alternative heroine who is not merely going to "die for," but shall "kill for," independence. Not exactly the kind of heroine acceptable to the present political order, especially with regard to patriarchy and class struggle.[34]

For middle class and bourgeois society, the implied audience of the novel, Mara is not interesting. Therefore her marginality in the text is quite understandable. More interestingly, even within the Communist Party and the orthodox left in general, Mara is a rather inappropriate heroine. According to Mara, *Wala po ng tinatawag na peaceful revolution.* "There is no such thing as a 'peaceful revolution.' " *Ang pagbabago, ang rebolusyon . . . di po maiiwasang maging madugo. Gaya ng panganganak.* "With change, with revolution . . . blood (violence) cannot be avoided. Like childbirth." It is this heroine who harbors *hinanakit*, albeit suppressed, against the men in the New People's Army who attach more importance to "the revolution" and revolutionary time which marches forward in a disciplined linear fashion, than to women's activities such as childbirth which are considered an obstruction to its class-determined political objectives. In addition, Tagalog, the language in which Mara articulates her ideas, is also rather inappropriate to the leaders of the left who theorize only in English because their implied audience does not include people like Mara. Most official party documents are written in English.

In conclusion, in this essay I have demonstrated Lualhati Bautista's effort to present alternative Filipina heroines and articulate subaltern voices which, because they break from the dominant discourses of patriarchy, whether colonialist, nationalist or leftist, are often not allowed to speak.

NOTES

I would like to thank Michael Peletz, Geoffrey Robinson, Amin Sweeney and David Lloyd for providing challenging and insightful comments. Most especially I would like to thank Aihwa Ong and Sylvia Tiwon who inspired me to think critically and creatively and without whose editorial support this essay would not have been possible.

1. This is important because she is one of the few highly-acclaimed women writers in the Philippines who did not attend elite convent schools.

2. This is also important because *Liwayway* is associated with "popular" as opposed to "intellectual" literature. It publishes mostly Tagalog fiction, as opposed to the more elite magazines which publish works in the English language. *Liwayway* is also associated with the *bakya* (literally, wooden slippers) culture referring to "lower class, provincial, popular tastes." In Malay, for example, the equivalent of *bakya* is *kampungan*. I suppose the equivalent in the Indonesian context would be people who read *Pos Kota* as opposed to those who read *Kompas*.

3. All translations in this essay are mine.

4. Her novels *Dekada '70, 'Gapo (Olongapo)*, and *Bata, Bata Paano Ka Ginawa* all won the grand prize for novels from the Carlos Palanca Memorial Awards for Literature, the highest literary award in the Philippines. Her other works include film scripts: *Sakada* (1976); *Bulaklak sa City Jail* (1984); *Kung Mahawi Man Ang Ulap* (1984); *Sex Object* (1985); TV dramas: *Daga Sa Timba Ng Tubig* (1975); *Isang Kabanata sa Libro ng Buhay ni Leilani Cruzaldo* (1987); short stories: *Tatlong Kuwento sa Buhay ni Julian Candelabra* (1982) and *Buwan, Buwan, Hulugan mo ako ng Sundang* (1983).

5. *Veritas*, Book Reviews, September 16, 1984.

6. For more extraordinary alternative heroines in Pramoedya's works, see for example the unforgettable characters of Nyai Ontosoroh in *Bumi Manusia*, Surati in *Anak Semua Bangsa*, Ang San Mei and Prinses Kasiruta in *Jejak Langkah*, and Sitti Soendari in *Rumah Kaca*.

7. Kartini, a nineteenth-century Javanese princess, called for women's emancipation. Sylvia Tiwon argues that in *Gadis Pantai*, Pramoedya has created an alternative heroine, a Kartini of the masses. See Tiwon (1992) for a thought-provoking analysis of how Kartini, who died after childbirth and was never really a "mother," has been portrayed by the New Order as the "model" national mother (*ibu kita Kartini*).

8. The translation is mine, from the Indonesian original by Pramoedya Ananta Toer, *Gadis Pantai* (1987).

9. Interview in Indonesian by Vedi R. Hadiz of Benedict Anderson, in *Politik, Budaya dan Perubahan Social: Ben Anderson Dalam Studi Politik Indonesia* (1992). The rest of the translations in this essay are from the Tagalog language.

10. For informative writings on the Martial Law period, see for example, Anderson (1988); Hawes (1987); Davis (1989); Kessler (1988); Rosenberg (1979); and Bello (1977, 1987).

11. Noetics is the study of the shaping, communication, transmission and retrieval of knowledge. It includes the study not only of printed texts but also of oral traditions and other means by which knowledge is articulated. For an illuminating discussion of this, see Sweeney (1987).

12. The kind of racism which, as Rosaldo argues, is "more often found in corridor talk than in published writings." I quote the following incident because it is the kind of cultural arrogance which I too have encountered countless times: "Allow me to make the problem of cultural invisibility rather more concrete by telling

about what happened when I was a graduate student contemplating fieldwork in the Philippines. A teacher warned me that Filipinos are 'people without culture.' Meaning to be helpful, he suggested doing fieldwork in Madagascar because people there have 'rich' cultures" (1989:197). For further discussion of American "imperialist nostalgia" for the Philippines, see Salman (1991).

13. For a splendid critique of the linear emplotment of Philippine history by colonial scholars and even well-intentioned nationalist and leftist historians, which conceals the roles played by popular movements outside the discursive formations of the universal, secular, nation-state, see, for example, Reynaldo Ileto, "Outlines of a Non-Linear Emplotment of Philippine History" (1988b). See also Ileto (1979a, 1982, 1988a). For a brilliant analysis of gender and nationalism, see Rafael (1984, 1993). For excellent work on local politics, see Kerkvliet (1990, 1991).

14. For an excellent account of theory and practice in postcolonial literatures in which marginal or absent participants, "borderline figures" and previously "unspoken subjects" become the central problematic of analysis, see Ashcroft et al. (1989).

15. See Dipesh Chakrabarty's brilliant essay, "Postcoloniality and the Artifice of History: Who Speaks for 'Indian' Pasts?" (1992). The issues which Chakrabarty raises for Indian scholars are also important for Filipino scholars trying to write an alternative history. As Chakrabarty writes, "The 'greats' and the models of the historian's enterprise are always at least culturally 'European.' [In the case of the Philippines, it would be 'American'.] 'They' produce their work in relative ignorance of non-Western histories, and this does not seem to affect the quality of their work. This is a gesture, however, that 'we' cannot return. We cannot even afford an equality or symmetry of ignorance at this level without taking the risk of appearing 'old-fashioned' or 'outdated' " (1992:2).

16. Writing a polite academic article on violence against Filipina women seems so benign when juxtaposed with everyday reality. I am reminded, for example, of opening a Singaporean newspaper and seeing advertisements for Filipina migrant laborers "on sale." The ads had photographs of these women and below their individual photos, a price tag—$150–$300 per month—and a description of their virtuous qualities as good, cheap laborers. I am also reminded of a family who were former neighbors in Pangasinan. They had received a letter to pick up their young, beautiful daughter, who had decided to return home after working for two years as a migrant laborer in Saudi Arabia, from the airport in Manila. When they got to the airport, they were given a coffin, in which their daughter's body, chopped up into pieces, was delivered. The Philippine Commission on Migrant Workers could do nothing. Or the unforgettable but sadly common story in the news a few years ago of an American man who murdered his Filipina mail-order bride without remorse, because, according to him, "he [had] bought her, owned her, and could do whatever he wanted." For an excellent analysis of the Filipino male (in particular Ilokano) migrant's experience in the Middle East, see Margold, this volume.

17. See, for example, Kintanar (1992); Mananzan (1987, 1988); Barrios (1990).

18. See "Fraternal Foes: Rival Strategies Split the Communists," in *Far Eastern Economic Review,* January 14, 1993.

19. When I was in elementary and high school in Dagupan City, Pangasinan,

the teachers, determined to teach us proper English, set a fine of fifty cents for each Tagalog word spoken. But the fine for Pangasinan, a dialect, was higher—seventy-five cents per word. There was a designated student spy-cum-money collector for each class whose job was to eavesdrop, collect the money, and report to the teachers.

20. The *asuang* is one of the most powerful and frightening supernatural beings in Filipino belief systems. There are several varying narratives, but the main theme is that she is an extraordinarily beautiful woman with very long, dark hair who is "normal" by day but can turn into nonhuman forms at night, flying around looking for victims to suck, usually pregnant women or men. She has a long tongue with a needle which can penetrate *atap* roofs and suck the fetus from a pregnant woman. She usually leaves the lower half of her human body on the ground, while the upper half travels. In order to capture her, one must put vinegar, garlic, and pepper in her lower abdomen so that she cannot return to her body and make it whole again. I mention this belief because it is very popular and part of belief systems about women's access to magical and supernatural powers (similar to the Malay concept of *keramat*) which has been suppressed and demonized by Catholicism, and only occasionally comes out in nervous comments by modern literary critics about powerful women acting as "men" or as "nonhumans." For readings on the *asuang*, see, for example, Lynch (1949); Pertierra (1983); Ramos (1971a).

21. For evocative stories of the querida's social position in the middle and upper-middle class Filipino family, see, for example, Nick Joaquin's "Three Generations," and Kerima Polotan's "The Chieftest Mourner," in Croghan (1975). For an interesting discussion of the consequences of Spanish colonialism on sexuality and gender in the Lowland Visayas, see Blanc-Szanton (1990).

22. For a historical analysis of the transformation of these haciendero provincial oligarchies into national elites, see Anderson (1988).

23. For further discussion of the traditional Maria Clara character, see Nakpil (1962).

24. See, for example, Rosca (1988); Rosario Cruz Lucero's "Family Rites," Ruth Elynia Mabanglo's "Regla sa Buwan ng Hunyo," and Aida Santos's "Isang Gabi: Erotica" in Salanga ed. (1987); Barrios (1990).

25. For a fascinating alternative representation of a traditional, populist form of local female power and sexuality in the cult of the Tadtarin during the Feast of St. John juxtaposed with disciplined Spanish Catholic colonial morality, see Nick Joaquin's short story, "The Summer Solstice" (1952).

26. For a satirical account of the Catholic training to become *mahinhin*, especially among the elite, see Rosario Cruz Lucero's short story, "Tales of a Catholic Girls' School" in *Herstory*, pp. 1–11, Manila: St. Scholastica's College, Institute of Women's Studies, 1990.

27. "Salvage" was a term coined in the 1970s to refer to extrajudicial killings by government armed forces against civilians. Like several English words which have acquired an inverted meaning in the Philippine context, "salvage" (meaning "to be saved from a wreck," "to be rescued") came to mean "extrajudicial killing" by the military.

28. Having been born and raised in Dagupan City, Pangasinan, Central Luzon, where I finished high school, and having been to Manila only a few times, I was

initially attracted to *Dekada '70* and to novels set in Manila because I was interested in critically reading Tagalog novels and the construction of its nationalist rhetoric (I learned Tagalog as a foreign language, my native tongue is Pangasinan). Tagalog literature attempts to represent all of "Philippine literature," which other language groups find problematic.

29. I owe this phrase to Vicente Rafael's 1984 essay entitled, "Language, Identity and Gender in Rizal's *Noli*."

30. In reality Aquino (Corazon Cojuangco) was not really an "inexperienced housewife" but an astute businesswoman with plenty of experience running her family's sugar plantation, Hacienda Luisita. For a scathing critique of Corazon Aquino and the middle-class uprising of 1986, see Anderson (1988). See also Vokes (1989); Dahm (1991); Magno (1990).

31. The literary analyses of *Dekada '70* of which I am aware are those of Garcellano (1987); Reyes (1990); Kintanar (1990).

32. This question is inspired by Spivak's 1988 article, "Can the Subaltern Speak?", which problematizes the position that "valorizes the concrete experience of the oppressed, while being so uncritical about the historical role of the intellectual" who claims to speak of (or for) the subaltern woman (275).

33. Here, Ileto's critique of nationalist historians, including leftist intellectuals, is instructive. In the essay, "Outlines of a Non-Linear Emplotment of Philippine History," Ileto argues that "While Constantino and the NDF look upon the masses as the real 'makers of history,' the masses are not allowed to speak" (1988:135).

34. This theme of insubordinate women is quite common in Malay oral traditions. In a beautiful oral narration of *Puteri Babi* ("Pig Princess") by an old peasant woman from Johor (Leper bt. Abdul Hamid 1975), she closes her narration by saying, *Dulu banyak cerita. Tapi semua cerita perintah raja.* "In the old days there were a lot of stories. But all the stories were ordered (commissioned) by the ruler." Today's cultural scene is not much different. Pig-type women heroines who are poor (*sekin/miskin*), dirty (*kotor*), who bring about chaos (*semua dikubang dia*) and disorder (*kacau*) continue to speak, as Alan Feldman has argued elsewhere, "from a position of having been narrated and edited by others—by political institutions, by concepts of historical causality, and possibly by violence" (1991:13). I would like to thank Prof. Amin Sweeney who generously shared with us several of these oral narratives about insubordinate women in Malay society which he had collected and transcribed while teaching in Malaysia.

REFERENCES

Anderson, Benedict R. O'G. 1988. "Cacique Democracy in the Philippines: Its Origins and Dreams." *New Left Review,* May–June.

Angeles, Leonora. 1989. "Getting the Right Mix of Feminism and Nationalism: The Politics of the Women's Movement in the Philippines." M. A. thesis, Diliman, University of the Philippines.

Ashcroft, Bill, Gareth Griffiths, and Hellen Tiffin, eds. 1989. *The Empire Writes Back: Theory and Practice in Post-Colonial Literatures.* London: Routledge.

Barrios, Joi. 1990. *Ang Pagiging Babae ay Pamumuhay sa Panahon ng Digma* (To Be a Woman Is to Live in a Time of War). Manila: St. Scholastica's College.

Bautista, Lualhati. 1988. *Dekada '70*. Manila: Carmelo and Bauermann Printing Corporation.

———. 1989. "From Rocking the Cradle to Rocking the Boat." In Maria Asuncion Azcuna, Sr. Mary John Mananzan, and Fe Mangahas, eds., *Sarilaya: Women in Arts and Media*, pp. 86–90. Manila: St. Scholastica's College.

Bello, Walden. 1987. *U.S. Sponsored Low-Intensity Conflict in the Philippines*. San Francisco: Institute for Food and Development Policy.

———. 1992. "The Philippine Progressive Movement Today: A Preliminary Study on the State of the Left." *Philippine Alternatives* 1(2):2–4.

Blanc-Szanton, Cristina. 1990. "Collision of Cultures: Historical Reformulations of Gender in the Lowland Visayas, Philippines." In Jane M. Atkinson and Shelly Errington, eds., *Power and Difference: Gender in Island Southeast Asia,* pp. 345–384. Stanford: Stanford University Press.

Bonner, Raymond. 1987. *Waltzing with a Dictator: The Marcoses and the Making of American Policy.* New York: Times Books.

Chakrabarty, Dipesh. 1992. "Postcoloniality and the Artifice of History: Who Speaks for 'Indian' Pasts?" *Representations* 37 (Winter 1992):1–26.

Croghan, Richard V. 1975. *The Development of Philippine Literature in English (since 1900)*. Quezon City: Alemar-Phoenix Publishing House.

Dahm, Bernhard, ed. 1991. *Economy and Politics in the Philippines under Corazon Aquino.* Hamburg: Institute fur Asienkunde.

Davis, Leonard. 1989. *Revolutionary Struggle in the Philippines*. New York: St. Martin's Press.

De Dios, Aurora. 1988. "Women in History: Out of the Shadows, Filipina Women as Historical Footnotes," Paper presented to Conference at Women's Resource and Research Center, Manila, February.

Evasco, Marjorie. 1985. "A Dream of Pintadas." *Solidarity* 104–105:55–70.

Feldman, Alan. 1991. *Formations of Violence: The Narrative of the Body and Political Terror in Northern Ireland.* Chicago: University of Chicago Press.

Foulcher, Keith. 1990. "The Construction of an Indonesian National Culture: Patterns of Hegemony and Resistance." In Arief Budiman, ed., *State and Civil Society in Indonesia,* pp. 301–320. Clayton, Victoria: Monash Papers on Southeast Asia, No. 22.

Garcellano, Edel. 1987. "*Dekada '70* and the Search for a Method." In *First Person Plural.* Published by the author.

Hadiz, Vedi. 1992. *Politik, Budaya dan Perubahan Sosial: Ben Anderson Dalam Studi Politik Indonesia.* Jakarta: Penerbit Gramedia Pustaka Utama.

Hawes, Gary. 1987. *The Philippine State and the Marcos Regime: The Politics of Export.* Ithaca: Cornell University Press.

Ileto, Reynaldo C. 1979a. *Pasyon and Revolution: Popular Movements in the Philippines, 1840–1910.* Quezon City: Ateneo de Manila University Press.

———. 1979b. "Tagalog Poetry and Perceptions of the Past in the War Against Spain." In Anthony Reid and David Marr, eds., *Perceptions of the Past in Southeast Asia,* pp. 379–400. Singapore: Heinemann.

———. 1982. "Rizal and the Underside of Philippine History." In David Wyatt and

Alexander Woodside, eds., *Moral Order and Question of Change: Essays on Southeast Asia*, pp. 274–337. New Haven: Yale University Press.

———. 1988a. "Cholera and the Origins of the American Sanitary Order in the Philippines." In David Arnold, ed., *Imperial Medicine and Indigenous Societies*, pp. 125–148. Manchester: Manchester University Press.

———. 1988b. "Outlines of a Non-Linear Emplotment of Philippine History." In Lim Teck Ghee, ed., *Reflections on Development in Southeast Asia*, pp. 130–159. Singapore: Institute of Southeast Asian Studies.

Joaquin, Nick. 1952. "The Summer Solstice." In *Prose and Poems*. Manila: Graphic House.

Kerkvliet, Benedict, ed. 1990. *Everyday Politics in the Philippines: Class and Status Relations in a Central Luzon Village*. Berkeley: University of California Press.

———. 1991. *From Marcos to Aquino: Local Perspectives on Political Transition in the Philippines*. Quezon City: Ateneo de Manila University Press.

Kessler, Richard. 1988. *Rebellion and Repression in the Philippines*. New Haven: Yale University Press.

Kintanar, Thelma, ed. 1990. "Tracing the Rizal Tradition in the Filipino Novel." *Tenggara* 25.

———. 1992. *Feminist Perspectives on Philippine Literary Texts*. Diliman: University of the Philippines Press.

Leper bt. Abdul Hamid. 1973. "Puteri Babi." Oral narrative. Johor. Transcribed by Amin Sweeney.

Lucero, Rosario Cruz. 1990. *Herstory*. Manila: Institute of Women's Studies, St. Scholastica's College.

Lumbera, Bienvenido. 1984. *Revaluation: Essays in Philippine Literature, Cinema, and Popular Culture*. Manila: Index Publishing Co.

———. 1988. "Foreword." In Lualhati Bautista, *Dekada '70*. Manila: Carmelo and Bauermann Printing Corporation.

Lynch, Frank, S. J. 1949. "Ang Mga Asuang: A Bicol Belief." *Philippine Social Sciences and Humanities Review* 14 (December 1949): pp. 401–428.

Magno, Alexander. 1990. *Power Without Form: Essays on the Filipino State and Politics*. Manila: Kalikasan Press.

Mananzan, Mary John, OSB. 1987. *Essays on Women*. Manila: St. Scholastica's College.

———. 1988. *Women and Religion*. Manila: St. Scholastica's College.

Nakpil, Carmen Guerrero. 1962. "Maria Clara." In *Woman Enough and Other Essays*. Manila: Vibal Publishing House.

Pertierra, Raul. 1983. "Viscera-Suckers and Female Sociality: The Philippine Asuang." *Philippine Studies* 31:319–337.

Pramoedya Ananta Toer. 1981. *Bumi Manusia*. Kuala Lumpur: Wira Karya.

———. 1982. *Anak Semua Bangsa*. Kuala Lumpur: Wira Karya.

———. 1986. *Jejak Langkah*. Kuala Lumpur: Wira Karya.

———. 1987. *Gadis Pantai*. Jakarta: Hasta Mitra.

———. 1988. *Rumah Kaca*. Kuala Lumpur: Wira Karya.

Rafael, Vicente. 1993. "White Love: Surveillance and Nationalist Resistance in the United States Colonization of the Philippines." In Amy Kaplan and Donald

Pease, eds., *The Cultures of United States Imperialism*, pp. 185–218. Durham: Duke University Press.

———. 1984. "Language, Identity and Gender in Rizal's *Noli*." *Review of Malaysian and Indonesian Affairs* 18 (winter 1984): 110–140.

Ramos, Maximo D. 1971a. *The Asuang Syncrasy in Philippine Folklore*. Manila: Philippine Folklore Society.

———. 1971b. *Creatures of Philippine Lower Mythology*. Quezon City: University of the Philippines Press.

Reyes, Soledad. 1982. *Nobelang Tagalog, 1905–1975: Tradisyon at Modernismo*. Manila: Ateneo de Manila University Press.

———. 1987. *Noli Me Tangere, A Century After: An Interdisciplinary Perspective*. Quezon City: Ateneo de Manila University Press.

———. 1990. "Desire as Subversion in the Novels of Lualhati Bautista." *Tenggara* 25.

Rizal, Jose. 1961. *Noli Me Tangere*. Trans. by Leon Ma. (Maria) Guerrero. London: Longmans.

Rosaldo, Renato. 1989. "Imperialist Nostalgia." In *Culture and Truth: The Remaking of Social Analysis*, pp. 68–87. Boston: Beacon Press.

Rosca, Ninotchka. 1988. *State of War: A Novel*. New York: Norton.

Rosenberg, David, ed. 1979. *Marcos and Martial Law in the Philippines*. Ithaca: Cornell University Press.

Said, Edward. 1993. *Culture and Imperialism*. New York: Knopf.

Salanga, Alfredo Navarro and Esther Pacheco, eds. 1986. *Versus: Philippine Protest Poetry, 1983–1986*. Quezon City: Ateneo de Manila University Press.

———, et al., eds. 1987. *Kamao: Mga Tula ng Protesta (Protest Poetry), 1970–1986*. Manila: Cultural Center of the Philippines.

Salman, Michael. 1991. "In Our Orientalist Imagination: Historiography and the Culture of Colonialism in the U.S." *Radical History Review* 50 (spring 1991): 221–232.

Spivak, Gayatri Chakravorty. 1988. "Can the Subaltern Speak?," In Cary Nelson and Lawrence Grossberg, eds., *Marxism and the Interpretation of Culture*, pp. 271–313. Chicago: University of Illinois Press.

Sweeney, Amin. 1987. *A Full Hearing: Orality and Literacy in the Malay World*. Berkeley: University of California Press.

Tiglao, Rigoberto. 1993. "Fraternal Foes: Rival Strategies Split the Communists." *Far Eastern Economic Review* (January 14) 18–19.

Tiwon, Sylvia. 1995. "Models and Maniacs: Articulating the Female in Indonesia." In Laurie Sears, ed., *Fantasies of the Feminine: Sex and Death in Indonesia*. Durham: Duke University Press.

Vokes, R. W. A., ed. *The Philippines Under Aquino*. Occasional Paper no. 11. Canterbury: University of Kent, Centre for South-east Asian Studies.

EIGHT

Attack of the Widow Ghosts: Gender, Death, and Modernity in Northeast Thailand

Mary Beth Mills

Mary Beth Mills examines some of the local meanings and material consequences of modernity in northeast Thailand, a region situated at the margins of the national polity and culture, and subject to profoundly transformative changes associated with the monetization of the economy and the attendant decline in the viability of a broad range of village-based social, economic, and other institutions. Mills's essay illustrates that local understandings of gender are most profitably viewed against the backdrop of national developments, especially the deeply ambivalent nature of nationalist discourses bearing on modernity, progress, and the like. Her analysis of the outbreak of "hysteria" focusing on maurauding, sexually voracious "widow ghosts" bent on consuming male hosts reveals that official, state-sponsored discourses on modernity and progress do not resonate with the lived experiences of Thai citizens, the majority of whom experience wage labor, out-migration, and other aspects of "development" in decidedly threatening and otherwise negative terms. Local Thai fears of widow ghosts and the beliefs and practices associated with them are thus interpreted as constituting an alternative, largely counterhegemonic discourse on modernity, the meanings of which are in some ways similar both to capitalist-era South American narratives and practices bearing on the Devil (Taussig 1980), and to various aspects of large-scale spirit possession ("mass hysteria") on the shop floors of modern factories in Free Trade Zones in Selangor and other parts of Malaysia (Ong 1987, 1988). In all three cases we see a ritual dramatization of subalterns' fears, anxieties, and ambivalences about dealing with the wider (capitalist) world. In Mills's case we also see a clear dramatization of tensions between males and females, and of male fears, anxieties, and ambivalences toward women and their sexualities and embodied powers in particular—all of which reveal that in Thai culture women are viewed as having the capacity to both save and devour men. More generally, the trope of man-hungry (female) ghosts suggests that, for Thais, modernization has heavy gender ramifications, especially in marital and cross-generational terms; and that the modernization-driven transformation of gender relations is seen as putting everyone's lives in greater jeopardy, even though capitalism itself is not. Because widow ghosts do not "take issue" with capitalism and modernity and do in fact confine their "critique" to the transformation of gender relations that is linked to capitalism, they simultaneously resist and bolster the very structures against which they are arrayed (see also Krier, this volume).

In the dry season of 1990, for a period of about six weeks, villagers in the northeast of Thailand came to believe that they were in imminent danger of attack by marauding "widow ghosts" (*phii mae maai*).[1] Rural communities throughout the region called Isan, erected large, carved wooden penises, often two to three feet long or more, on village gateposts and at the entrances of most houses in an attempt to ward off these deadly female spirits. *Phii mae maai*, it was believed, were roaming the countryside looking for men to kill and take as "husbands." The fearsome power of these spirits reflects, in part, Northeast Thai cultural understandings of gender difference and the dangers inherent in female sexuality. But the gender symbolism which underlies widow ghost attacks does not explain why the fear of these spirits became a sudden, regionwide phenomenon in April and May of 1990.

To understand the massive scale of this episode, we need to see how local beliefs in these spirits and their deathly powers came also to represent some fundamental dilemmas in the contemporary experience of Northeastern peasant producers. In order to earn the cash income that is essential to sustain household production and reproduction, Isan villagers have turned increasingly to wage work outside their home communities. Labor migration by men as well as women (especially unmarried youth) provides a key source of cash earnings for rural families at the same time that it allows some villagers to participate in the prestigious domain of Thailand's modern urban centers. On the other hand, migration for wage work has introduced new strains into village social relations. These relate partly to the prolonged absence of many household members, as well as to the competing demands made on migrant earnings by obligations to rural kin and the attractions of commodity-oriented consumption. Furthermore, customary patterns of generational authority and gender role expectations are often challenged by the mobility and economic autonomy of village members who are off working in distant places. The widow ghost scare played directly upon these tensions within rural households through the explosive idiom of female sexual powers and appetites rampaging out of control; yet, the scale of the episode suggests that the *phii mae maai* also spoke to a more profound sense of rural distress. The explicitly gendered messages of impending widow ghost attacks can be read as a more general text, a symbolic dramatization of villagers' fears and experiences of vulnerability as a politically and economically subordinate population within the wider Thai society.

More than a static text, however, this episode provides insight into the dynamics of cultural production: the active construction and negotiation of meaning in everyday life. I draw here on the critical theory of Raymond Williams (1977) and his identification of the complex relationship between, to use his own terms, dominant, residual and emergent culture. In any society the hegemonic reach of dominant meanings and practices over subordinate groups can be extensive but is never complete; the persistence of traditional (residual) forms as well as the production of new (emergent) ideas and understandings provide the basis for alternative and at least potentially oppositional interpretations to arise. In a recent restatement of Williams's ideas, William Roseberry (1989:45) argues that to understand the dynamics of cultural production and the creation of meaning in social life, it is crucial to identify the points at which lived experience breaks with the representations of dominant cultural forms. It is in this gap between meaning and experience that the possibility exists for people to construct new, alternative understandings of themselves and the world around them.

It is essential, however, to note that the production of these alternative understandings, no less than the forms and representations of dominant cultures, are contingent processes shaped by specific social and historical contexts. Analyses which seek to uncover signs of class-based "resistance" in every moment of social conflict risk losing sight of the variety of cultural meanings involved and the often limited range of choices available to social actors (cf. Scott 1985). The structural inequities entailed in market relations, lack of available credit, and widespread dependence upon powerful patrons, including local merchants and state officials, present the peasant farmers and small commodity producers of Isan with few viable avenues of opposition. Furthermore, local perceptions of exploitation and disadvantage must compete with and are often mediated by powerful messages within the dominant national culture which contrast rural poverty and the practice of "traditional" ways (*chiwit samai kaw*) with the social and economic comforts of life in more "modern" urban centers (*chiwit than samai*).

The widow ghost scare of 1990 reflected the ambivalent response of Isan villagers to the profound social and economic transformations that they confront as a subordinate population in contemporary Thai society. In order to understand the dynamics at work here, I prefer to follow the suggestion of Aihwa Ong who, in reference to newly industrialized workers around the globe, has argued that their varied responses to the experience of subordination can be seen as "cultural struggles." Encounters with new forms of control and domination, rather than provoking explicit resistance to structures of power, tend to find expression in localized struggles over "cultural meanings, values and goals" (Ong 1991:281). While the cultural meanings which people appropriate or seek to defend may challenge existing arrangements of political and economic power, they are just as likely to promote understandings (or to return to Williams's term "structures of feeling") that are limited, fragmentary and ambivalent (ibid.).

In the following I examine the threat of widow ghost attacks in Northeastern Thailand as one such instance of local cultural production or struggle. I discuss villagers' constructions of and responses to these deadly spirits in terms of three areas of cultural production that the episode served to highlight. These are, first, local commentaries on the problematic linkage between gendered meanings and images of modernity; second, the particular dangers of overseas labor migration; and third, the uneasy relationship between sources of local knowledge and the prestige of information emanating from the dominant culture, particularly that conveyed by the mass media. I argue that what I call the "widow ghost scare" captured the imagination of communities throughout Northeast Thailand not only because it expressed the fears and frustrations of a subordinate peasant population but also because it played directly on the break between dominant representations of "modernity" in Thai society and villagers' own experiences of social change. My discussion is based primarily upon observations in the community of Baan Naa Sakae, a Theravada Buddhist, ethnic-Lao, rice-growing village in Mahasarakham province where I resided at the time that *phii mae maai* became a matter of regionwide concern.[2]

During the past century the people of Isan, the majority of whom are of Lao ethnicity, have been incorporated into the Thai nation-state. This consolidation of state authority, as in other regions of the country, was accompanied by the spread of commercial capitalism, the impact of which has accelerated since the end of the Second World War. During the past several decades, rural Northeastern communities have become firmly integrated into the national and transnational market economy both as producers of cash crops (most notably cassava and kenaf) and as cheap migrant workers for Bangkok's expanding industrial and service sectors. While the labor of Northeastern peasants has contributed to the high rates of economic growth that Thailand has enjoyed in recent years—averaging over 7 percent annual growth between 1960 and 1985, with even higher rates in the late 1980s—they have not shared equally in the resulting prosperity (Suchart 1989:17). National measures of Thailand's economic boom only mask a reality of widening disparities between a primarily urban (i.e., Bangkok) elite and the country's majority rural population, of whom the inhabitants of Isan consistently represent the poorest regional segment (Suntaree 1989:22–23; Saneh 1983:15).

Throughout most of the twentieth century, this extension of both Central Thai state authority and capitalist relations of production into the daily lives of Northeastern villagers has been depicted as a necessary movement toward national "modernity" and away from localized "tradition." Dominant forms of cultural production—such as the rhetoric of state officials and policy analysts, or the more pervasive imagery disseminated in the popular media—frequently contrast the "modern" institutions and practices located in urban centers of power with the "traditional" ways of rural communities and regional minorities. I use the terms "modern" and "traditional" for the Thai and Lao terms *than samai* or *samai mai* and *samai kon* or *samai kaw*. These translate as "in step with the times" or "new times" and "times before" or "old times." This language is employed by people at all levels of Thai society in reference to perceived differences not only between the present and the past, but also to contrast the status and prestige of images and practices which originate in the dominant culture of the urban-based middle and upper classes as against the customs and beliefs of rural communities and regional minorities. These concepts provide a common ideological framework for explaining ongoing disparities in the distribution of wealth and power as matters of having (or lacking) knowledge and experience of "modern" ways rather than as inequities of class, gender, ethnicity and/or regional underdevelopment.[3]

The cultural prestige associated with urban "modernity" (against the purported backwardness and ignorance of peasant "tradition") has been most widely disseminated in Thailand through standardized public education, mass-consumer markets, and perhaps most powerfully, by the pervasive presence of television and other forms of national media production. Consequently, the rural inhabitants of communities like Baan Naa Sakae are well aware of the physical comforts and material conveniences which define a *samai mai* consumer lifestyle at the same time that they find themselves excluded from full participation in this primarily urban form of social status. As a result, *than samai* styles and commodities within the Bangkok-based dominant culture have become more and more important markers of status and economic success in rural communities. This is particularly obvious in the construction of new village houses that imitate urban architectural styles by incorporating such features as a ground-level story enclosed by concrete walls, glass windows, machine-tooled shutters and other trim. In addition, a variety of commodity items and modern technologies may also be deployed by rural households in displays of wealth and status. The most desirable of these include televisions, trucks, motorcycles, refrigerators, electric fans, and stereo players.

The glamor and prestige associated with the acquisition of such "modern" commodities can, however, obscure the extent to which rural households must participate in market transactions as a matter of economic necessity. Many basic requirements of household production and

reproduction—including fertilizers and seeds, school fees, bus fares, medi-
cines, even many essential food items and clothing—must be purchased
either on a daily, weekly or seasonal basis. Although the Northeastern sta-
ple crop of glutinous rice continues to be grown almost entirely for subsistence and not for sale, rice production alone is not sufficient to ensure
economic survival. Having access to a cash income is imperative for rural
families. Most also raise cash crops (cassava and kenaf being the most common) but this is rarely a secure source of income, given the unpredictability of world markets. In Baan Naa Sakae, like other Northeastern communities, many households have turned to labor migration as a way to
supplement (or in some cases replace) cash earnings from crop production. Even wealthier village families often have members working in Bangkok or elsewhere; their wages provide a kind of cash reserve that can be
utilized to reinforce household claims to wealth and social standing in the
community. Nevertheless villagers' participation in these "modern" mar-
ket-based forms of production and employment carries with it considerable
risk; successes or failures are subject to impersonal systems of knowledge
and power (such things as employment contracts, labor laws and international markets) over which rural farmers and migrant laborers have little
or no means of control.[4] Consequently a gap exists between the urban-
based production of meanings about Thai modernity—characterized by
glamorous images of material wealth and the sophisticated use of market
commodities—and villagers' own experiences of disadvantage and marginalization. The deep anxiety with which people all over Isan responded to
the threat of widow ghost attacks was both an example and an expression
of this sense of vulnerability in their dealings with the wider society. At the
same time, however, it was an occasion to affirm the significance of village
life and village meanings for interpreting social experience and to question, if only partially or implicitly, the moral authority of change, or "progress," as defined by the dominant or "modern" Thai culture.

ATTACK OF THE WIDOW GHOSTS

In April 1990, I returned to Baan Naa Sakae village after a few days' absence to find the entire community of two hundred households festooned
with wooden phalluses in all shapes and sizes. Ranging from the crudest
wooden shafts to carefully carved images complete with coconut shell testi-
cles and fishnet pubic hair, they adorned virtually every house and residential compound. The phalluses, I was told, were to protect residents, especially boys and men, from "nightmare deaths" (*lai taai*) at the hands of
malevolent "widow ghosts" (*phii mae maai*).

Certain spirits (*phii rai*) are a recognized source of death, illness, and
other misfortunes in Thai and Isan culture. *Phii* of many sorts permeate

the social space of Northeastern villages. Every community has a spirit guardian (*phii puu taa*) of somewhat vague ancestral origins; other spirits are attached to plots of land or to unusual features of the local landscape. Although any *phii* can act upon the living, the spirits of the dead are especially unpredictable and most likely to present a significant danger. In the Northeastern belief system any death risks loosing the deceased's spirit (*phii*), with its unpredictable powers and potential malevolence, on the lives of kin and neighbors left behind. Funerary rites held prior to and for several days after the cremation of a corpse serve to ensure the full separation of the deceased from the living and to start the former on the path toward rebirth. Sudden and/or violent death can produce a particularly dangerous and uncontrollable *phii*, especially if the victim was young and had not gained the experience and moral discipline that are features of mature age. Among the most dangerous are *phii phrai*, the spirit of a child and mother who die during pregnancy or in childbirth, and *phii tai hoeng*, the ghost of someone who has died suddenly and usually in the prime of life (Tambiah 1970:315–316).

A widow ghost is the sexually voracious spirit of a woman who has met an untimely and probably violent death. They are therefore similar in conception to other dangerous spirits. To my knowledge, there is no record of "widow ghosts" in the ethnographic literature on Northeast Thailand but, if this is the spirit held responsible when an otherwise healthy man dies in his sleep, it is not surprising that *phii mae maai* are rarely encountered. During the regionwide scare of 1990 the residents of Baan Naa Sakae could not identify the specific origin of the *phii mae maai* threatening them but several villagers pointed to a character in a television drama as a kind of *phii mae maai*. The character in the show had been raped and then abandoned to die by her attackers. She returned as a beautiful but malevolent spirit who, like the *phii mae maai* of news reports, attacked men indiscriminately and often with fatal consequences. In Isan-Lao as well as Thai, *mae maai* means "widow" but it can be used colloquially to refer to any woman who has lost a husband whether through death, divorce or desertion. This broader connotation of the term underlies the identification of the rape victim in the television drama as a widow ghost. The value attached to female purity and virginity in Thai and Isan cultural ideals, while not always upheld in practice, means that at one level a single act of sexual intercourse between a woman and a man (whether by consent or not) establishes a marital bond. In the television drama, the conjugal union implied by the act of sexual intercourse was ruptured by the violence of the attack, the woman's abandonment and subsequent death, effectively making her a "widow." A *phii mae maai* is thus a female spirit of sexual experience whose carnal appetite is both virtually unquenchable and potentially fatal to the living who become its targets. *Phii mae maai* roam the countryside looking, as villagers said, for new "husbands." A widow ghost is thought to come to a man in a dream, often taking the form of a young and beautiful woman; she lies down upon him, draining him of strength and life but leaving no other sign. To the victim's friends and family, the man simply goes to sleep one night and never wakes up.

The unnatural and voracious appetites of widow ghosts present a frightening image of female powers of generation and sexuality run violently amok. Both Lao and Thai gender systems attribute potentially harmful powers to female sexuality when not contained within the marital relationship and circumscribed by appropriate displays of physical modesty and/or maternal solicitude. By contrast, male sexual powers pose little danger to the social fabric and phallic representations can be employed to preserve or restore spiritual strength, and physical and social health. This dichotomy is explicit in the way Northeasterners reacted to the widow ghost threats. The wooden phalluses which Baan Naa Sakae villagers hung on gateposts and on the steps entering their homes were envisioned as protective devices. At a crudely functional level, informants described these giant penises as decoys that would distract the interest of any *phii mae maai* which might come looking for a husband. The greedy ghosts would take their pleasure with the wooden penises and be satisfied, leaving the men of that household asleep, safe in their beds.

At another level, however, the phalluses invoked understandings of male sexual potency as a positive force for social and cosmological regeneration. The same kind of wooden phalluses are familiar to Isan villagers as props in the annual rocket festival, where they appear in the company of large bamboo rockets which are fired into the air to call down the first rains after the long dry season. Furthermore, several informants referred to the phalluses as *palat khik,* the term for a particular class of penis-shaped amulets that men may wear on strings around their waists as protection against loss of virility and physical vitality. Such amulets may be sacralized by famous monks (Tambiah 1984: 228). They also evoke the powers of stone *lingam,* phallic shrines of Indic origin which can still be found in different parts of the country, often on the grounds of old Buddhist temples. These represent the linkage of cosmic and human fertility in the *devaraja* or divine kingship, aspects of which continue to shape popular Thai conceptions of royal authority (Tambiah 1976: 98–101).

The phalluses I saw both in Baan Naa Sakae village, as well as in dozens of other communities in the region, were only the most dramatic and collective response by villagers to the widow ghost threat.[5] Talk of widow ghost attacks had in fact been growing in the area for the preceding two to three weeks. This was triggered by revelations in the national news that over two hundred Thai men had died mysteriously while working in Singapore since 1983. Beginning in late March national newspapers and television broadcasts publicized these deaths, cases of what medical experts have called "Sudden Unexplained Nocturnal Death" (SUND), a rare syndrome often described as a kind of adult "crib death" that afflicts men from different parts of Southeast Asia.[6] Most news stories focused on the deaths in Singapore, but as the coverage continued through April and into May the press noted that sleeping deaths of Thai workers had occurred in Brunei and many Middle Eastern nations as well. For several weeks the news media were preoccupied with the need to find the cause of this malady. Several government commissions, research teams, and expert panels traveled to and from Singapore searching for answers. As reports of more sleeping deaths came to light, the press coverage reached a fever pitch of speculation. Theories flew about thick and fast. Chemical poisoning from unsafe cooking procedures, vitamin B deficiency, bootleg alcohol, unhealthy work and living conditions—all were proposed as potential causes. Unlike the medical experts and government officials, however, villagers in the Northeast of Thailand had no difficulty explaining these sleeping deaths: the dead men were the victims of *phii mae maai*. According to older men and women in Baan Naa Sakae, in the past *lai taai* deaths were very unusual; no one had heard of any such victims for at least the preceding ten years and probably longer. Moreover the rash of deaths reported in the media and the wide geographical area affected had no precedent in living memory.

Initially, then, residents of Baan Naa Sakae reacted to the radio and television news reports with concern for the welfare of the almost two dozen men—sons, brothers, husbands, fathers—who were away working in Singapore or other countries. Soon, however, many began to fear for their own safety, especially when the national media began to report not only cases of overseas deaths but also a few that had recently occurred in Isan. The most anxious tended to be men who had been to Singapore or who had tried to go there sometime in the past, as well as a few who were preparing to go for the first time. The first protective measures began in early April even before the wooden phalluses appeared on doorsteps and gateways. A number of village men started to wear red nail polish, some on only one finger, others on several. Most in this group had experience with overseas migration. For example, Pho Sit, a man in his late forties, was among the first to paint his nails. He had traveled to Singapore several years earlier but was deported soon after his arrival because an illegal job agency had provided him with faulty papers. I also began to see some of this same group wearing women's clothes in the evening. One man in his mid-thirties, who had spent three or four years on construction sites in Singapore, even donned a long black wig on several occasions. During the weeks that followed, full or partial transvestism remained an infrequent tactic limited to a few adult men on a few evenings. Thus costumes like that of Pho Dam—who appeared at the height of the scare in a brassiere and a woman's *phaa sin* (a sarong-like skirt) with his cheeks and lips heavily rouged—were noteworthy but relatively rare. Nonetheless, as reports of nightmare deaths continued, anxieties in Baan Naa Sakae grew; throughout April and into May more and more villagers began painting one or more fingernails with red polish, including children and many women. No one suggested that these latter groups were likely "husbands" for *phii mae maai*, but given the general unpredictability of malevolent spirits most people in the community preferred to adopt whatever precautions they could.

A variety of additional protective techniques were also employed. These included several all-night drinking and gambling parties to help men avoid sleeping on certain nights, tying a red or multicolored string about one's wrist to prevent the soul's "vital essence" (*khwan*) from leaving the body, as well as the wooden penis images already mentioned. Villagers' explanations of these tactics often shared the same substitution logic as that of the phallic decoys. The nail painting and the transvestism were, as residents readily admitted, attempts at disguise to trick the widow ghost into thinking a man was a woman and therefore not a potential victim. Two of the most common measures, the nail painting and the wrist string, required the services of a living widow (to apply the polish or tie the string). In this way, people told me, the ghosts would see that another widow had already claimed that person and so leave him alone.

These were always older women well past menopause. Women at this stage in life have often relinquished some of the day-to-day responsibilities of household cares to their adult children and begin to spend more time attending temple ceremonies, listening to monks' sermons and making daily offerings of food. At the same time older matrons, such as these widows, are not required to uphold the same strict code of physical modesty that is expected of younger women; elderly women in particular will frequently work around their homes or visit neighboring compounds while clothed only from the waist down. They also enjoy greater license than younger women to participate in the ribald verbal exchanges and witty double entendre that is a primary form of humor in the Northeast. Moreover, age, for women as for men, entails a degree of social status; reverence for an elder's wisdom and experience is expressed (at least by superficial deference and more often with real respect) in any relations between senior and junior. Older women's claims to such age-based standing is not altered by the death or other loss of a husband. Widows are not expected or required to seek alternate sources of male protection or authority; in Baan Naa Sakae the vast majority of older women who have lost husbands continue to live in their own homes, sometimes, but not always, with a married daughter or son in residence. These women are fully active in the community, both socially and economically; however, the strains on household income and assets that often accompany the loss of an adult male (especially if still in his prime years of productive labor) usually mean that such female heads of household have neither the time nor resources to participate in local politics and community decision making. The latter are areas of social interaction in which their husbands were more likely to have been involved at least at some level. Thus living widows represent a category of female sexual experience and social independence that poses no threat to local men. Finally, as mothers of children grown to adulthood and as active supporters of the Buddhist faith, these women have earned considerable religious merit of their own; this status may also contribute to their ability to save men from the sexual predations of other (spirit) "widows."

Over a period of five or six weeks, rumors and predictions of widow ghost attacks circulated freely in Baan Naa Sakae. These were prompted on at least one occasion by dreams, as when a local man dreamed of being seduced by a strange woman. More often, however, villagers told me that their concerns were based on local radio broadcasts. These were usually shows conducted in the Isan dialect, mixing news reports with traditional horoscope and other sorts of regional entertainment.[7] On several occasions men in the village stayed up all night, gathering in groups to gamble and drink, because they said radio reports indicated that those nights were especially dangerous. Local anxiety reached its peak when one man had a seizure after napping in the sun on a day identified as one when no one should sleep. A week or so later, women in the village were alarmed by rumors that the widow ghosts had taken enough husbands and now wanted some "bosom friends" (*siaw*) to keep them company.

Nevertheless, I do not mean to imply that people in Baan Naa Sakae were paralyzed by fear during these weeks. Responses to the widow ghost threat presented many opportunities for community entertainment. Several of the village's more energetic and witty widows became the centers of lively groups that would gather in the early evenings to have their nails painted or wrists tied amidst much joking and laughter. Moreover, some of the protective tactics employed by villagers, notably the wooden phalluses and male transvestism, are more familiar as features of community festivals where they contribute to an atmosphere of bawdy license and symbolic reversal that is enjoyed by all. Although deployed here against the serious threat of *phii mae maai*, they did not thereby lose all their humorous associations. In a similar fashion, public discussion of widow ghosts often involved jokes and ribald banter. As the weeks passed, toward the middle of May, media stories about nightmare deaths grew less and less frequent and finally disappeared altogether. By the end of the month most Baan Naa Sakae households had taken down the wooden phalluses; the nail polish and special wrist strings faded away soon thereafter.

Widow ghosts may serve to explain a particular form of death that afflicts some men in Northeast Thailand but the problem remains: how does one account for the massive scale of the response? How is it that this particular form of gendered death came to threaten an entire region comprising a third of the area and population of Thailand? As with any cultural phenomenon, the widow ghost scare involves multiple levels of meaning. In the following discussion I will show how the widow ghost threat reflected emergent tensions in contemporary Isan household and gender relations. More profoundly, however, the gendered idiom of the episode served to highlight a central dilemma of Isan peasant life: as villagers attempt to pursue the standards and symbols of modern wealth, comfort and status, they encounter major obstacles in the day-to-day realities of political and economic dependence, exploitation, and poverty. In both content and structure, the widow ghost scare did more than speak to these fears and frustrations; it also offered a reinterpretation, however temporary and limited, of the consequences of social change and the meaning of modernity in rural life.

GENDERED MODERNITY, GENDERED DEATH

By threatening the well-being of men, the widow ghost scare invoked an idiom of gender and sexuality which is already rife with contradictions in contemporary Thai and Isan experience. On the one hand, gendered meanings help explain why widow ghosts are considered dangerous to men; the power of female sexuality to harm the spiritual potency and physical well-being of men is a feature of cultural beliefs in many parts of Thailand, and indeed throughout much of Southeast Asia.[8] In addition, gender meanings and images, particularly those concerning women and women's bodies, have become key points of tension in present-day Thailand concerning the meanings and consequences of modern life. The threat of widow ghost attacks became a regional phenomenon, not only because it highlighted common problems of overseas migration, but because it addressed a similar gap between dominant meanings and villagers' experience of gender relations and sexuality. Specifically, this episode highlighted tensions in the way gender images have come to represent modernity and progress in contemporary Thai culture.

As is true for many Southeast Asian societies, gender identity does not determine an individual's social identity along rigid or easily predictable lines. In everyday life Baan Naa Sakae men and women share the burden of many domestic tasks and farm chores. Similarly, practices such as equal inheritance of land by sons and daughters, marriage payments from the groom to the bride's family and a preference for postmarital residence with the wife's parents (at least in the initial stage of a union) provide many women with access to key economic resources and the emotional support of close kin throughout their lives. While men, as husbands and fathers, are the recognized "heads" of households and occupy most positions of community leadership, women nonetheless exercise considerable economic and personal autonomy in their roles as respected mothers and the managers of household finances.

If gender difference is often muted in everyday interaction, it remains an important aspect of Northeastern Thai social life. Gender meanings are manifested subtly but directly in a body code which stresses the limitation of contact between men and women and the special necessity of controlling the movement of female bodies.[9] The key element I want to highlight here is the way these gender-appropriate body codes make clear a close association between spatial mobility and sexual activity. This linkage draws in turn upon key cultural understandings about the differential moral status of male and female sexuality. In general, spatial mobility is perceived as a natural and appropriate characteristic for men, while women's bodies and their movement are subject to far greater restrictions.

The highest social and spiritual reverence is reserved for men who forgo sexual activity as members of the Buddhist monkhood, but for the majority lay population sexual prowess is a positive aspect of masculine identity (cf. Keyes 1986).[10] Visits to massage parlors and brothels (for those with the money to do so) or telling bawdy stories and participating in exchanges of sexual banter are features of male peer group activity and act, along with drinking and gambling, as markers of masculine strength and sociality. Female sexuality on the other hand presents a more troublesome moral problem. Women are spiritually and ritually subordinate to men; they cannot ordain as monks, only as inferior nuns (*mae chii*), because it is believed their biological sex binds them more closely than men to worldly attachments and desires (Kirsch 1982). Although women make important contributions to ritual and religious life as mothers of monks, as nurturers of the faith and their families (Keyes 1984), when female sexuality is not contained within a conjugal relationship it is considered immoral and the social equivalent of prostitution. Monogamy is the only acceptable practice for women. Prostitutes and other "loose" women may be described as "having many husbands" (*mii phua laai khon*) but the derogatory connotation of this phrase does not carry over to the male equivalent. A man with "many wives" is more an object of admiration, especially among other men.

Furthermore, both men and women attribute a polluting and destructive capacity to female genitalia and bodily fluids that can be dangerous to the physical and spiritual well-being of men (cf. Thitsa 1980). For example, women's underwear and lower garments, such as the *phaa sin* skirt, should not come into contact with men and more importantly with men's heads, the most ritually pure part of the body. Even when washing or hanging clothes to dry women must be careful to keep their lower garments separate and on a level beneath any men's laundry. Drying underwear and *phaa sin* are generally hung at waist height or lower and in a spot slightly out of the way, as it is believed that a man may suffer headaches or other physical harm if he walks under the washline (ibid.; see also Irvine 1984:320). Similarly, sacred objects such as the protective amulets which men often wear can also be damaged, their magical effectiveness destroyed by contact with women's lower garments or if a woman steps over them (Terweil 1975).[11]

In everyday life the destructive powers of female sexuality remain a passive force. These polluting effects are inherent in the female body and not subject to women's volition or control; however, standards for proper social behavior ensure that women's garments and bodies do not inadvertently threaten male potency. In addition to the care taken with laundry, etiquette prohibits such potentially polluting actions as stepping over food (meals are generally prepared and served on the floor) or sitting on a cushion that is normally used as a pillow for the head. Moreover, Baan Naa Sakae women are usually careful to avoid any sort of public physical contact with men as this can be (and generally is) construed as sexual interest on their part. Even long-married couples rarely touch each other in public. In the case of widow ghosts, however, these patterns of proper behavior are inverted as the passive force of female sexuality is transformed into the fearsomely active powers of sexually voracious and deadly spirit beings. *Phii mae maai* take the initiative, seeking out "husbands" and seducing them. This is a reversal not only of proper courting practices but also of the proper hierarchy of male and female bodies; the *phii mae maai* are thought to lie on top of their chosen "husbands" in contrast to the more usual positioning of the man above the woman in sexual intercourse. The Baan Naa Sakae man who dreamed of a strange woman seducing him reported that she lay upon his chest, her weight almost suffocating him. Widow ghosts thus provide an object lesson in the unnatural and dangerous consequences of allowing women to roam freely, their bodies and sexual powers unconstrained by the controls of society or of men.

However, this is exactly the problem that currently confronts Northeastern understandings of gender and gender relations. Not only are men leaving village homes to find work overseas or in the cities; rural women are also moving into wage labor in Bangkok and other urban centers. In fact, surveys of recent migrants to metropolitan Bangkok over the past fifteen years show women outnumbering men by almost two to one (Aphichat 1979; Wilson 1983:58). Beginning in the late 1960s, roughly equal numbers of men and women have left Baan Naa Sakae to find jobs in Bangkok where they may work for periods of a few months to several years. Some marry and settle permanently in the city, but most eventually return home.

This mobility has involved well over half the community's households. Like many Third World nations, Thailand's strategy for economic development has focused on attracting transnational capital investment through export-oriented manufacturing as well as services for international tourism. The economic boom that Thailand has enjoyed, especially since the 1970s, was made possible by cheap labor moving into the Bangkok metropolitan area from the outlying provinces. Among these rural-urban migrants—most of whom work in the city on a temporary or circulating basis—it is women, usually young and unmarried, who constitute the primary labor force in the areas of greatest economic growth: textile and garment manufacturing and the service industries (including the commercial sex trade) (Bell 1992).

Although long-distance mobility has historically been an acceptable, even a valued aspect of masculine identity, the same is not true for cultural understandings of female gender roles. In the Northeast, geographical mobility is associated with male obligations to the state, such as corvée labor duty (in the nineteenth century) and present-day military service; more informal "traveling" (*pai thiaw*) is also a common practice among young rural men who may thereby seek opportunities for social and economic advancement (perhaps by searching out new farmland or acquiring a skilled trade). Travel of any distance offers a chance to gain greater knowledge and experience of the world as well as to look for attractive women to court (cf. Kirsch 1966). In Baan Naa Sakae, the experience of long-distance travel, the acquisition of new job skills and the ability to survive and communicate in a foreign society were all matters of considerable pride among men returning from work overseas.[12] By contrast the new geographical mobility of young unmarried women challenges the customary male monopoly over these sources of prestige. Bangkok employment provides young women with direct access not only to a cash income but also to an experience of independence and self-sufficiency that no previous generation of rural women has ever shared. At one level the migration of young women from Baan Naa Sakae to Bangkok (and more rarely overseas)[13] can be and is seen as appropriate gender behavior—i.e., dutiful daughters upholding their obligations to help support parents and younger siblings. But this movement also raises tensions that are absent or much less problematic in the case of migrant sons. These conflicts most often take the form of parental and community concerns that the experience of personal and economic autonomy undermines the sexual propriety and moral safety of women living away from home. Parents worry about the physical safety of absent sons and daughters alike but usually only daughters are considered at risk for inappropriate sexual activity. Virginity (or at least its appearance) is an important part of a young woman's reputation in the village but, in the absence of parental supervision, the sexual propriety of women working in Bangkok becomes a matter for uncertainty and speculation.

This situation is exacerbated by the fact that within the dominant culture, women or women's bodies represent powerful images of modernity and progress. The active, mobile, beautiful, "modern Thai woman" is celebrated and promoted in the entertainment media, beauty contests, shopping malls, beauty salons and a wide range of advertisements, all of which tend to link feminine beauty and sexual attractiveness to the acquisition and display of the latest market commodities (Van Esterik 1988; Mills 1993). Such symbols of modern style and commodified status proliferate wildly in urban Thai settings; however, the beautiful modern woman is also a familiar figure to most rural audiences for whom television is an increasingly commonplace form of entertainment. Urban employment promises village youth the opportunity to participate in these images of modern style and physical beauty; indeed a colloquial term for migrants heading to the city refers to those "going to get (white) skin" (*pai aw phiw*). Pale coloring is perhaps the single most important criterion of beauty (both for men and women) in Thailand and one which peasant farmers working in their fields cannot easily achieve.

There is, however, a flip side to this glamorized image of modern female beauty and sexual attractiveness. Only a fine line separates it from the stigma and moral degradation of the prostitute. The prostitute is, of course, another prolific image of female sexuality in present-day Thailand. Northeastern villagers are well aware that commercial sex services proliferate in urban areas.[14] A majority of the women working in the sex trade come from rural backgrounds and many are native to Isan. Although to my knowledge no women from Baan Naa Sakae worked in the sex industry, the possible sexual experience of these young migrants in the city was a common subject of community gossip. Villagers' fears of widow ghosts bring into play these conflicting meanings of female sexuality in contemporary Thailand. The idea of sexually promiscuous women roaming the country with murderous intent turns the seductive image of the modern, mobile Thai woman on its head. Female labor migration serves as an important economic resource for many rural households but it also provokes widespread ambivalence. Women's new geographical mobility and wage earning power challenges the economic and moral authority of parents and particularly men—both fathers and potential suitors—over female productive and reproductive capacities. Moreover, in Thai popular culture a steady stream of (advertising and other) images highlights the "modern" (*than samai*) woman's autonomy and freedom of movement. *Phii mae maai*, with their rapacious and uncontrollable appetites, translate these same characteristics of modern womanhood into frightening harbingers of death and destruction.

WAGE LABOR, WAGERED LIVES

The widow ghost episode addressed more than masculine distress in the face of rural women's increased economic and social independence. News reports of mysterious deaths among Thai workers in Singapore triggered widespread anxiety because these cases resonated with Northeastern villagers' more general perceptions of vulnerability in their relations with the wider Thai society. This sense of danger and risk is particularly acute in the context of overseas labor migration. Since the late 1970s, hundreds of thousands of Thai men have gone abroad on temporary labor contracts, the large majority heading to destinations in the Middle East. According to the Thai Department of Labor, the number of individuals leaving for international contract work rose from less than 4,000 in 1977 to over 85,000 in 1986, with the number peaking in 1982 at 108,000 (Charit 1987:6; cf. Witayakorn 1986). This is only a conservative estimate of the total overseas migration, because the existence of many unlicensed employment agencies has meant that an unknown number of Thai migrants are not accounted for in official statistics. Northeastern men have long made up a significant proportion of Thailand's labor exports, representing between one-quarter and one-half of all overseas workers, according to one survey in the mid-1980s (cf. Charit 1987:7).[15] By 1990 in Baan Naa Sakae these figures were reflected in the fact that approximately 50 percent of all adult men (age 25–45) had gone, tried to go or were at the time working outside Thailand.

The main attraction of overseas work lies in the high wages paid for contract labor, much higher than anything an unskilled or semiskilled worker could hope to earn if he remained in Thailand. In the early to mid-1980s—the peak period for migration among Baan Naa Sakae men—the high exchange rates for Middle Eastern currencies meant that a man could earn as much as ten or fifteen thousand baht every month (U.S.$400 to $600). Monthly remittances of between 7,000 and 10,000 baht, transferred directly into Thai bank accounts, were not at all uncommon among this group. This provided the men's families with an income well above what their village neighbors could earn through farming or even from wage labor in Bangkok, where the minimum daily wage only rose above 70 baht (U.S.$2.80) in 1987. For example, two local men, by working overseas for nearly a decade, earned enough money to build substantial "modern" houses and educate their children through college. But most men from Baan Naa Sake who worked overseas only did so for one or two contract periods, a total of two to four years on average. These migrants' earnings have financed the construction of numerous houses, the purchase of motorcycles, televisions, refrigerators, electric fans and a variety of other large consumer items. In a few cases returning migrants have used their money to buy new farmland, small freight trucks or mechanical plows.[16]

Despite the seductive potential for material gain, the decision to work overseas is not made lightly. To begin with, finding a job abroad can be very expensive. The first men from Baan Naa Sakae to go overseas in the late 1970s paid relatively small advance fees, a little over 10,000 baht (around U.S.$400 to $500) in most cases; however, as the number of applicants rose in the 1980s, employment agencies began to charge the equivalent of between one thousand and two thousand dollars (U.S.) for arranging jobs, travel, passports and work permits. Only the richest families had ready access to such large sums of money. Although less well documented than in other regions of Thailand, economic stratification is a widespread feature of Northeastern rural communities (cf. Turton 1989; also Tarr 1988). Landlessness and tenancy affect only a small proportion of households in Isan but disparities of wealth and social influence between larger and smaller landowners are commonplace. Baan Naa Sakae is no exception. In 1990, approximately one-third of village households owned more than 45 *rai* (18 acres) of land, enough in many cases to plant both rice and cash crops as well as to raise cattle which can provide a steady income and act as a reserve of wealth. The relative comfort of these families contrasted with the daily struggle of poorer households, usually those with holdings of less than 20 *rai* (8 acres)—another third of the community—who had to supplement subsistence rice production and small amounts of cash crops with occasional day labor.

Given these economic circumstances, it is not surprising that most village households have had to go into debt in order to finance a husband's or son's search for overseas employment. If, as was often the case, they could not raise the funds from relatives, families often turned to merchants in nearby market towns; but these creditors routinely demand very high rates of interest on their loans—anywhere from 5 to 10 percent per month. Such high initial costs put overseas work beyond the reach of Baan Naa Sakae's poorest families, while it dramatically increased the risk for those who had enough resources to support a loan but no margin to fall back on in case of failure. For the majority the risks have paid off. After enduring difficult working and living conditions, as well as the strange language, food and customs of another society, many Baan Naa Sakae migrants were able not only to pay off their debts but to return with significant sums of cash and modern commodities.

The successes of the first men to go overseas inspired similar ambitions in friends and neighbors, but the hardships and difficulties of other Baan Naa Sakae migrants present a very different picture. In 1990 20 percent of village households with members who had gone or attempted to go overseas reported they had been cheated at least once in the process. Usually this meant that an agent, who claimed to be recruiting workers, collected the advance fee and then disappeared never to be seen again. Pho Som's experience, while worse than most, demonstrates the risks villagers run when choosing to work overseas. He was cheated four times by various job agencies; as a result he lost not only the money borrowed to pay the advance fees but also several thousand baht more that he spent making numerous trips back and forth to Bangkok (a day's journey from Baan Naa Sakae either way) to do the initial paperwork and later to try to recover his money. Finally he was able to go to Singapore but ten days after his arrival he was deported because the last employment agency had not provided him with the proper work permit. When I met Pho Som in 1990 he and his wife had been forced to sell all their land and water buffalo to pay debts of more than 100,000 baht (U.S.$4,000); they lived in a tiny, ramshackle hut and survived by renting a little farmland supplemented by occasional remittances from two teenage daughters working in Bangkok. In other cases, hopeful migrants were never able to leave the country and their families were forced to sell whatever they could—land, livestock, tools—to pay off the debts. Other village members arrived in Singapore or someplace in the Middle East only to discover either, like Pho Som, that their papers were not in order or that employers refused to pay their wages or broke job contracts with impunity. Some returned home with barely enough money to cover their debts; others were still paying these off years later. In this way a half dozen local families have been reduced to penury.

Besides the monetary risks, a few Baan Naa Sakae men were injured, became ill, or got into legal difficulties while overseas and had to be sent home. Thus, for example, Mae Thong told me about her son who was caught distilling alcohol while working in Saudi Arabia; he was publicly flogged and then deported to Thailand "with no money and still in his underwear the way he was caught." It cost her 3,000 baht (U.S.$120) to meet him at the Bangkok airport, buy him clothes and bring him back home. Furthermore, during the decade and a half since local men began to go overseas, at least three community members had died while working abroad. The most recent of these deaths occurred just one month before the widow ghost scare began. In February 1990, a man in his late twenties died in a traffic accident while employed in Israel. His body was flown back to Bangkok where his parents had to go to collect it for cremation back in the village. It was barely six weeks later that the unexplained deaths of Thai men in Singapore became national news. Whether by personal experience or that of their neighbors, many villagers in Baan Naa Sakae have seen the promises of wealth and new opportunities through overseas employment replaced by economic hardship, exploitation, trickery, and even death.

The widow ghost scare played directly on this gap between widespread aspirations for material and status gains through overseas migration and the very real possibilities of failure. The news of Thai overseas workers dying in their sleep served as a dramatic reminder to villagers that they risk potential disaster when moving into a world beyond their knowledge and control. In this context, the threat of widow ghost attacks symbolizes the way exploitative economic relations and cultural demands for commodity consumption devour the physical and economic vitality of Northeastern men. A striking example of these fears emerged at the beginning of the widow ghost outbreak in stories about the Thai Queen and a dream she was said to have had. According to these rumors, the Queen had dreamed that there were no men left in Thailand; the widow ghosts had taken away the entire adult male population, leaving only women, children and the elderly still alive.

In the Northeast, as in the rest of Thailand, dreams are a respected means of predicting the future or receiving messages from ancestral or other spirits. In the ordinary course of events most people review their dreams for clues about the next winning lottery number.[17] However, in the case of rumors concerning the Queen's dream a much more urgent matter was at stake: here was a warning of the potential for personal and collective disaster that participation in modern institutions and economic relations could or would entail. A nation without men is a sterile and ultimately lifeless society, unable to sustain or reproduce itself for the future. Members of Baan Naa Sakae village were well aware that the decision to migrate overseas involves the possibility of economic ruin and even death. The reports of mysterious sleeping deaths among Thai men working overseas placed these chances of disaster into sharp relief, both for individual migrants and their families. The Queen's dream went a step further and implied that these fears and experiences of personal vulnerability might extend to the nation as a whole. For the residents of Baan Naa Sakae, malevolent widow ghosts represent the risks that rural men and their families run by participating in modern economic relations like overseas migration. While my informants did not make the connection themselves, their accounts of the Queen's dream suggest that for Northeastern peasants the consequences of modernity may assume a very different form than the life-enhancing images of economic and social "progress" promoted in the dominant culture.

DOMINANT CULTURE AND LOCAL KNOWLEDGE

The widow ghost scare can be understood as a local response to the gaps villagers perceive between popular conceptions of and aspirations for "modernity" and their own lived experiences of exploitation and insecurity. In its symbolic content the episode questioned the moral status of dominant cultural meanings regarding both labor migration and "modern" under-standings of gender and sexuality. At the same time, the structure of the six-week episode reflected similar disjunctures between meaning and expe-rience in the life of Isan villagers. Specifically, the widow ghost scare high-lighted the subordination of local sources of knowledge and authority to systems of expertise that lie outside villagers' control. For example, the widow ghost scare was initiated not by any local cases of nightmare deaths but by reports of these in the national news. In addition, advice gleaned from radio broadcasts, rather than villagers' own assessments of imminent danger, helped to determine the timing and even the choice of particular protective strategies, such as the setting up of wooden phalluses or the identification of specific days and nights when people were not supposed to go to sleep. Residents of Baan Naa Sakae themselves acknowledged the power of the wider society to shape local perceptions. As one man admitted at the height of the scare: "We Northeasterners are great followers of the news. If it says to stand, we stand; if it says to sit, we sit." According to this speaker, it was better to follow whatever suggestions were offered in order to be sure, to "protect ourselves ahead of time."

In this way responses to threatening *phii mae maai* were triggered by information originating outside the community's experience or control. By contrast, the protective actions themselves served to reinforce the village community and its traditions as a place of refuge for its members and a source of support and moral order in a dangerous and uncertain world. For example, the tying of red and multicolored strings around the wrist was an adaptation of a key Northeastern ritual of healing and blessing, the *su khwan*. In this rite a white string is fastened about a person's wrist in order to bind the vital essence or soul (*khwan*) to the body, thereby ensur-ing his or her safety and well-being. The full ceremony involves a variety of preparations and must be conducted by a lay ritual expert (*mo sut*). A for-mal *su khwan* is usually held when someone is about to enter into a new social identity (through marriage or ordination, for example) or at the beginning of a journey, when an individual is preparing to leave the safety of the village community. It can also be performed as a healing ritual to call the soul back into the body (Tambiah 1970:223 ff). *Su khwan* rites are of Lao origin and their continued practice throughout Northeast Thailand is a conscious marker of ethnic pride and identity in Lao-speaking commu-nities like Baan Naa Sakae. The way in which people received strings from widows most closely resembled an informal version of the *su khwan* in which an older man or woman, or a venerated monk binds a supplicant's wrist to bestow a blessing for safety and good health.

Perhaps more dramatically, the wooden phalluses presented a similar statement of collective, local identity. The widow ghosts placed the whole community in jeopardy; no family was too rich or too poor, too powerful or too humble to be safe without the protective phallic images. In addition, the fact that these phalluses are more commonly used as objects of bawdy play during the annual rocket festival (*bun bang fai*), strengthens their power as symbols of communal unity. The *bun bang fai* is another consciously Isan ritual held at the end of the long dry season; its high point is a contest in which rockets made of long bamboo sections loaded with gunpowder are fired into the sky, partly as offerings to the village guardian spirit. The rockets help to ensure plentiful rains and an abundant rice crop for the year to come. The phallic imagery of the rockets calling down rain from the sky is supplemented by carved wooden phalluses, similar to the ones used as protection against the *phii mae maai*, which villagers use as props in the raucous banter and joking that takes place during *bun bang fai* celebrations (cf. Condominas 1975:265). It is probably not a coincidence—although no one in the village commented on the connection— that the celebration of *bun bang fai* appeared to mark the end of the widow ghost scare in Baan Naa Sakae. The rocket festival is a rite of fertility symbolizing the power of human (and specifically male, phallic) activity to bring forth life at the same time that it strengthens the collective bond between village members and the community's guardian spirit. The latter, when properly respected and cared for, provides a key bulwark against the potential incursions of malevolent spirits as well as other dangers which may threaten the livelihood of peasant agriculturalists. In different ways, then, reactions to the widow ghost scare called upon the efficacy and moral centrality of local forms of knowledge and communal identity in the face of external threats.

However, this remained an implicit affirmation. Throughout the episode, many residents tended to downplay the extent of any threat, at least when talking to me. This was especially true of those higher status community members whose social position derived mainly from their association with "modern" standards and practices, usually through their higher education and/or employment in the civil service. The embarrassment that the episode caused some people in Baan Naa Sakae was related to the fact that, as an educated foreigner, I represented particularly strong associations with modernity and its high social status. At the same time it reflected the ambivalence with which many people in Isan assess local practices and traditions against the prestige of "modern" beliefs and attitudes in the dominant culture.

It is in relation to this ambivalence between local and dominant sources of knowledge that one can also assess what might otherwise seem a puzzling failure of people in Baan Naa Sakae to mobilize the authority and power of Buddhism against the threat of widow ghosts. *Phii mai maai*, like other malevolent spirits, are traditionally believed to act outside the scope of Buddhist ceremonies, which focus on the accumulation of religious merit (*bun*); protection from *phii rai* usually requires different kinds of ritual action presided over by lay experts or, in some cases, spirit mediums (cf. Tambiah 1970:286). Still, in Baan Naa Sakae, monks are frequently involved in merit-making ceremonies immediately prior to the performance of a rite directed at deflecting misfortune or distress due to spirit activity. But the monks of Baan Naa Sakae, the spiritual and ritual foci of community life at most other times, had little or no role to play during the scare. Nor was there any noticeable change or increase in merit-making activities by villagers during this time. While no one said so directly, it was my impression that in local eyes the many "traditional" (read "superstitious") characteristics of the widow ghost scare created an embarrassing gap between local fears and an increasing awareness of and interest in more doctrinally pure forms of Buddhist practice.[18] In only one case that I know of did any villager approach local monks in response to the threat of *phii mae maai*: a man in his fifties with two sons working in Singapore, asked the oldest monk at the village temple to bless two white *su khwan* strings which he then mailed to his sons to wear as protection.

CONCLUSION

Ultimately, the widow ghost scare had only minor, temporary effects on Baan Naa Sakae villagers' participation in migration streams and other "modern" forms of social and economic activities. The most noticeable change was that a few men decided not to go work in Singapore; however, most of them later went to Bangkok instead. Nor did the collective threat posed by these spirits mobilize community energy to address or protest more systematically the problems of social and economic subordination that many rural households face. Despite the regional scale of the phenomenon it did not herald (not even in the form of rumor) the kind of social upheaval or protest movement that has periodically arisen in the Northeast. Since the late nineteenth century, Isan has been the site of one large and several small millennial Buddhist movements led by local figures claiming prophetic and other spiritual powers (*phuu mii bun*). These movements sought, albeit unsuccessfully, to counter the growing presence of state authority and a capitalist economy in the region (cf. Keyes 1967; Chattip 1984). By contrast, the widow ghost scare offered neither prophetic figures nor an explicit rejection of the moral and material conditions of contemporary Thai society, rallying points that were characteristic of these earlier movements. Even less did it resemble the specific program and clear-cut organization of the communist revolutionaries who conducted an armed insurgency in the Northeast (and other regions) during the 1960s and 1970s. As an example of peasant "resistance" the widow ghost scare is weak at best.

The episode is much better understood as a case of cultural struggle. Attacking widow ghosts represent an alternative interpretation of the consequences of "modernity" in Thailand and one that resonates more closely with the actual experiences of Northeastern peasants than do the images of comfort and convenience promoted in the dominant culture. Anthropologists have often identified malevolent spirits as vehicles for expressing the ambivalence and distress that may accompany social and economic transformation. For example, in a Northern Thai case, Anan Ganjanapan (1984) noted that early twentieth-century accusations of *phii ka'*—a form of spirit possession that turns its victims into sorcerers—reflected growing social and economic differentiation within rural communities due to the consolidation of large landholdings. Stephen Griffiths (1988) reports similar beliefs in witches and sorcerers as an expression of the profound social tensions resulting from long-term overseas migration in an Ilocano village in the Philippines. It is perhaps a sign of the alienating effects of social change in Northeast Thailand that none of the more common origins of supernatural attacks—local historical figures, deceased ancestral spirits, or the possessed hosts of sorcerous demons—were connected to the *phii mae mai*. The widow ghosts remained a diffuse and unlocatable menace much like the power that institutions of global capitalism and the nation-state wield over the lives of village residents. In this way *phii mae mai* are akin to accounts of Devil beliefs among miners and plantation workers in Latin America, where satanic destruction threatened those in transition from precapitalist to capitalist forms of labor and production (Taussig 1980), or to rumors of "construction sacrifice" in different parts of Indonesia, in which state officials and their foreign agents were believed to be seeking human heads from the local population to place under the foundations of major construction projects (Drake 1989; Erb 1991; Forth 1991). Aihwa Ong's (1987) study of spirit possession among neophyte factory workers in Malaysia offers an especially apt comparison to the Isan experience. Ong found that incidents of mass possession in transnational factories challenged the moral legitimacy of industrial discipline and the depersonalized forms of control Malay women encountered through wage employment; however, the momentary effectiveness of spirit possession in shutting down production lines did not contribute to a broader reworking of an inequitable social order.

The threat of attacking widow ghosts in Northeast Thailand highlighted several important gaps between dominant meanings of modernity and villagers' own experiences of dependence and exploitation. But the resulting assessments of modern images and institutions were in no way revolutionary. Widow ghost beliefs offered at best only a temporary and largely implicit critique of the political and material disparities that mark Northeasterners' experiences in contemporary Thai society. This is hardly surprising given the tremendous reach of dominant ideas and cultural authority in Thailand today. The widow ghost threat did not constitute a rejection of the styles and standards of modernity; it was instead a momentary break, which placed into sharp relief the tensions and disjunctures that permeate Northeastern social relations both within rural communities and as subordinate members of the wider nation. For people in Baan Naa Sakae, an outright rejection of modern institutions and ideas is economically and conceptually unfeasible. As is reflected in the widow ghost episode itself, daily life in the rural Northeast is already profoundly shaped by the rhythms and relations of commodity production, modern media, and (less obvious from this account but equally true) the institutions and authority of the Thai nation-state.

The significance of the widow ghost phenomenon is not diminished, however, by the continuing subordination of Northeastern village life to ideological and economic forces of the wider Thai society. What is interesting and instructive about the widow ghost scare is how it revealed, on the one hand, an explicit critique of the transformation of household and gender relations by capitalist modes of production and, on the other hand, more fundamental (if still implicit) sources of tension and ambivalence in popular experiences of modernity. While such conflicts fueled the dramatic episode, they found no resolution in it. The *phii mae maai* attacks offer useful insights into ongoing dilemmas in contemporary peasant life. However, for the people of Baan Naa Sakae and other communities like it, the widow ghost episode did not offer any effective alternatives to the hegemonic forms and practices of modernity that they now confront.

NOTES

1. This study is based on research conducted in Thailand during 1987–88 and 1989–90. Financial support for the research and writing was provided at different stages by doctoral fellowships from the National Science Foundation (U.S.) and the Social Sciences and Humanities Research Council of Canada; and by Social Science Research Council and Fulbright-Hays doctoral dissertation research grants. Additional support was received from the Center for Southeast Asian Studies (through a grant from the Luce Foundation) and the Department of Anthropology at the University of California, Berkeley. I have benefited greatly from the comments of Herbert P. Phillips, Ara Wilson and Linda Green on an earlier version of this paper. I am especially grateful to Aihwa Ong and Michael Peletz for their thoughtful criticisms and suggestions. Of course, any shortcomings or errors that remain are entirely my own.

2. Baan Naa Sakae is a pseudonym, as are all names of individuals cited in the text.

3. In contrast to the ignorance and backwardness frequently associated with the traditions of rural populations, the twentieth-century Thai state has sought to

promote (or one might argue, "invent" [Hobsbawm 1983]) a number of national "traditions." Based on the symbolic trilogy of "Country, Religion and King," these "traditional" images and practices constitute an ideological foundation for constructing and disseminating a Thai "national identity" (cf. Girling 1981; Keyes 1989).

4. My understanding of villagers' risk in the face of modern social life draws here upon the work of Anthony Giddens (1990), in particular his discussion of the vulnerability of individuals in modern societies to "expert systems," impersonal institutions which operate according to expert knowledge unavailable to ordinary citizens and over which they can exercise little or no control. As a result all modern individuals live with a degree of uncertainty and (potential) insecurity (Giddens 1990:92 ff). What Giddens fails to address adequately is how and with what effects certain groups or segments of modern societies are systematically disadvantaged in their access to politically and economically important areas of knowledge and control.

5. During this same period of time in the spring of 1990 I saw similar phalluses set up to ward off widow ghost attacks in every village that I visited or passed through. This was true of all the communities within the area immediately surrounding Baan Naa Sakae as well as villages in several different provinces through which I traveled in April and May, including Kalasin, Khon Kaen, Roi Et, Yasothon, and Ubol Ratchathani.

6. There have been a number of Western-style medical studies of this phenomenon in recent years focusing in particular on Southeast Asian refugees relocated to the United States. See for example Kirschner et al. (1986); Munger (1987); and Goh et al. (1990).

7. Radio stations in Thailand are owned and operated either by the national government or the Thai army. Commercial sponsors can rent broadcast time but it is not clear to me whether the broadcasts which included news about widow ghost attacks were scripted by private or state agents.

8. Although conceptualized in different ways, many Southeast Asian cultures distinguish between male and female sexuality and reproductive powers, attributing special, often polluting forces to that of women. See for example several contributions to the volume edited by Jane Atkinson and Shelly Errington (1990).

9. I draw here on the work of Penny Van Esterik who has suggested that the gender system in Thai society is deeply intertwined with the way bodies are conceptualized, mobilized and experienced (cf. Van Esterik 1990).

10. In Thai (and Isan) Buddhism, only adult males can ordain as monks; however, their vows of worldly detachment prohibit sexual activity and for the period of their ordination monks are classed as members of a "gender" or category of person (*phet yang song*) that is quite separate from that of lay men (*phet chaai*) (Keyes 1986:86). In Baan Naa Sakae, the local monks were not deemed to be in any danger from the widow ghosts, perhaps because of this classificatory difference but also because of the spiritual merit and power that monks accumulate through their ascetic practices. Indeed the Buddhist temple was the only part of the village where protective wooden phalluses were not hung.

11. Amulets are worn by Thai men (and to a lesser extent women) in all regions of the country. However, the high price which the more powerful of these sacred

objects can command means that their use is more extensive among urban populations than in rural areas (see Tambiah 1984:228–229).

12. In most cases, however, these experiences did not in themselves contribute
to an improvement in returned migrants' social status unless accompanied by significant cash savings or remittances. A few men in Baan Naa Sakae were able to
turn truck-driving skills acquired overseas into a form of livelihood back home by
purchasing a freight truck with their earnings. When referring to overseas experiences, Baan Naa Sakae men revealed an ambivalence similar to that which Jane
Margold (this volume) found among returned Filipino migrants. Pride in their own
skills and competence warred with memories of fear, loneliness, and resentment
against the harsh discipline, racist employers, and difficult living and working conditions.

13. The movement of Thai women into overseas employment has not occurred
on the same scale as that of men. Since the late 1980s a growing number of women,
usually of rural background and many from the Northeast, have gone abroad to
work as domestic servants primarily in Hong Kong (Nayana Suphaphung, personal
communication). More often employment overseas for Thai women involves work,
either by force or by choice, in the commercial sex trade. See for example Siriporn
Skrobanek (1985). In 1990 no women then living in Baan Naa Sakae had ever
been overseas and only one woman born to a local family had done so. This woman,
now in her forties, had gone to work near one of the U.S. military bases during the
Vietnam War. She married an American and later moved with him to the United
States.

14. Thailand has an enormous sex industry. Estimates range from official figures of 80,000 to well over one million sex workers (see Muecke 1992:892–893;
Truong 1990:181).

15. The enthusiastic support of the Thai government for this type of labor mobility is no doubt related to the substantial wage remittances that have flowed into
the country as a result. The earnings of these workers as remitted through Thai
banks (not counting cash and goods carried in by returning migrants) constitute a
significant proportion of Thai foreign exchange earnings. In fact, for most of the
1980s these were roughly equivalent to the value of rice exports, or more than 800
million U.S. dollars annually (NSO 1988:17, 64).

16. This pattern of expenditures, heavily weighted toward consumer items
rather than productive resources, is comparable to that found in an official survey
of returned migrants (cf. Witayakorn 1986:332).

17. Playing the underground lottery, although officially illegal, is a widespread
form of gambling throughout Thailand. Many people in Baan Naa Sakae wagered
small amounts in the bimonthly drawing. Winning selections are based upon the
first or last digits of numbers announced in the national (legal) lottery. Dreams are
among the most common sources for lucky numbers, sometimes with startling results. For example, one schoolteacher residing in Baan Naa Sakae dreamed that
the village guardian spirit told him the next winning numbers. He wagered heavily
in the next drawing and won 10,000 baht (U.S.$400).

18. Buddhism in Isan is an important point of community identification—especially through the village temple and annual festivals—at the same time that it
clearly links each village to the wider national society. Monks are residents in village

temples and themselves are often natives of these communities but as members of the ordained Sangha, they are involved in a hierarchy of authority that encompasses the entire nation. Buddhism, moreover, is explicitly proclaimed by the Thai state as one of the cornerstones of a national identity. Purifying reforms of regional practices have periodically shaped state religious policy over the course of Thai national development. While I am unaware of any special campaigns or programs of this nature that might have affected the events with which this paper is concerned, a number of women and a few older men from Baan Naa Sakae at the time were active participants in meditation and dharma classes being held at the temple of a neighboring village. The prestige of this temple and its abbot, reflected in the recent construction of an elaborate new ordination hall (*boot*), was a source of considerable envy in Baan Naa Sakae, where many felt that their own temple seemed decrepit and their monks somewhat lacking in spiritual achievements by comparison.

REFERENCES

Anan Ganjanapan. 1984. "The Idiom of Phii Ka': Peasant Conception of Class Differentiation in Northern Thailand." *Mankind* 14(4):325–329.

Aphichat Chamratrithirong, Krittaya Archavanitkul, and Uraiwan Kanungsukkasem. 1979. *Recent Migrants in Bangkok Metropolis: A Follow-up Study of Migrants, Adjustment, Assimilation and Integration.* Bangkok: Mahidol University, Institute for Population and Social Research.

Atkinson, Jane M., and Shelly Errington, eds. 1990. *Power and Difference: Gender in Island Southeast Asia.* Stanford: Stanford University Press.

Bell, Peter F. 1992. "Gender and Industrialization in Thailand." Paper presented at Association of Asian Studies, Washington, D.C.

Charit Tingsabadh. 1987. "Maximising Development Benefits from Labour Migration: Thailand Country Study." New Delhi: Asian Employment Programme, ILO-ARTEP.

Chattip Nartsupha. 1984. "The Ideology of Holy Men Revolts in North East Thailand." In Andrew Turton and Shigeharu Tanabe, eds., *History and Peasant Consciousness in Southeast Asia.* Senri Ethnological Series no. 13. Osaka: National Museum of Ethnology.

Condominas, Georges. 1975. "*Phiban* Cults in Rural Laos." In G. William Skinner and A. Thomas Kirsch, eds., *Change and Persistence in Thai Society.* Ithaca: Cornell University Press.

Drake, Richard Allen. 1989. "Construction Sacrifice and Kidnapping Rumor Panics in Borneo." *Oceania* 59:269–279.

Erb, Maribeth. 1991. "Construction Sacrifice, Rumors and Kidnapping Scares in Manggarai: Further Comparative Notes from Flores." *Oceania* 62:114–127.

Forth, Gregory. 1991. "Construction Sacrifice and Head-hunting Rumours in Central Flores (Eastern Indonesia): A Comparative Note." *Oceania* 61:257–266.

Giddens, Anthony. 1990. *The Consequences of Modernity.* Stanford: Stanford University Press.

Girling, John L. S. 1981. *Thailand: Society and Politics.* Ithaca: Cornell University Press.

Goh, K. T., T. C. Chao, and C. H. Chew. 1990. "Sudden Nocturnal Deaths among Thai Construction Workers in Singapore." *Lancet* 335 (8698): 1154.

Griffiths, Stephen. 1988. *Emigrants, Entrepreneurs, and Evil Spirits: Life in a Philippine Village.* Honolulu: University of Hawaii Press.

Hobsbawm, Eric. 1983. "Introduction: Inventing Traditions." In Eric Hobsbawm and Terence Ranger, eds., *The Invention of Tradition,* pp. 1–14. New York: Cambridge University Press.

Irvine, Walter. 1984. "Decline of Village Spirit Cults and Growth of Urban Spirit Mediumship: The Persistence of Spirit Beliefs, the Position of Women and Modernization." *Mankind* 14(4):315–324.

Keyes, Charles F. 1967. "Isan: Regionalism in Northeastern Thailand." Data Paper no. 65. Ithaca: Cornell University, Southeast Asia Program.

———. 1984. "Mother or Mistress but Never a Monk: Buddhist Notions of Female Gender in Rural Thailand." *American Ethnologist* 11(2):223–241.

———. 1986. "Ambiguous Gender: Male Initiation in a Northern Thai Buddhist Society." In Caroline Walker Bynum, Stevan Harrell, and Paula Richman, eds., *Gender and Religion: On the Complexity of Symbols,* pp. 66–96. Boston: Beacon Press.

———. 1989. *Thailand: Buddhist Kingdom as Modern Nation-State.* Boulder: Westview Press.

Kirsch, A. Thomas. 1966. "Development and Mobility Among the Phu Thai of Northeast Thailand." *Asian Survey* 6: 370–378.

———. 1982. "Buddhism, Sex Roles and the Thai Economy." In Penny Van Esterik, ed., *Women of Southeast Asia,* pp. 16–41. Dekalb, Ill.: Northern Illinois University, Center for Southeast Asian Studies.

Kirschner, R. H., F. A. Echner, and R. C. Baron. 1986. "The Cardiac Pathology of Sudden Unexplained Nocturnal Death in Southeast Asian Refugees." *Journal of the American Medical Association* 256 (19):2700–2705.

Mills, Mary Elizabeth. 1993. " 'We Are Not Like Our Mothers': Migrants, Modernity and Identity in Northeast Thailand." Ph.D. diss., University of California, Berkeley.

Muecke, Marjorie. 1992. "Mother Sold Food, Daughter Sells Her Body: The Cultural Continuity of Prostitution." *Social Science and Medicine* 35(7):891–901.

Munger, R. G. 1987. "Sudden Death in Sleep of Laotian-Hmong Refugees in Thailand: A Case-Control Study." *American Journal of Public Health* 77 (9):1187–1190.

NSO (National Statistical Office). 1988. *Key Statistics of Thailand 1988.* Bangkok: Office of the Prime Minister.

Ong, Aihwa. 1987. *Spirits of Resistance and Capitalist Discipline: Factory Women in Malaysia.* Albany: SUNY Press.

———. 1991. "The Gender and Labor Politics of Postmodernity." *Annual Review of Anthropology* 20: 279–309.

Roseberry, William. 1989. *Anthropologies and Histories: Essays in Culture, History, and Political Economy.* New Brunswick: Rutgers University Press.

Saneh Chamarik. 1983. "Problems of Development in Thai Political Setting [sic]." Paper no. 14. Bangkok: Thammasat University, Thai Khadi Research Institute.

Scott, James C. 1985. *Weapons of the Weak: Everyday Forms of Peasant Resistance.* New Haven: Yale University Press.

Skrobanek, Siriporn. 1985. "In Pursuit of an Illusion: Thai Women in Europe." *Southeast Asia Chronicle* 96:7–12.

Suchart Prasith-rathsint, ed. 1989. *Thailand's National Development: Social and Economic Background.* Bangkok: Thai University Research Association and CIDA.

Suntaree Komin. 1989. *Social Dimensions of Industrialization in Thailand.* Bangkok: National Institute of Development Administration.

Tambiah, Stanley J. 1970. *Buddhism and the Spirit Cults in North-East Thailand.* Cambridge: Cambridge University Press.

——. 1976. *World Conqueror and World Renouncer: A Study of Buddhism and Policy in Thailand Against a Historical Background.* Cambridge: Cambridge University Press.

——. 1984. *The Buddhist Saints of the Forest and the Cult of Amulets: A Study in Charisma, Hagiography, Sectarianism and Millenial Buddhism.* Cambridge: Cambridge University Press.

Tarr, Chou Meng. 1988. "The Nature of Structural Contradictions in Peasant Communities of Northeastern Thailand." *Southeast Asian Journal of Social Science* 16(1):26–62.

Taussig, Michael T. 1980. *The Devil and Commodity Fetishism in South America.* Chapel Hill: University of North Carolina Press.

Terweil, Baas J. 1975. *Monks and Magic: An Analysis of Religious Ceremonies in Central Thailand.* London: Curzon Press.

Thitsa, Khin. 1980. "Providence and Prostitution: Image and Reality for Women in Buddhist Thailand." London: CHANGE, International Reports.

Truong, Thanh-Dam. 1990. *Sex, Money and Morality: Prostitution and Tourism in Southeast Asia.* London: Zed Books Ltd.

Turton, Andrew. 1989. "Local Powers and Rural Differentiation." In Gillian Hart, Andrew Turton and Benjamin White, eds., *Agrarian Transformations: Local Processes and the State in Southeast Asia,* pp. 70–97. Berkeley: University of California Press.

Van Esterik, Penny. 1988. *Gender and Development in Thailand: Deconstructing Display.* Toronto: York University, Thai Studies Project, Department of Anthropology.

——. 1990. "Foreign Bodies, Diseased Bodies, No Bodies: Thai Prostitution and Gender Identity." Paper presented at Conference on Sexuality and Gender in East and Southeast Asia, University of California, Los Angeles.

Williams, Raymond. 1977. *Marxism and Literature.* Oxford: Oxford University Press.

Wilson, Constance M. 1983. *Thailand: A Handbook of Historical Statistics.* Boston: G. K. Hall and Company.

Witayakorn Chiengkal. 1986. "Thailand." In Godfrey Gunatilleke, ed., *Migration of Asian Workers to the Arab World,* pp. 306–337. Tokyo: The United Nations University.

NINE

Narratives of Masculinity and Transnational Migration: Filipino Workers in the Middle East

Jane A. Margold

Jane Margold's essay links late capitalist forms of labor control with changes in the lived masculinity of migrant men from the Ilocos region of the Philippines. She explores the limitations of conventional theories concerning the acquisition of male identity (encapsulated in psychoanalytic, "machismo," and/or "wildman" models), each of which is shown to be inadequate with respect to capturing the dynamic experiences and subjectivities of Filipino male migrants in the Arab Gulf countries. Drawing upon a rich literature devoted to describing and analyzing the incorporation of Third World women into fluid global labor markets, Margold examines the effects on subaltern male workers of intersecting variables of culture, class, nationality, and power, especially the ways in which these workers are both treated and referred to by their Gulf employers as "tools," "slaves," and "dogs." As Margold makes clear, the experiences of the Ilokano worker abroad (which include fraudulent contracts, deskilling, etc.) are not only degrading and humiliating; they also constitute a painful inversion of the men's premigratory experiences in their homelands, which are characterized both by the according of prestige to travelers and by a malleable and fluid masculinity embedded within a larger system of gender symmetry. The "crises of masculinity" these workers experience in Saudi Arabia and other Gulf states thus stem not only, or even primarily, from government-imposed restrictions on their sexualities, but more importantly from state-backed constraints on their very voices and emotions, many of which reflect broadly dispersed Saudi and other Middle Eastern perceptions of Filipinos as dark(er) skinned Asian Others bent on (or at least constitutionally inclined toward) transgressing all that is held sacred in a capitalist controlled, theocratic state. In short, the extreme caution and self-control expected and demanded of the Filipino worker abroad virtually presupposes his further (re)socialization insofar as it divests him of public voice and renders him utterly ineffectual, except as raw energy fit for rapid recycling in and out of the Gulf (and other forms of channelization by multinational locations and domination). The resocialization forcibly im-

posed on displaced Ilokanos thus entails their denigration as human beings, just as it provides yet another example of how capital silences subaltern speech. It also leads to a disintegrating sense of self and the dismemberment of their masculinity—all of which is clear from the migrants' narratives of public dismemberment and execution (including, most notably, their identification with the condemned). Reduced to body instrumentality and body parts, some Ilokanos joke uncomfortably about offering themselves as mail-order bridegrooms to Filipina-Americans—as an alternative to migrant work. Such imaginings suggest a reworking of their liminal status as anonymous subaltern male bodies.

I n a performance piece entitled "1991," the Mexican-American protagonist identifies himself as a migrant poet, a "high-tech Aztec" who wanders through the borderlands of pastiche cultures and multiple epochs. The male subjectivity he enacts is fragmented and self-parodic. Standing astride an imaginary line on stage, the poet reflects that his "manhood" is "perfectly bisected" by the border between Mexico and the United States. No bodily integrity or unitary consciousness is possible for this liminal male self. The poet exits stage as he entered, the perplexed child of *desmodernidad:* chaos, motherlessness and late modernity.[1]

FRACTURED IDENTITIES AND FLEXIBLE LABOR REGIMES

The migrant poet's performance of his splintered, uncertain masculinity raises questions about the effects of international migration on the gender identities of subaltern men. For Mexican migrants, the prospect of betraying their own culture while "trespassing" in the society of the other is the paramount source of tension (Anzaldua 1987). Although the Filipino labor migrants whose narratives are analyzed here are not viewed by their communities as "cultural traitors," their quest for international employment still exposes them to analogous psychic risks. Like their Mexican counterparts, they are cast as transgressors in the countries that buy their labor. Their migration stories are threaded through with a similar sense of bodily sacrifice, psychic disintegration and startled outrage at the negative images ("dogs," "tools," "slaves") that assault them in the international workplace.

Scholars investigating the incorporation of Third World women into the fluid global labor markets of the last two decades have rejected the more static, unicausal approaches to gender-role formation, insisting instead on analyzing the interplay of culture, class, nationality and power with engenderment (Ong 1987, 1990, 1991; Enloe 1989). In applying their insights to the ethnographic case of peasant men who migrate from the Philippines' Ilocos region to the wealthy Arab Gulf states, I argue that geopolitics and geoeconomics can crucially transfigure masculine identities. Drawing on anthropological fieldwork conducted in 1987 and 1989–1990 in a heavily migratory village in the northern Philippines, I seek to show that the sense of manhood that develops locally may be partially disassembled when the migrant is incorporated into the lowest ranks of the global labor force. There, he is ghettoized, ordered to work at top speed and quickly repatriated, often before his economic gains outweigh his feelings of shock.

As we will see, the Ilokano men attempt to retain an observing eye and a critical voice while encountering an industrial work environment they experience as emotionally and bodily threatening. These perceptions become apparent in the excerpts below. I then consider the applicability of several Western theories of masculinity to peasant-migrants who straddle often contradictory worlds of subsistence production and deeply commodified relations.

BIOGRAPHIES OF MALE UPHEAVAL

If a Muslim is caught stealing, they will cut off his hand. For the [non-Muslim] Filipino, they will parade him around the city for hours, chained to whatever he stole. With a police escort. Until he gets on the airplane [to be deported], he is chained so every one can see he is a thief. A fellow Filipino! Of course we feel pity and shame.
— Ruben, a carpenter in his twenties who worked in Saudi Arabia.

The Filipino is used to his independent ways. . . . Here, in the Philippines, you can do what you want, make trouble, work, sleep, you are free to move. You can bring your body anywhere you like. . . . We carry that freeness in our body, so when there is something we cannot accept, it is hard to keep silent.
—Rogelio, a tricycle (small transport vehicle) driver and small farmer who worked in Iraq.

Embedded in the narratives of Ilokano male returnees from the Gulf is a pattern of personal crisis experienced abroad, of work and public incidents the men perceived as assaults to their sense of manhood. Tales of unusual punishments overseas (whippings, amputations, beheadings) alternate with some migrants' confessions of their fears of homosexual rape by employers—a worry unimaginable in the Philippines, where attitudes toward gay men (*bakla*) are tolerant.

Overtly hostile local youths are a further bitter surprise to men from a country in which invidious racial distinctions are made, but not openly or confrontatively. Disquieting, too, to the peasant-migrants are power clashes with labor recruiters, employers and impatient supervisors, who treat workers like robots or tools. A story volunteered by a returned migrant named Avelino reveals his disorientation at the techniques of intimidation he encountered overseas:

> My first day there, I almost got into trouble. Our foreman, an Italian . . . asked me to give him a hammer. Hammer is called in Arabic, *jacus*. . . During my first day, how do I know he means hammer when he said *jacus?* So I don't know what to hand him. He's getting angry. But still I don't get what he means, so how could I give him? Then he got the hammer [*here, Avelino mimed coming so close and shaking the tool in my face that I could not help but rear back in alarm*] and told me [*gritting his teeth in imitation*]: *jacus, jacus, jacus*.

Workers of several nationalities witnessed the angry gesture:

> There are Egyptian, Pakistani, Eritrean, Indian [workers] watching. And we are five Filipinos in that group . . . at that point, I was in a place of humiliation. I decided, it was our first day. I grabbed the hammer from him. . . . Then I throw it, almost hitting his feet. I tell him, this is *martillo* [*gritting his teeth*]. *Martillo, martillo*. Then I again got the hammer and almost hit him with it.

The critical qualifier "almost," repeated several times, points to the cautious self-control that orchestrated this performance. If the foreman's shaking of the hammer in Avelino's face is an impulsive aggressive display, Avelino's response is much more choreographed. He tosses the hammer so as to miss the boss's feet, thereby de-escalating the conflict. And Avelino "almost" hits the foreman, but only in fantasy, judging from the foreman's reaction:

> You know what happened? He was very much surprised, not afraid. Not angry. He said: 'what, *martillo?*' It is also *martillo* in Italy. We have the common name! [*laughs delightedly*.] Yes, Philippines, *martillo*. Italy, *martillo*. [*He grins and nods, repeating the word, first enunciating it sharply in Ilokano, then with a lingering, Italian accent*.] So right after that, when he saw my response, that Filipinos are not cowardly, ready to fight, management conducted a meeting. They said in the meeting: these are the characteristics of the Filipino. They are sensitive, but they have brains. . . . They respect us because if we hear insults, we will make trouble instantly. Particularly the Europeans, they underestimate us. But then they find out that we have a brain . . . after that, no more trouble.

Avelino's and other migrants' accounts of such experiences are a potentially instructive means for exploring the impact of a sharply patriarchal industrial culture on men from a Southeast Asian country where androcentrism is more subtle. Yet, current approaches to the study of masculinity focus heavily on childhood, neglecting both adult psychological plasticity and the capacity of more powerful men to resocialize the subordinate male, divesting him of public voice and rendering him ineffectual except as raw energy.

PSYCHOANALYTIC, HYPERMASCULINITY AND WILD MAN MODELS

In the contemporary literature on male gender, three interrelated formulations tend to dominate: first, psychoanalytic approaches, which would link the migrants' expressed fears of bodily assaults to their unresolved Oedipal tensions and castration anxieties (Mitchell 1990; Gregor 1985); second, hypermasculinity models, which are also psychoanalytically oriented but are preoccupied with analysis of machismo and its variants (cf. Gilmore 1990; Limon 1989; Brandes 1980; Herzfeld 1985); and third, the neoromantic notion of the "wild man" (Boscaglia 1991), which also relies on psychodevelopmental notions of manhood acquisition, and diagnoses the problem of masculine identity in the advanced industrial age as the result of the boy child's interrupted closeness with his emotionally distant father.

The first two approaches offer valuable insights into male emotional development. The scholars of hypermasculinity, moreover, attempt to avoid universalized assumptions, providing rich ethnographic studies of the development of male sexuality and styles of communication. Yet they tend to focus too exclusively on personality development within the family and local cultural community. Thus, their applicability to men compelled by economics to operate within an internationally stratified labor force is limited: machismo characterizes Ilokano men to some extent but they cannot sustain that stance abroad, as will be shown below.

The third and newest perspective promises that the late-modern male psyche—constantly in flux, inserted (as the migrants are) into "radically discontinuous realities" (Pred and Watts 1992:71)—can be healed by men sweating side by side in teepees and thumping on drums to unleash "the wild man within" (Boscaglia 1991). As much as this approach envies the emotivity of men who stay close to nature, it fails to recognize that releasing the internal savage is not a prerogative for brown-skinned male laborers working in countries that are ambivalent about their presence. Representations of the man of color as untamed beast have historically been a pretext for imperialism, as Michael Taussig argues in his study of the profusion of contradictory images ("timid and treacherous," "magical and monstrous," "childlike, animallike") that the Spaniards and Portuguese projected upon the colonized to mask the irrationality of terrorizing and killing the very labor upon whom they depended (1987:77, 85, 97, 99).

Throughout Spanish and American colonial rule in the Philippines, wild-man images of the Filipino as "headhunter," "monkey" and "maniac . . . run[ning] amuck" persisted, leaving their residues in the postcolonial setting (Bogardus 1929; Foster 1932:445). In the Philippines of the early 1990s, however, it is no longer race but class that sets the boundaries of emotional expression. The angry elite man can vent his wrath in private, maintaining a public persona that is well-spoken and smoothly self-possessed, whereas the angry lower-class man, with less opportunity to conceal his rage, arouses horror. If he raises his voice or brandishes a knife, neighbors will hide themselves in panic, fearful that the slip in self-control will become a plunge into the abyss.[2] In the Philippines, an aggressive, challenging masculinity is an ideal, but it must be subtly conveyed, held in reserve, beneath the surface of a good-humored, obliging exterior.

Given the sociohistorical and cultural constructions of emotional display, power, and man/woman relations, the prevailing Western paradigms for conceptualizing the development of social manhood cannot be applied globally. Psychoanalytic and hypermasculinity models, with their emphasis on Oedipal conflict and competition between men, shed only partial light on the development of masculinity in a region where friendship groups (*barkada*) and individual male friendships are lifelong associations, and it is not unusual for unmarried men in their twenties and thirties to sleep at night in groups, without raising alarms or even thoughts of homosexuality. The distance between male bodies is not cathected with fear. Historically, masculinity has not been defined by male biological markers of difference from women (larger size, greater muscularity) but by qualities of mind (which women may possess, but without comparable social validation). Masculinity in the Philippines has asserted itself in persuasive words that assuage and reason cogently, and in grace and emotional accessibility. In the Ilocos, male eloquence is highly appreciated (as in Crete, cf. Herzfeld 1985). A powerful manhood has resided in men of gallant words (*gaki; galante a lalaki*) and men of magnetic character (*batom-balani:* magic stones), whose charisma attracted a following.

Male socialization, analyzed as a process of emotional repression and detachment from others (Lyttleton 1983–84), fails to account for a masculinity that seeks intimacy and reckons a feeling of trust and oneness with another (including other men) as a highly desirable state (*pakikiisa*, in Tagalog). Ilokano men practice empathetic relational skills as a matter of cultural expectations. Long-standing economic uncertainty throughout the region has deepened the need to maintain personal and familial networks through interchanges of affection. Indigenous psychologists argue that Western-style psychodynamic analyses cannot be imported to the Philippines; a culturally-relevant psychology, they contend, can only be developed through extensive investigation of locally normative behavior, cognition and emotion (Enriquez 1990).

The existing research on gender in the Philippines confirms that the contrastive identity proposed by the prevailing theories of masculinity does not hold up among the peoples studied (e.g., Blanc-Szanton 1990). In an exemplary essay, Cristina Blanc-Szanton cautions that within a particular cultural group, women's and men's relative positions may have differed historically, regionally, by class and with respect to specific realms of social activity (1990). While attending to these distinctions in the Visayan region, she documents a variety of ways in which gender symmetry has been culturally thematized among the Ilonggo, a people who display the national talent for imaginatively refashioning the ideals of conduct imposed upon them by Hispano-Catholic (Rafael 1988) and American colonialism.[3]

Following Blanc-Szanton, it will be useful to consider a brief history of male gender in the Ilocos before pointing to an alternative paradigm for conceptualizing Ilokano masculinity.

COLONIAL AND ILOKANO PERSPECTIVES ON ILOKANO MANHOOD

Despite the occasional claim that Ilokano men did not differ from other Filipinos (Millan y Villanueva 1891:94), certain consistencies and distinctive traits emerge from reading the Spanish accounts of a culture that was less syncretic than that of the Tagalogs and Visayans, as a result of the Ilocos region's geographic inaccessibility.

By the mid-eighteenth century, the Ilocos provinces had been only lightly Christianized, as a Spanish missionary attested in 1756, commenting that the locals were tremendously affable—hardly "wild men"—but tough (*duro*) and obstinate (*terco*) in resisting the colonial religion (Carrillo 1895). Familial honor (*dayaw*) and an accompanying sensitivity to and respect for the power of the word were major preoccupations of the ancient and colonized Ilokano male; his concern with courtesy and diplomatic social relations did not derive from the Hispanic notions of honor and shame (Zialcita 1989; Foronda and Foronda 1972). Similarly, notions of equality and fraternity did not arrive with the Americans (Nieto 1898), despite the colonizers' habit of crediting themselves with bringing democratic notions to the Philippines (Anthony 1931). By the late nineteenth century, at the onset of American influence, the Ilokanos had been stereotyped as comparable to the people of Galicia[4] (the mountainous northwest of Spain): they were sober, frugal, tenacious and hardworking (Millan y Villaneuva 1891:4).

Claims were also made for the greater "temperance" of local custom, which probably meant that the people of the Ilocos were more like the Spaniards than other Filipinos. Docility vanished abruptly, however, when independence became a possibility. An intense, prolonged struggle against the American invasion of the Ilocos followed the Spanish American War (cf. Scott 1986; Trafton 1990).

Turning to indigenous accounts of Ilokano life, which provide a clearer portrait of masculinity and male-female relations, the Ilokano journalist and historian Isabelo de los Reyes emphasized a gentle, sweet character as a manly ideal, combined with industriousness, common sense and a profound respect for elders (1888:153). The socially-respected Ilokano thought before he spoke; verbal insults were punished more severely than bodily assaults and the slanderer was not forgiven (Zialcita 1989; Foronda and Foronda 1972).

To win an Ilokana, whom de los Reyes described (perhaps teasingly) as "surly, churlish" (*arisca*) compared to Tagalog women, the suitor had to display his capacity to provide well, his freedom from vices (1888:141–142), and his sincerity and loyalty. Graceful rhetoric was essential in wooing a potential bride; the chosen woman had to be approached with an attitude of entreaty, a moving voice and clear, concise yet emotionally convincing phrasing (1888:142).

Ilokano masculinity, then, blended social sensitivity with an emphasis on verbality that would make labor migration throughout this century particularly painful. Racial slights hounded the agricultural laborers who worked in the U.S. during the 1920s and 1930s (Bulosan n.d.; Wood c. 1931). Compounding the debasement of Ilokano masculinity was the men's expectation that prestige should be accorded the traveler who had experienced life widely. Male honor in the Ilocos had long been predicated upon heroic quests, as the Ilokanos' epic poem *Lam-ang* indicates. The acquisition of male prestige through travel was still a motivating force for men in the early part of the twentieth century. As a future migrant wrote, after watching a crowd excitedly greet a man who had just returned from the U.S.: "I was thrilled and inspired . . . In my fancy, I made the trip to America and I, too, returned a hero . . . in the style of our . . . old legends [in which] a . . . man had gone forth to slay the winged giants and flying devils in the days before history" (Buaken 1948:41, 40).

In the contemporary rural Ilocos, dreams of male distinction coexist with daily practices that reinforce mutuality and interdependence in domestic and subsistence tasks. While boys compete with each other,[5] they are not allowed to act aggressively toward little girls. Child-rearing practices train boys as well as girls in obedience and social nurturance (Lagmay 1983). Small girls (aged seven and older) play managerial games, reflecting women's entry into professional and business domains (albeit at lower levels than men). Men often cook, sweep and do some child care, while women perform many agricultural chores.

Contemporary Ilokanas initially say that the ideal husband attends to his household and familial duties, including, most importantly, securing their economic stability. However, "the good provider is not such an exciting topic: he's mostly praised when he's dead," women commented. Ilokanas, of all classes, have "sidelines" or multiple small businesses utilized not merely to supplement a spouse's income but often to support the household. The widow of a town mayor, a woman considered rich by rural standards, revealed that she had never known her husband's income, nor received money from him. Her extensive entrepreneurial activities had not only sustained six children, but covered the costs of feeding the mayor's frequent guests. Reliance on the wife for household support was common. In one town, women pointed to at least fifteen "housebands"—"domesticated husbands"—who stayed home and performed most domestic tasks, while their wives brought in cash.

Intrigued by the theme of defining good and bad husbands, women specified tenderness (*managayat*), good character (*nasingpet*) and, with some embarrassment, attractive looks.[6] In jokes about courting, men are scrutinized for "funny" physical characteristics, just as the young bride in the Ilokano epic *Lam-ang*, insists on watching her husband walk in front of her so that she can study his movements and body, even after he has demonstrated his heroism and supernatural powers.[7] Male bodily comportment becomes a metonymic predictor of male sexual and generative capacity, another sine qua non of powerful masculinity.

In the Ilocos, where kinship is reckoned bilaterally, fathering children and thereby founding a line of descent has been an important means of asserting political claims (Rafael 1988). Hence, the "Saudi Syndrome,"[8] as the Philippine media termed the overseas worker's "haunting" fear of his wife's infidelity (Arcinas et al. 1986:67), had a double edge: male absence not only endangered the worker's control over his wife's and daughters' sexuality, but limited the number of children that could be produced.

Married men who were childless before going to "Saudi" pressured their wives into pregnancy when they returned (or cut short women's employment abroad). Daughters were as desired as sons. Ilokanos view the marriage of daughters as an opportunity to extend familial networks of assistance and influence, not as a financial burden. There is thus no preference for sons. Indeed, male children are more costly: ideally, fathers help sons by contributing to the male dowry (*sab-ong*) that Ilokanas historically expected.[9]

Parent-son bonds also tend to be close, so that a son who fails to marry may remain comfortably in his parents' household all his adult life. As an extreme example of Ilokano filial devotion, Ferdinand Marcos never stopped calling his mother "Mommy" and refused to have her buried if he could not be present at her funeral (Ellison 1988:86).

In these and other ways, the perspectives on masculinity reviewed earlier are challenged by Ilokano practice. A full consideration of the ways in which male-female interactions shape Ilokano manhood merits an essay in itself. However, ethnographic data show that men and women in the Ilocos are viewed as having complementary roles. The phallus is not seen as a central symbol of male difference and dominance (Mitchell 1990). Among the defining characteristics of the Ilokano male are verbal graces, emotional availability, a capacity for deep friendship with other men, and a willingness to be involved closely with children.

MASCULINITY APPROACHED ECOLOGICALLY

A decidedly minority viewpoint on the acquisition of social manhood proposes a move beyond phallocentricity and toward a more "ecological" contemplation of the culturally particular ways in which the male body is schooled politically and economically (Corrigan 1988:153). In several autobiographical essays, an English analyst traces his own instruction in the "right" gestures, postures and announcements of presence (Corrigan 1988, 1983–84). Years of arm-twisting and other rough punishments at public school taught the working-class boy "to be effortlessly there—not [a] grubby little pusher," to speak as if he knew, to "bray" with masterly confidence (Corrigan 1988:144).

Building on Phillip Corrigan's attention to the whole male body in the acquisition of masculinity, I consider a broader architecture of adult male identity than the existing paradigms would allow. Male sexuality cannot be ignored, to be sure; cross-societally and pan-historically, suppression of the sexuality and generativity of male labor migrants has been a condition of their entry into particular countries or segments of labor markets (see van Onselen 1982; Lasker 1931). The ethnographic cases indicate, however, that restrictions on sexual expression in the Gulf are not more significant in tearing down and reassembling a masculine sense of self than the restraints employers place upon the men's voice, emotions and other distinctive attributes. The proposition argued here is that claims that castration anxiety is the "motor of male subjectivity" (Morgan 1991) or that the Filipino man is macho or patriarchal, fail to express or exhaust more fluid, contingent gender identities.

Below, I direct attention to shifts in production arrangements in the Philippines and the Arab Gulf as constituent elements of Ilokano masculinity. In the late twentieth century, the labor regimes that transnational corporations (TNCs) have established globally have been characterized as newly "flexible" in their strategies for capital accumulation and as "deterritorialized" in their capacity to relocate wherever profits are maximum and political costs minimal (Ong 1991; Coronil and Skurski 1991:334). While flexible recruitment and managerial tactics may characterize the TNCs in the Middle East, I accentuate their opposite tendency, arguing that subaltern males are rigidly regimented by late-stage industrial capital.

To substantiate this claim, I inquire briefly into evolving labor relations in the Philippines, then assess the effects on Ilokano masculinity of work sites that constrict men bodily and silence them, thus removing a critical cultural means of asserting male gender identity.

THE POLITICAL ECONOMY OF FOREIGN DEBT AND POVERTY

Structural defects in the Philippine economy, such as failures of land reform and extreme inequalities in the accumulation and distribution of wealth, have converged over the past two decades to progressively impoverish the majority of Filipinos (Fulleros-Santos and Lee 1991), reducing per capita income by almost 19 percent between 1981 and the downfall of Marcos in 1986 (Montes 1989a:58).

In the early 1990s, however, foreign debt is what most drastically affected the grassroots, by raising prices, reducing basic commodity subsidies, depressing wages and slashing employment (Montes 1989b; Fulleros-Santos and Lee 1991). Expanding industries have hired women, banking on their lack of labor militancy (Salva 1991:1). By 1991, women made up 90 percent of the employees in the free trade zones (FTZs) (Hildebrand 1991).

In the Ilocos, a mountainous area far from the FTZs, underemployed young men had become a fixture in the late 1980s, as a result of huge price fluctuations in the region's cash crops (garlic, tobacco), long-standing overpopulation and the failure of urban areas to absorb more than a few of the available workers. The Ilokano word *standby* (unemployed) captured the reality of men lingering in village rest houses, joking uncomfortably about becoming mail-order bridegrooms for Filipinas in the U.S.

LABOR MIGRATION AND THE DEBT CRISIS

Seeking employment overseas became an increasingly attractive household option when news of the oil-fueled construction boom in the Arab Gulf reached the Ilocos. The government actively encouraged the labor outflow; remittances earned dollars.

By 1975, temporary migration to the Gulf surpassed permanent emigration to the U.S. and Canada, which had previously been the major destinations. Between 1975 and 1983, Saudi Arabia was the largest recruiter of Filipino labor; together Saudi Arabia, Kuwait and the United Arab Emirates were the destinations for about 90 percent of the contract workers (Arcinas n.d.:3). Approximately three out of four of these migrants were men, with most employed as construction or menial service workers (ibid.:10).[10] A parallel migration exported women to the Gulf, largely as domestic workers, and to the affluent countries of Asia and Europe. Demand for less-skilled male workers peaked in the early 1980s in the Gulf, when many of the construction projects neared completion. Prospects for renewing contracts were unpromising: falling oil revenues caused retrenchment, and competition was fierce among the many Asian labor-exporting states (ibid.:63).

In a buyers' market, reports were abundant of gross overcharges by re-cruiters, contract substitutions, sudden layoffs and other abuses. Attempts at work stoppage, sick-outs and other conventional expressions of discon-tent were received with impatience and contempt in the highly-system-atized industrial work place. "Work or go home," the men were told if they attempted to negotiate with management. The migrants had no labor rights: union activity was banned throughout the Gulf.[11] Islamic courts were reputedly protective of workers, but access to them was logistically difficult for the Ilokano migrants and little help could be offered by under-staffed Philippine consulates and embassies. The peasant migrants were thus left unprotected in an industrial environment bent on extracting their bodily energy while containing and immobilizing its human source.

A brief review of the material and political interests at stake in the Gulf will assist in explaining the fragmented, severed sense of masculine self the men suffered upon being inserted into labor regimes that positioned them as interstitial, to be utilized and repatriated at the pleasure of their hosts.

THE IMPORT OF FOREIGN LABOR TO THE MIDDLE EAST

The oil boom of the 1970s drew a massive tide of foreign labor to thinly populated countries; by the 1980s, foreigners accounted for an overwhelm-ing 70 to 80 percent of the workforce in most of the Gulf states (Owen 1985:4). For complex reasons of nationalist, religious, class and gender politics, Asian workers came to be preferred over foreign Arab laborers at the lower levels of the workforce. Non-Muslim Asians were unlikely to es-pouse pan-Arabist, pan-Islamic ideals, staking moral claims to citizenship, and potentially exacerbating religious tensions by allying with local Shiite communities at a time when Gulf rulers had to deal delicately with the Islamic radicalism of their younger, more educated citizens (Eickelman 1989). While the Gulf state governments hired (through agencies) only a small percentage of the migrants, as street sweepers, gardeners and other menial workers, TNCs and other Gulf employers synchronized their inter-ests with those of the dominant families. TNCs could not operate locally without Gulf citizens as partners and agents.

The Gulf political elite, in turn, when their other interests did not con-flict, acceded to the TNCs' restless worldwide search for the most cost-effective labor. Asian workers, rather than foreign Arabs from the countries that earlier in the century had supplied less-skilled laborers (e.g., Tunisia and Egypt) were recruited into the lowest rungs of the workforce. Wages could be keyed to deteriorating conditions in the countries of origin, re-sulting in a meticulously-stratified labor force, with Euro-American techno-crats on top, foreign Arabs in the middle and Asians on the lowest tier (Owen 1985).

Asians were also easier to regulate socially: racial distinctiveness made it easier to enforce policies that segregated foreigners' housing. The Filipinos, like many other migrant groups, preferred to live with each other, socially insulating themselves from their unwelcoming surroundings. Yet, problematically, their self- and externally-imposed ghettoization exposed them to public notice, and to constant monitoring aimed at preventing them from transgressing the boundaries of the narrow social space allotted them.

A watchful environment closed in around them at city construction sites and desert work camps, which were set up to maximize productivity by tightly controlling individuals' time, space and movements. The typical project operated at high efficiency, with an intensification of working hours, militarization of discipline and rapid expulsion of the workforce, often every eighteen months (Guzman 1985:13). The lightning speed of these industrial arrangements, which orbited men away from their homelands, instantly set them to work and ejected them out of the Gulf before they could regain their equilibrium, instilled new forms of alienation. The migrants rarely saw a finished project and often were propelled home before their profits matched their expenses. Some expressed a visceral sense of disintegration, as sponsors and agents pocketed percentages of their earnings. "Drop by drop," the men said, "it is as if these people melt you away." (*Isu nga i-dribol-dribol da ti tattao.*)

The emotional tone in the Gulf seemed assaultive to the Ilokano men. "You have to dance to their music," the migrants said with dismay, indicating the difficulty of stepping fast enough to the orders of officials, police, and employers.

"Dancing" was also the trope men invoked when they were able, in some cases, to make friends with their employers. "He could dance with us," an Ilokano truck driver said approvingly of his Saudi Arabian boss. "He invited us to his house to eat. He treated me respectfully, as a man older than he."

Mutual "dancing," with neither permanently in the lead, stood as a metonymy for the close emotional relationships the Ilokano men expected to have with one another. The expectation was rarely met, however, within the industrial culture.

At work sites, "strict," "irritable" job superiors chipped away at the cheerful demeanor the Ilokanos maintained as an emotional amulet against adversity. Preoccupied with construction schedules, these bosses offered few of the token indulgences that reduced class frictions in the Philippines. Contractual relations unsettled men accustomed to an easy camaraderie.

Returnees from the Gulf thus reacted strongly to the tensions of the foreign work site and to transnational strains on their affective ties. These collisions, in which culture, class, gender, and familial ideologies intermingled, struck the men as experiences of "agony," "sacrifice" and "torment":

There is only one thing we talk about at night in the barracks. [*emphatically*] Our agony. How we want to go home to our families, after earning big money. Nobody goes to Saudi out of choice. You sacrifice for the [economic improvement] of your family. . . . So if some employers take advantage of your weakness and do not pay full wages, you are tormented. You cannot say anything because they speak Arabic. You have no way to explain.

UNCERTAIN PASSAGES

The entire trajectory of industrial work relations seemed off-kilter to the peasant-migrants. Human immediacies and needs were ignored in the circulation of bodies through time and space. A mechanic, who considered himself "lucky" to have worked at his own trade in the Gulf, described the dislocation of workers who arrived overseas to find that they had been recruited for jobs they knew little about:

> The people . . . cannot read Arabic, so they don't know what is on the visa. A poor man reaches his destination . . . [*high, outraged voice*] "Why? This is not my position that I applied for." [*Voice turns severe.*] "You are here. [*The words are pounded out, one by one, emphatically.*] You . . . must . . . work."

De-skilling was as common as fraudulent contracts that forced men to learn jobs on the spot or be deported, with no means of paying off their usurious creditors in the Philippines. In countries with a long history of industrialization, de-skilling has been linked with class and political impotence. Over time, English workers developed a discursive means of externalizing the source of their misery, blaming it on "the despots of capital" who destroyed the nostalgic dream of organizing labor so that work and domestic life were a smoothly flowing unity (Alexander 1990:38). For migrants from a rural area in a largely agricultural country, no systematic articulation of capital's tendency to select only certain elements of workers and discard others had gained widespread usage.

Without an effective means of exteriorization, the men found that the slurs they heard on the job or in the street eroded their masculine self-confidence, already chastened by the lack of demand for male labor in the Philippines. "You tell them you are a degree-holder," said one man disconsolately. "You say you teach in the high school, farming skills. 'A teacher?' they say. 'Okay, you—you will be good at cleaning the streets.' "

National and racial sensitivities, submerged in the homogeneity of the rural Ilocos, resurfaced. A hierarchy of difference positioned Asians as a lower Other than the expatriate Arabs, then distinguished among the Asians, endowing them with imagined cultural attributes that sought to explain their differing pay. Filipinos were said to be "cleaner" and hence deserving of higher wages than Bangladeshis and Sri Lankans. But the Ilokanos did not miss the implication of contamination and of a treacherous, unruly carnality that police reaffirmed by waylaying them and asking them to display marriage licenses even when their companions were not Arab but Asian women.

The notion that they were "cleaner" than certain other migrants was relative to an absolute standard that was set beyond their reach. Orientalism proceeded eastward, from the Arab to the Asian world, in search of new terrain to penetrate. Petrodollars facilitated the repositioning of the wealthiest Gulf citizens far away from the poorer, darker, Asian Others and closer to the occidental nations. In the void, those from economically dispossessed countries, such as the Philippines, were represented as bestialized or as apparatuses, stripped of human voice.

"The Arabs say that Filipinos are like dogs," men lamented, indicating their awareness that Arabs considered dogs the most loathsome of creatures: homeless and scavenging. "On the streets, they yell at us that we *are* dogs," said a migrant who was particularly embittered after being jailed overseas. "Filipinos are treated like slaves, made to work in the sun even when it is too hot to touch a piece of metal," he added.

One man recalled working at a construction site when he and his workmates were told to fill in for a crew whose crane had broken down: "They lent *us* along with the equipment." The men, he stressed, were equated with tools.

The institutional means for redress was virtually nil for the Asian migrants. Ensuring an unimpeded flow of labor did not entail socially acknowledging the presence of the Asians by granting them political entitlements. Indeed, Gulf states, intent on indigenizing the local workforce, officially denied their continued dependence on foreign labor in successive five-year plans (Askari 1990).

The net impact for the Ilokano men was to render them structurally invisible, while paradoxically their physical visibility continued to draw unwanted attention. "In the street, when the Arab teenagers are driving their cars, they throw Pepsi cans. You can't go to the authorities, because they don't believe the Filipino's complaints," men said.

> So you keep silent. At home, no one tells the whole story, that Saudi is for the Arab only, not for people of other races. They print articles there: "Manila: The Sin City of Asia." The good things are not acknowledged, that we are educated, that we know more English and work more efficiently than these other [migrants]. That the Filipino has a brain.

AFFIRMATIONS OF NONEXISTENCE

Social erasure of the migrants resurrected earlier struggles against colonialism. As a scathing editorial in a 1912 newspaper delineated the relationship, the American conqueror "paraded" through the streets, "rich, strong and wise," while the "poor, colored, weak" masses hid "in suspicious shacks," "ignorant and scorned" (Stanley 1974:166–167).

Almost a century later, when multinational capitalism had expanded prodigiously, finding its workforce all over the globe (Jameson 1984:78), social and political effacement were again the crucial issues. Mobilizing against the new labor situation presented greater difficulties, however, because neither workers nor transnational capital paused long enough in a single locus for labor to marshall its organizational resources and clearly identify its enemy.

Unlike the Filipinos who early in the century achieved a stunning mastery of the conqueror's language and sufficient perception of his systems of meaning to contest and sabotage his rule, the peasant-migrants catapulted to the Gulf rarely learned more than a functional Arabic, were baffled by the politics that isolated them as aliens, and did not sustain engagements with particular superordinates long enough to assess and manipulate their weaknesses. The distinctiveness of the regimes of power that rotated the migrants from the unemployment of the Ilocos to the intensive production zones of the Gulf lay in an elusive yet forceful agency. The matrices of power were obscure, yet the terrain they bounded was tightly-patrolled. Particular skills and the bodies that housed them could be summoned at a moment's notice from anywhere in the world. As the bodies cycled rapidly in and out of the Gulf, individual rights were suspended; persons segregated; sexuality frozen by multiple, interlocking regulations; color stigmatized and intelligence discounted. Yet who or what was in command had no name to the workers. One man recalled his work in Libya:

> Many people, many Filipinos, were afraid . . . especially if [they] were assigned in the desert places. . . . In the city, it's somewhat . . . civilized. But . . . in the desert . . . it's full of thieves, full of wicked people. They are hungry. . . . There's no law in the desert. If . . . they catch you doing not nice in their eyes . . . [*matter-of-fact voice*] they will just shoot you and leave you there. [*nervous laugh*] That's it. So I risked my life going to such places. Just to [*savors the word*] EARN. Just to save [*slow, drawn-out*] MONEY. [*Laughs*].

The theme of danger recurs throughout his brief tale, yet most peculiar, from his perspective, is the local people's obliviousness, as if by refusing to conceptualize the threat they avoid its shadow:

> This province where I work is . . . on the border of Chad and Libya. Even in the noontime, we hear cannons . . . and jets, coming to that ill-fated place. With bombs. . . . Imagine, eh? The people maybe cut to pieces? And the natives, they say, "Oh no worry." [*His voice goes falsetto in ironic imitation.*] Oh no worry. That's the will of Allah.

In such accounts, power does not radiate from any single center, but is dispersed throughout all public spaces in the Gulf region, occluding and deflecting opposition because agency is hidden, unidentifiable. Landing amidst an unknown war, the migrant cannot assign its peril to a colonizing nation, the "despots of capital" (Alexander 1990:38) or any other single force.

Tales of dismemberment and bodily mutilation were volunteered by three or four men I came to know in the Ilocos village where I lived. My neighbor Avelino was cooking dinner for his wife and me when he announced, in the midst of a conversation about "Saudi":

> One memorable experience I had there in Saudi [Arabia]. I witnessed a criminal execution. There [in] the most crowded [area], they execute the most severe penalty . . . capital punishment is for rape, killing . . . and now drug pushing, too. I don't know the crime of the man executed in the heart of the city. But we [were there] working when they blocked the streets, the arteries. All the openings were blocked. . . .

Avelino paused, having remapped the city—ordinarily a locus of vitality—as a place of inescapable death. The heart of the city, its arteries, its flows, had been cut off abruptly by an unseen force. A dislocating, dreamlike logic set in. Instead of fleeing the space of death, the migrant recounted rushing toward it, ascending excitedly above it, floating anchorless and alone above the crowd:

> We were two hundred meters away, but when I learned that somebody would be beheaded, I was so curious. I was running, running to see. There were so many people. I even looked for a higher place. I even climbed a truck so I could see. . . . It was thirty feet up. I could see clearly. . . . They made [the criminal] sit. I don't know why. There was no resistance to him. They bring him here . . . there. No resistance. Whatever they do, he'll obey.

Drawing on the religious resources of his own culture, Avelino attempted to frame this jarring spectacle within moral terms that lent a redemptive significance to the taking of a life. He reached the central portion of the narrative: "The criminal's attire is all white. He's wrapped with a white towel. Like Jesus Christ, the criminal's wrapped in white. Clean. He's clean. He'll be washed of his sins."

But the framework the speaker had erected began to disintegrate; the syntactic connections cracked as the denouement arrived:

> Then, the man was executed. All the people watching . . . even on the roof of buildings, people. Windows, roof, balcony, streets, people. They watch. He's asked to go like this [*bends head*]. Then a sword. What I imagined before, it was like an ax. But it was a sword. Very very sharp. Like a samurai sword, but wider.

The graphic details can be elided here, but the lack of closure bears underscoring. The death of the condemned was not mentioned. There was no catharsis, no exorcism of feeling, no resolution—only an ebbing away of affect, as he reached the end of his story:

> After the execution, the people clap their hands and shout. They enjoy very much. While I, because I am not used to that scene, my knees tremble. I feel them tremble. . . . The law executes. So that the people avoid the same crime. . . . Then when they execute . . . I worry that I'll fall. I go down. I feel a little dizzy. I'm not happy like those people who clapped their hands. They enjoyed. I was not happy.

Ethnographic inquiry elicited further accounts of lives and limbs ritualistically undone. The details of this folklore of disjuncture varied, but it was a story volunteered by male returnees from the Arab Gulf, not by women.[12]

While the men spoke admiringly of the public "orderliness" of Saudi, their enthusiasm for the state's order-keeping apparatus was more guarded and ambivalent. In many of the men's comments, an uneasy approval was apparent, suggesting an internalization of the disciplines imposed in transmigration, a self-policing that defended against external surveillance. "It is good that they have the people watch such [spectacles of punishment]," men said. "Maybe, in the Philippines, we would not have toughs and trouble-makers if we had these [displays]."

Other male migrants, however, voiced a feeling of identification with the condemned. A former construction worker recalled an afternoon of strolling around the city with his friends, window-shopping, when the streets were suddenly blocked off. "Rumors began to roam," he remembered. "It is a Filipino, they are saying. So we are already feeling ashamed. *Kliftic* is thief in Arabic. Filipino, *kliftic,* we hear. We look at each other with grim faces."

Like the migrant who rushed to the scene of execution, this man, too, reported being drawn to the spectacle. But he and his companions went reluctantly:

> We keep walking toward the place [of punishment]. But not energetically, ah? Very slow movement in the body. The feeling is very sorry. Maybe if it is a Filipino, we will turn back, we cannot watch. But then we get to the place where they are putting the convict out of a van, a black van. And we see, it is a Pakistani! [*laughs*] All the Filipinos are smiling again, laughing, because it is a Pakistani. Some are even jumping, yay!

Yet the relief was short-lived. The speaker suddenly emptied his narrative of human subjects, focusing instead on a body part, the hand (of the Pakistani), which had been rendered passive and homeless by the disciplining state. The migrant referred not to "the Pakistani's hand," nor "his hand," but to "the hand," detaching it from its owner as he reflected matter-of-factly: "It is the hand that is cut off. With first aid, which is available there, the loss of the hand does not kill. But," he noted, with an uncomfortable, distancing humor that separated him from the victim, "for the head, there is no first aid."

Such chronicles of disjuncture and loss reveal the Ilokano workers' sense of being caught up in an overwhelmingly intrusive industrial environment. Their narrations of their experience overseas recouped a male identity that was highly contingent. To an appreciative audience, their masculinity could be presented as adventuresome, striving and imbued with a moral aim: securing their family's future. Yet, for men who felt that their earnings had been shamefully small, the family was no longer a warm, enfolding community.

As an extreme example of disturbed social functioning, a returned migrant installed his Filipina mistress from "Saudi" in his household, explaining publicly that she would be his newly-pregnant wife's helper. Other men exerted an aggressive control over wives and children, commenting that their wives had been "too soft," "indecisive," or "weak-minded": depictions that surprised the Ilokanas, although most remained silent.

With female migration increasing, men no longer had an exclusive hold on the prestige once associated with male travel. In the Ilocos (and elsewhere in Southeast Asia [Siegel 1969]), male status had long derived not from the sexual division of labor but from the cosmopolitan knowledge that men gleaned from their regional and international journeys. Remarkably, male migrants to the Middle East had hardly spoken publicly of their trips. Even wives were often surprised to hear the details that emerged during my interviews with the men. In a society where verbal prowess is an important aspect of male social esteem, the returned migrants were caught in a contradictory, ironic situation. By remaining silent about the humiliations they had endured overseas, the men could trade upon the cultural notion that foreign travel had imbued them with new social and political skills. Yet, without a display of those skills, the returnees could not be sure that their trip to Saudi had conveyed a higher status upon them in the eyes of their village and town mates.

Ethnographic inquiry over time indicated that even for those who profited financially from their migration, the experience of desexualization and dehumanization had led to a psychological withdrawal from their local community. Returned male migrants tended to remain at home when not actively working. The world outside the domestic household failed to affirm the peasant-migrant as an integral whole. Quite the opposite, as I have argued: the international political economy that interpenetrated with individual lives had splintering effects, selecting muscles and energy and denying human totalities. The Ilokano migrant caught up in the labor markets of the late twentieth century did surround himself with a protective margin of reason, critiquing the inequities he perceived. But his cultural commentary was a fragile insulation against the stigmatizing gaze of states and the expropriations of a newly fluid form of transnational capital, which no longer "advanced," "marched," "penetrated," or "thrusted" as the old Marxian metaphors would have it—but was now "delocalized," "footloose," "deterritorialized," "dispersed" (Lipietz 1986; Coronil and Skurski 1991) and especially difficult to rally against.

Identity is always precarious and provisional, never fixed. But until the global political economy opens new spaces for the self-assertion of the subaltern male, the Ilokano migrant is likely to remain liminal, unable to resuture himself into a seamless whole.

NOTES

I am indebted to Aihwa Ong, Michael Peletz, Lynn Kwiatkowsi, Nadine Fernandez, Matthew Gutmann, James N. Anderson and the anonymous reviewers of the University of California Press for their helpful comments. I am solely responsible, however, for any flaws in interpretation or failures to incorporate suggestions. Fulbright-Hays funded the research in the Philippines upon which this essay is based. An earlier, abbreviated version of this essay was published in *Masculinities* 2,3 (fall 1994): 18–36.

1. The word is an amalgam of *desmadre* (motherlessness/chaos) and *modernidad* (modernity), according to the program notes for Guillermo Gomez-Pena's "1991." It is likely that it comes from Roger Bartra's *Cage of Melancholy* (1992), as Matt Gutmann kindly pointed out.

2. In a village in the Ilocos, neighbors helped a young man flee into the night, moments after hearing him tell the father of his pregnant girlfriend that he had "not been the first to touch her." Several men restrained the father as the young man ran to the house of a friend with a motorbike and sped away, abandoning all his possessions and a good job as a baker's helper. The father's anger frightened all concerned. No one doubted that the young man would be killed.

3. American colonial officials were shocked by peasant women who "swear like any man and smoke cigars in public" (Halsema 1983:15). In the early 1990s, the village Ilokana casually ignores the boundaries set by a highly differentiated notion of femininity/masculinity. When she walks to her fields, she may be wearing a flounced skirt with long pants underneath, carrying a harvesting knife and chewing on a cigar.

4. Other stereotypes of Galicians that the author may have drawn upon are provided by Unamuno, who, like Camilo Millan, viewed the Galician character as

shaped by landscape. Writing in 1912 (later than Camilo Millan), Unamuno never-theless codified what was probably a widespread view of Galicians. Galicians, to Unamuno, were suspicious, given to joking and complaining, displayed a sensitivity that seemed feminine (*una susceptibilidad feminina*) and retained paganism to a larger extent than other regional peoples (Unamuno 1959:72–75). With the ex-ception of the last trait, he could be reiterating common characterizations of Ilo-kanos.

5. Mothers note their sons' habit of lining up to urinate together to see who can propel a stream the highest and furthest. Boys also take pride at being "big enough" to be the first in the age group to be circumcised (an operation per-formed on eleven- to thirteen-year-olds).

6. A typical comment discounted the importance of looks, but pointed out that women's susceptibility to rogues could only be explained by the Ilokanas' taste for good looks and charm. Thus, a variety of cads were capable of attracting women: the *malalaki*, or *maingel a lalaki*, like wine that is highly intoxicating, but referring to courage in fighting; the *sabongero*, who spends all his time at cockfights; the *mannakiringor* and *napudot ti panagul-ulona* (violent noisemakers, hotheads), the *bartekero* (a hard drinker, which is not limited to men), the *sugalero* (gambler), the *babaero* (playboy, womanizer) and the *mananggundaway* (exploiter of women). Of this nightmarish but tolerated bunch, only the *mammalit* or *reypis* (rapist) could not compensate for his deviance with looks or magnetism.

7. She is merciless in her critique, complaining about his clumsiness, messy hair, the size and prominence of his backside, the way his hips sway, while he tries jokingly to convince her to accept him as he is. He criticizes her physically as well, but much more gently.

8. "Saudi" in Ilokano and Tagalog refers not only to Saudi Arabia but generi-cally to the Middle East.

9. In a situation of widespread poverty, the *sab-ong* is now expected only from *Hawaiianos*, the relatively affluent retirees who marry young brides in the Philip-pines after spending their work lives as agricultural laborers in the U.S. Their social security pensions are a key attraction for the young brides. Even where the groom's resources preclude a dowry, his family pays for the wedding. If the man's side is unable to provide a feast, there may be quiet negotiations in which the bride's family provides some cash. But the more face-saving solution is to have the couple elope.

10. The situation of professional migrants working in well-paid prestigious jobs is not discussed here. The percentage they represented of Filipino overseas workers declined rapidly from 53 percent in 1975 to about 16 percent in 1980 (Arcinas n.d.:14).

11. Kuwait was an exception, but residence requirements precluded foreigners' entry into labor unions.

12. Television, according to the men, made these scenes of punishment avail-able to female household workers who did not have days off or who lived far from cities where these displays took place. But the women said that they did not have access to television, "did not have time" to watch or saw television only with the children of their employers. Thus, they did not see or know about "such frightening things."

REFERENCES

Alexander, Sally. 1990. "Women, Class and Sexual Differences in the 1830s and 1840s: Some Reflections on the Writing of a Feminist History." In Terry Lovell, ed., *British Feminist Thought*, pp. 28–50. London: Basil Blackwell.

Anthony, Donald Elliot. 1931. "Filipino Labor in Central California." *Sociology and Social Research.* 15(2):49–156.

Anzaldua, Gloria. 1987. *Borderlands/La Frontera.* San Francisco: Spinsters/Aunt Lute.

Arcinas, Fe R., n.d. (c. 1983). *Asian Migrant Workers to the Gulf Region: The Philippine Case.* Quezon City: University of the Philippines, Department of Social Sciences.

Arcinas, Fe R., Cynthia Banzon-Bautista, and Randolf S. David. 1986. *The Odyssey of the Filipino Migrant Workers to the Gulf Region.* Quezon City: University of the Philippines, Department of Social Sciences.

Askari, Hossein. 1990. *Saudi Arabia's Economy: Oil and the Search for Economic Development.* Greenwich, Conn.: JAI Press.

Bartra, Roger. 1992. *The Cage of Melancholy.* New Brunswick: Rutgers University Press.

Birks, J. S., and C. A. Sinclair. 1980. *Arab Manpower.* London: Croom Helm.

Blanc-Szanton, Cristina. 1990. "Collision of Cultures: Historical Reformulations of Gender in the Lowland Visayas, Philippines." In Jane M. Atkinson and Shelly Errington, eds., *Power and Difference: Gender in Island Southeast Asia,* pp. 345–384. Stanford: Stanford University Press.

Bogardus, Emory. 1929. "American Attitudes Toward Filipinos." *Sociology and Social Research.* 14(1):59–69.

Boscaglia, Maurizia. 1991. "A Moving Story: Masculine Tears and the Humanity of Televised Emotions." Paper presented at Modern Language Association Convention, San Francisco.

Brandes, Stanley. 1980. *Metaphors of Masculinity.* Philadelphia: University of Pennsylvania Press.

Buaken, Manuel. 1948. *I Have Lived with the American People.* Caldwell, Idaho: Caxton Printers.

Bulosan, Carlos. n.d. *America Is in the Heart.* New York: Harcourt, Brace and Co.

Carillo, Fr. Manuel. [1756] 1895. "Breve Relación de las Misiones de las quatro naciones, llamadas Igorrotes, Tinguianes, Apayaos y Adanes." In W. E. Retana, ed., *Archivo del Bibliófilo Filipino,* vol. 1, pp. 32–34. Madrid: N.P.

Coronil, Fernando, and Julie Skurski. 1991. "Dismembering and Remembering the Nation: The Semantics of Political Violence in Venezuela." *Comparative Studies in Society and History* 33(2):288–337.

Corrigan, Phillip. 1988. "The Making of the Boy: Meditations on What Grammar School Did With, To, and For My Body." *Journal of Education* 170(3):142–161.

———. 1983–84. "My(?) Body, My Self(?): Coming to See with My Masculine Eyes." *Resource for Feminist Research* 12(4).

de los Reyes y Florentino, Isabelo. 1888. *Artículos Varios Sobre Etnografía, Historia y Costumbres de Filipinas.* Manila: J. A. Ramos.

Eickelman, Dale F. 1989. *The Middle East: An Anthropological Approach.* Englewood Cliffs: Prentice Hall.

Ellison, Katherine. 1988. *Imelda*. New York: McGraw Hill.

Ellison, Ralph. 1960. *The Invisible Man*. New York: New American Library, Signet Books.

Enloe, Cynthia. 1989. *Bananas, Beaches and Bases: Making Feminist Sense of International Politics*. Berkeley: University of California Press.

Enriquez, Virgilio. 1990. *Indigenous Psychology*. Quezon City: Philippine Psychology Research and Training House.

Findley, Sally. 1987. *Rural Development and Migration*. Boulder: Westview Press.

Foronda, Marcelino, and Juan A. Foronda. 1972. "The Establishment of the First Missionary Centers in Ilocos, 1572–1612." In Marcelino Foronda and Juan A. Foronda, eds., *Samtoy: Essays on Iloko History and Culture*, pp. 1–65. Manila: United Publishing.

Foster, Nellie. 1932. "Legal Status of Filipino Intermarriages in California." *Sociology and Social Research* 16(5):441–454.

Fulleros-Santos, Aida, and Lynn F. Lee. 1991. "A Treadmill of Poverty for Filipino Women." *Pulso ng Bayan* 48:2–10.

Gilmore, David. 1990. *Manhood in the Making: Cultural Concepts of Masculinity*. New Haven: Yale University Press.

Gomez-Pena, Guillermo. 1991. *"1991," a Performance Piece*. Nov. 8, 1991. University of California, Berkeley.

Gregor, Thomas. 1985. *Anxious Pleasures: The Sexual Life of an Amazonian People*. Chicago: University of Chicago Press.

Guzman, Arnel de. 1985. "Filipino Labor Outmigration: A Preliminary Analysis." *Kasarinlan* 1(1):11–20.

Halsema, J. 1983. "E. J. Halsema: Colonial Engineer (1)." *Bulletin of the American Historical Collection* 11(2):7–33.

Hawes, Gary. 1990. "Theories of Peasant Revolution: A Critique and Contribution from the Philippines." *World Politics* 42(2):261–298.

Herzfeld, Michael. 1985. *The Poetics of Manhood*. Princeton: Princeton University Press.

Hildebrand, Dale. 1991. *To Pay Is to Die*. Davao City, Philippines: Philippine International Forum.

Jameson, Frederic. 1984. "Postmodernism, or the Cultural Logic of Late Capitalism." *New Left Review* 146:53–92.

Lagmay, Leticia A. 1983. *Cruz-na-Ligas: Early Socialization in an Urbanizing Community*. Quezon City: University of the Philippines Press.

Lasker, Bruno. 1931. *Filipino Immigration*. Chicago: University of Chicago Press.

Limon, Jose. 1989. "Carne, Carnales and the Carnivalesque: Bakhtinian Batos, Disorder and Narrative Discourses." *American Ethnologist* 16(3):471–486.

Lipietz, Alain. 1986. "New Tendencies in the International Division of Labor: Regimes of Accumulation and Modes of Regulation." In A. Scott and M. Storper, eds., *Production, Work and Territory*, pp. 16–39. Boston: Allen and Unwin.

Luciani, Giacomo. 1990. "Allocation vs. Production States: A Theoretical Framework," In *The Arab State*, pp. 65–84. London: Routledge.

Lyttleton, Ned. 1983–84. "Men's Liberation, Men Against Sexism and Major Dividing Lines." *Resource for Feminist Research* 12(4):33–34.

Millan y Villanueva, Camilo. 1891. *Ilocos Norte. Descripción General de Dicha Provincia.* Manila: El Eco de Filipinas.

Mitchell, Juliet. 1990. "Feminine Sexuality: Jacques Lacan and the Ecole Freudienne: Introduction-I." In Terry Lovell, ed., *British Feminist Thought,* pp. 196–210. London: Basil Blackwell.

Montes, Manuel. 1989a. "Emerging Economic Issues: Recovery and Democratization." In R. W. A. Vokes, ed., *The Philippines Under Aquino,* pp. 53–70. Occasional Paper no. 11. Canterbury: University of Kent, Centre for South-East Asian Studies.

——— 1989b. "Four Points Regarding the Philippine Foreign Debt Issue." In R. W. A. Vokes, ed., *The Philippines Under Aquino,* pp. 71–82. Occasional Paper no. 11. Canterbury: University of Kent, Centre for South-East Asian Studies.

Morgan, Thais. 1991. "Powers of Male Masochism: The Construction of Masculinities in Euripedes' *Bacchae* and Peter Shaffer's *Equus.*" Paper presented at Modern Language Association Convention, San Francisco.

Nieto, Fr. José. 1898. "Extracto de la Memoria del Padre Fr. Jose Nieto, agustino, sobre la insurreción de Sarrat de 1815." In W. E. Retana, ed., *Archivo del Bibliófilo Filipino,* vol. 4, pp. 171–179. Madrid: N.p.

Ong, Aihwa. 1987. *Spirits of Resistance and Capitalist Discipline: Factory Women in Malaysia.* Albany: SUNY Press.

———. 1990. "Japanese Factories, Malay Workers: Class and Sexual Metaphors in West Malaysia." In Jane M. Atkinson and Shelly Errington, eds., *Power and Difference: Gender in Island Southeast Asia,* pp. 385–422. Stanford: Stanford University Press.

———. 1991. "The Gender and Labor Politics of Postmodernity." *Annual Review of Anthropology* 20:279–309.

Owen, Roger. 1985. *Migrant Workers in the Gulf.* London: Minority Rights Group Ltd.

Pred, Allan, and Michael J. Watts. 1992. *Reworking Modernity: Capitalisms and Symbolic Discontent.* New Brunswick: Rutgers University Press.

Rafael, Vicente. 1988. *Contracting Colonialism.* Ithaca: Cornell University Press.

Salva, Rai. 1991. "Women Through a Man's Eye." *Pulso ng Bayan* 48:1.

Scott, William Henry. 1986. *Ilocano Responses to American Aggression, 1900–1901.* Quezon City: New Day Publishers.

Siegel, James T. 1969. *The Rope of God.* Berkeley: University of California Press.

Stanley, Peter. 1974. *A Nation in the Making.* Cambridge, Mass.: Harvard University Press.

Stoler, Ann L. 1991. "Carnal Knowledge and Imperial Power: Gender, Race and Morality in Colonial Asia." In Micaela di Leonardo, ed., *Gender at the Crossroads of Knowledge: Feminist Anthropology in the Postmodern Era,* pp. 51–101. Berkeley: University of California Press.

Taussig, Michael T. 1987. *Shamanism, Colonialism and the Wild Man.* Chicago: University of Chicago Press.

Trafton, William Oliver. 1990. *We Thought We Could Whip Them in Two Weeks.* Quezon City: New Day Publishers.

Unamuno, Miguel de. 1959. *Andanzas y Visiones Espanolas.* Madrid: Espasa-Calpe, S. A.

van Onselen, Charles. 1982. *Studies in the Social and Economic History of Witswatersrang, 1886–1914.* Vol. 2, "Nineveh." Harlow, Essex: Longman House.

Wilson, Elizabeth. 1990. "Psychoanalysis: Psychic Law and Order?" In Terry Lovell, ed., *British Feminist Thought,* pp. 211–226. London: Basil Blackwell.

Wood, James Earl. c. 1929–31. James Earl Wood Papers. Bancroft Library. University of California, Berkeley.

Zialcita, Fernando N. 1989. *Notions of Justice.* Quezon City: Ateneo de Manila University Press.

INDEX

ABIM (*Angkatan Belia Islam Malaysia,* Islamic Youth Movement of Malaysia), 162, 174–75, 179, 180, 181–82

Aborigines, 89–90

Abortion, in Singapore, 200, 212–13n11

Abu-Lughod, Lila, 53

Acehnese, 47n14, 91

Adat (legal system): age distinction in, 148, 154n18; described, 69n2; egalitarian ideology of, 53–54, 67, 164; gendered hierarchy of, 51, 53, 56–57, 64, 130–31; Islamic law versus, 127, 152n2, 163–67; LKAAM discourse on, 143, 144; matrilineal versus bilateral, 80–81; Minangkabau women's control of, 129, 130, 140–42, 150–51; PKK impact on, 147, 148; as property forum, 56, 70–71n13, 130–31, 164

Adat council, 56, 70–71n13

Adat perpatih, 80–81

Adat temenggong, 81

Adultery, by Javanese women, 39, 40, 45, 47n19

Affinal exchange: in Negeri Sembilan marriage, 84–87

African Americans, 105

African states, 6, 95, 175

Akal (reason): concept of, 91–93; dominant view of, 30–31, 47n14, 55, 93–94, 165; historical precedents for, 94, 116n20; of Minangkabau women, 153–54n14; practical view of, 95–96, 186, 190n29. See also *Nafsu* (passion)

Alcoholic intake, 89, 96, 117n24

Alternative hegemony, defined, 14n2

American colonialism, 278, 280, 288–89

Anak dara (virgins), 166

Anan Ganjanapan, 267

Andaman Islanders, 83

Anderson, Benedict, 19, 28, 29, 30, 67–68, 229–30

Angeles, Leonora, 233

Anthropology, 1–2, 9, 77–79, 114n1

Anwar Ibrahim, 175, 182, 185

Appadurai, Arjun, 8

Aquino, Corazon, 218, 227, 234, 240n30

Arab Gulf countries. *See* Middle East

Arisan (cooperative credit association), 37

Asceticism. *See* Self-control

Asuang (female spirit), 223, 239n20

Atkinson, Jane, 7–8

Avelino (pseud.), 277, 290

Baan Naa Sakae (pseud.): consumerism in, 248–49; overseas workers from, 260–62; travel mobility in, 258, 270n12; widow ghost scare in, 250, 252–54; wooden phalluses in, 249, 251. *See also* Thailand, northeast

Babcock, Barbara, 11

Balfour, Arthur, 210n3

Bali, 82

Bangkok, 247, 248, 257–58

Banks, David, 168

Baralek adat (ritual), 54

Barkada (friendship groups), 279

unwed motherhood versus, 202,
214n18–19. *See also* Lee Kuan Yew
Pork prohibition, 89, 90, 116n17
Postcolonial nations: crisis narratives of,
196; defined, 13–14n1; domesticity ideology of, 125–26, 152n1; female bodies in,
6–7, 12, 201, 213n14; gender contestation in, 1–3; narrative resistance in, 218–
19; new gender categories of, 124, 125;
political culture of, 161; positionally de-
fined masculinity of, 102, 103, 104–5;
soft nationalism of, 184–86, 190n25;
Westernization of, 203–4, 208–9
Power. *See* Spiritual potency
*Power and Difference: Gender in Island Southeast
Asia* (Atkinson and Errington, ed.), 7–8
Pramoedya Ananta Toer, 217–18
Pred, Allan, 2
Prestige/stigma system: defined, 114n6; in
Java, 8, 25, 26, 43–44; self-control in,
88–89; silence in, 67–68; wealth in, 25,
109. *See also* Spiritual potency
Prindiville, Joanne, 134
Priyayi (elites), 20–21, 26–27, 31, 46n8
Prostitutes, 38, 259
Pusako (lineage property), 54

Querida system, 224
Qur'an, 92, 133–34, 138, 139, 170, 177

Race, as reproduction crisis category, 198,
203, 204, 210n3, 215n22
Rafael, Vicente, 219–20, 225
Raffles, Thomas Stamford, 19, 23, 24
Rajo (pseud.), 134
Ramadan, 89
Ranji bako (paternal genealogies), 55,
70n11–12
Rapat balai (village meeting), 57
Reason. See *Akal* (reason)
Relational/positional dichotomy, 100,
103–5
Religious resurgence, 187. *See also* Islamic re-
surgence (*Dakwa* movement)
REPELITA, 135
Rethinking Anthropology (Leach), 77
Reyes, Soledad, 222
Rice production, 132–33, 153n9, 249, 265
Rizal, Jose, 218, 225
A Room of One's Own (Woolf), 229
The Rope of God (Siegel), 47n14

Rosaldo, Michelle, 79
Rosaldo, Renato, 219, 237–38n12
Roseberry, William, 246
Rosen, Lawrence, 47n14
Rubin, Gayle, 78
Rukunegara (Malay state ideology), 167–68

Sabbah, Fatna, 179
Sab-ong (male dowry), 282, 294n9
Said, Edward, 206, 216, 218–19
Sapokat (*kaum* meeting), 57
Saudara saudari (siblings), 173
Saudi Arabia, 274, 284, 290–91
"Saudi Syndrome," 282, 294n8
Schneider, David M., 77, 79, 128
Scott, James, 162, 188n1
Self-control: absence of, 89–90, 116n18; am-
bivalent ideology of, 39–40, 41; Islamic
discourse on, 30–31; in marketplace, 36–
37, 39; as moral virtue, 88–89, 90; spiri-
tual potency and, 20, 21, 28, 29, 40; as
status indicator, 19, 29, 30, 35; subordi-
nate Javanese view of, 32, 34–35. See
also *Akal* (reason)
Semangat (life forces), 97
*Sexual Meanings: The Cultural Construction of
Gender and Sexuality* (Ortner and
Whitehead), 101
Sexual potency, money and, 33–35, 36–37,
39, 45
Shafi'i law, 164
Shapiro, Judith, 79
Shockley, William, 210n3
Siapno, Jacqueline, 216
Sidiam, West Sumatra, 52, 56, 69n5
Siegel, James T., 14n3, 47n14
Singapore: Confucian refiguration in, 195,
203–4, 205–7, 214n20; economic
growth in, 2, 3; English language threat
to, 204–5; importation of Chinese to,
215n22; Mandarin campaign in, 204,
208, 214–15n21; nation trope of, 209n1;
population regeneration focus of, 196–
97; school admissions policy of, 200,
211–12n8, 212n9–10; sleeping death in,
251–52, 260. *See also* Lee Kuan Yew
Singaporean women: child-bearing duty of,
201, 213n13; reproduction incentives
for, 200–201, 211n7, 212–13n11; reproductive rates of, 195, 197, 198
Sisters of Islam, 185–86

Index:	Patricia Deminna
Composition:	Maple-Vail Book Manufacturing
Text:	10/12 Baskerville
Display:	Baskerville
Printing and binding:	Maple-Vail Book Manufacturing